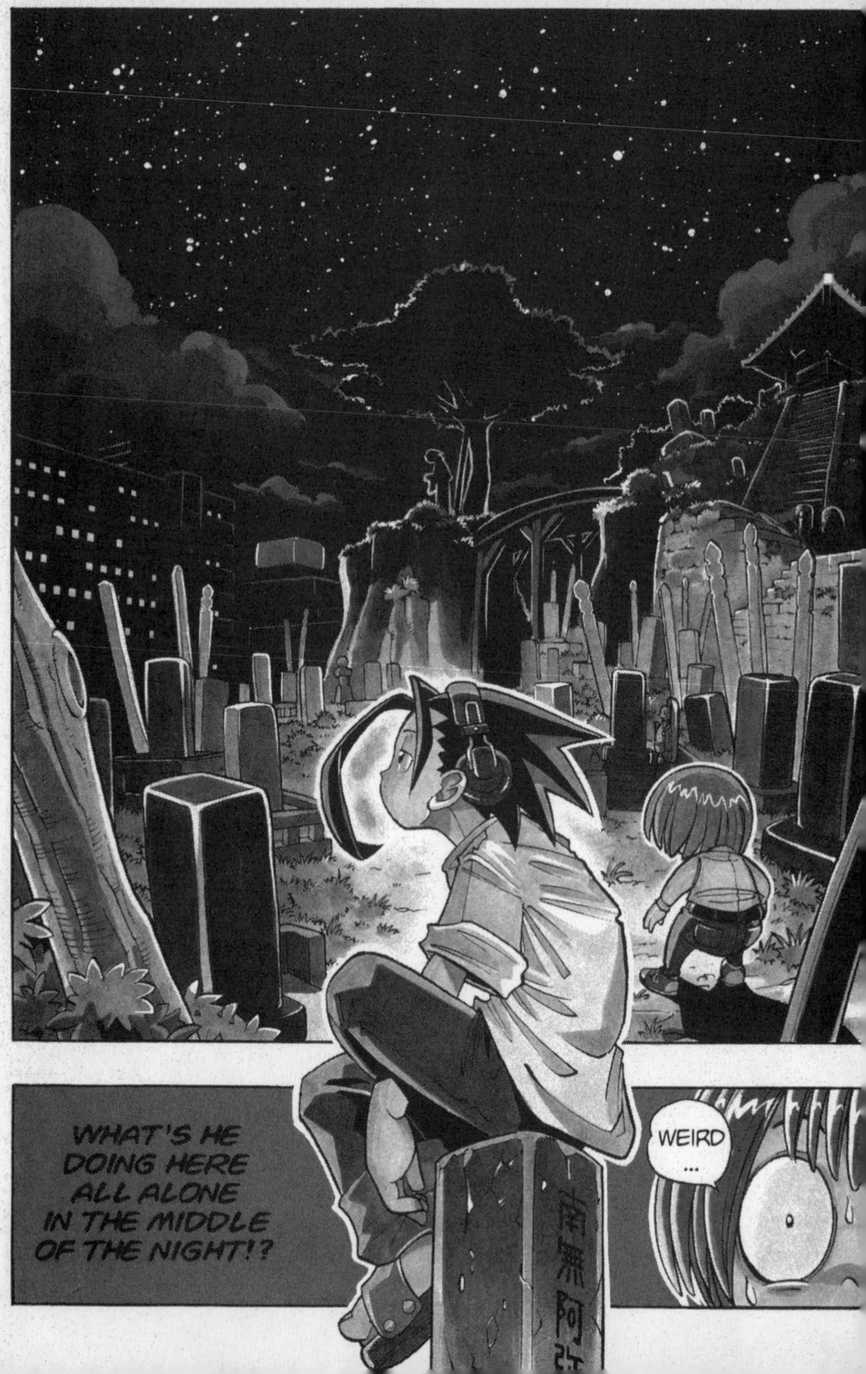
WEIRD ...
WHAT'S HE DOING HERE ALL ALONE IN THE MIDDLE OF THE NIGHT!?

SHAMAN
KING
1

LEAVES

READ THIS WAY

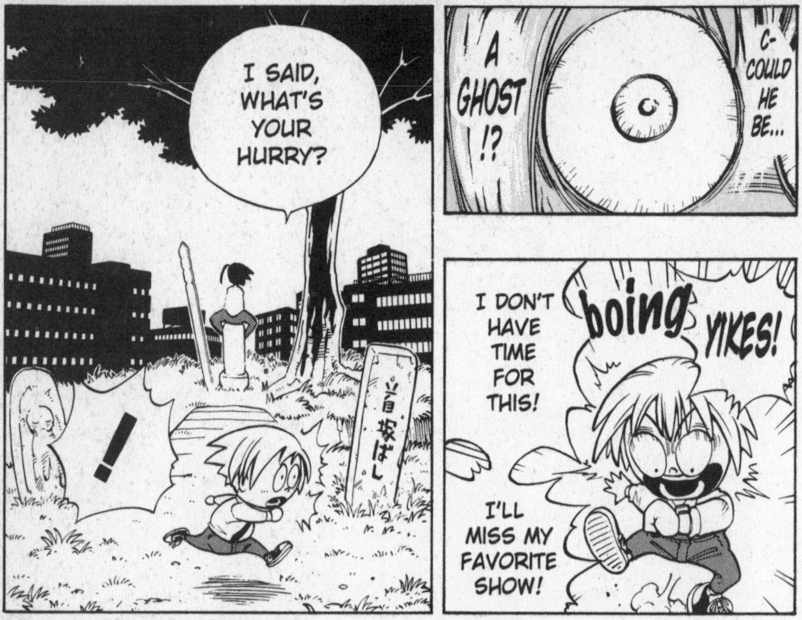
C-COULD HE BE...
A GHOST!?
YIKES!
boing
I DON'T HAVE TIME FOR THIS!
I'LL MISS MY FAVORITE SHOW!
I SAID, WHAT'S YOUR HURRY?
!
首塚ばし

*Sign: Headstone Bridge

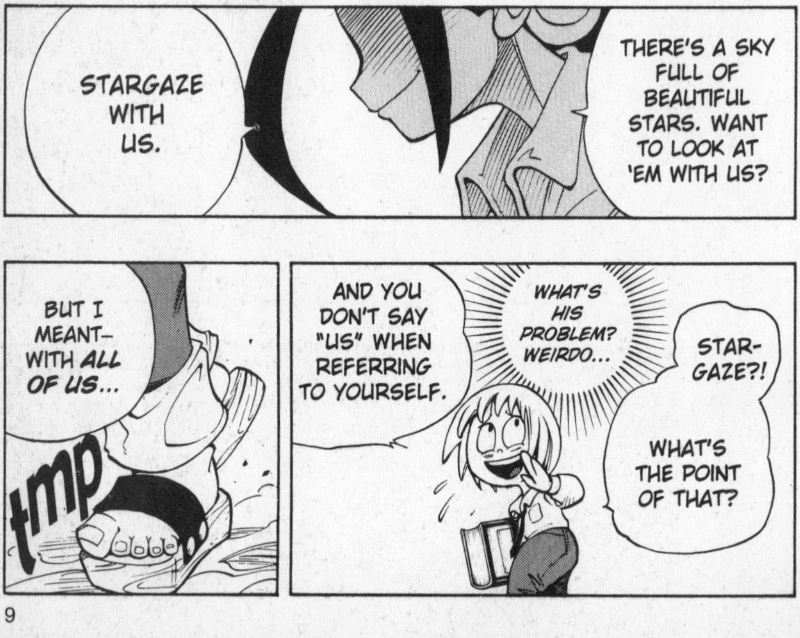
THERE'S A SKY FULL OF BEAUTIFUL STARS. WANT TO LOOK AT 'EM WITH US?
STARGAZE WITH US.
STAR-GAZE?!
WHAT'S THE POINT OF THAT?
WHAT'S HIS PROBLEM? WEIRDO...
AND YOU DON'T SAY "US" WHEN REFERRING TO YOURSELF.
BUT I MEANT— WITH ALL OF US...
tmp

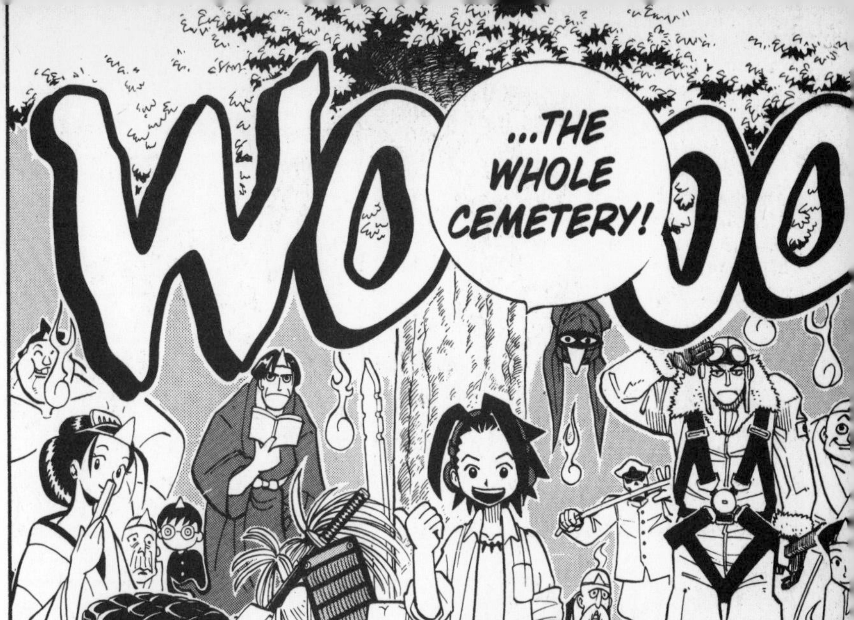
WO OO
...THE WHOLE CEMETERY!
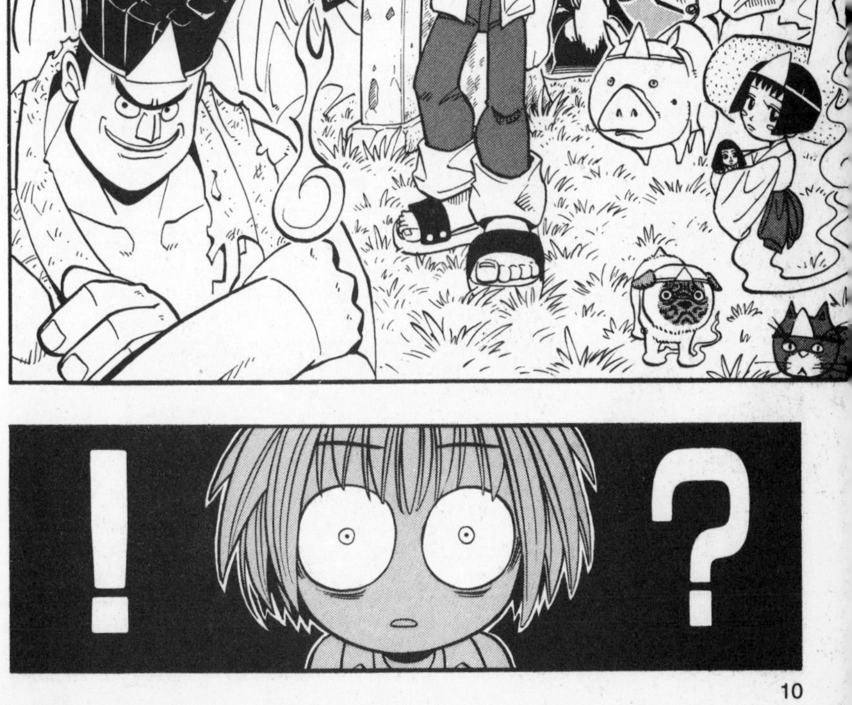
!
?

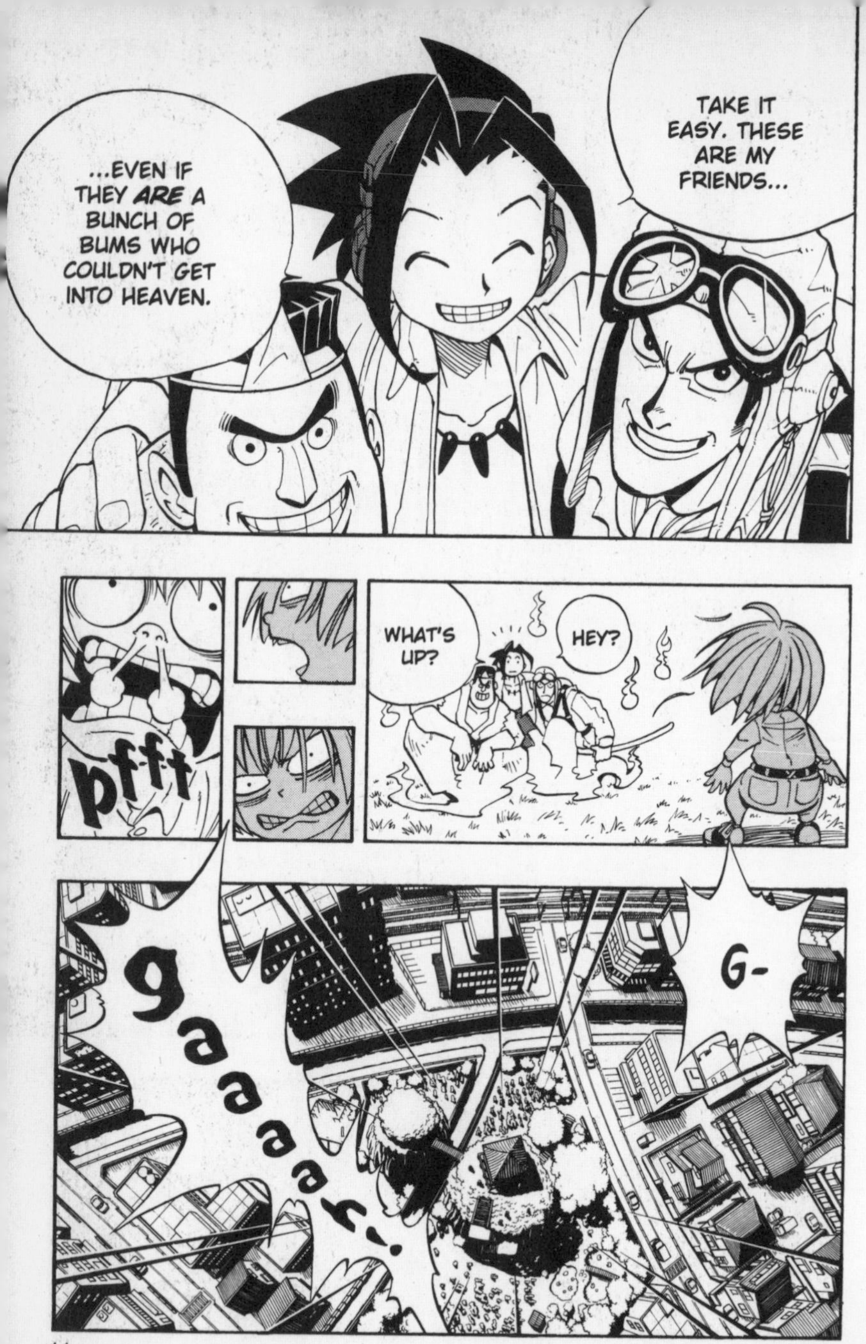
TAKE IT EASY. THESE ARE MY FRIENDS...
...EVEN IF THEY *ARE* A BUNCH OF BUMS WHO COULDN'T GET INTO HEAVEN.
HEY?
WHAT'S UP?
pfft
G-
gaaaah!

READ THIS WAY

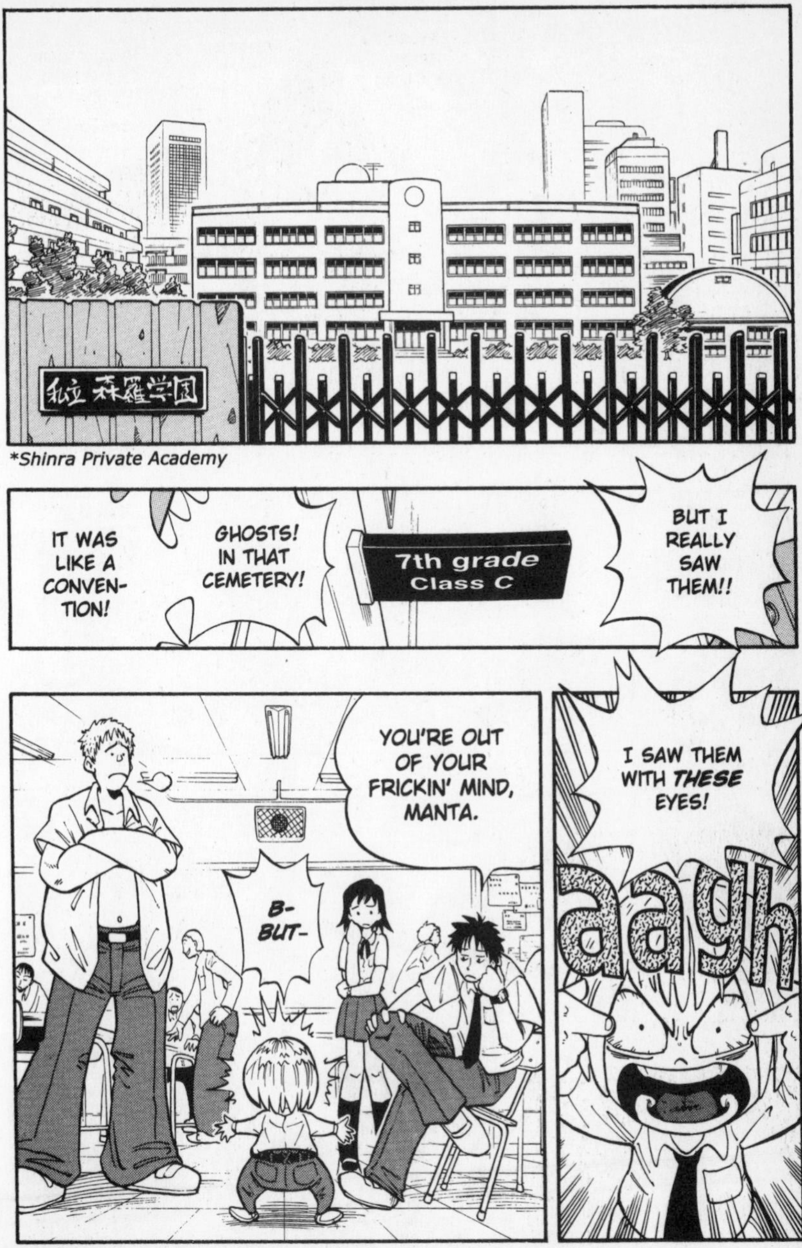
私立 森羅学園
*Shinra Private Academy
BUT I REALLY SAW THEM!!
7th grade Class C
GHOSTS! IN THAT CEMETERY!
IT WAS LIKE A CONVEN-TION!
I SAW THEM WITH *THESE* EYES!
aagh
YOU'RE OUT OF YOUR FRICKIN' MIND, MANTA.
B-BUT-

READ THIS WAY

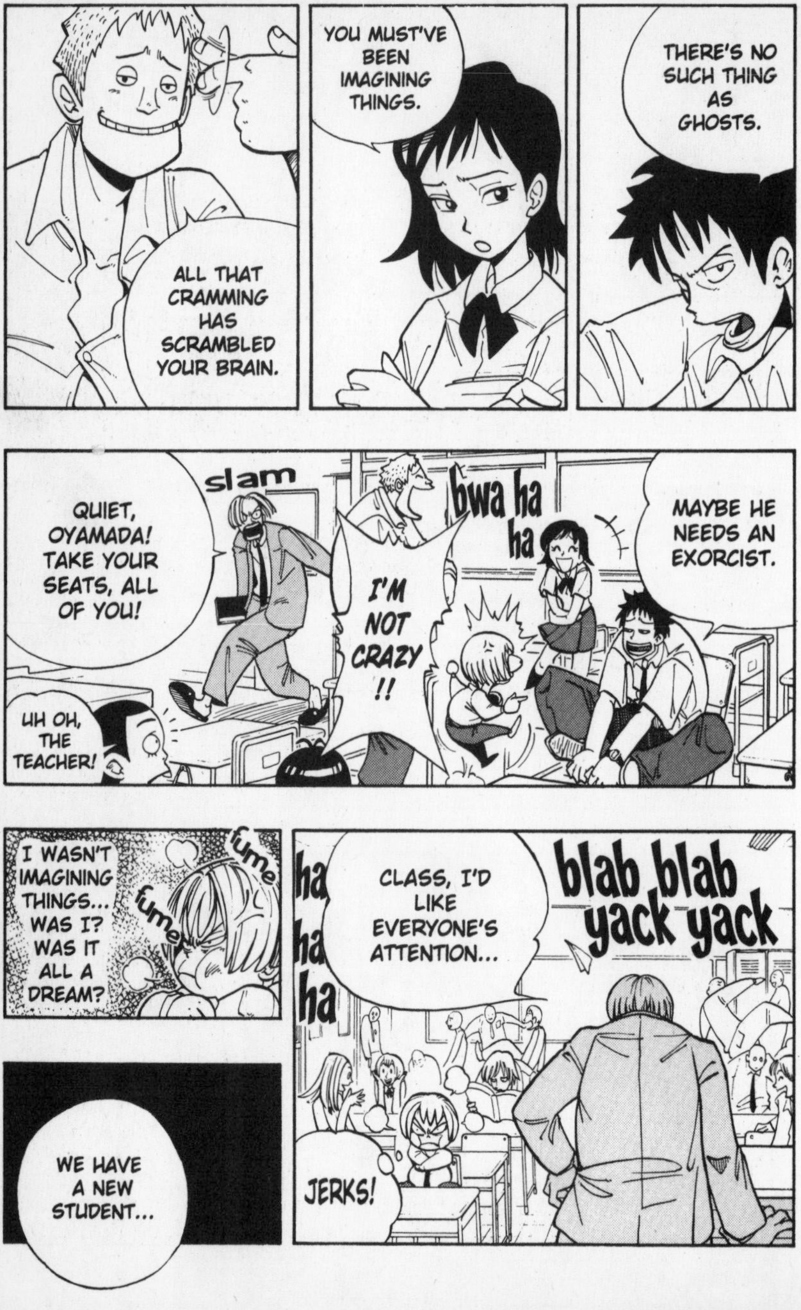
THERE'S NO SUCH THING AS GHOSTS.
YOU MUST'VE BEEN IMAGINING THINGS.
ALL THAT CRAMMING HAS SCRAMBLED YOUR BRAIN.
MAYBE HE NEEDS AN EXORCIST.
bwa ha ha
slam
I'M NOT CRAZY !!
QUIET, OYAMADA! TAKE YOUR SEATS, ALL OF YOU!
UH OH, THE TEACHER!
blab blab yack yack
CLASS, I'D LIKE EVERYONE'S ATTENTION...
ha ha ha
JERKS!
fume fume
I WASN'T IMAGINING THINGS... WAS I? WAS IT ALL A DREAM?
WE HAVE A NEW STUDENT...

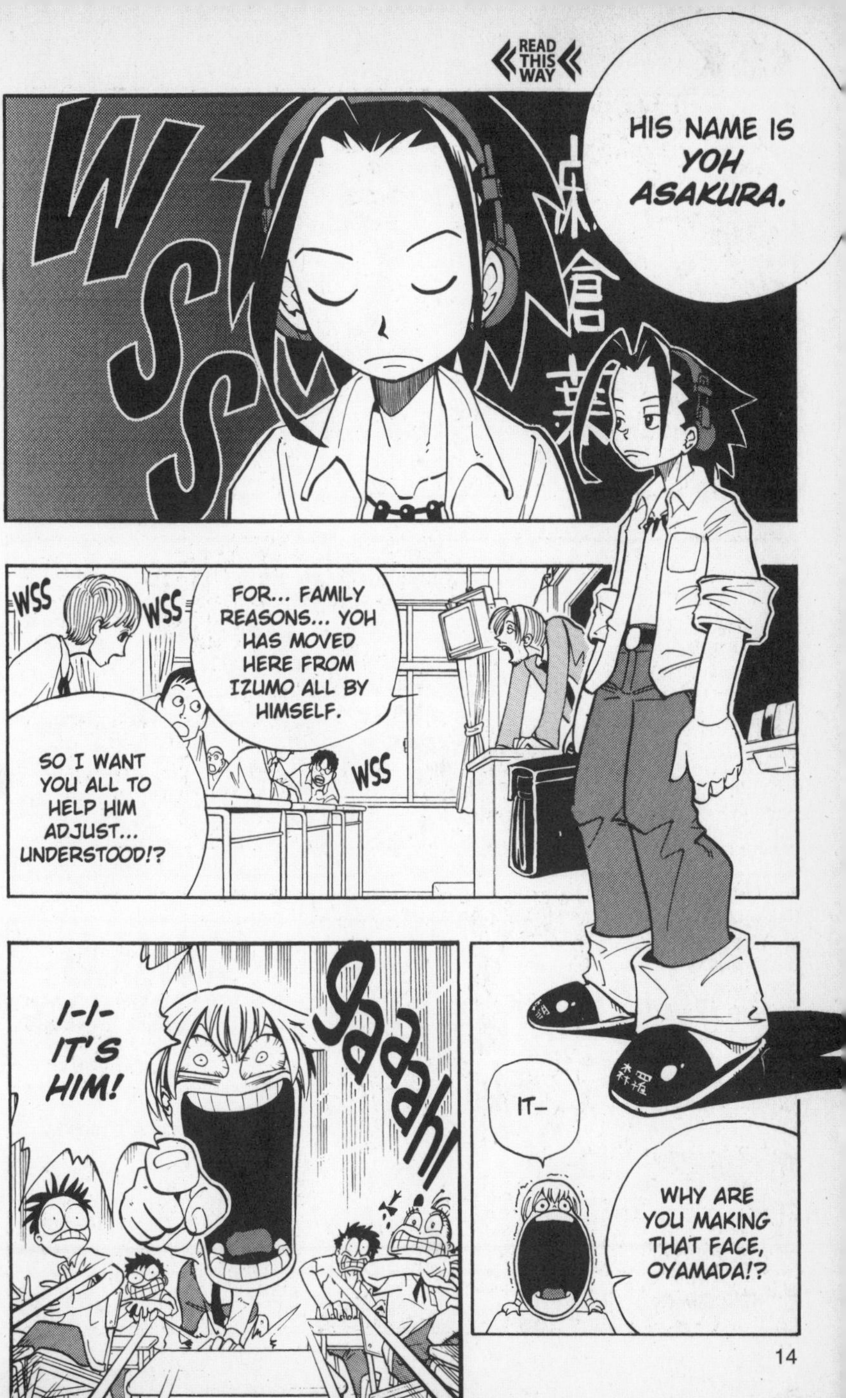
READ THIS WAY
HIS NAME IS YOH ASAKURA.
WSS
麻倉葉
FOR... FAMILY REASONS... YOH HAS MOVED HERE FROM IZUMO ALL BY HIMSELF.
WSS
WSS
SO I WANT YOU ALL TO HELP HIM ADJUST... UNDERSTOOD!?
WSS
IT–
WHY ARE YOU MAKING THAT FACE, OYAMADA!?
I-I-IT'S HIM!
Gaaah!

READ THIS WAY

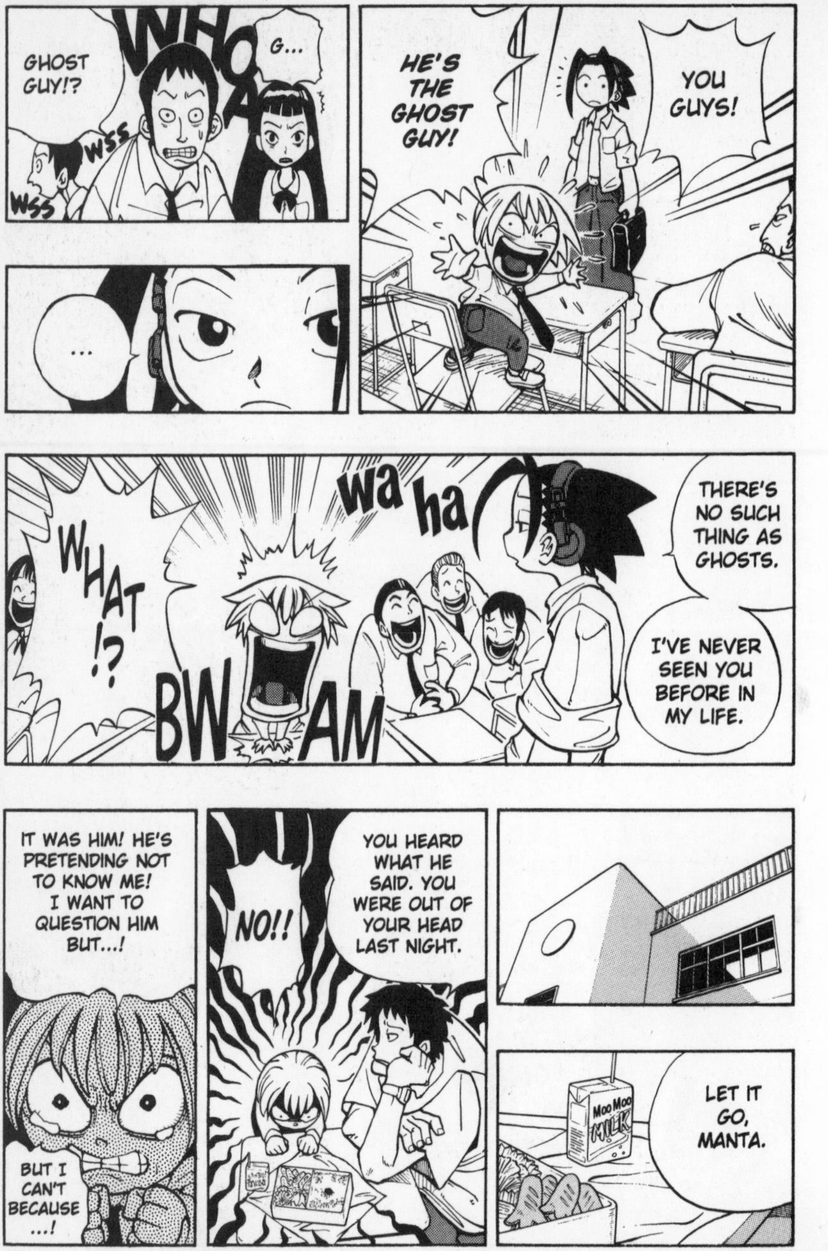

YOU GUYS!
HE'S THE GHOST GUY!
G...
WHOA
GHOST GUY!?
WSS
WSS
...
THERE'S NO SUCH THING AS GHOSTS.
I'VE NEVER SEEN YOU BEFORE IN MY LIFE.
wa ha
WHAT!?
BWAM
LET IT GO, MANTA.
MOO MOO MILK
YOU HEARD WHAT HE SAID. YOU WERE OUT OF YOUR HEAD LAST NIGHT.
NO!!
IT WAS HIM! HE'S PRETENDING NOT TO KNOW ME! I WANT TO QUESTION HIM BUT...!
BUT I CAN'T BECAUSE ...!

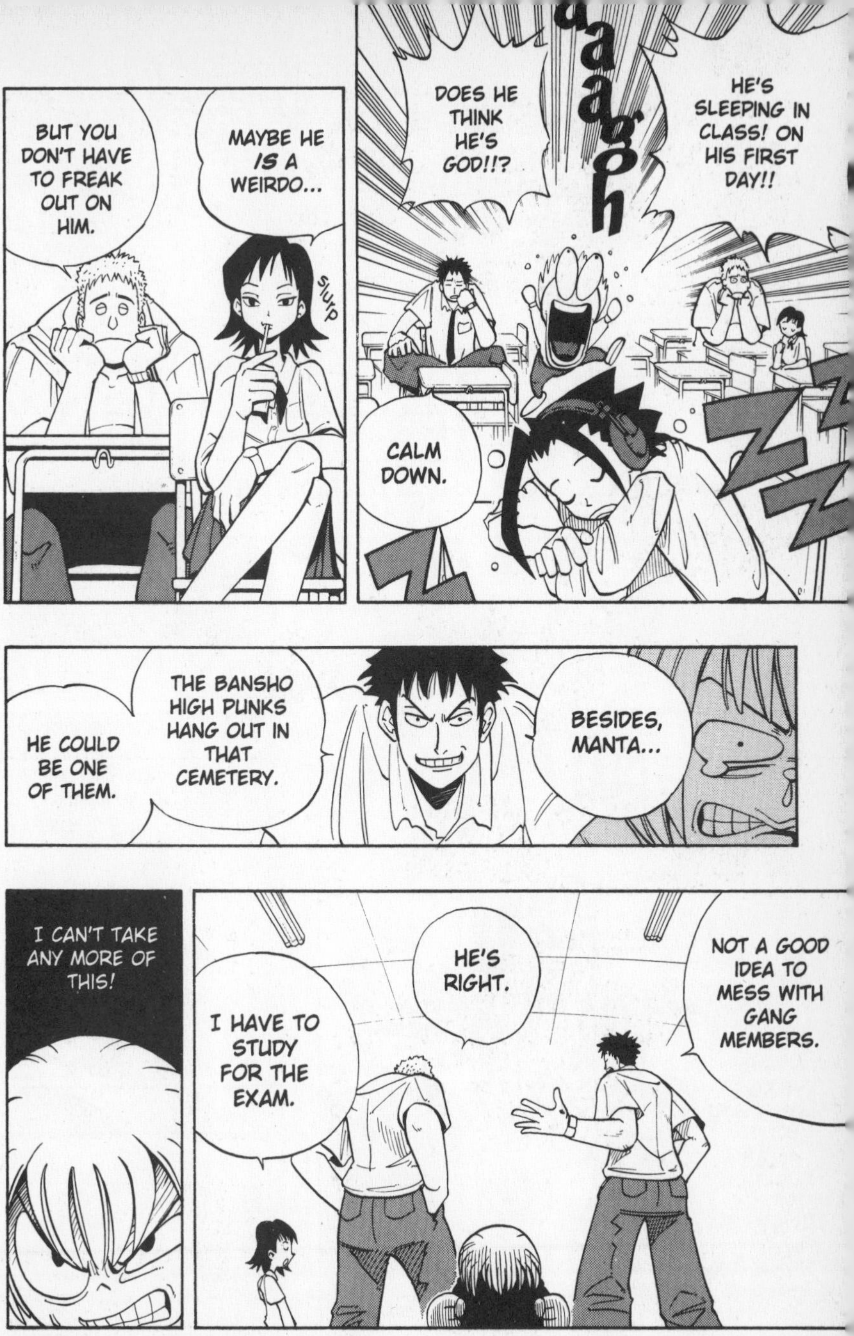
HE'S SLEEPING IN CLASS! ON HIS FIRST DAY!!
aaagh
DOES HE THINK HE'S GOD!!?
CALM DOWN.
MAYBE HE *IS* A WEIRDO...
SLURP
BUT YOU DON'T HAVE TO FREAK OUT ON HIM.
BESIDES, MANTA...
THE BANSHO HIGH PUNKS HANG OUT IN THAT CEMETERY.
HE COULD BE ONE OF THEM.
NOT A GOOD IDEA TO MESS WITH GANG MEMBERS.
HE'S RIGHT.
I HAVE TO STUDY FOR THE EXAM.
I CAN'T TAKE ANY MORE OF THIS!

READ THIS WAY

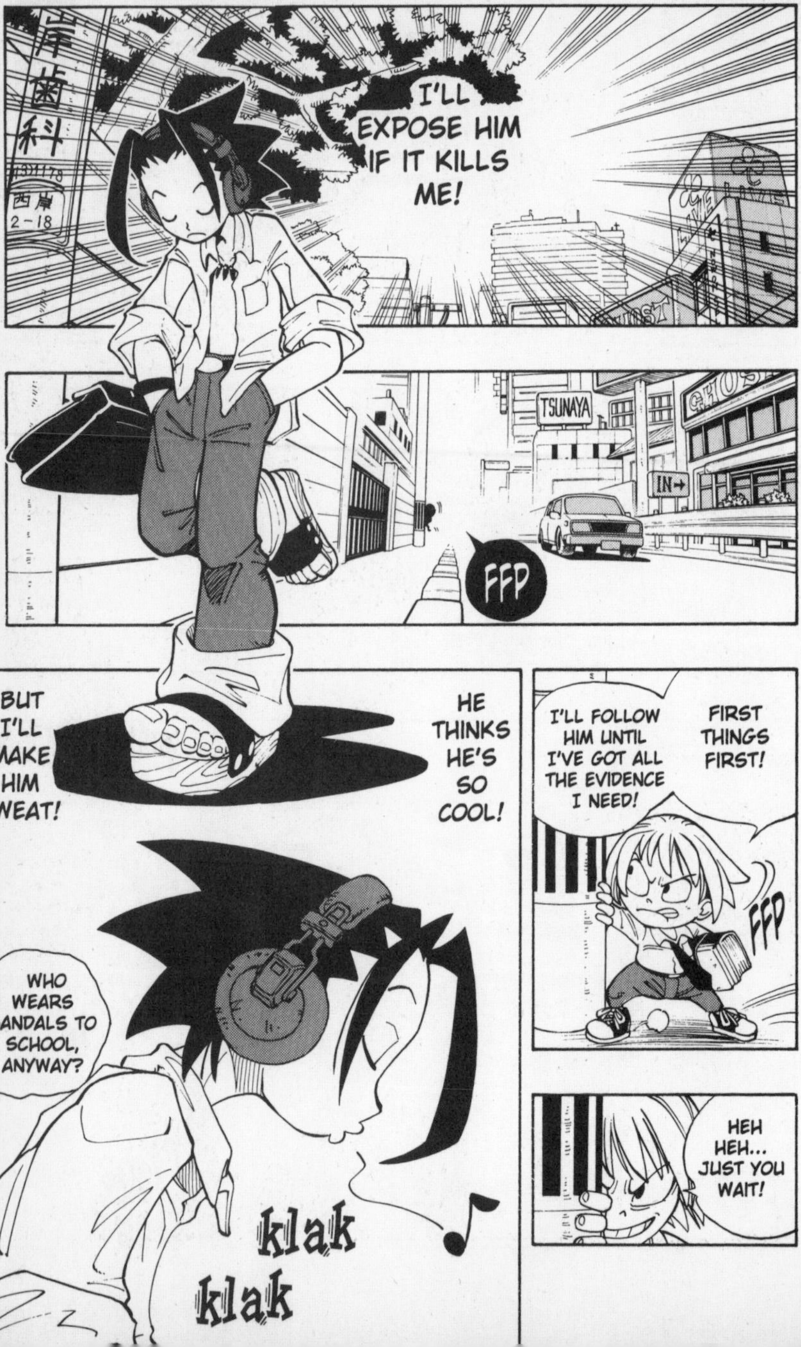

I'LL EXPOSE HIM IF IT KILLS ME!
TSUNAYA
IN→
FFP
FIRST THINGS FIRST!
I'LL FOLLOW HIM UNTIL I'VE GOT ALL THE EVIDENCE I NEED!
FFP
HEH HEH... JUST YOU WAIT!
HE THINKS HE'S SO COOL!
BUT I'LL MAKE HIM SWEAT!
WHO WEARS SANDALS TO SCHOOL, ANYWAY?
klak
klak

READ THIS WAY

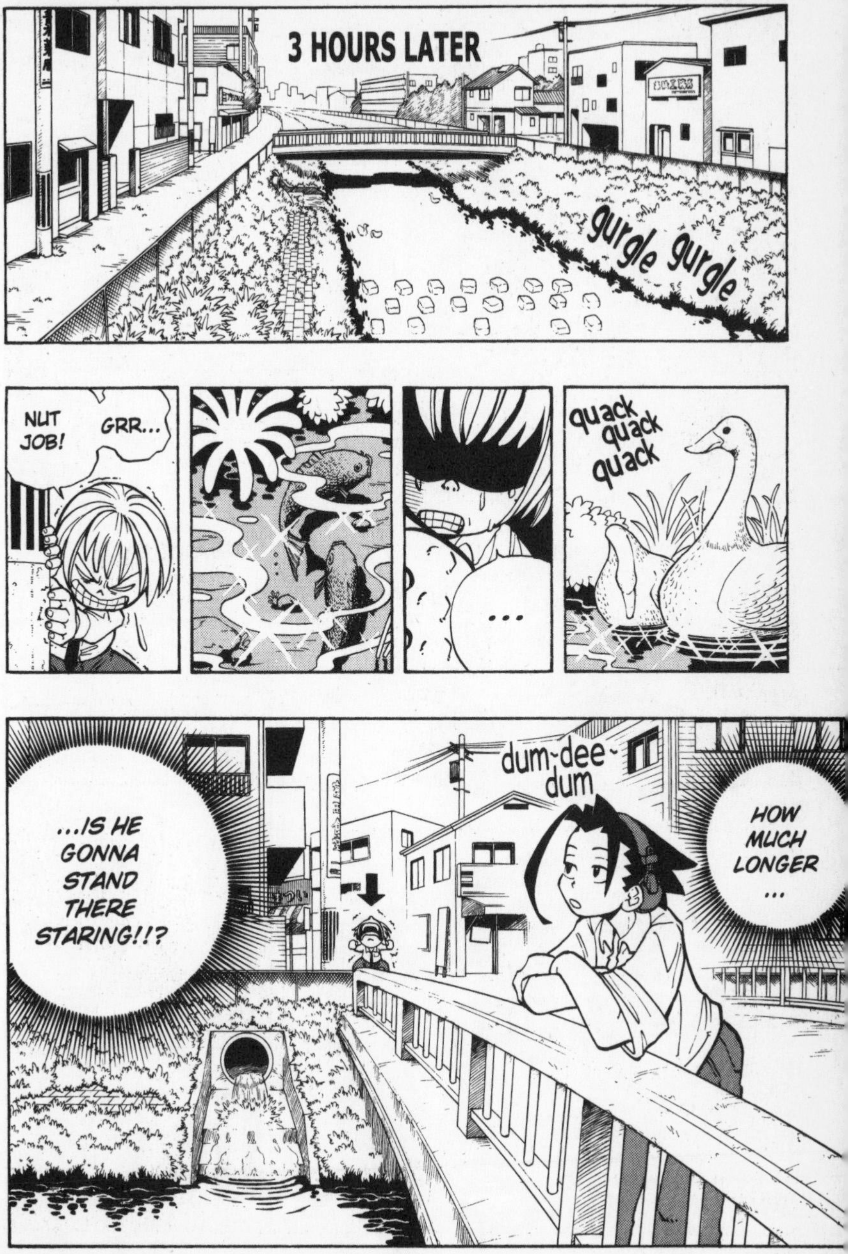
3 HOURS LATER
gurgle gurgle
quack quack quack
...
GRR...
NUT JOB!
HOW MUCH LONGER ...
dum-dee-dum
...IS HE GONNA STAND THERE STARING!!?

READ THIS WAY

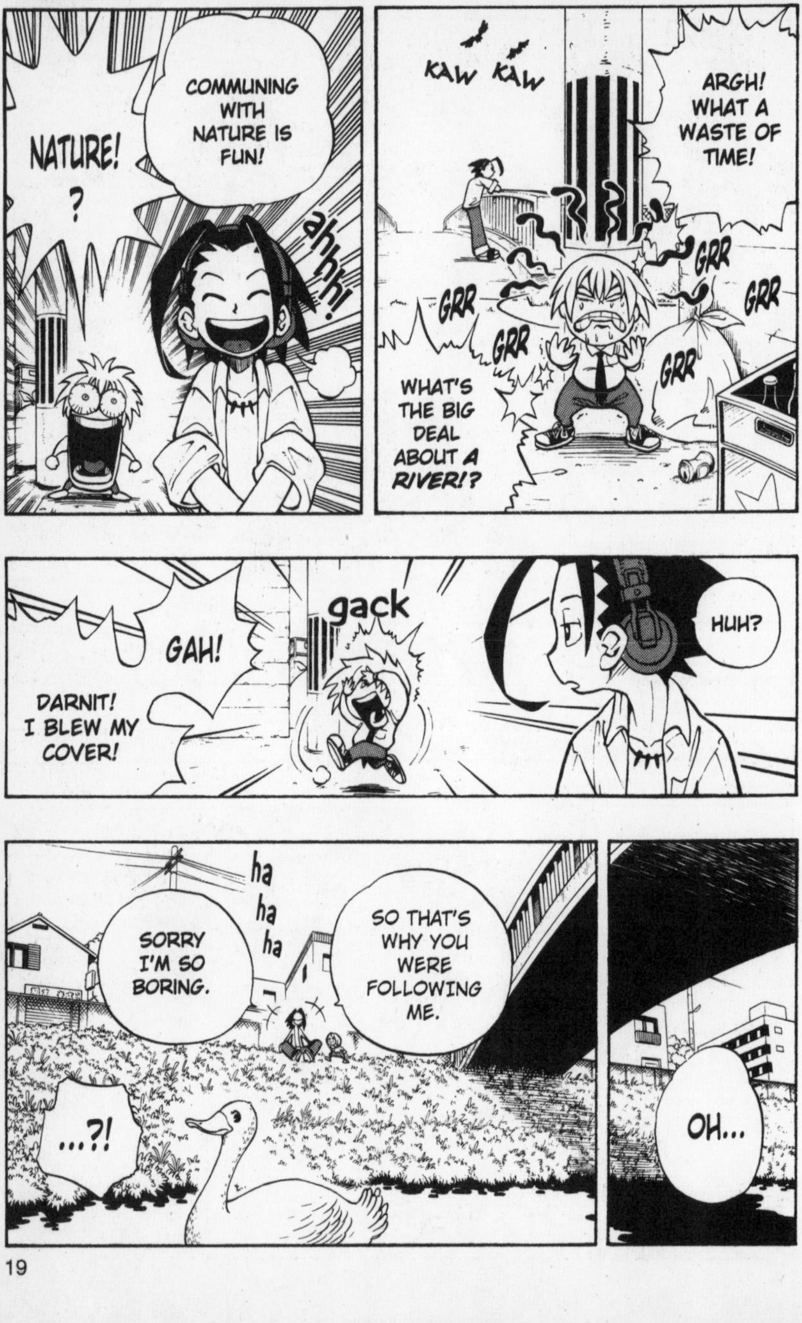

ARGH! WHAT A WASTE OF TIME!
KAW KAW
GRR
GRR
GRR
GRR
GRR
WHAT'S THE BIG DEAL ABOUT A *RIVER!?*
COMMUNING WITH NATURE IS FUN!
ahhh!
NATURE! ?
HUH?
gack
GAH!
DARNIT! I BLEW MY COVER!
OH...
SO THAT'S WHY YOU WERE FOLLOWING ME.
ha ha ha
SORRY I'M SO BORING.
...?!

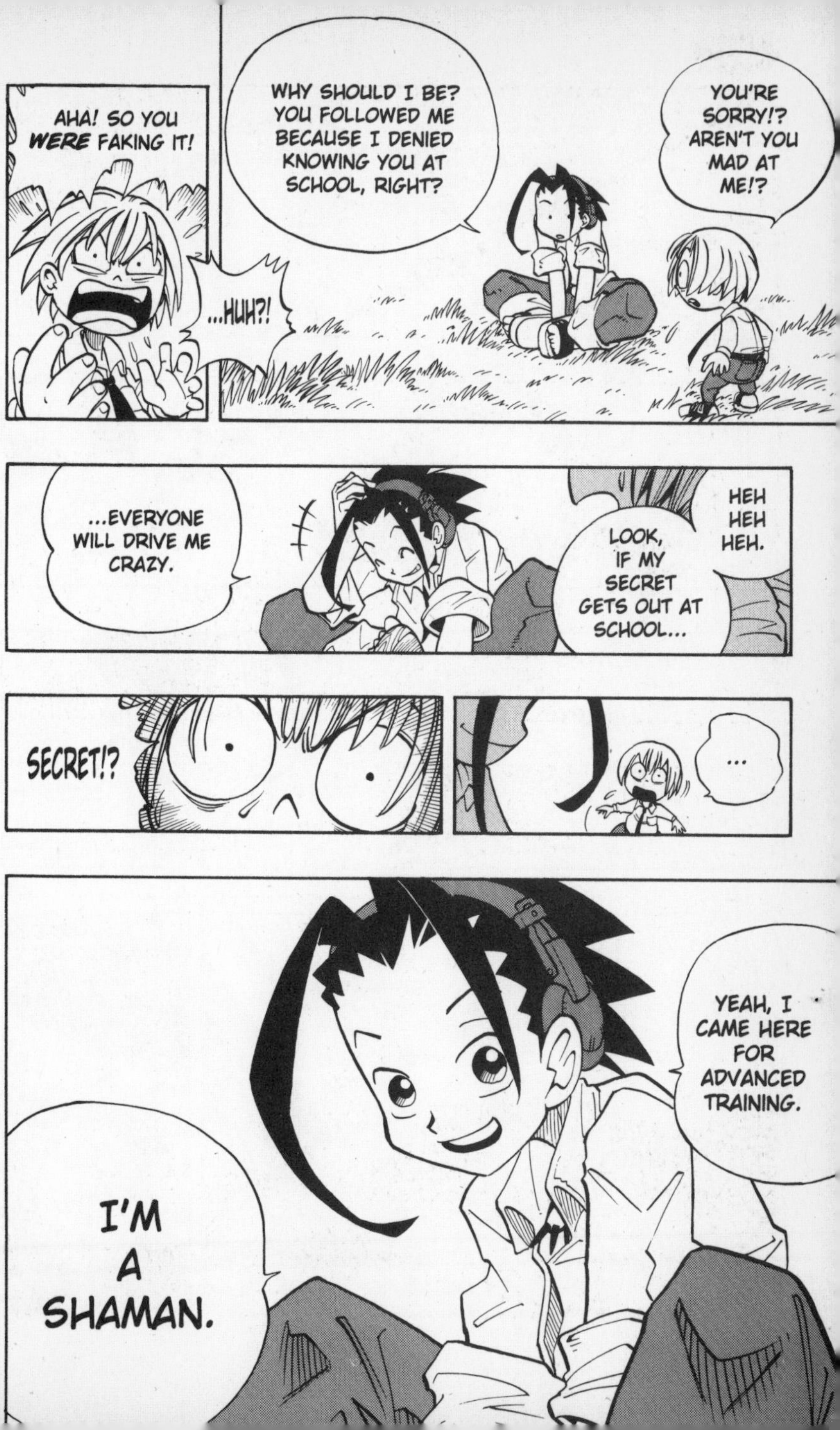
YOU'RE SORRY!? AREN'T YOU MAD AT ME!?
WHY SHOULD I BE? YOU FOLLOWED ME BECAUSE I DENIED KNOWING YOU AT SCHOOL, RIGHT?
...HUH?!
AHA! SO YOU *WERE* FAKING IT!
HEH HEH HEH.
LOOK, IF MY SECRET GETS OUT AT SCHOOL...
...EVERYONE WILL DRIVE ME CRAZY.
...
SECRET!?
YEAH, I CAME HERE FOR ADVANCED TRAINING.
I'M A SHAMAN.

READ THIS WAY

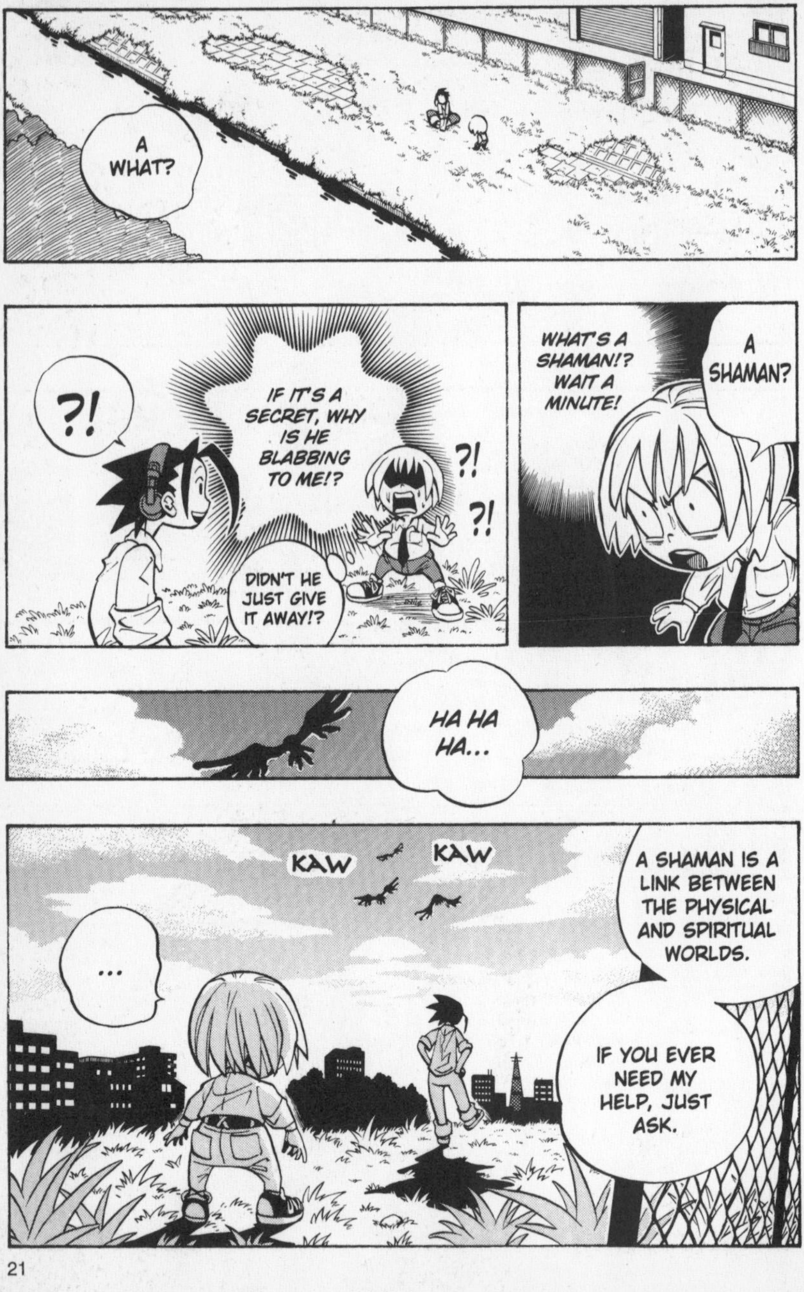

A WHAT?
A SHAMAN?
WHAT'S A SHAMAN!? WAIT A MINUTE!
IF IT'S A SECRET, WHY IS HE BLABBING TO ME!?
?! ?!
?!
DIDN'T HE JUST GIVE IT AWAY!?
HA HA HA...
A SHAMAN IS A LINK BETWEEN THE PHYSICAL AND SPIRITUAL WORLDS.
KAW
KAW
IF YOU EVER NEED MY HELP, JUST ASK.
...

READ THIS WAY

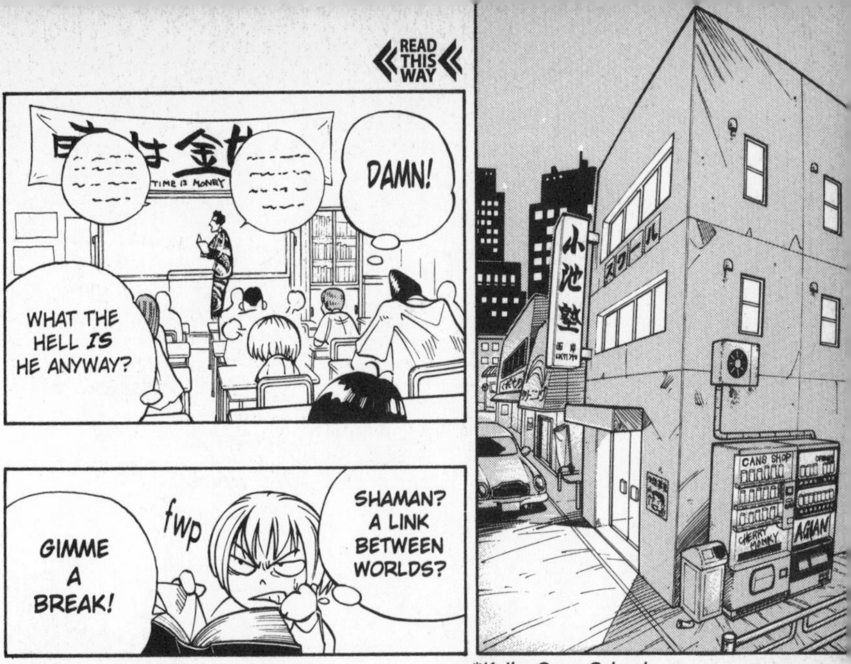
小池塾
CANS SHOP
CHERRY MONKY
TIME IS MONEY
DAMN!
WHAT THE HELL *IS* HE ANYWAY?
SHAMAN? A LINK BETWEEN WORLDS?
fwp
GIMME A BREAK!

*Koike Cram School

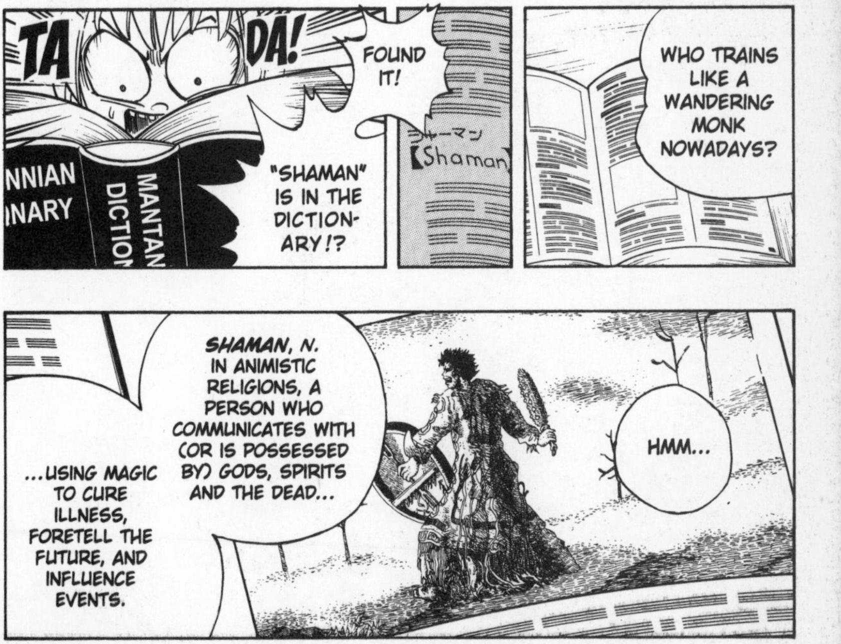
WHO TRAINS LIKE A WANDERING MONK NOWADAYS?
【Shaman】
TA
DA!
FOUND IT!
NNIAN
NARY
MANTAN
DICTIO
"SHAMAN" IS IN THE DICTION-ARY!?
HMM...
SHAMAN, N. IN ANIMISTIC RELIGIONS, A PERSON WHO COMMUNICATES WITH (OR IS POSSESSED BY) GODS, SPIRITS AND THE DEAD...
...USING MAGIC TO CURE ILLNESS, FORETELL THE FUTURE, AND INFLUENCE EVENTS.

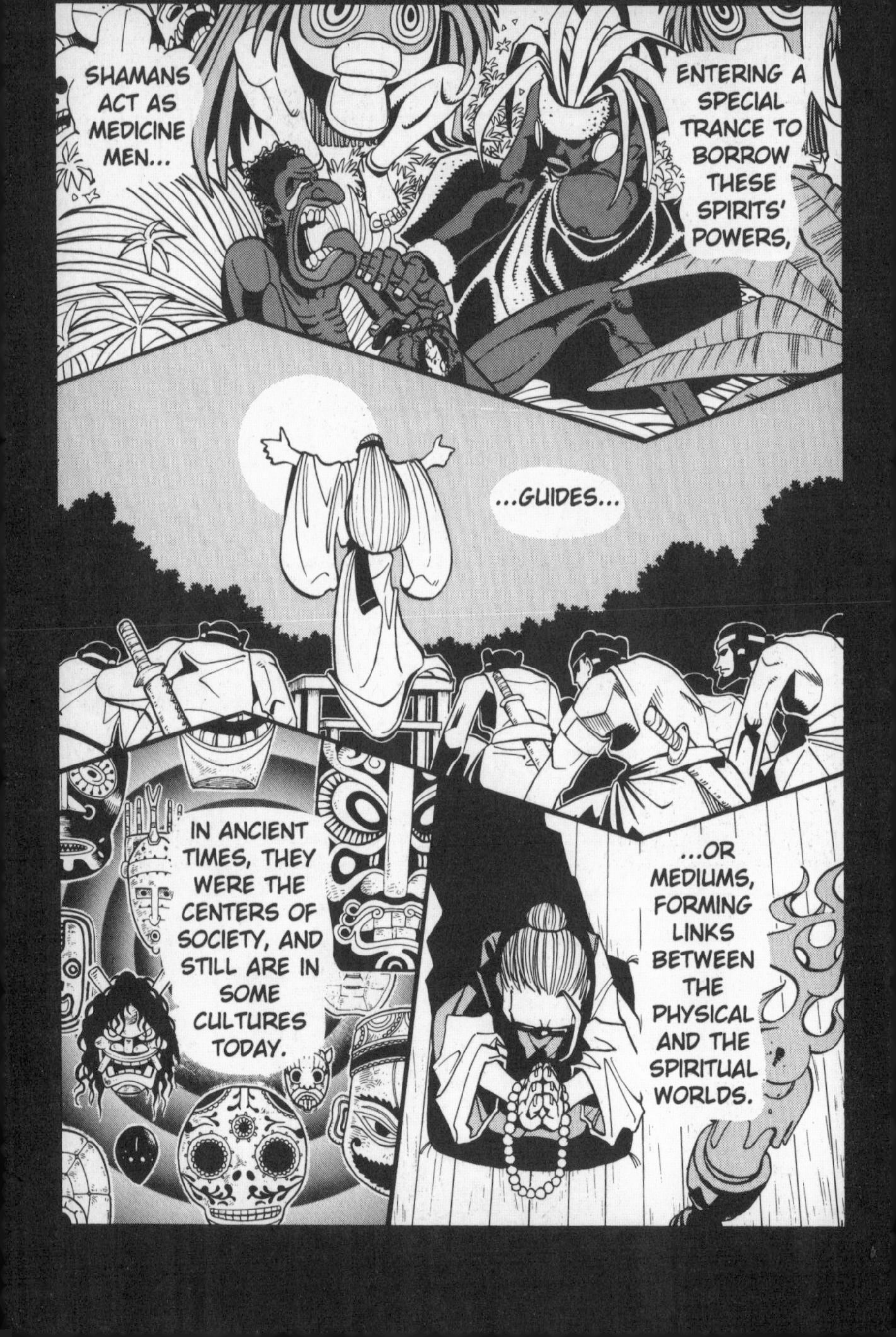
ENTERING A SPECIAL TRANCE TO BORROW THESE SPIRITS' POWERS,
SHAMANS ACT AS MEDICINE MEN...
...GUIDES...
...OR MEDIUMS, FORMING LINKS BETWEEN THE PHYSICAL AND THE SPIRITUAL WORLDS.
IN ANCIENT TIMES, THEY WERE THE CENTERS OF SOCIETY, AND STILL ARE IN SOME CULTURES TODAY.

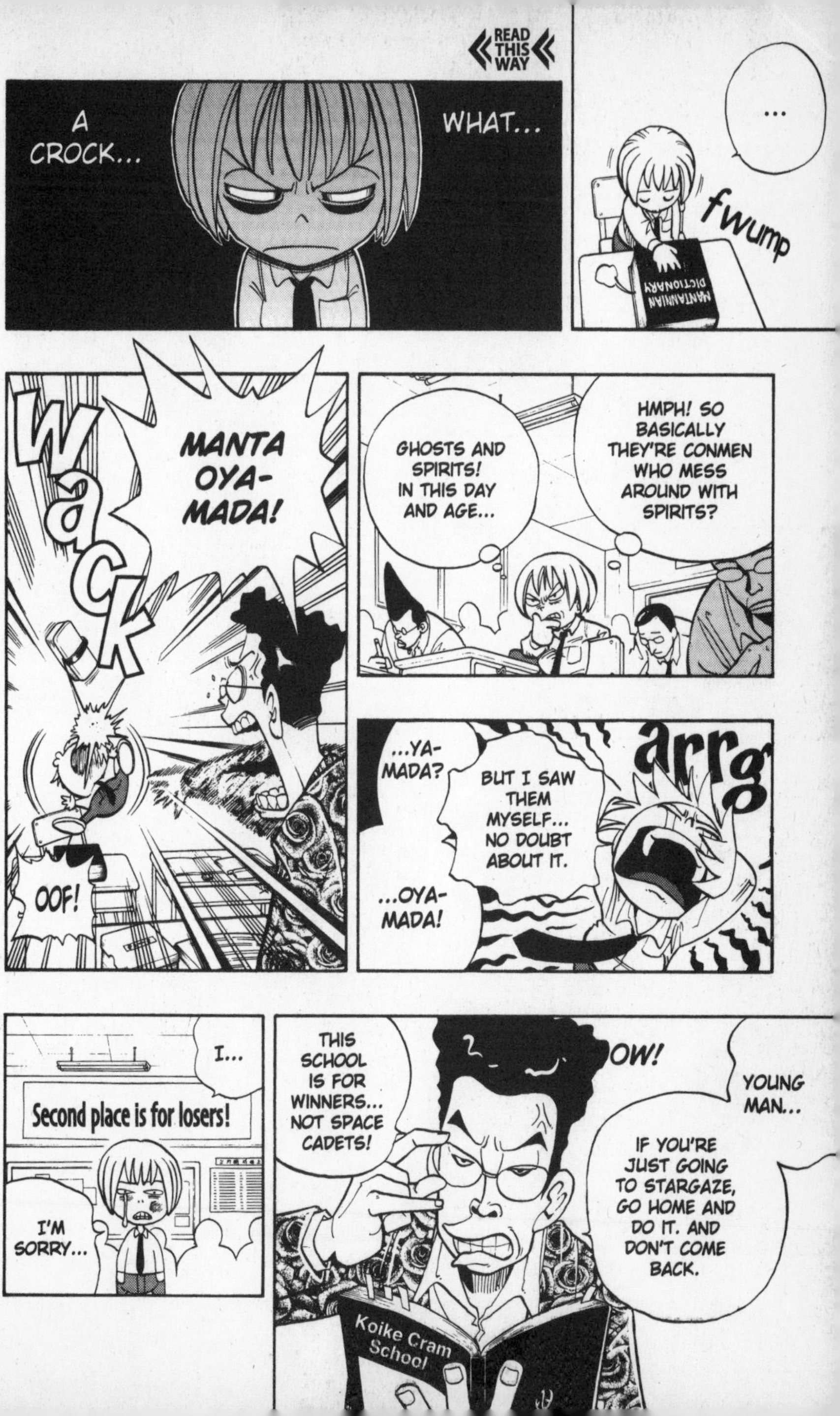
READ THIS WAY
...
fwump
WHAT...
A CROCK...
HMPH! SO BASICALLY THEY'RE CONMEN WHO MESS AROUND WITH SPIRITS?
GHOSTS AND SPIRITS! IN THIS DAY AND AGE...
arrg
BUT I SAW THEM MYSELF... NO DOUBT ABOUT IT.
...YA-MADA?
...OYA-MADA!
MANTA OYA-MADA!
Wack
OOF!
YOUNG MAN...
IF YOU'RE JUST GOING TO STARGAZE, GO HOME AND DO IT. AND DON'T COME BACK.
OW!
THIS SCHOOL IS FOR WINNERS... NOT SPACE CADETS!
Koike Cram School
I...
Second place is for losers!
I'M SORRY...

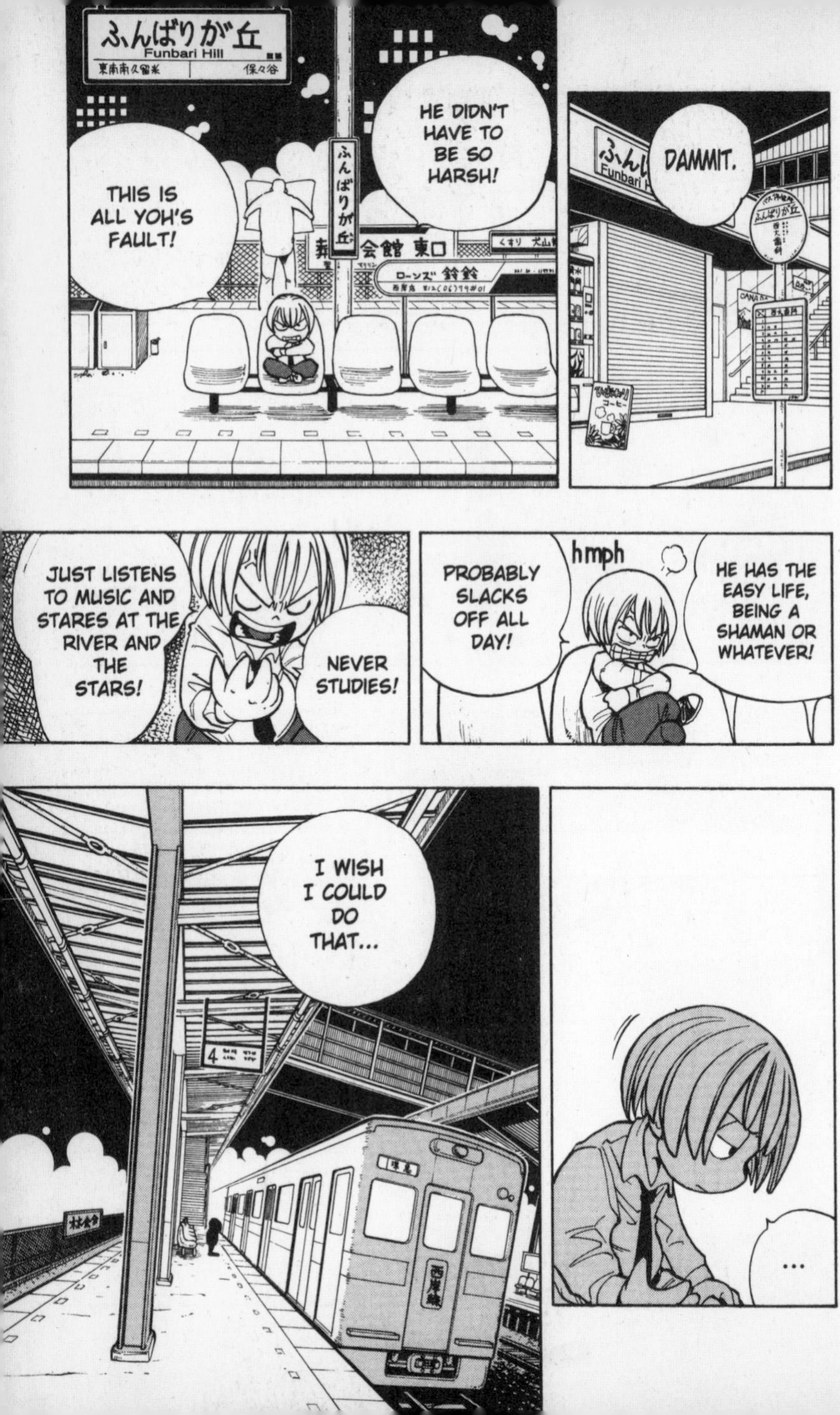
ふんばりが丘
Funbari Hill
東南南久留米
保々谷
DAMMIT.
HE DIDN'T HAVE TO BE SO HARSH!
THIS IS ALL YOH'S FAULT!
HE HAS THE EASY LIFE, BEING A SHAMAN OR WHATEVER!
hmph
PROBABLY SLACKS OFF ALL DAY!
NEVER STUDIES!
JUST LISTENS TO MUSIC AND STARES AT THE RIVER AND THE STARS!
...
I WISH I COULD DO THAT...

READ THIS WAY

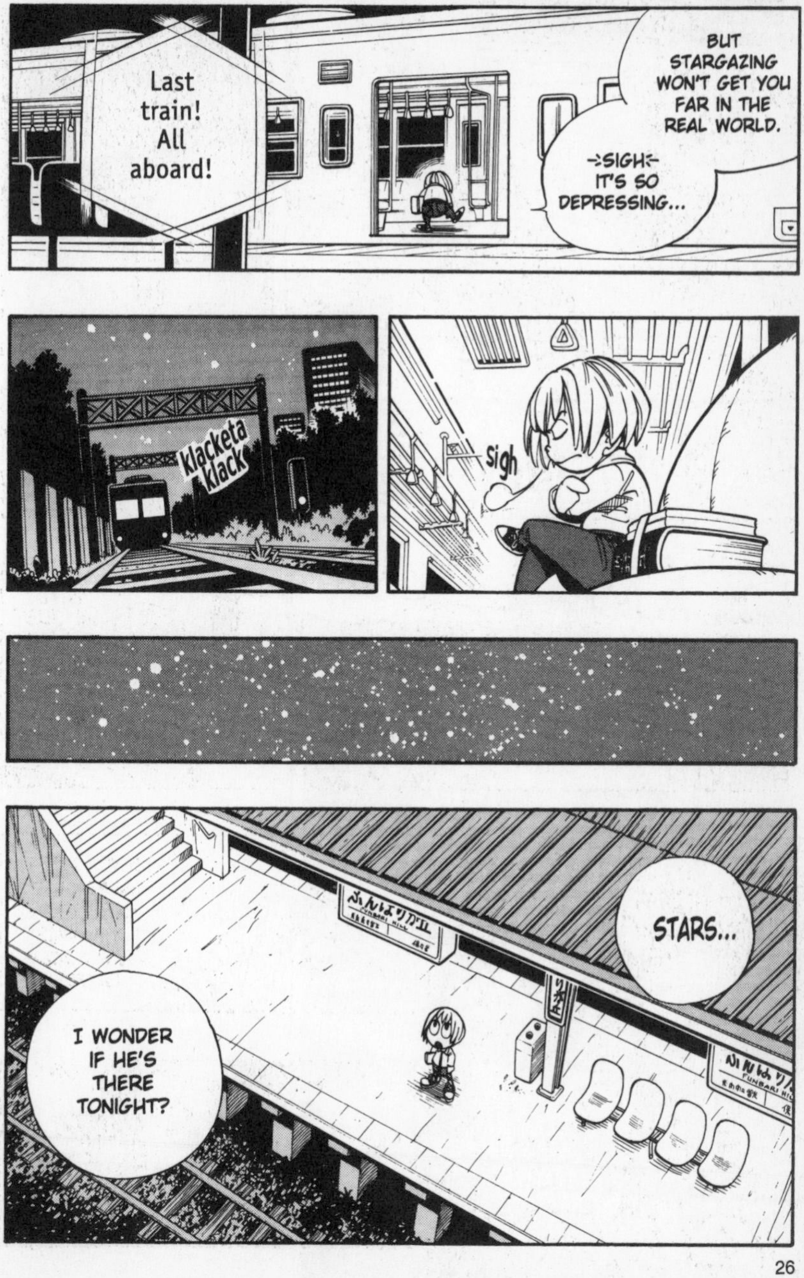

BUT STARGAZING WON'T GET YOU FAR IN THE REAL WORLD.
-SIGH- IT'S SO DEPRESSING...
Last train! All aboard!
sigh
klacketa klack
STARS...
I WONDER IF HE'S THERE TONIGHT?

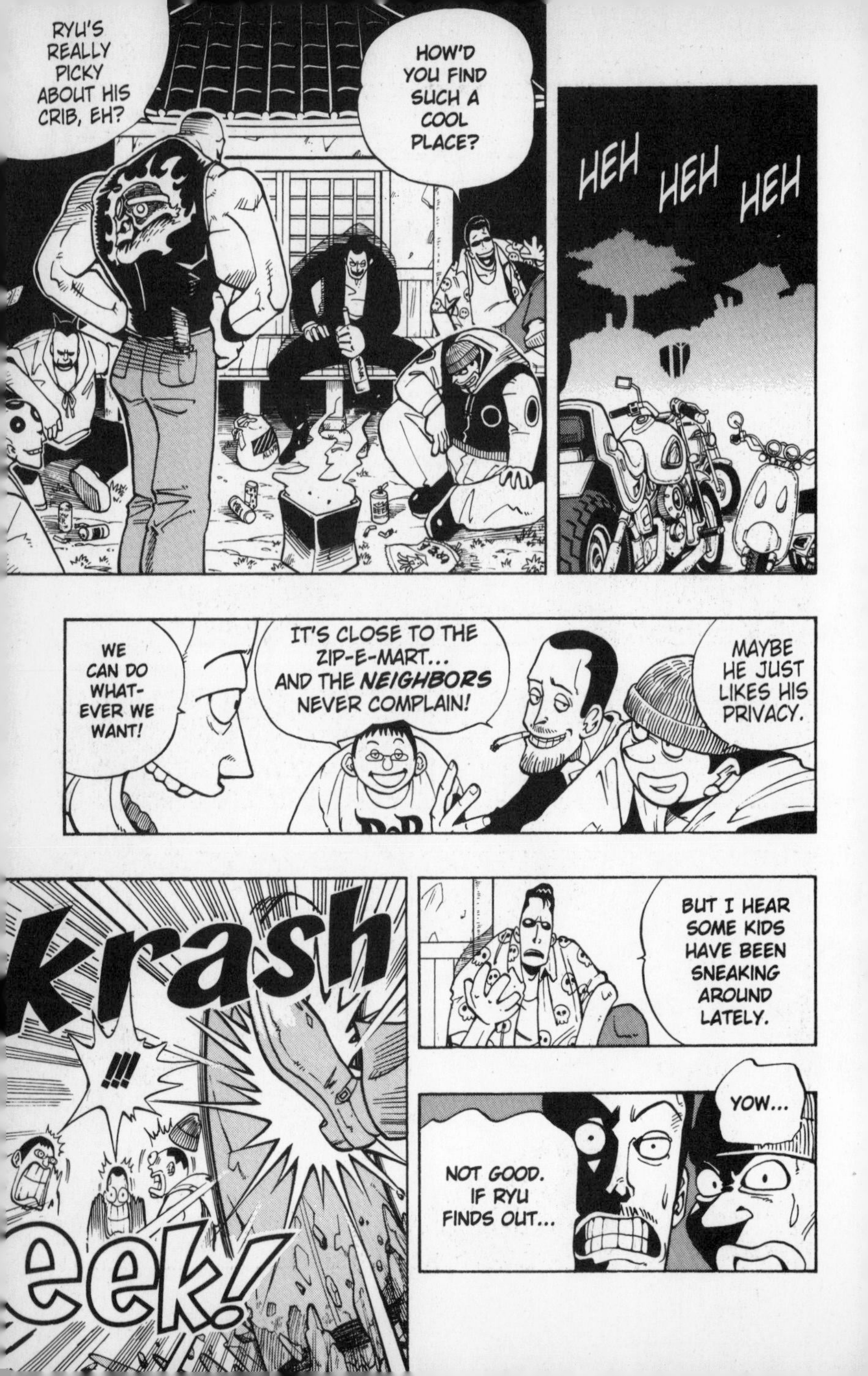
HEH HEH HEH
HOW'D YOU FIND SUCH A COOL PLACE?
RYU'S REALLY PICKY ABOUT HIS CRIB, EH?
MAYBE HE JUST LIKES HIS PRIVACY.
IT'S CLOSE TO THE ZIP-E-MART... AND THE NEIGHBORS NEVER COMPLAIN!
WE CAN DO WHAT-EVER WE WANT!
BUT I HEAR SOME KIDS HAVE BEEN SNEAKING AROUND LATELY.
YOW...
NOT GOOD. IF RYU FINDS OUT...
krash
!!!
eek!

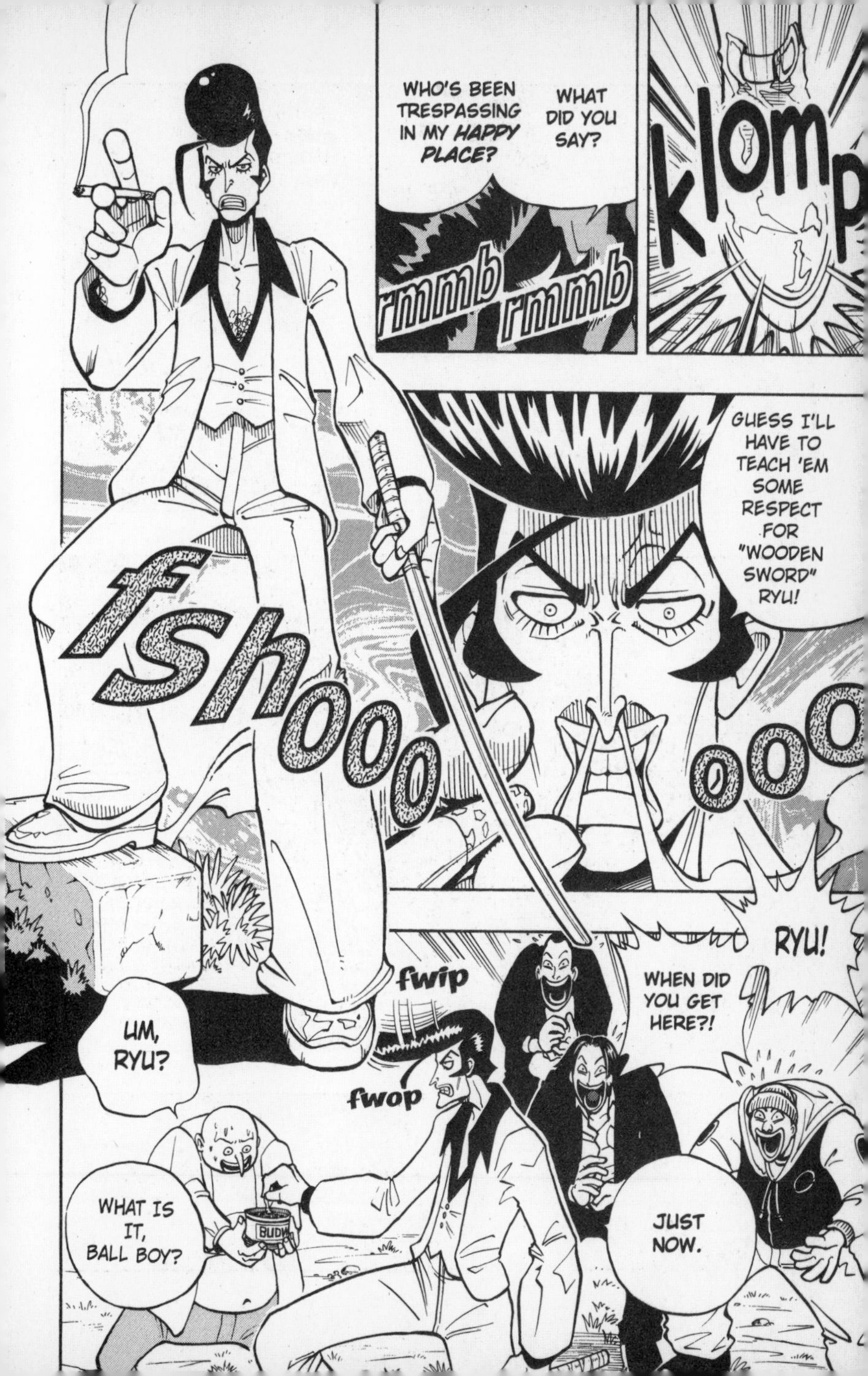
klomp
WHAT DID YOU SAY?
WHO'S BEEN TRESPASSING IN MY *HAPPY PLACE?*
rmmb rmmb
GUESS I'LL HAVE TO TEACH 'EM SOME RESPECT FOR "WOODEN SWORD" RYU!
fshoooooooo
RYU!
WHEN DID YOU GET HERE?!
JUST NOW.
fwip
fwop
UM, RYU?
WHAT IS IT, BALL BOY?

READ THIS WAY

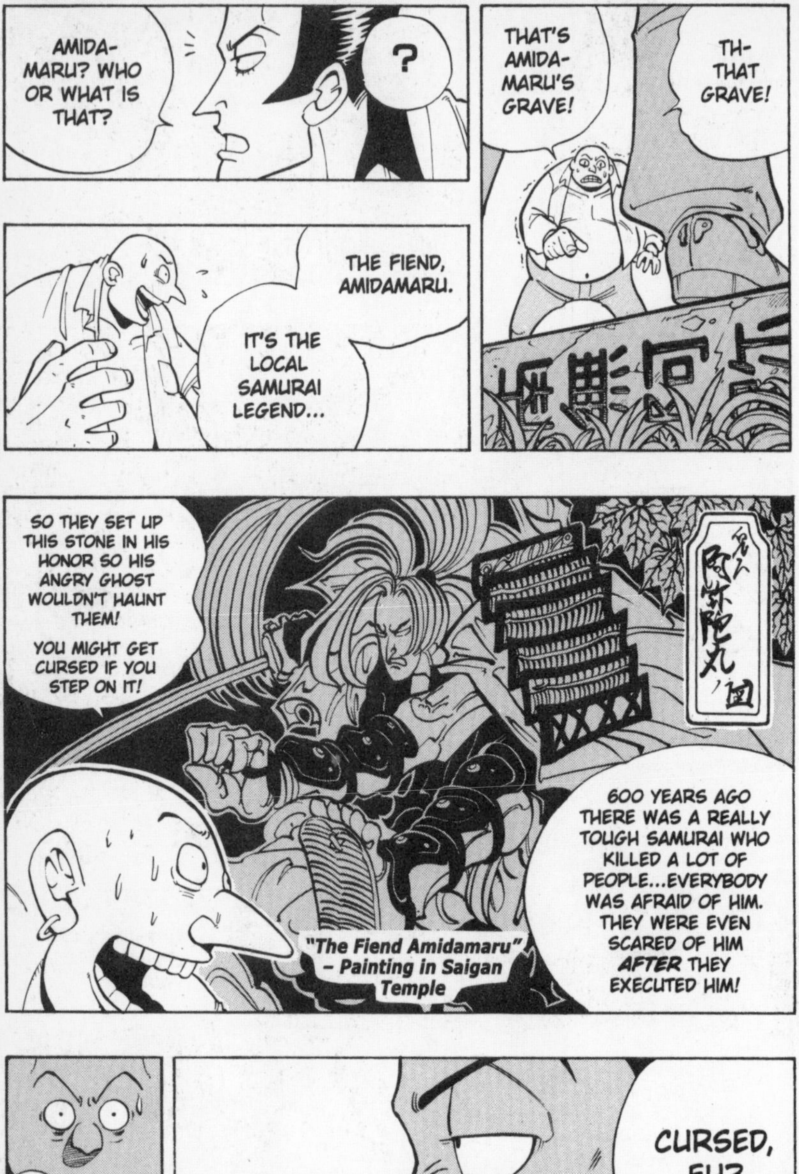
TH-THAT GRAVE!
THAT'S AMIDA-MARU'S GRAVE!
AMIDA-MARU? WHO OR WHAT IS THAT?
?
THE FIEND, AMIDAMARU.
IT'S THE LOCAL SAMURAI LEGEND...
600 YEARS AGO THERE WAS A REALLY TOUGH SAMURAI WHO KILLED A LOT OF PEOPLE...EVERYBODY WAS AFRAID OF HIM. THEY WERE EVEN SCARED OF HIM AFTER THEY EXECUTED HIM!
"The Fiend Amidamaru" – Painting in Saigan Temple
SO THEY SET UP THIS STONE IN HIS HONOR SO HIS ANGRY GHOST WOULDN'T HAUNT THEM!
YOU MIGHT GET CURSED IF YOU STEP ON IT!
CURSED, EH?
HUH?

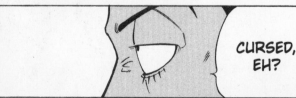

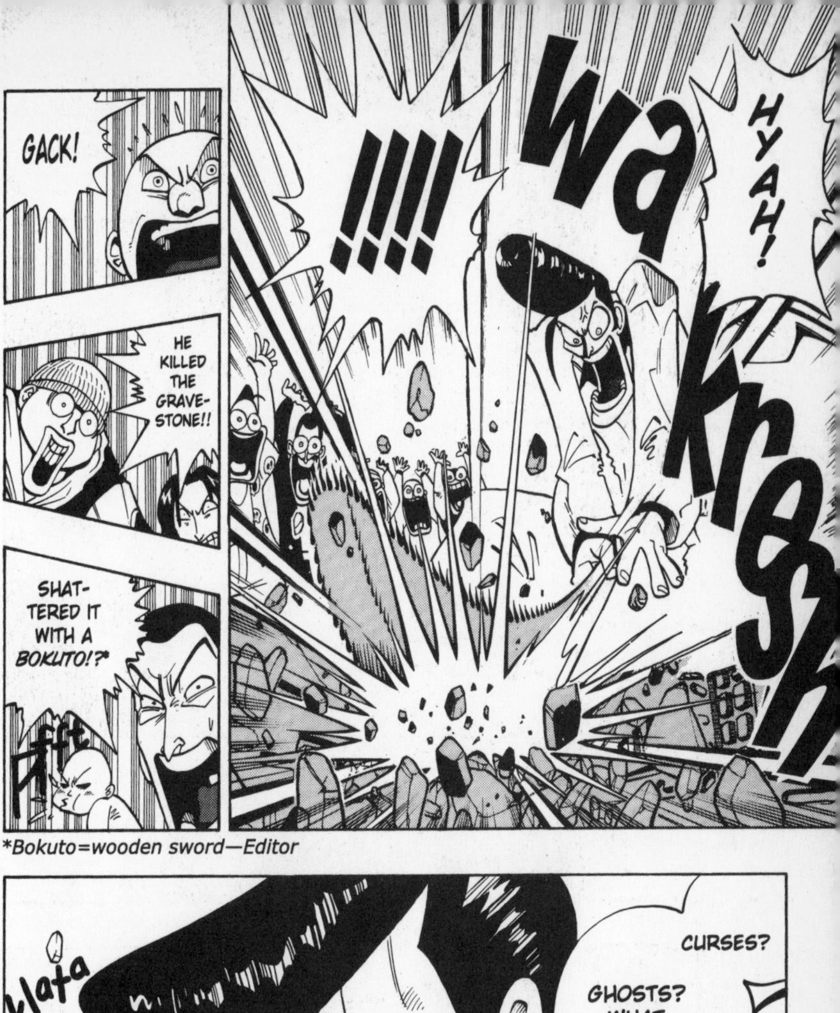
HYAH!
WA KRESH!
!!!!
GACK!
HE KILLED THE GRAVE-STONE!!
SHAT-TERED IT WITH A BOKUTO!?*
fft

*Bokuto=wooden sword—Editor

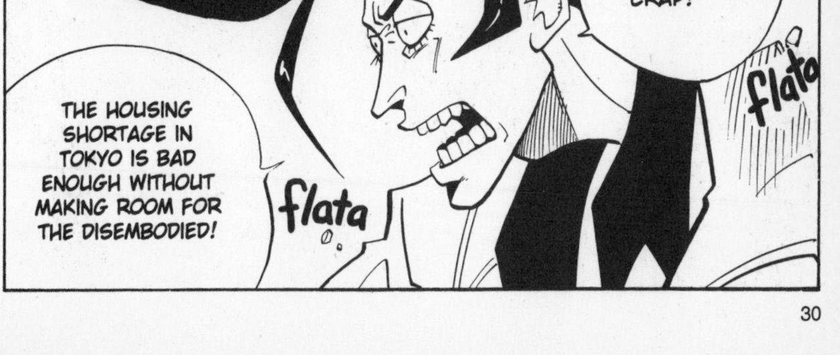
CURSES?
GHOSTS? WHAT CRAP!
flata
klata
THE HOUSING SHORTAGE IN TOKYO IS BAD ENOUGH WITHOUT MAKING ROOM FOR THE DISEMBODIED!
flata

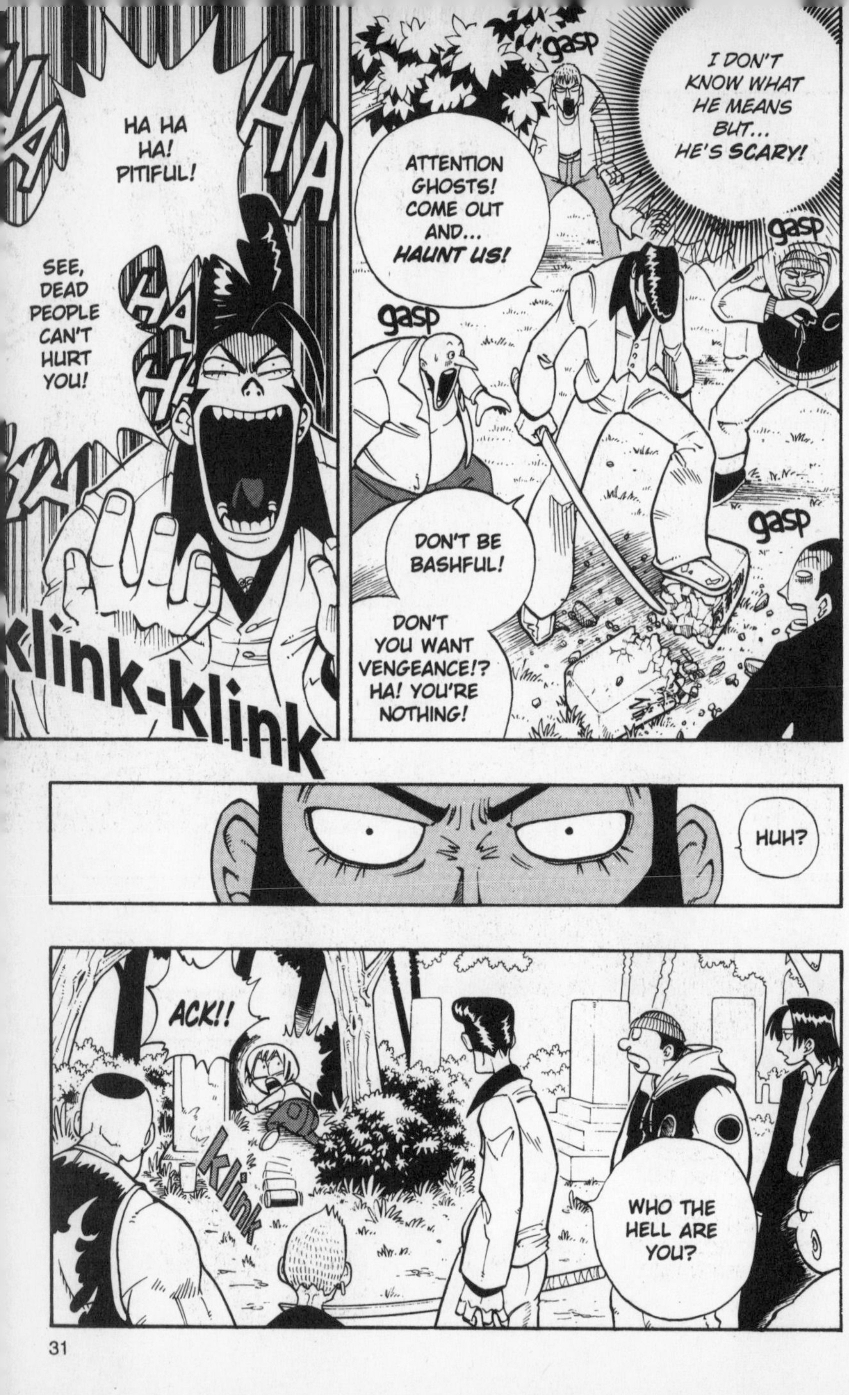
gasp
I DON'T KNOW WHAT HE MEANS BUT... HE'S SCARY!
gasp
ATTENTION GHOSTS! COME OUT AND... HAUNT US!
gasp
gasp
DON'T BE BASHFUL!
DON'T YOU WANT VENGEANCE!? HA! YOU'RE NOTHING!
HA HA
HA HA HA! PITIFUL!
HA HA HA
SEE, DEAD PEOPLE CAN'T HURT YOU!
klink-klink
HUH?
WHO THE HELL ARE YOU?
ACK!!
klink

READ THIS WAY

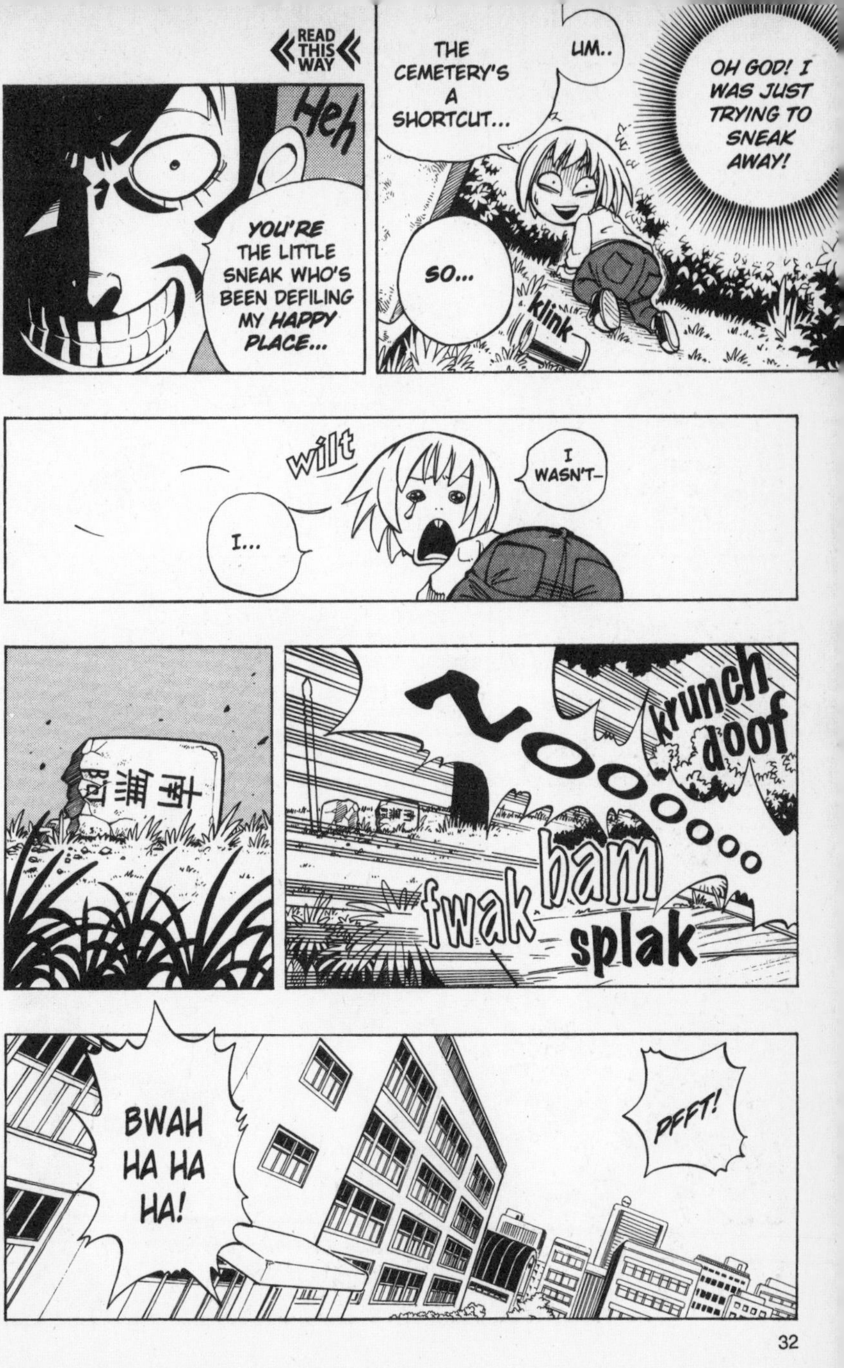
OH GOD! I WAS JUST TRYING TO SNEAK AWAY!
UM..
THE CEMETERY'S A SHORTCUT...
SO...
klink
Heh
YOU'RE THE LITTLE SNEAK WHO'S BEEN DEFILING MY HAPPY PLACE...
I WASN'T–
wilt
I...
krunch
doof
NOOOOOOO
bam
fwak
splak
PFFT!
BWAH HA HA HA!

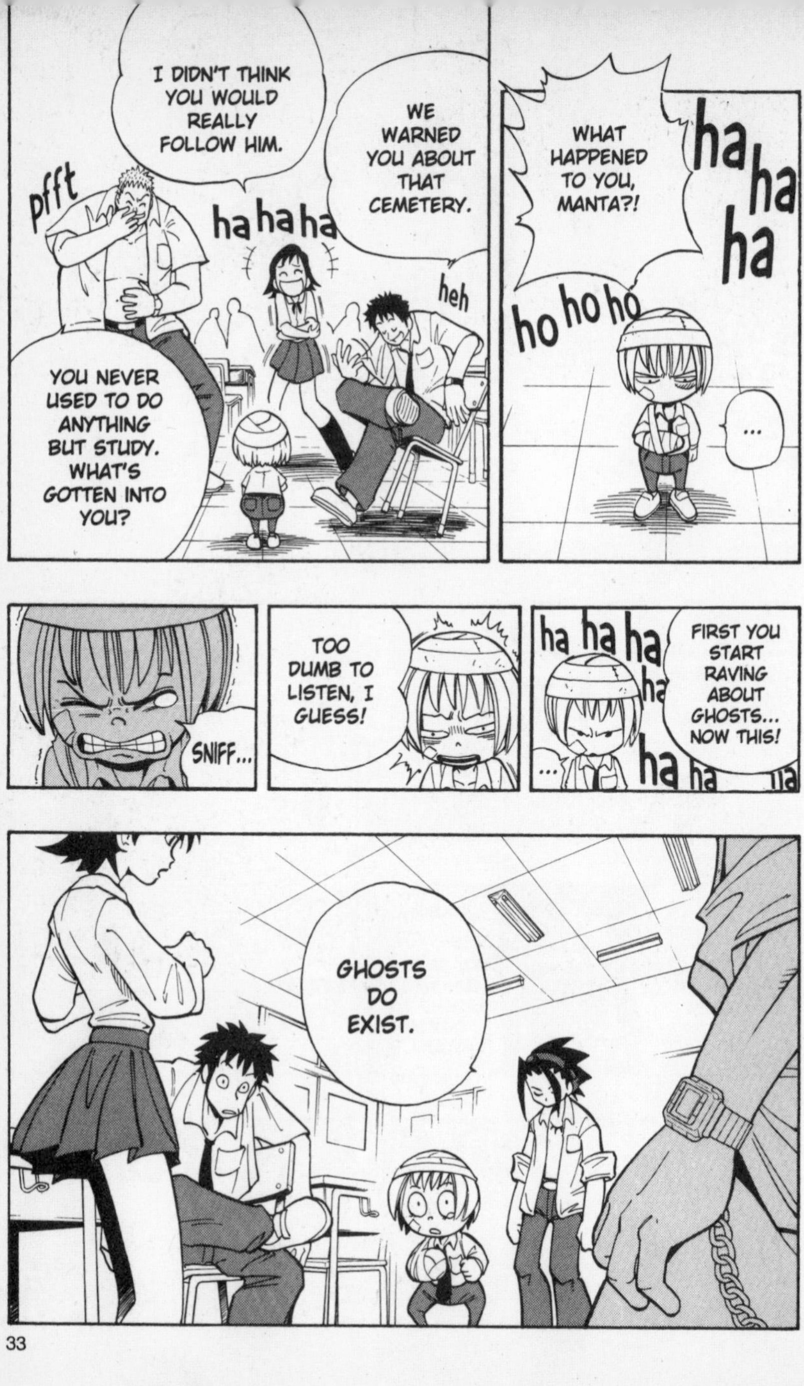
WHAT HAPPENED TO YOU, MANTA?!
ha ha ha
ho ho ho
...
WE WARNED YOU ABOUT THAT CEMETERY.
I DIDN'T THINK YOU WOULD REALLY FOLLOW HIM.
ha ha ha
heh
pfft
YOU NEVER USED TO DO ANYTHING BUT STUDY. WHAT'S GOTTEN INTO YOU?
FIRST YOU START RAVING ABOUT GHOSTS... NOW THIS!
ha ha ha ha
ha ha
...
TOO DUMB TO LISTEN, I GUESS!
SNIFF...
GHOSTS DO EXIST.

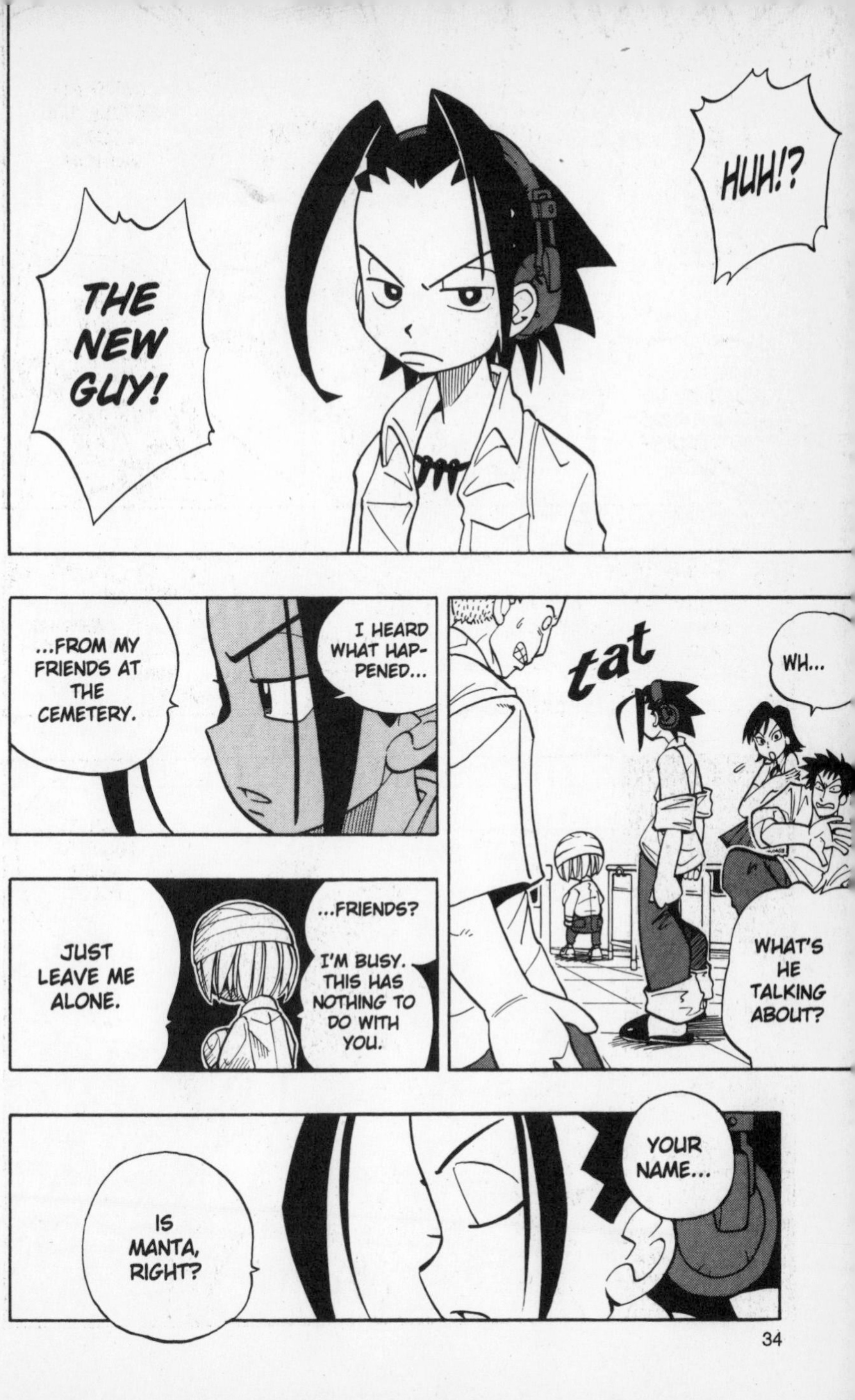
HUH!?
THE NEW GUY!
WH...
tat
WHAT'S HE TALKING ABOUT?
I HEARD WHAT HAP-PENED...
...FROM MY FRIENDS AT THE CEMETERY.
...FRIENDS?
I'M BUSY. THIS HAS NOTHING TO DO WITH YOU.
JUST LEAVE ME ALONE.
YOUR NAME...
IS MANTA, RIGHT?

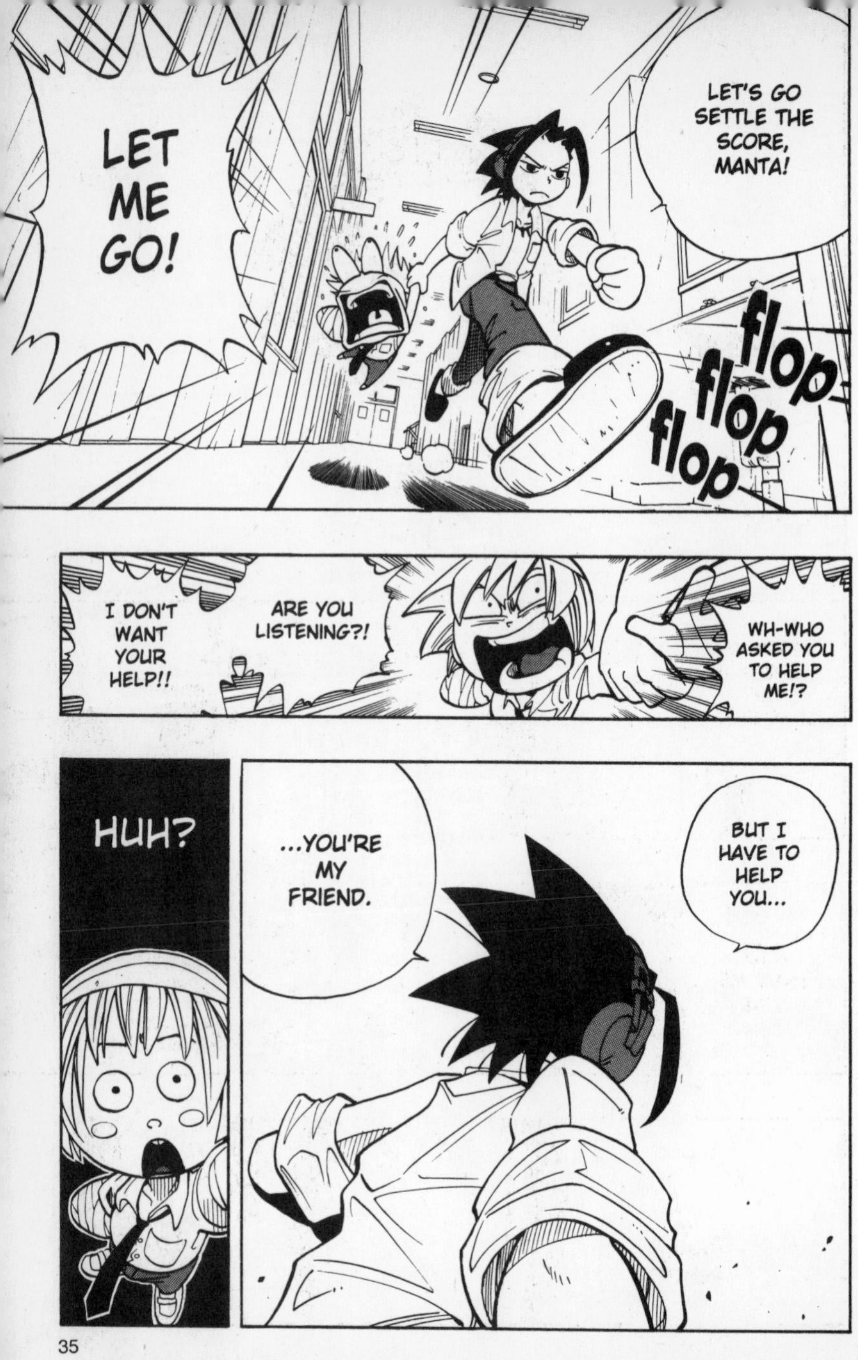
LET'S GO SETTLE THE SCORE, MANTA!
flop flop flop
LET ME GO!
WH-WHO ASKED YOU TO HELP ME!?
ARE YOU LISTENING?!
I DON'T WANT YOUR HELP!!
BUT I HAVE TO HELP YOU...
...YOU'RE MY FRIEND.
HUH?

READ THIS WAY

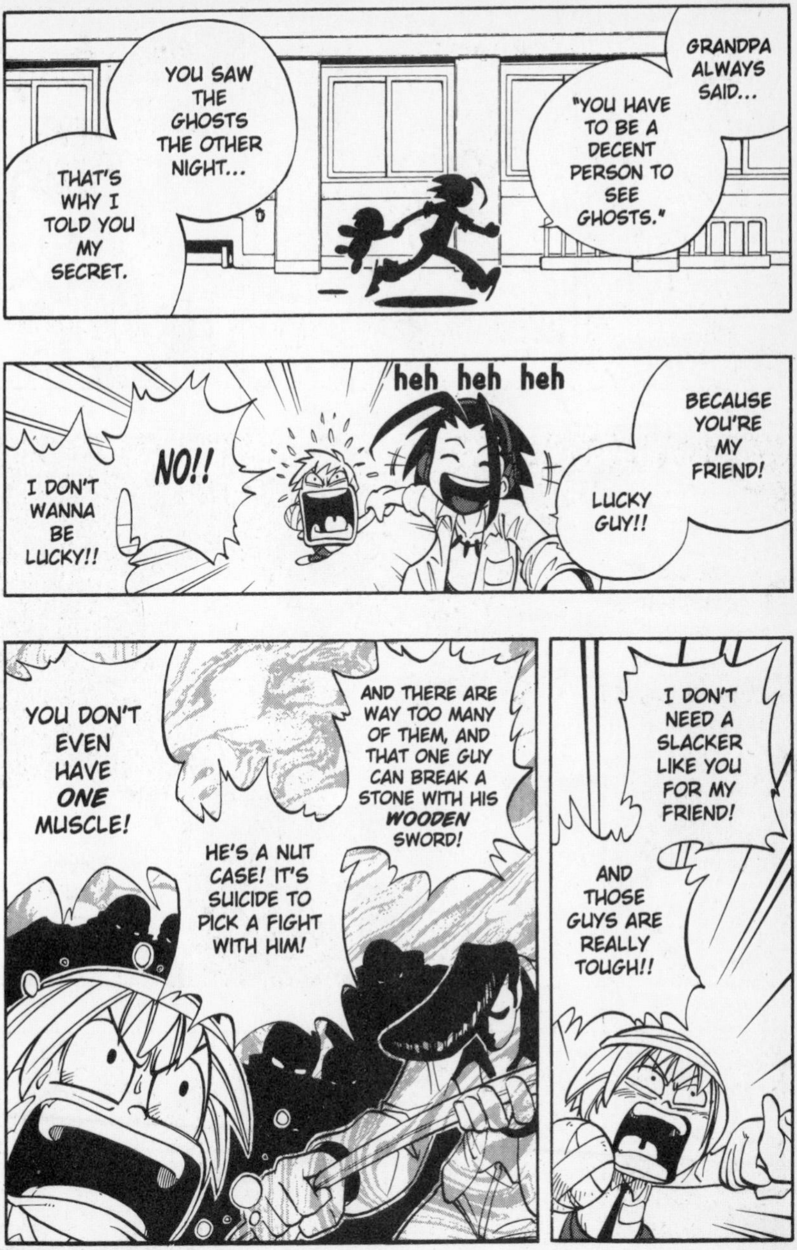
GRANDPA ALWAYS SAID...
"YOU HAVE TO BE A DECENT PERSON TO SEE GHOSTS."
YOU SAW THE GHOSTS THE OTHER NIGHT...
THAT'S WHY I TOLD YOU MY SECRET.
heh heh heh
BECAUSE YOU'RE MY FRIEND!
LUCKY GUY!!
NO!!
I DON'T WANNA BE LUCKY!!
I DON'T NEED A SLACKER LIKE YOU FOR MY FRIEND!
AND THOSE GUYS ARE REALLY TOUGH!!
AND THERE ARE WAY TOO MANY OF THEM, AND THAT ONE GUY CAN BREAK A STONE WITH HIS *WOODEN* SWORD!
YOU DON'T EVEN HAVE *ONE* MUSCLE!
HE'S A NUT CASE! IT'S SUICIDE TO PICK A FIGHT WITH HIM!

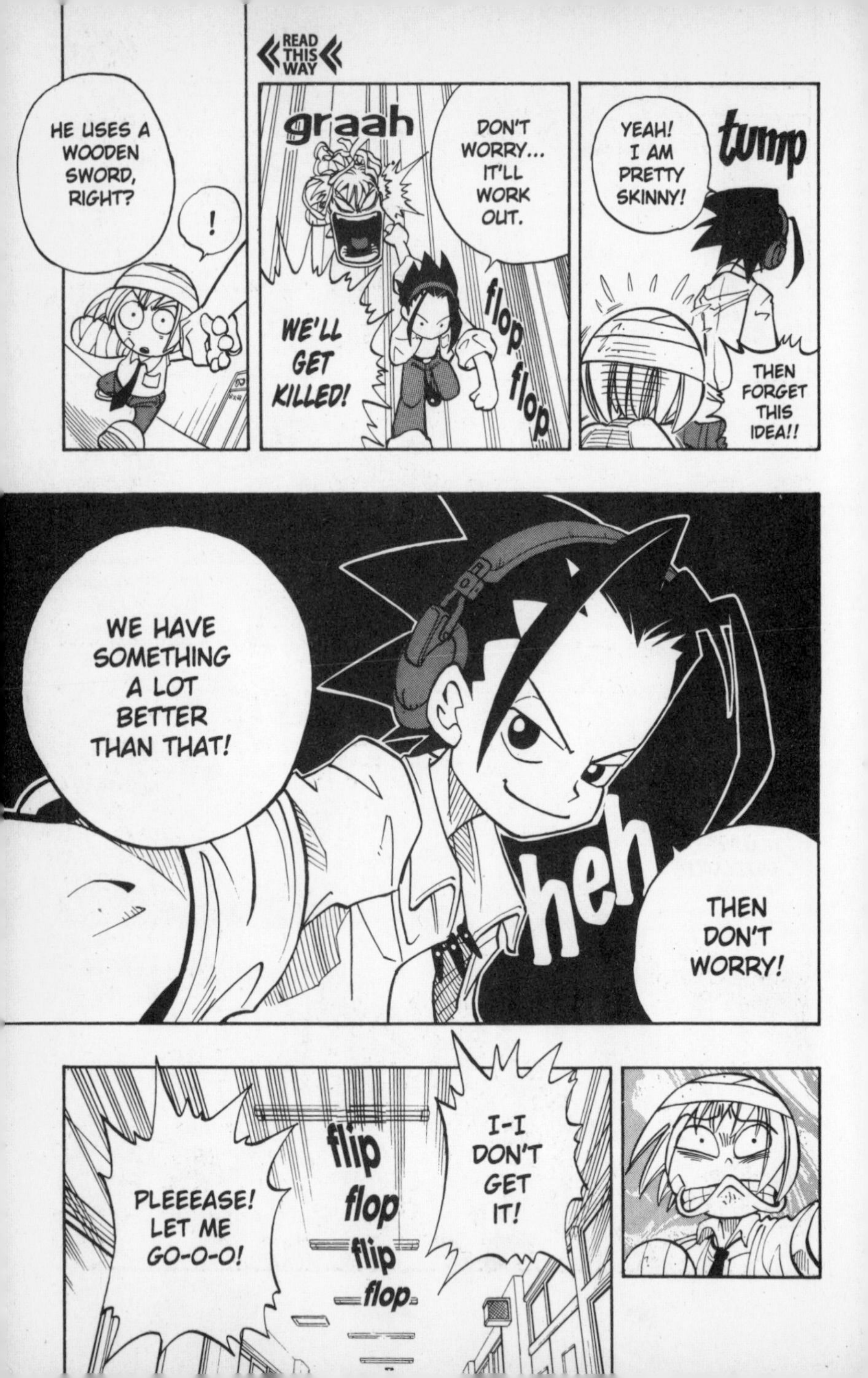
READ THIS WAY
YEAH! I AM PRETTY SKINNY!
tump
THEN FORGET THIS IDEA!!
graah
DON'T WORRY... IT'LL WORK OUT.
WE'LL GET KILLED!
flop flop
HE USES A WOODEN SWORD, RIGHT?
!
WE HAVE SOMETHING A LOT BETTER THAN THAT!
heh
THEN DON'T WORRY!
I-I DON'T GET IT!
flip
flop
flip
flop
PLEEEASE! LET ME GO-O-O!

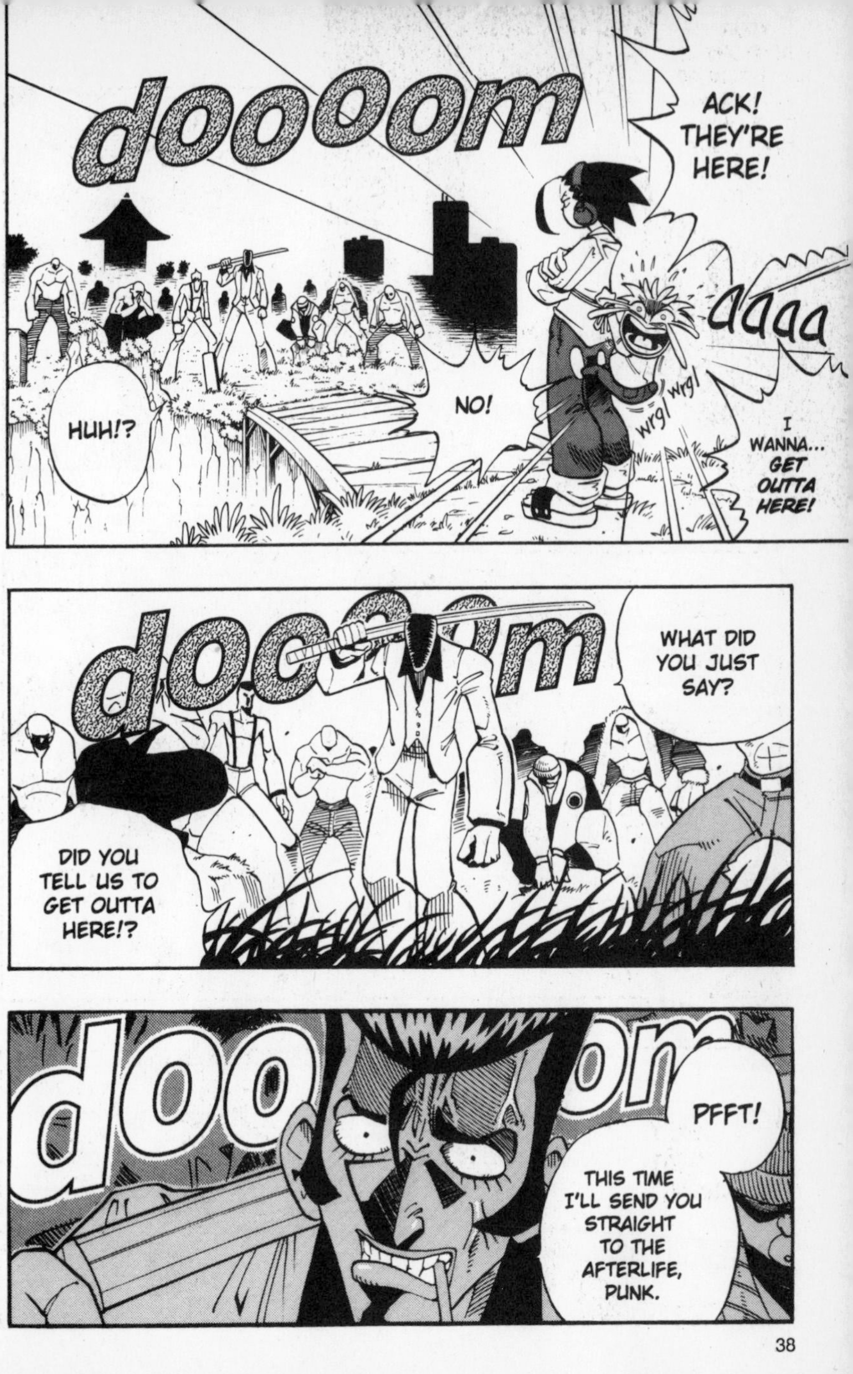
ACK! THEY'RE HERE!
aaaa
I WANNA... GET OUTTA HERE!
wrgl wrgl
NO!
dooooom
HUH!?
WHAT DID YOU JUST SAY?
DID YOU TELL US TO GET OUTTA HERE!?
PFFT!
THIS TIME I'LL SEND YOU STRAIGHT TO THE AFTERLIFE, PUNK.

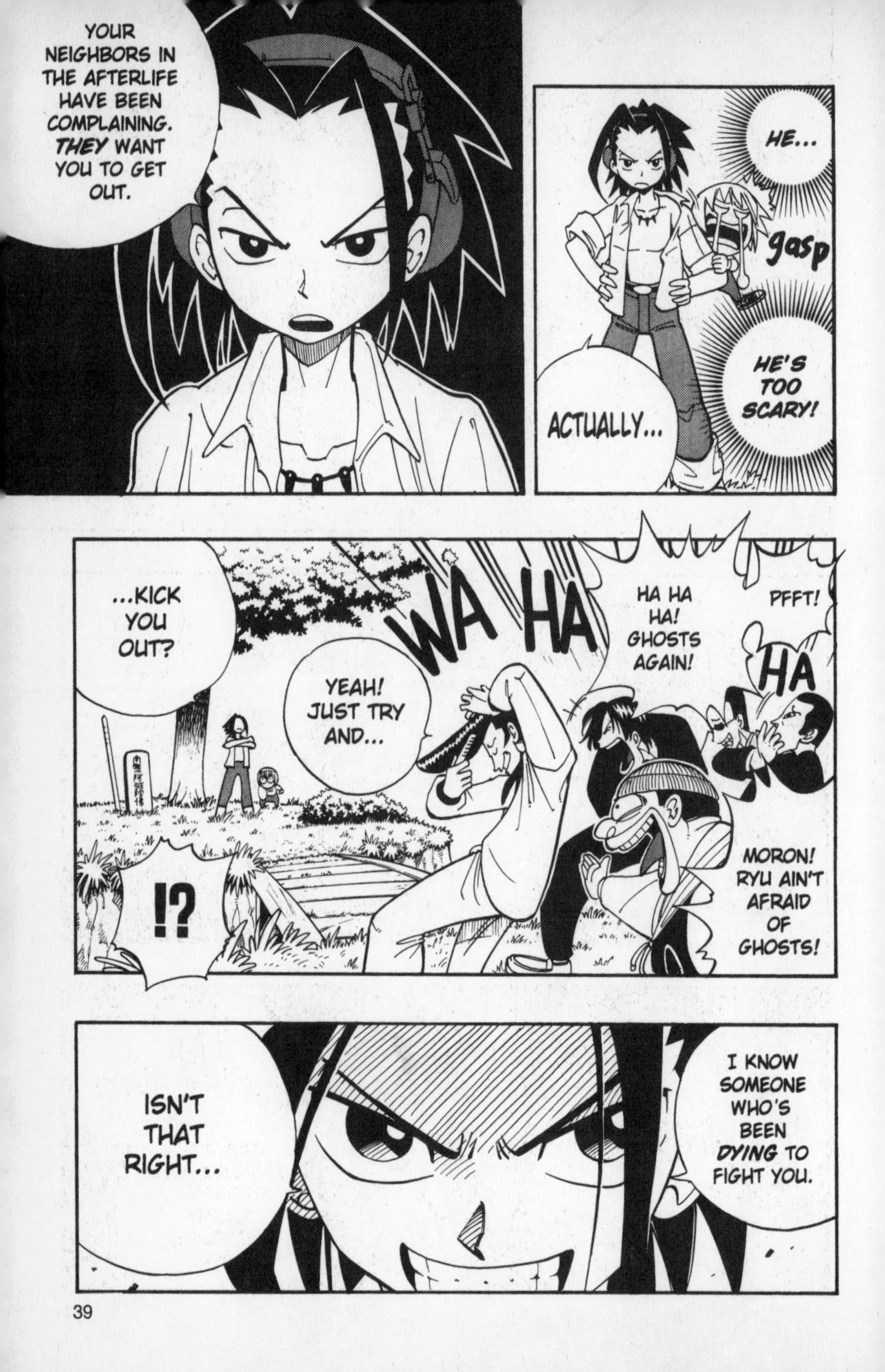
HE...
gasp
HE'S TOO SCARY!
ACTUALLY...
YOUR NEIGHBORS IN THE AFTERLIFE HAVE BEEN COMPLAINING. *THEY* WANT YOU TO GET OUT.
PFFT!
HA
HA HA HA! GHOSTS AGAIN!
WA HA
MORON! RYU AIN'T AFRAID OF GHOSTS!
YEAH! JUST TRY AND...
...KICK YOU OUT?
!?
I KNOW SOMEONE WHO'S BEEN *DYING* TO FIGHT YOU.
ISN'T THAT RIGHT...

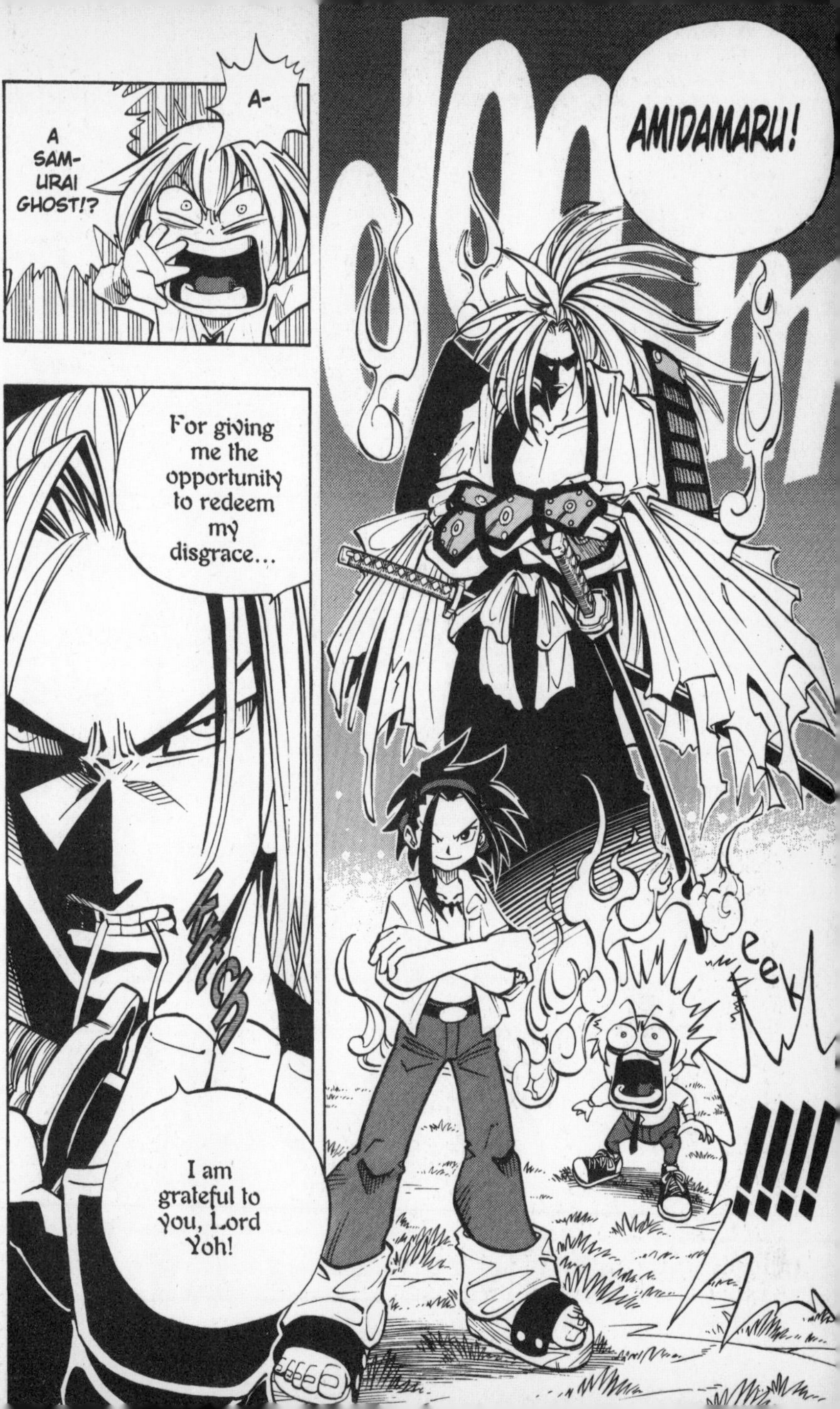
doom
AMIDAMARU!
eek!!!!
A-
A SAM-URAI GHOST!?
For giving me the opportunity to redeem my disgrace...
twitch
I am grateful to you, Lord Yoh!

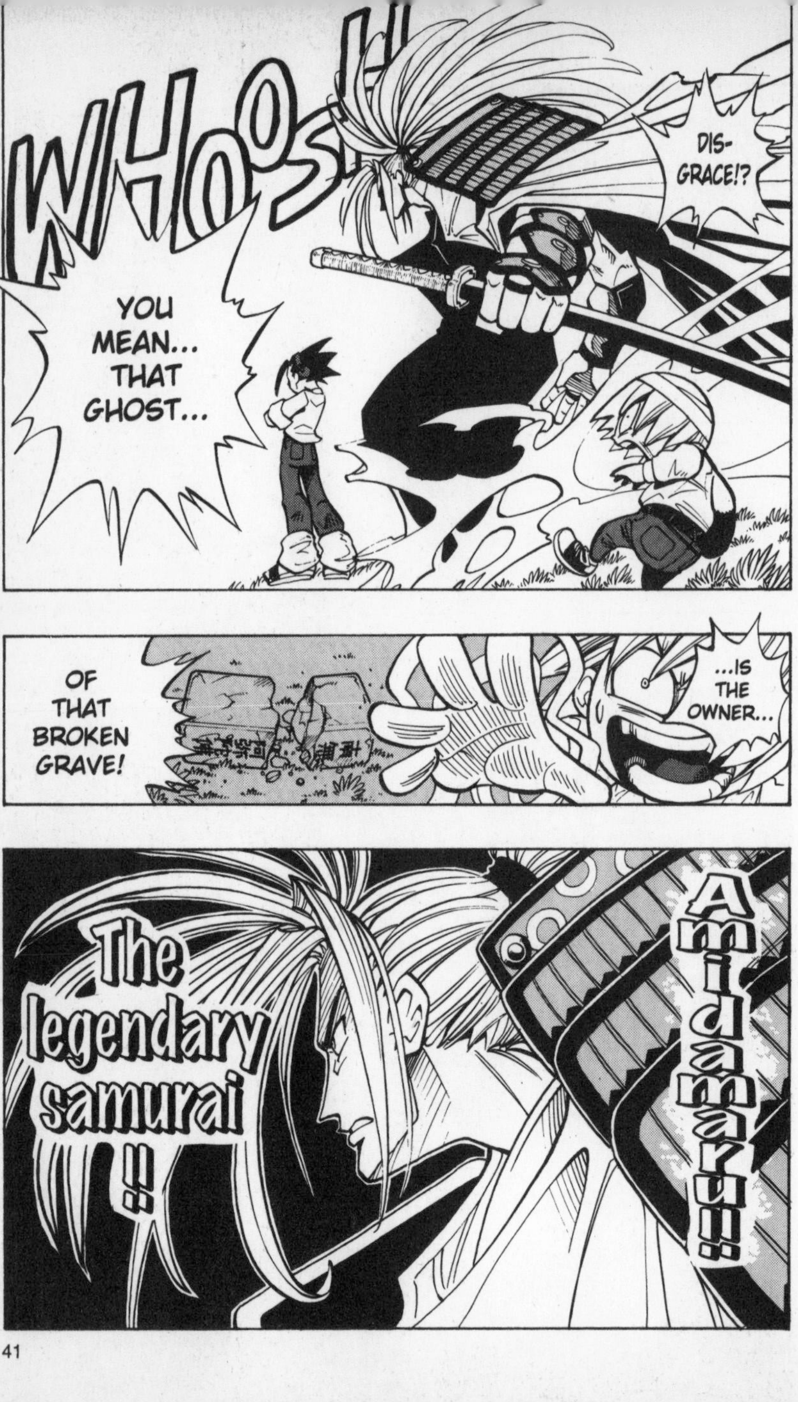
DIS-GRACE!?
WHOOSH!!
YOU MEAN... THAT GHOST...
...IS THE OWNER...
OF THAT BROKEN GRAVE!
Amidamaru!!
The legendary samurai !!

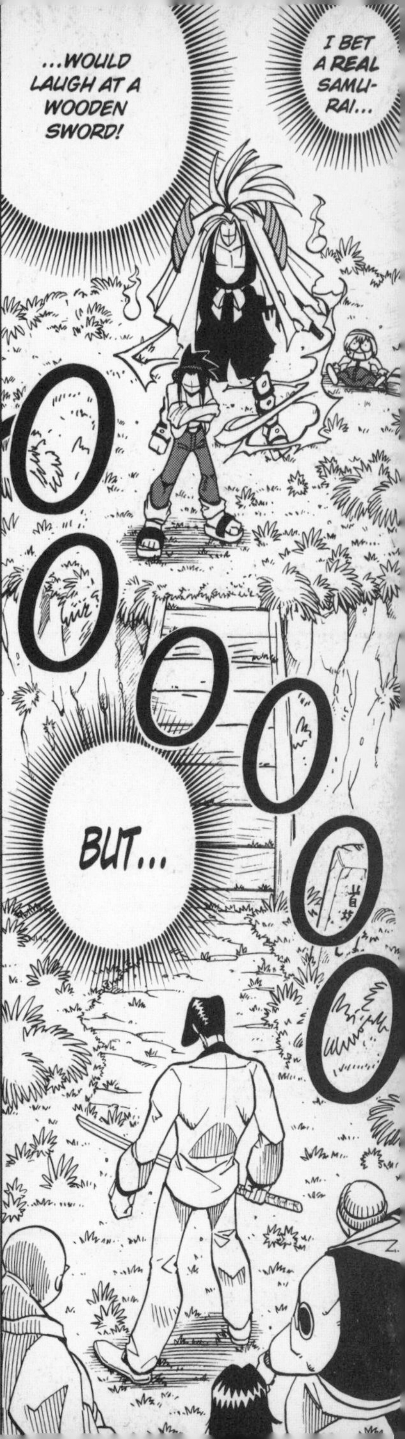
I BET A REAL SAMURAI...
...WOULD LAUGH AT A WOODEN SWORD!
BUT...

READ THIS WAY

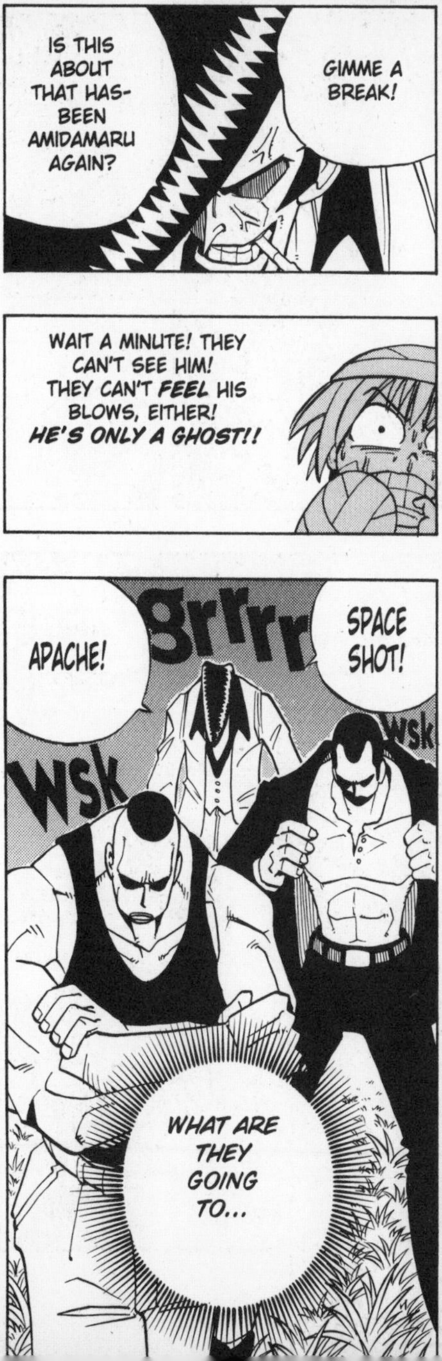
GIMME A BREAK!
IS THIS ABOUT THAT HAS-BEEN AMIDAMARU AGAIN?
WAIT A MINUTE! THEY CAN'T SEE HIM! THEY CAN'T FEEL HIS BLOWS, EITHER! HE'S ONLY A GHOST!!
SPACE SHOT!
grrrr
APACHE!
wsk
wsk
WHAT ARE THEY GOING TO...

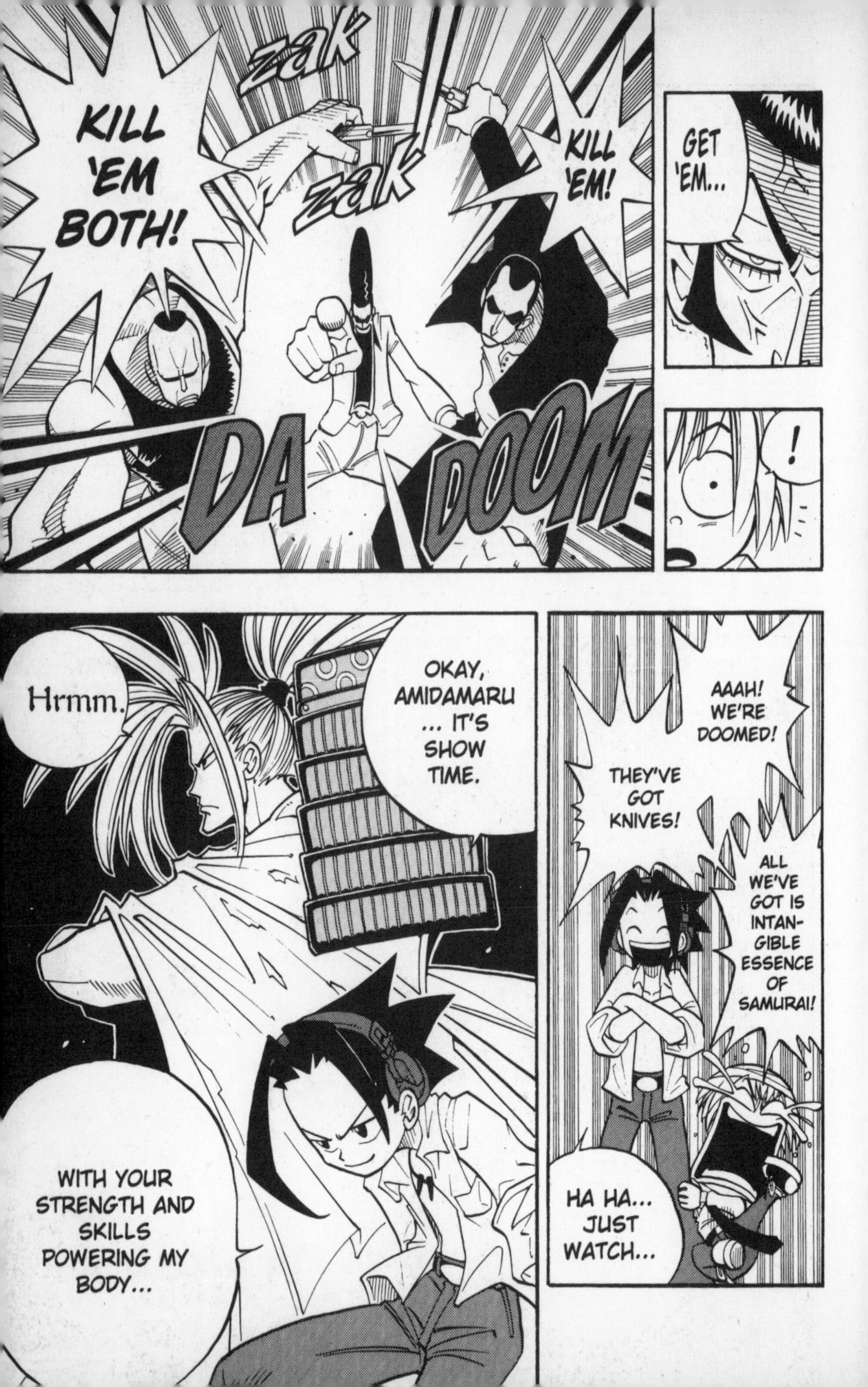
GET 'EM...
!
KILL 'EM!
ZAK
ZAK
KILL 'EM BOTH!
DA DOOM
AAAH! WE'RE DOOMED!
THEY'VE GOT KNIVES!
ALL WE'VE GOT IS INTANGIBLE ESSENCE OF SAMURAI!
HA HA... JUST WATCH...
OKAY, AMIDAMARU ... IT'S SHOW TIME.
Hrmm.
WITH YOUR STRENGTH AND SKILLS POWERING MY BODY...

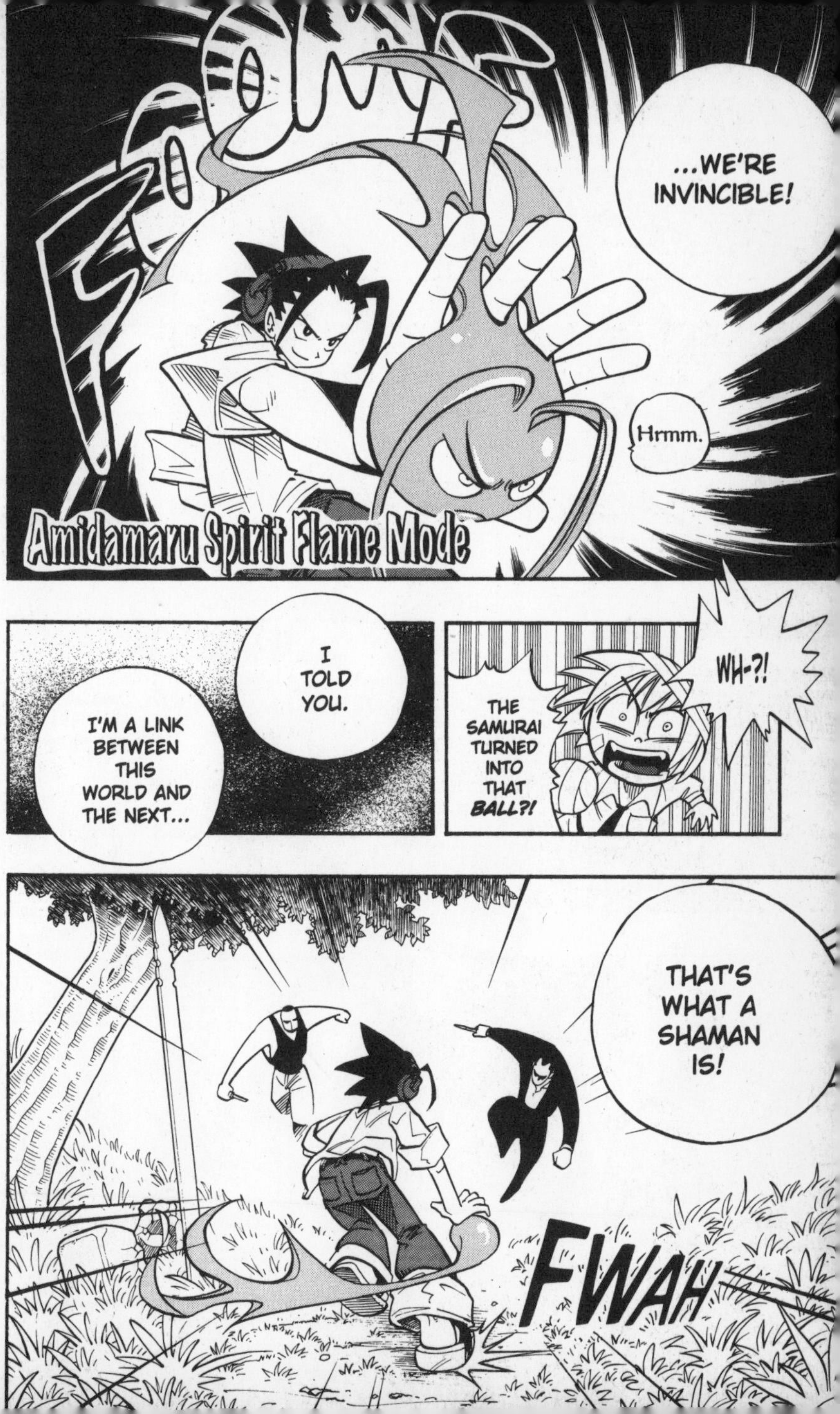
...WE'RE INVINCIBLE!
Hrmm.
Amidamaru Spirit Flame Mode
WH-?!
THE SAMURAI TURNED INTO THAT *BALL?!*
I TOLD YOU.
I'M A LINK BETWEEN THIS WORLD AND THE NEXT...
THAT'S WHAT A SHAMAN IS!
FWAH

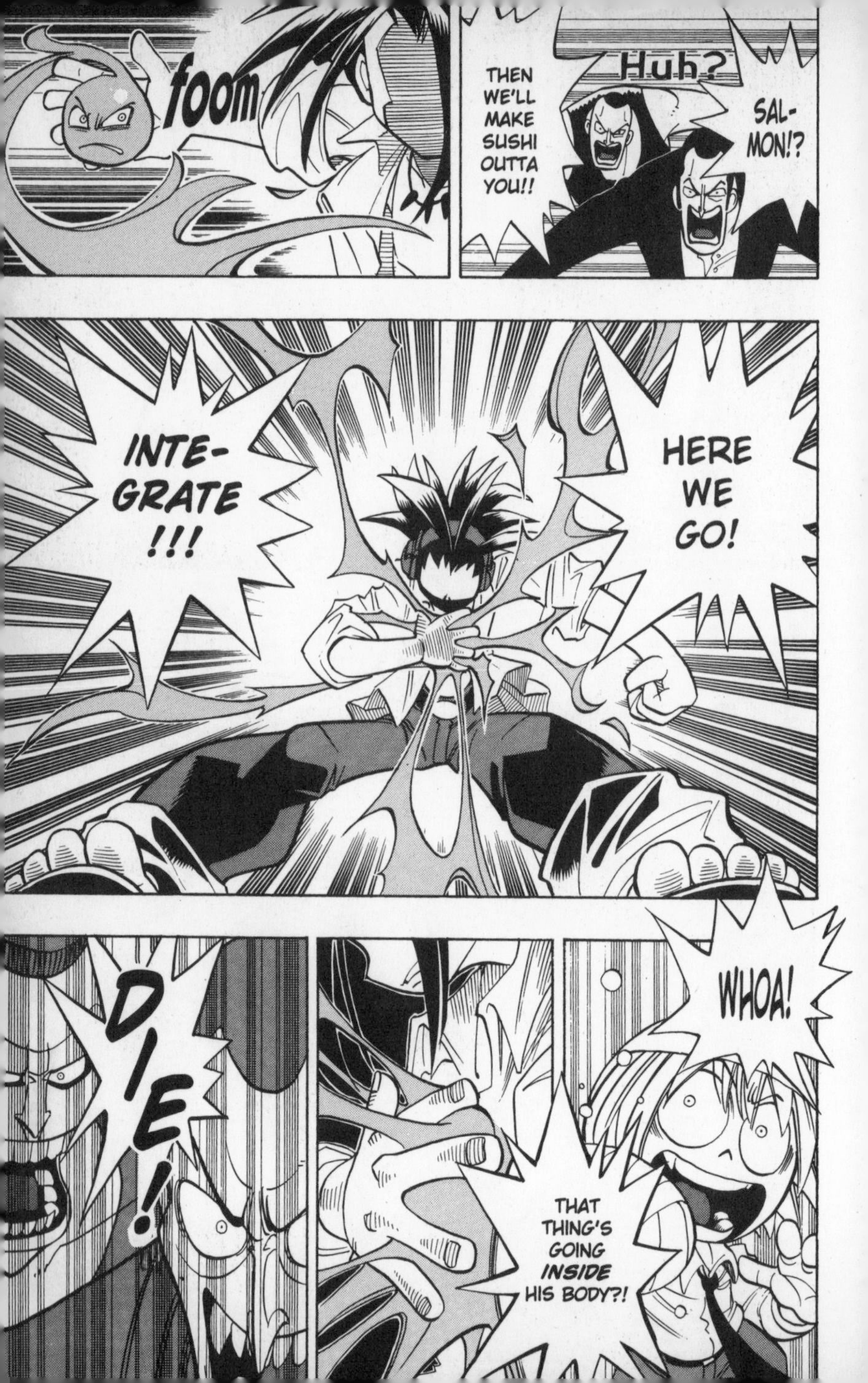
Huh?
SAL-MON!?
THEN WE'LL MAKE SUSHI OUTTA YOU!!
foom
HERE WE GO!
INTE-GRATE!!!
WHOA!
THAT THING'S GOING *INSIDE* HIS BODY?!
DIE!

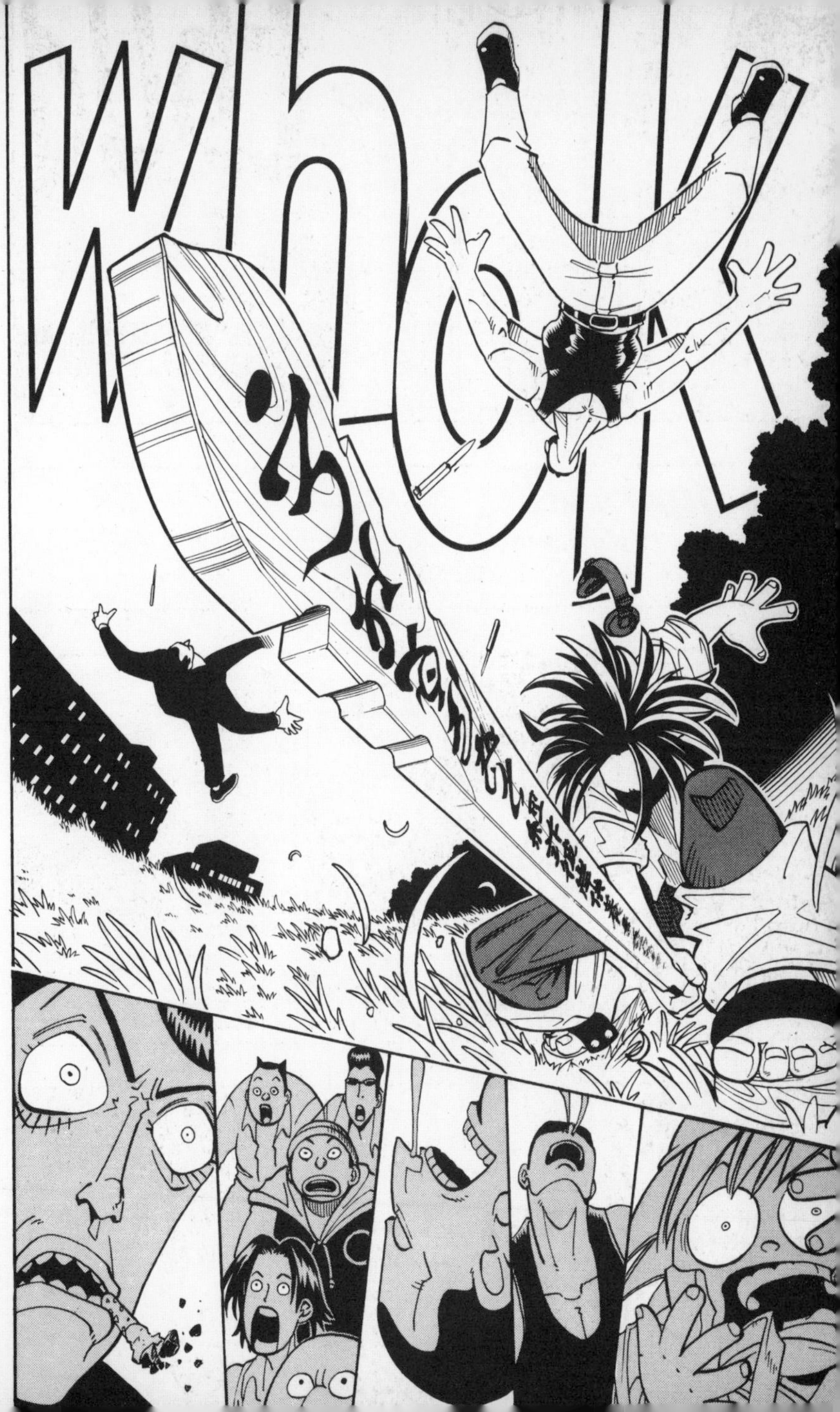
WhOK

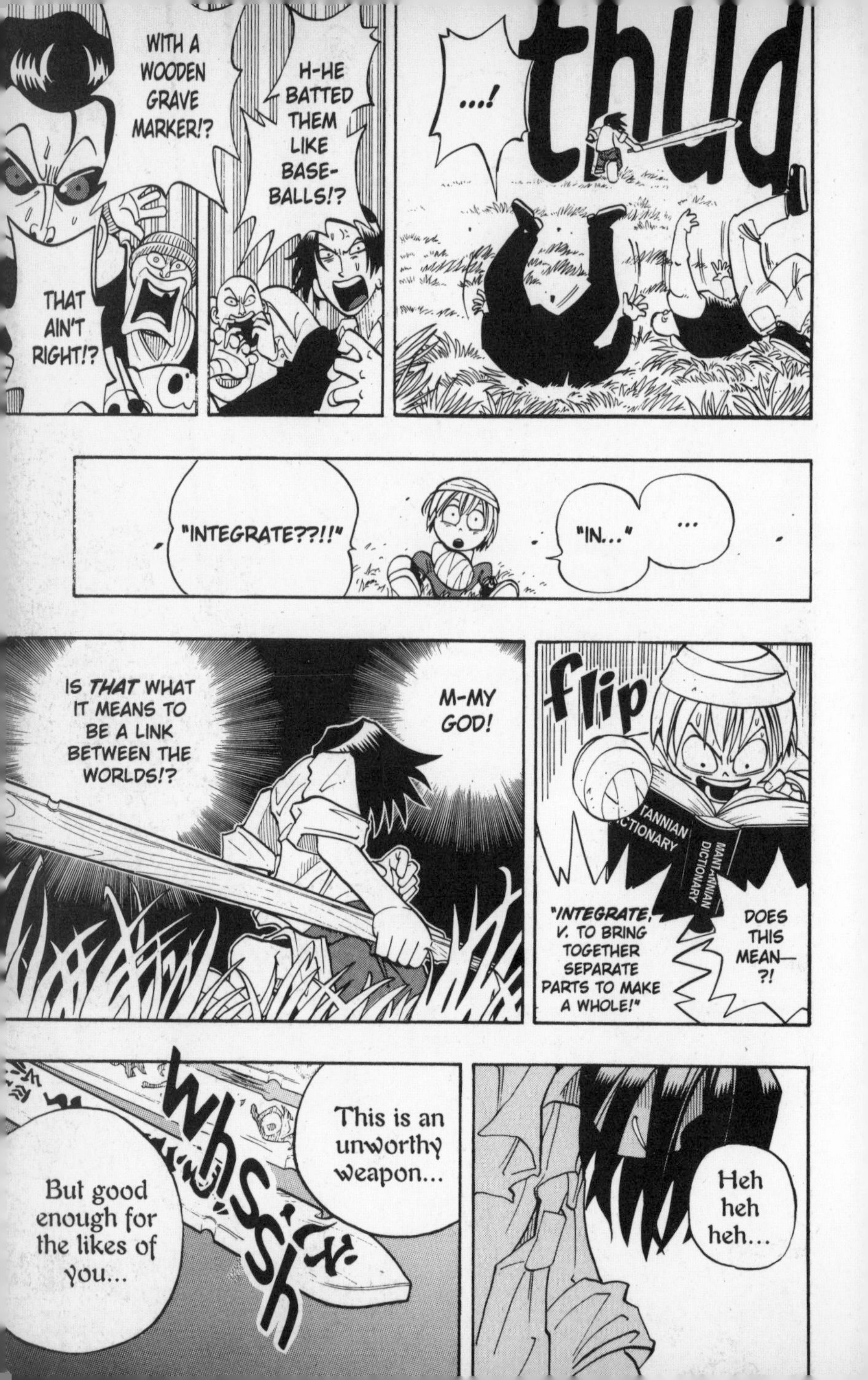
...!
thud
H-HE BATTED THEM LIKE BASE-BALLS!?
WITH A WOODEN GRAVE MARKER!?
THAT AIN'T RIGHT!?
...
"IN..."
"INTEGRATE??!!"
flip
"*INTEGRATE*, V. TO BRING TOGETHER SEPARATE PARTS TO MAKE A WHOLE!"
DOES THIS MEAN—?!
M-MY GOD!
IS *THAT* WHAT IT MEANS TO BE A LINK BETWEEN THE WORLDS!?
Heh heh heh...
This is an unworthy weapon...
But good enough for the likes of you...
whssh

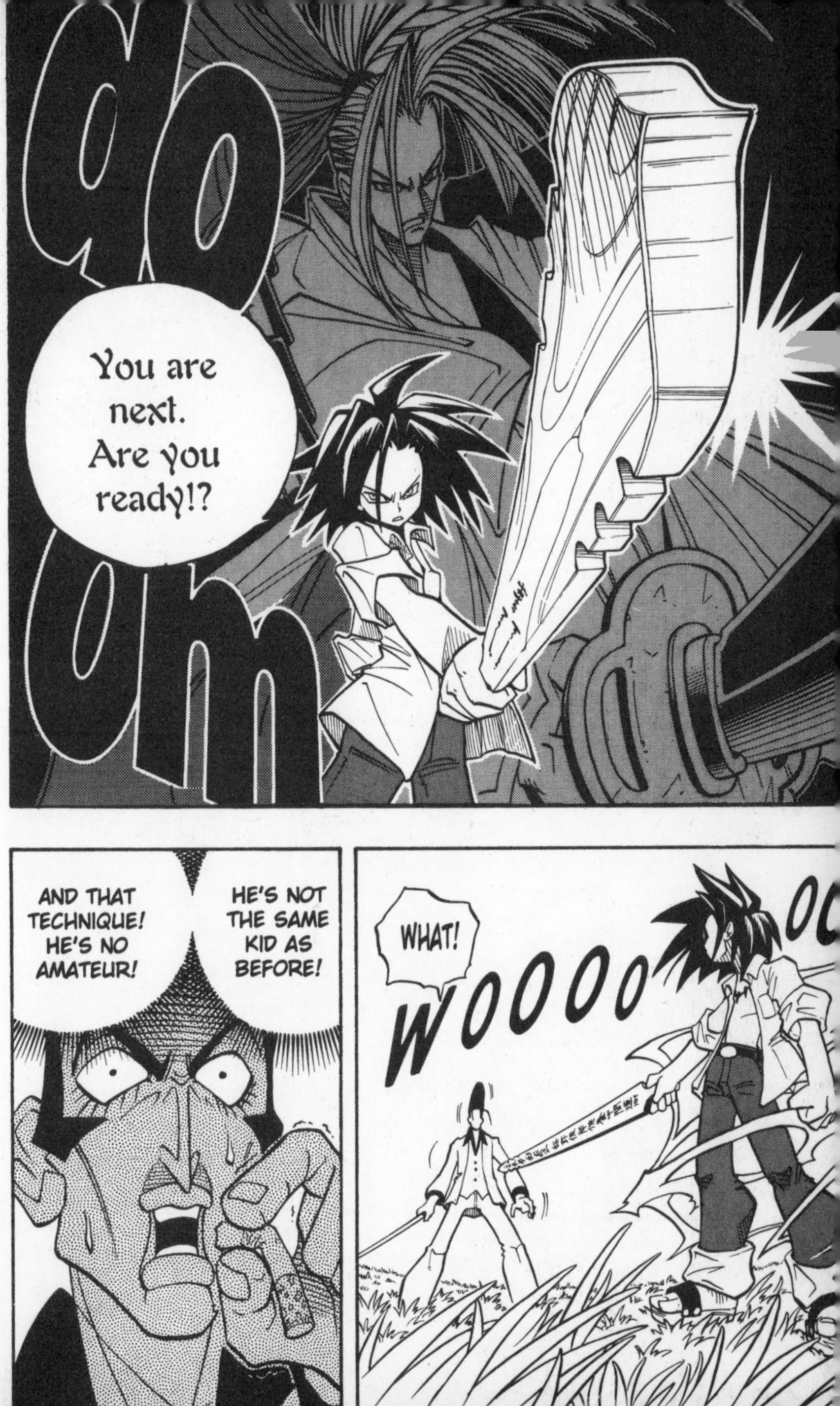
You are next. Are you ready!?
doom
WHAT!
WOOOO
HE'S NOT THE SAME KID AS BEFORE!
AND THAT TECHNIQUE! HE'S NO AMATEUR!

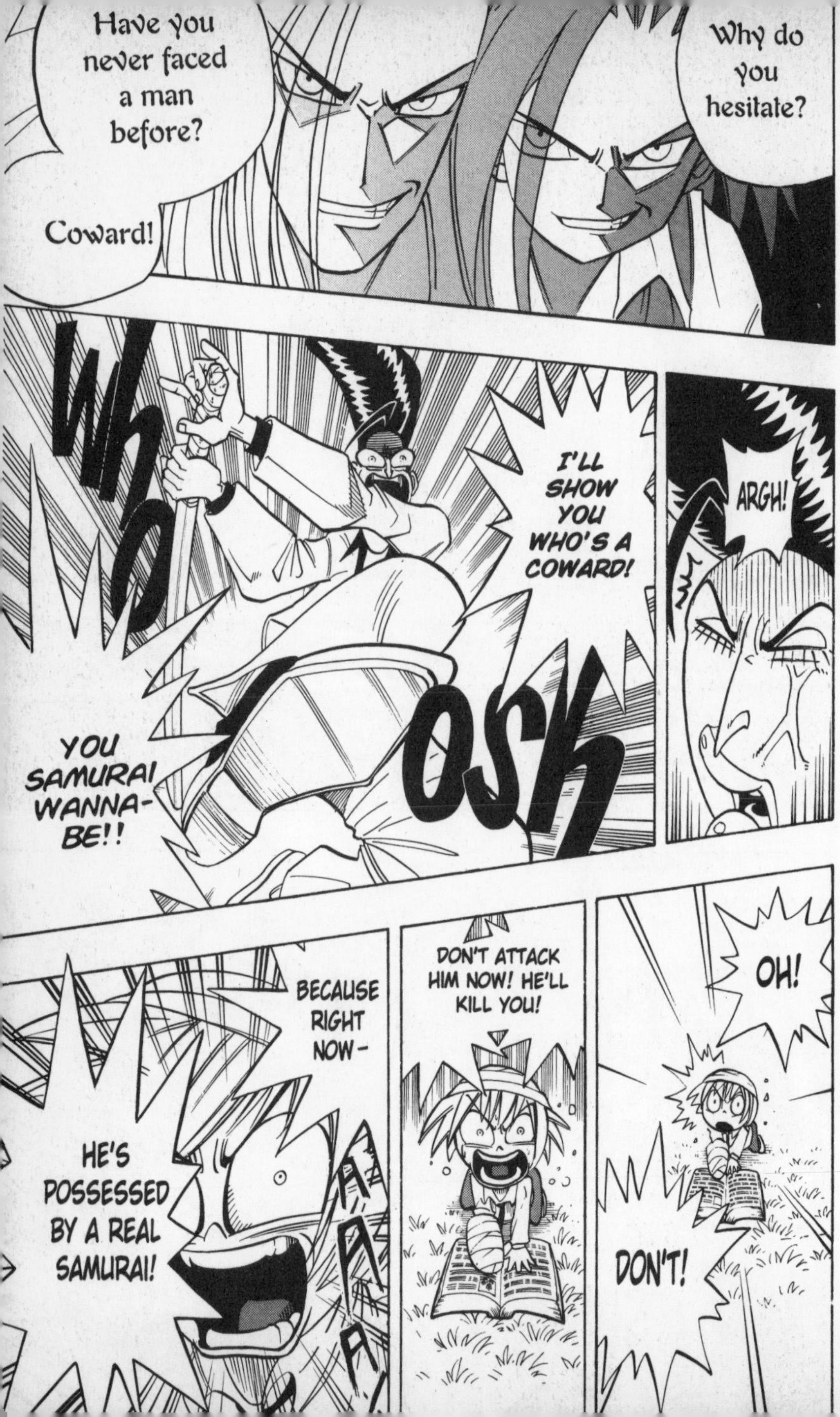

Why do you hesitate?
Have you never faced a man before?
Coward!
ARGH!
I'LL SHOW YOU WHO'S A COWARD!
Wh
O
OSh
YOU SAMURAI WANNA-BE!!
OH!
DON'T!
DON'T ATTACK HIM NOW! HE'LL KILL YOU!
BECAUSE RIGHT NOW-
HE'S POSSESSED BY A REAL SAMURAI!

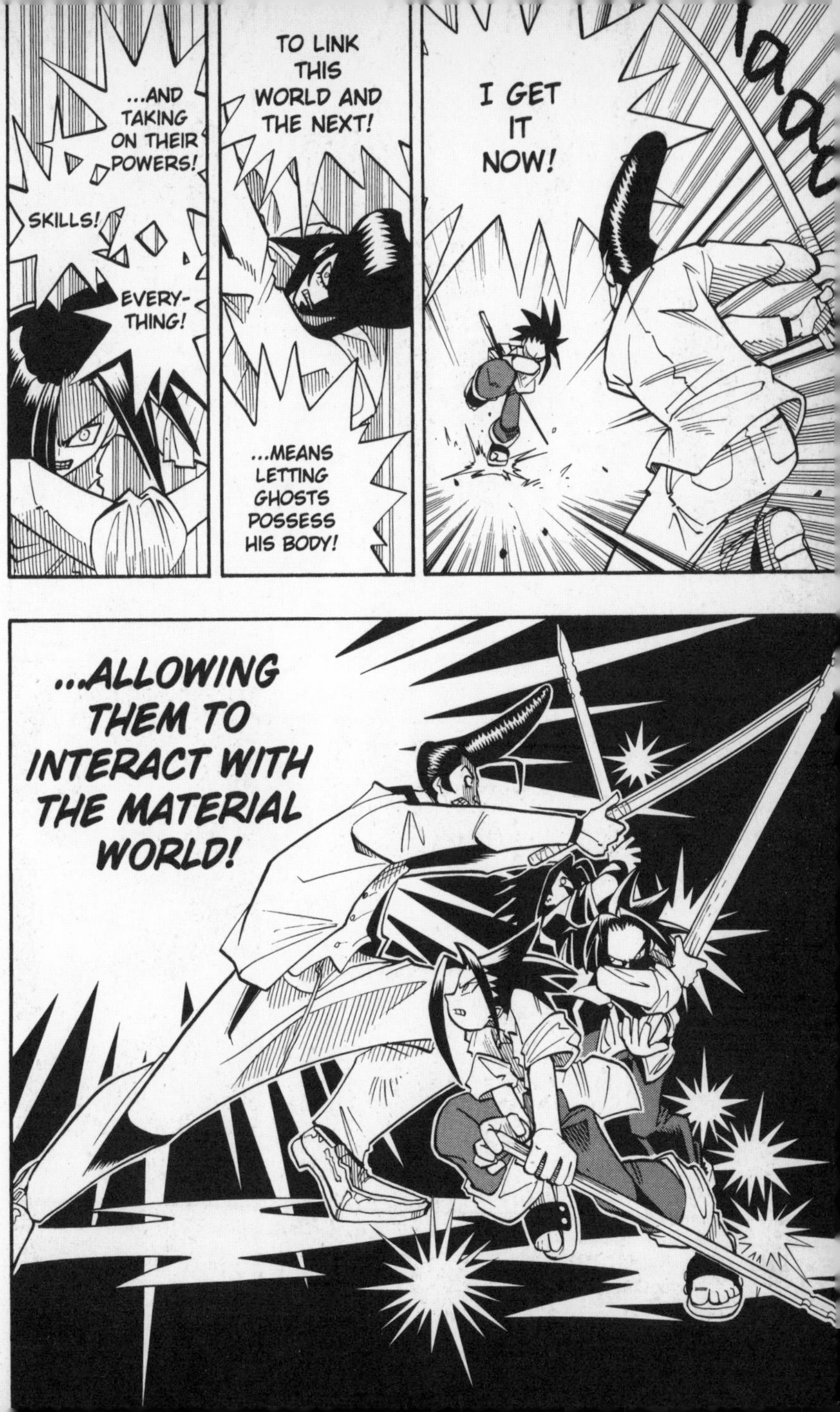
I GET IT NOW!
TO LINK THIS WORLD AND THE NEXT!
...MEANS LETTING GHOSTS POSSESS HIS BODY!
...AND TAKING ON THEIR POWERS!
SKILLS!
EVERYTHING!
...ALLOWING THEM TO INTERACT WITH THE MATERIAL WORLD!

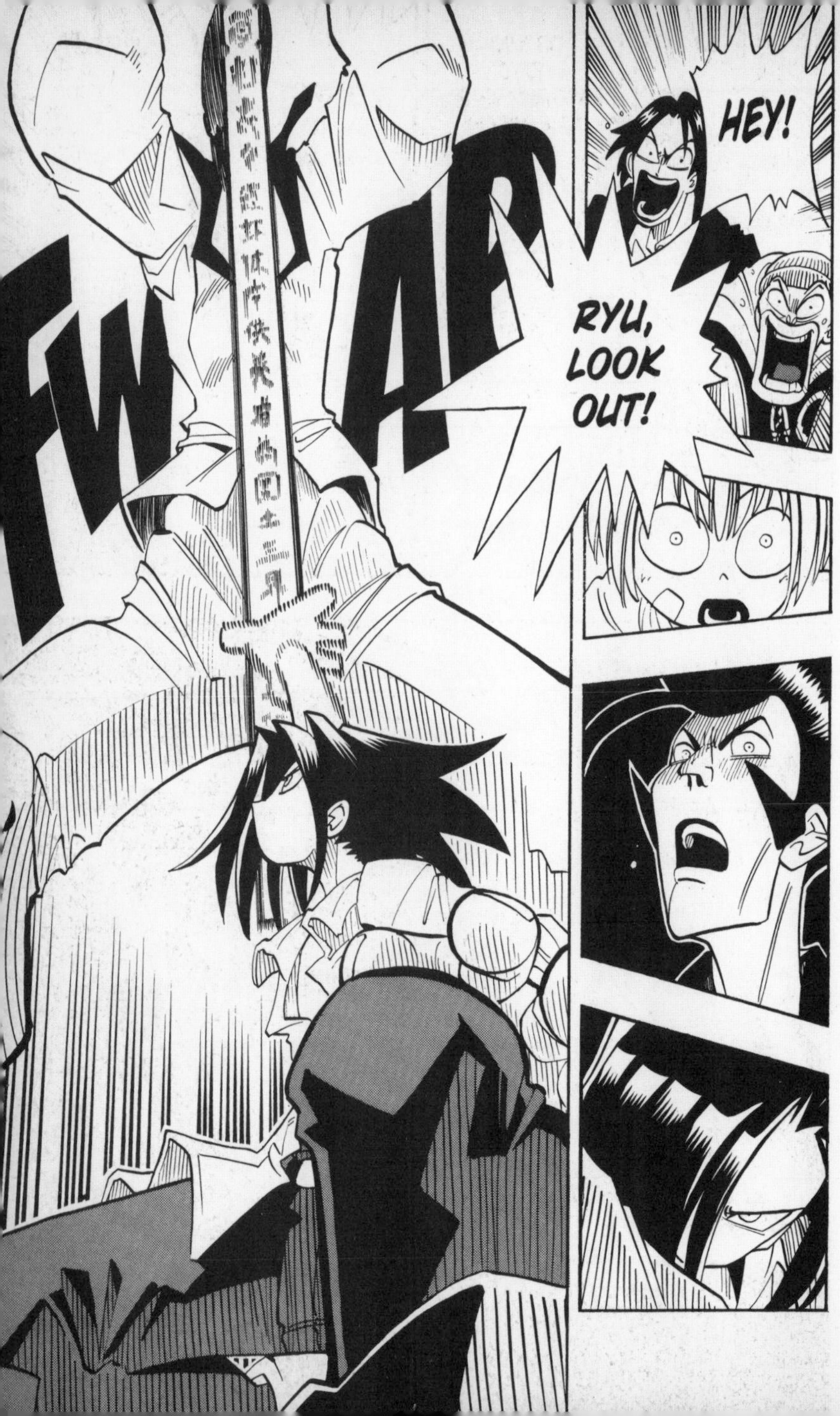
HEY!
RYU, LOOK OUT!
FWAP

READ THIS WAY

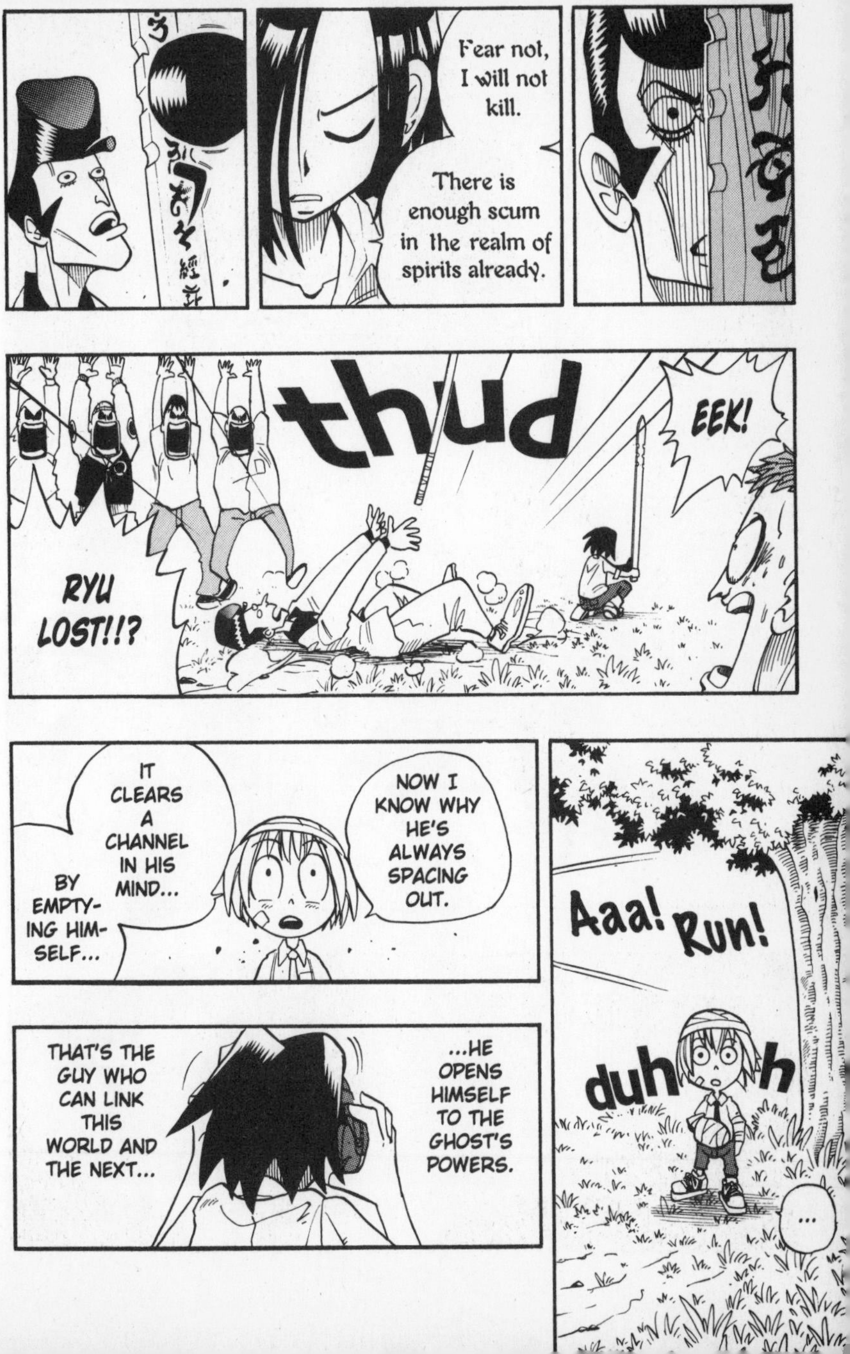

Fear not, I will not kill.
There is enough scum in the realm of spirits already.
EEK!
thud
RYU LOST!!?
Aaa! Run!
duh h
...
NOW I KNOW WHY HE'S ALWAYS SPACING OUT.
IT CLEARS A CHANNEL IN HIS MIND...
BY EMPTYING HIMSELF...
...HE OPENS HIMSELF TO THE GHOST'S POWERS.
THAT'S THE GUY WHO CAN LINK THIS WORLD AND THE NEXT...

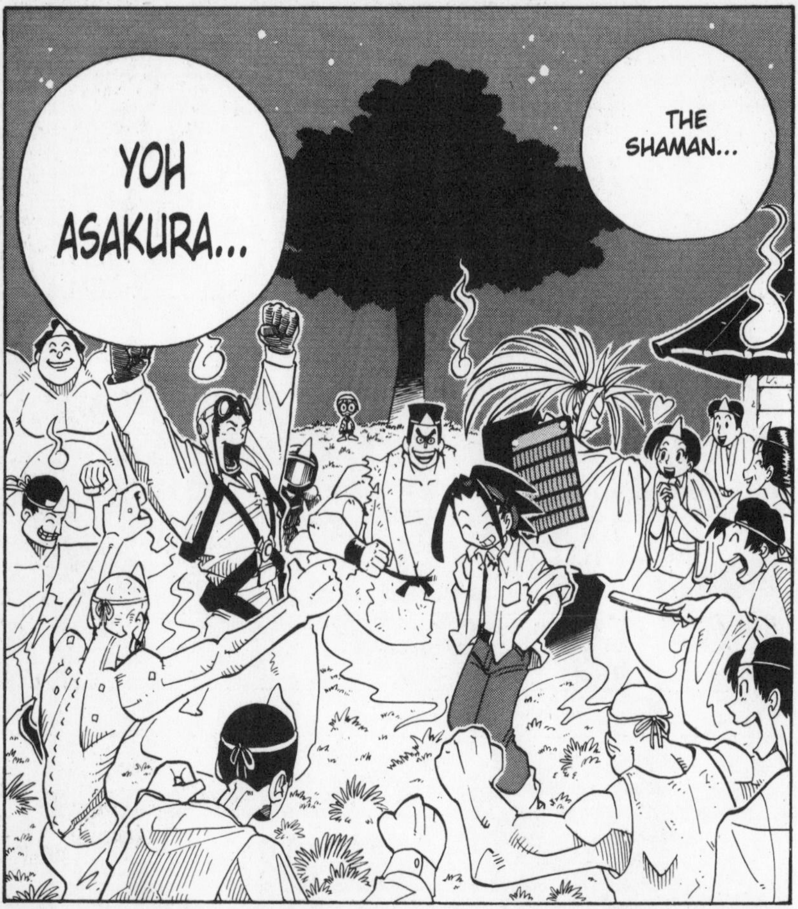
THE SHAMAN...
YOH ASAKURA...

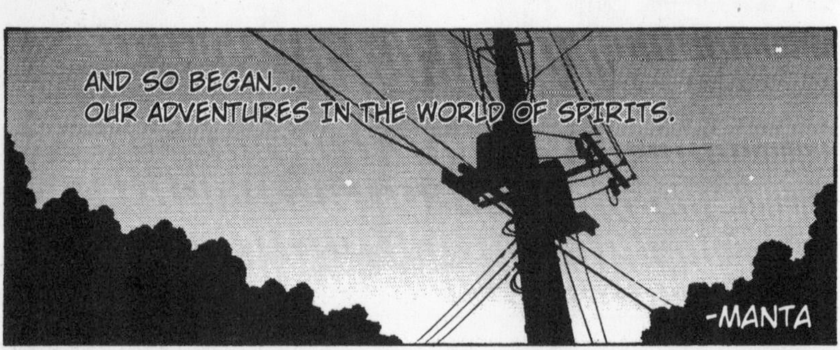
AND SO BEGAN...
OUR ADVENTURES IN THE WORLD OF SPIRITS.
-MANTA

SHAMAN KING CHARACTER FILE No.1

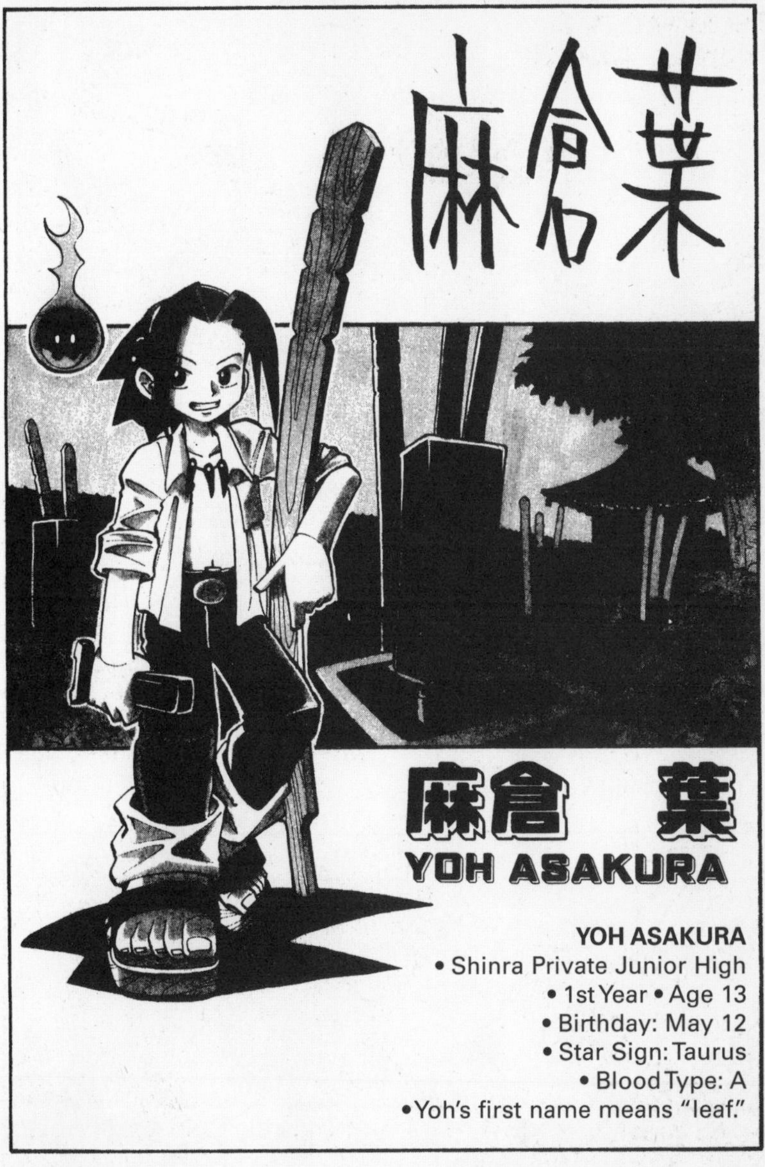
麻倉葉
麻倉 葉
YOH ASAKURA

YOH ASAKURA

• Shinra Private Junior High
• 1st Year • Age 13
• Birthday: May 12
• Star Sign: Taurus
• Blood Type: A
•Yoh's first name means "leaf."

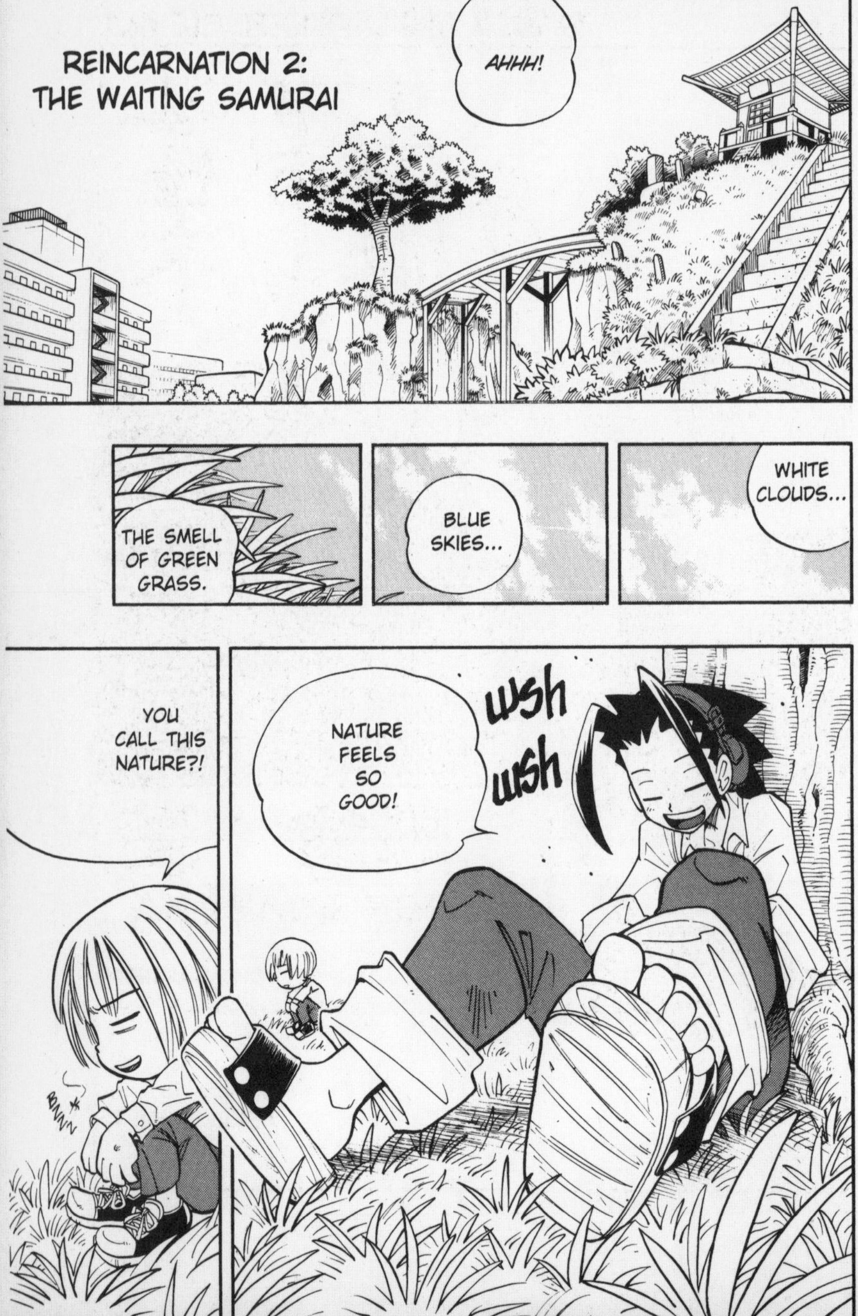
AHHH!
REINCARNATION 2: THE WAITING SAMURAI
WHITE CLOUDS...
BLUE SKIES...
THE SMELL OF GREEN GRASS.
WSH WSH
NATURE FEELS SO GOOD!
YOU CALL THIS NATURE?!

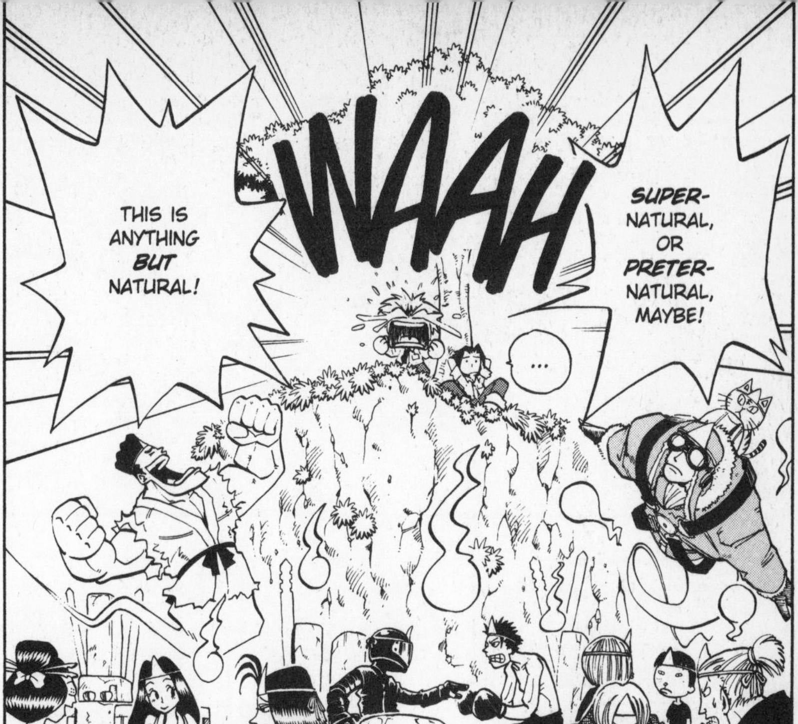
SUPER-NATURAL, OR PRETER-NATURAL, MAYBE!
WAAH
THIS IS ANYTHING BUT NATURAL!
...

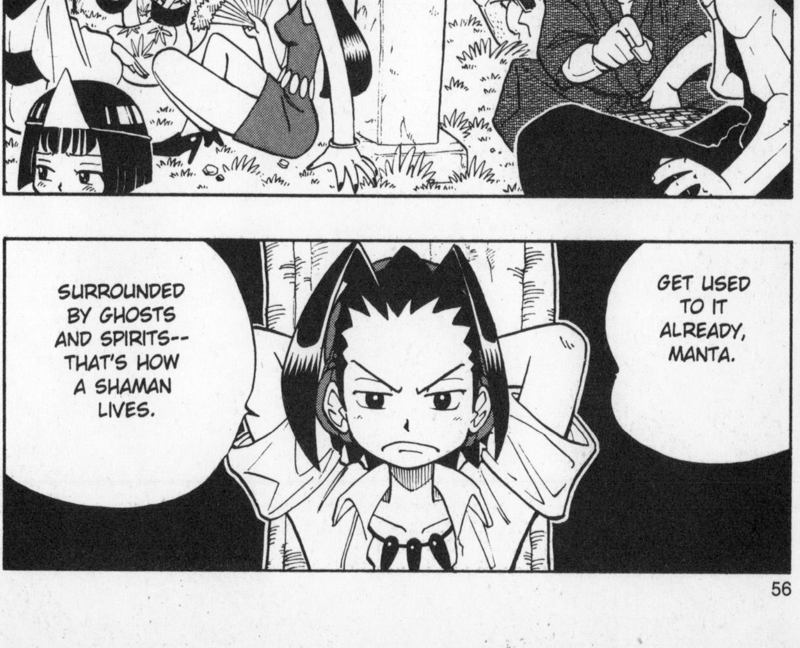
GET USED TO IT ALREADY, MANTA.
SURROUNDED BY GHOSTS AND SPIRITS-- THAT'S HOW A SHAMAN LIVES.

Reincarnation 2: The WAITING SAMURAI

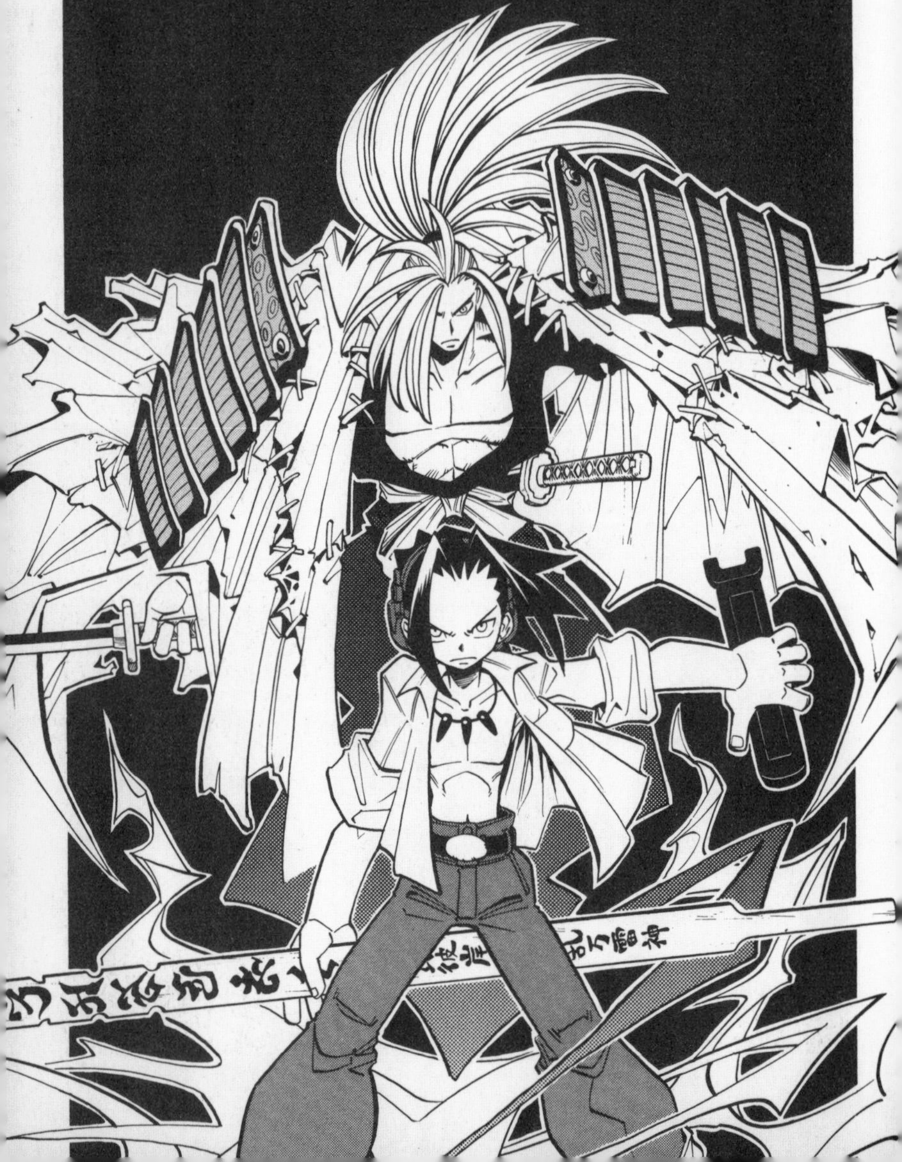

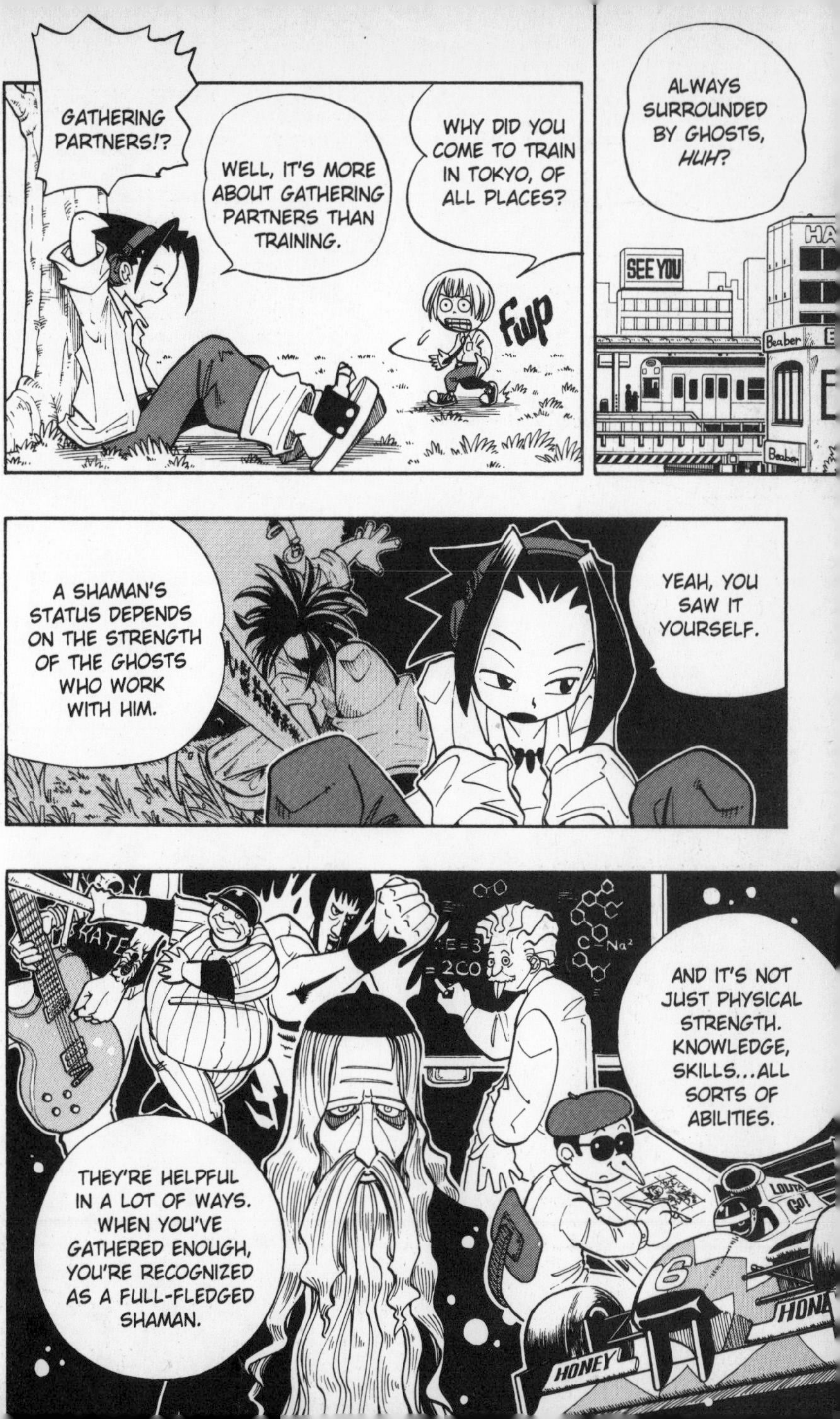
ALWAYS SURROUNDED BY GHOSTS, HUH?
SEE YOU
Beaber
Beaber
WHY DID YOU COME TO TRAIN IN TOKYO, OF ALL PLACES?
FWIP
WELL, IT'S MORE ABOUT GATHERING PARTNERS THAN TRAINING.
GATHERING PARTNERS!?
YEAH, YOU SAW IT YOURSELF.
A SHAMAN'S STATUS DEPENDS ON THE STRENGTH OF THE GHOSTS WHO WORK WITH HIM.
AND IT'S NOT JUST PHYSICAL STRENGTH. KNOWLEDGE, SKILLS...ALL SORTS OF ABILITIES.
THEY'RE HELPFUL IN A LOT OF WAYS. WHEN YOU'VE GATHERED ENOUGH, YOU'RE RECOGNIZED AS A FULL-FLEDGED SHAMAN.
HONEY

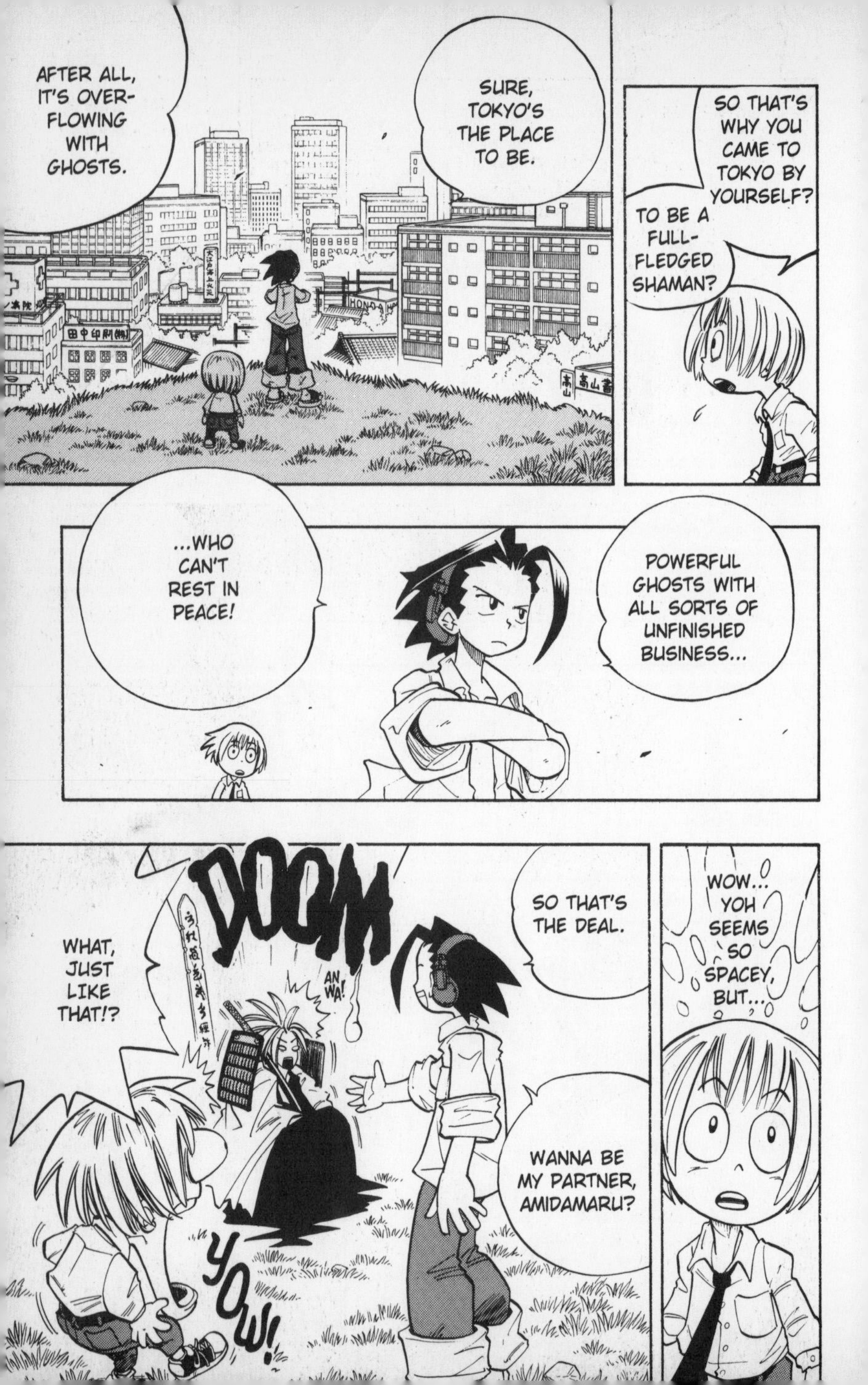
SO THAT'S WHY YOU CAME TO TOKYO BY YOURSELF?
TO BE A FULL-FLEDGED SHAMAN?
SURE, TOKYO'S THE PLACE TO BE.
AFTER ALL, IT'S OVER-FLOWING WITH GHOSTS.
田中印刷(株)
POWERFUL GHOSTS WITH ALL SORTS OF UNFINISHED BUSINESS...
...WHO CAN'T REST IN PEACE!
WOW... YOH SEEMS SO SPACEY, BUT...
SO THAT'S THE DEAL.
WANNA BE MY PARTNER, AMIDAMARU?
DOOM
AN WA!
WHAT, JUST LIKE THAT!?
YOW!

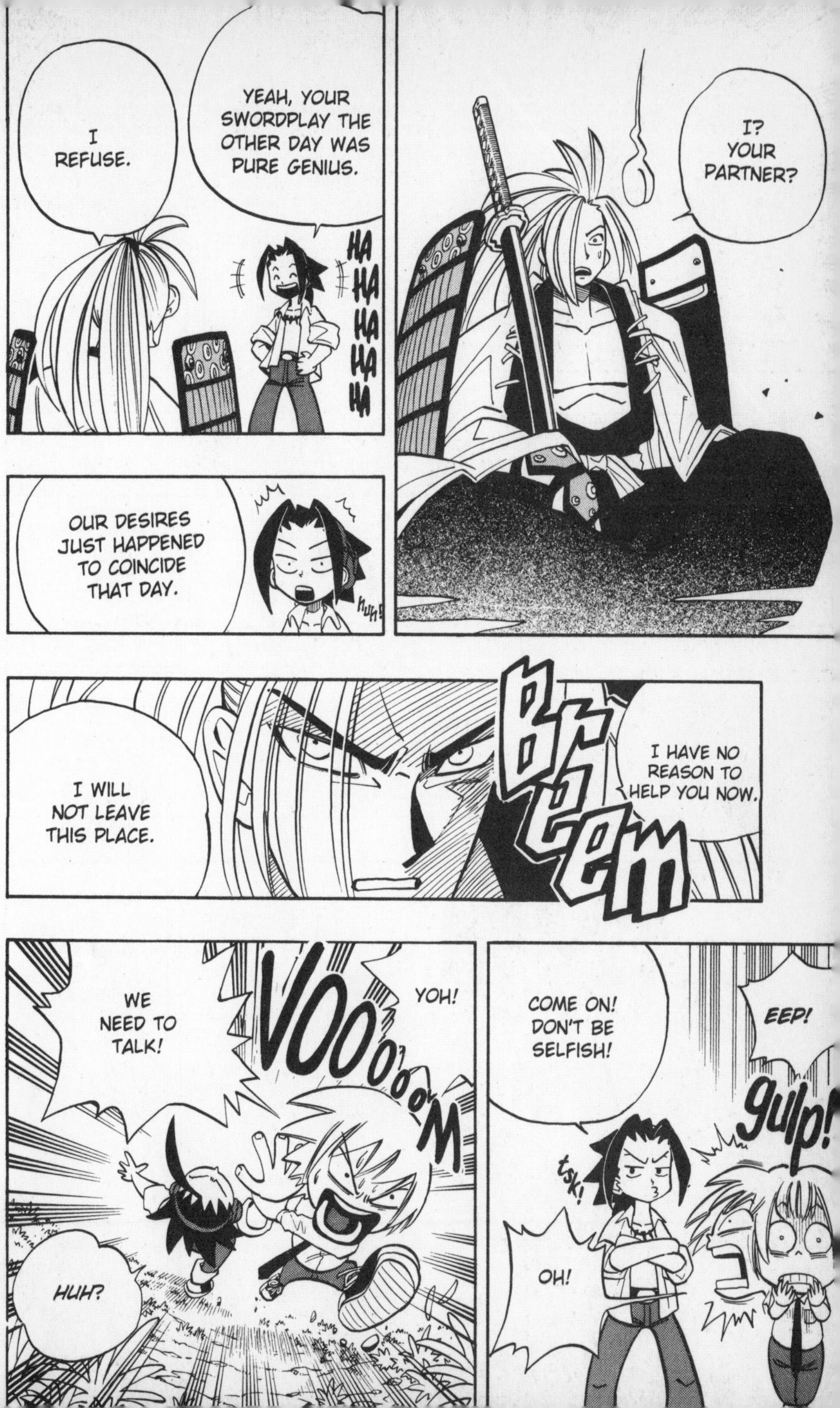
I? YOUR PARTNER?
YEAH, YOUR SWORDPLAY THE OTHER DAY WAS PURE GENIUS.
HA HA HA HA HA HA
I REFUSE.
huh!
OUR DESIRES JUST HAPPENED TO COINCIDE THAT DAY.
I HAVE NO REASON TO HELP YOU NOW.
Breem
I WILL NOT LEAVE THIS PLACE.
EEP!
gulp!
COME ON! DON'T BE SELFISH!
tsk!
OH!
YOH!
VOOooooM
WE NEED TO TALK!
HUH?

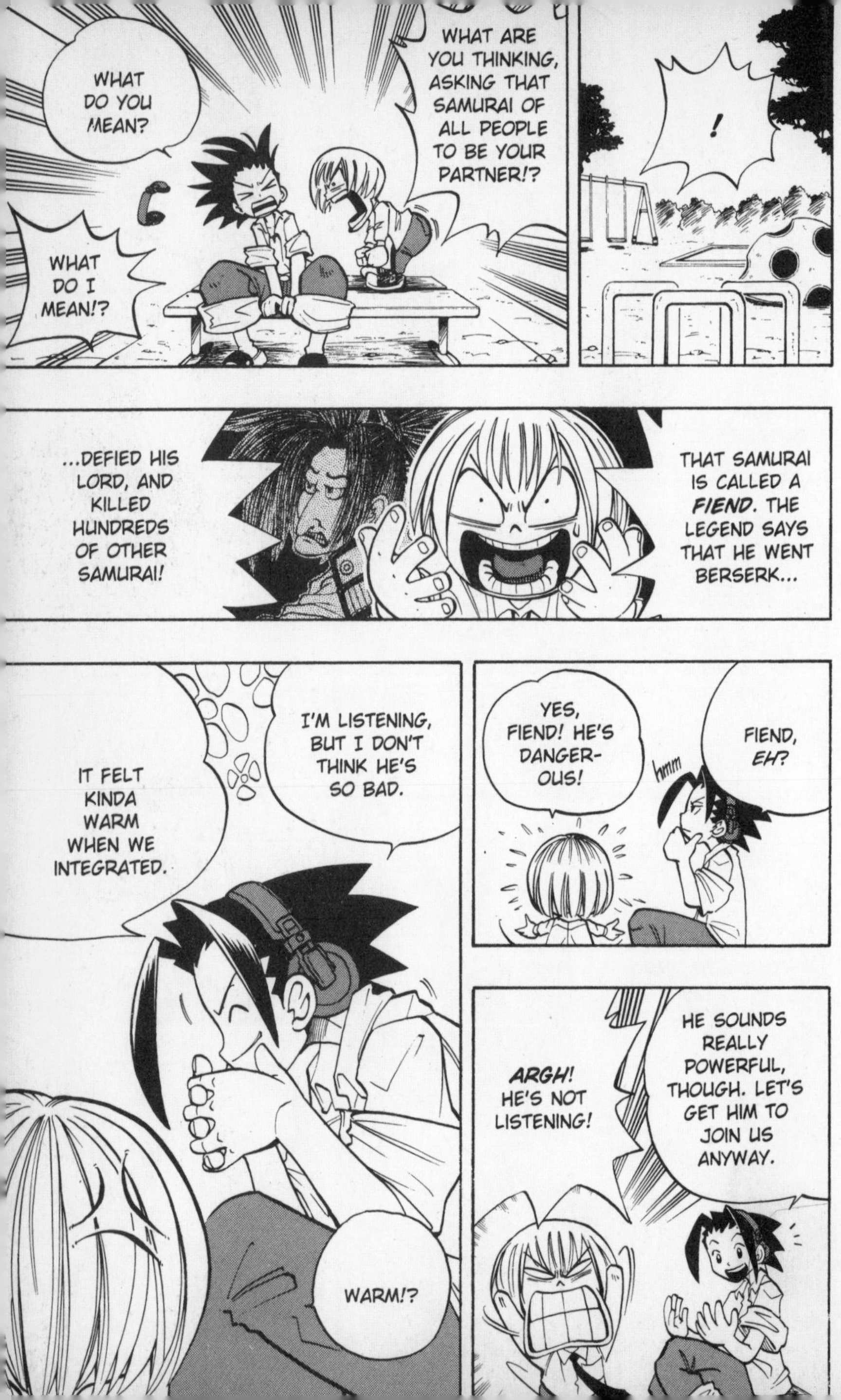
!
WHAT ARE YOU THINKING, ASKING THAT SAMURAI OF ALL PEOPLE TO BE YOUR PARTNER!?
WHAT DO YOU MEAN?
WHAT DO I MEAN!?
THAT SAMURAI IS CALLED A FIEND. THE LEGEND SAYS THAT HE WENT BERSERK...
...DEFIED HIS LORD, AND KILLED HUNDREDS OF OTHER SAMURAI!
FIEND, EH?
hmm
YES, FIEND! HE'S DANGER-OUS!
HE SOUNDS REALLY POWERFUL, THOUGH. LET'S GET HIM TO JOIN US ANYWAY.
ARGH! HE'S NOT LISTENING!
I'M LISTENING, BUT I DON'T THINK HE'S SO BAD.
IT FELT KINDA WARM WHEN WE INTEGRATED.
WARM!?

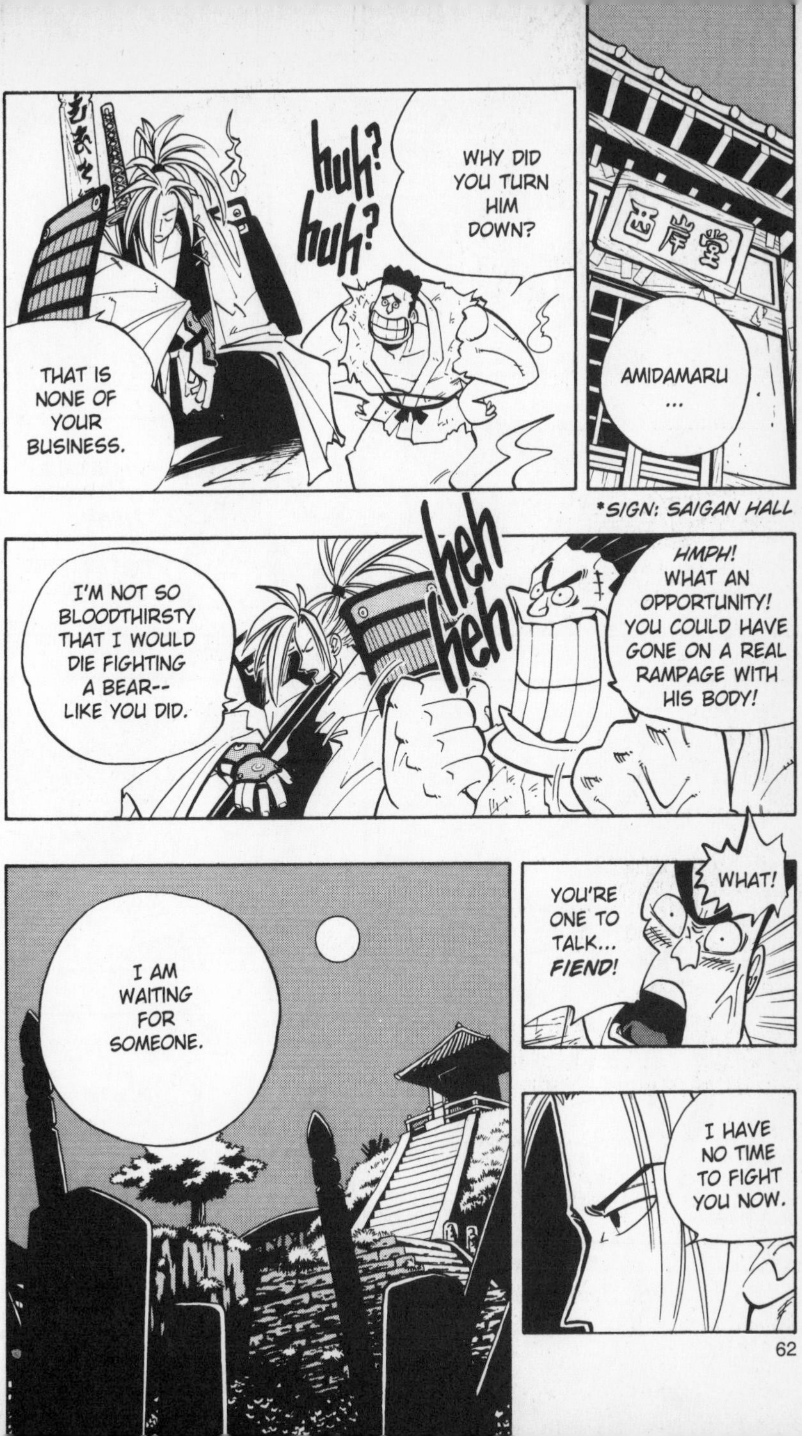
AMIDAMARU ...
*SIGN: SAIGAN HALL
WHY DID YOU TURN HIM DOWN?
huh? huh?
THAT IS NONE OF YOUR BUSINESS.
HMPH! WHAT AN OPPORTUNITY! YOU COULD HAVE GONE ON A REAL RAMPAGE WITH HIS BODY!
heh heh
I'M NOT SO BLOODTHIRSTY THAT I WOULD DIE FIGHTING A BEAR-- LIKE YOU DID.
WHAT!
YOU'RE ONE TO TALK... *FIEND*!
I HAVE NO TIME TO FIGHT YOU NOW.
I AM WAITING FOR SOMEONE.

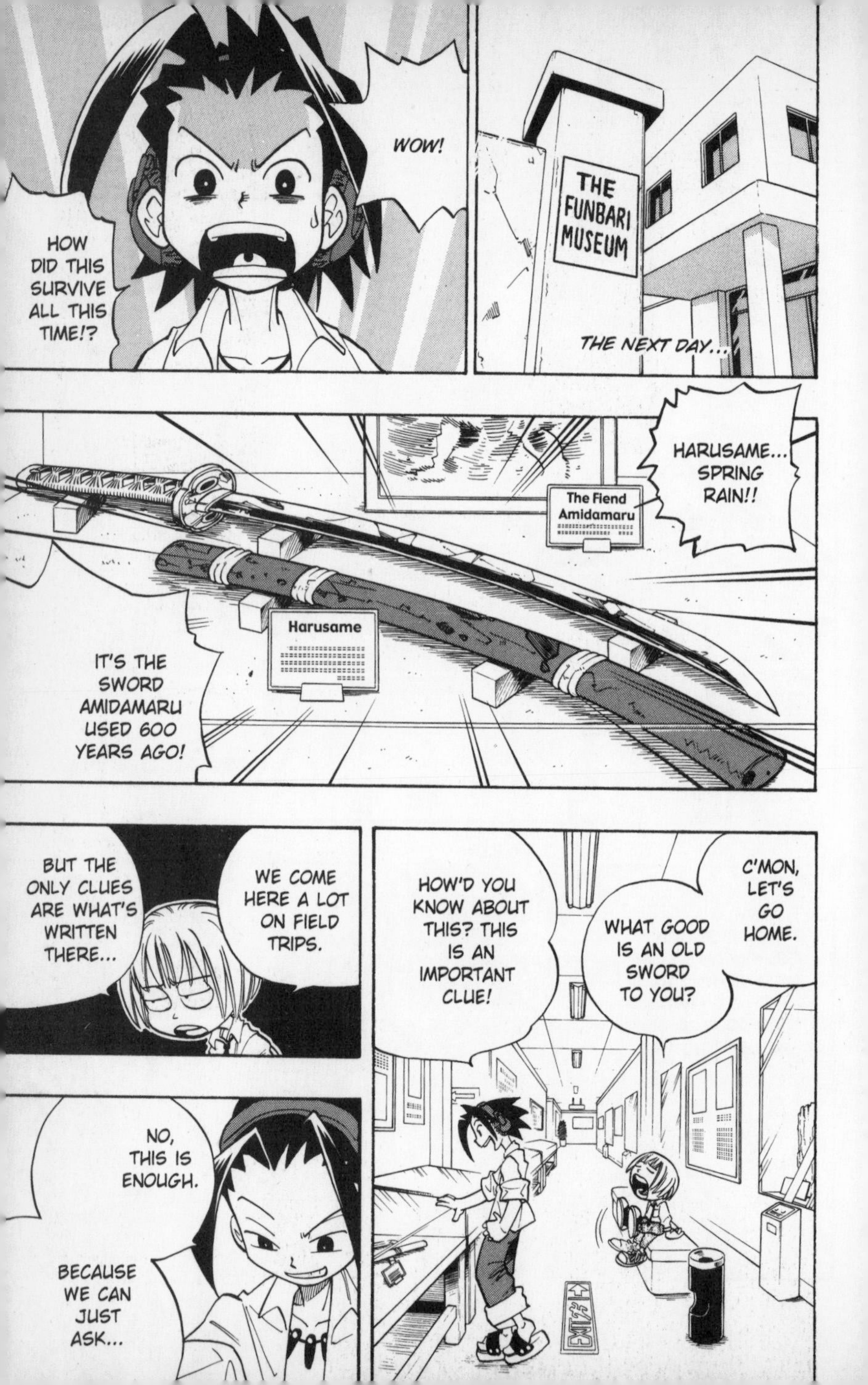
THE FUNBARI MUSEUM
THE NEXT DAY...
WOW!
HOW DID THIS SURVIVE ALL THIS TIME!?
HARUSAME... SPRING RAIN!!
The Fiend Amidamaru
Harusame
IT'S THE SWORD AMIDAMARU USED 600 YEARS AGO!
C'MON, LET'S GO HOME.
WHAT GOOD IS AN OLD SWORD TO YOU?
HOW'D YOU KNOW ABOUT THIS? THIS IS AN IMPORTANT CLUE!
WE COME HERE A LOT ON FIELD TRIPS.
BUT THE ONLY CLUES ARE WHAT'S WRITTEN THERE...
NO, THIS IS ENOUGH.
BECAUSE WE CAN JUST ASK...

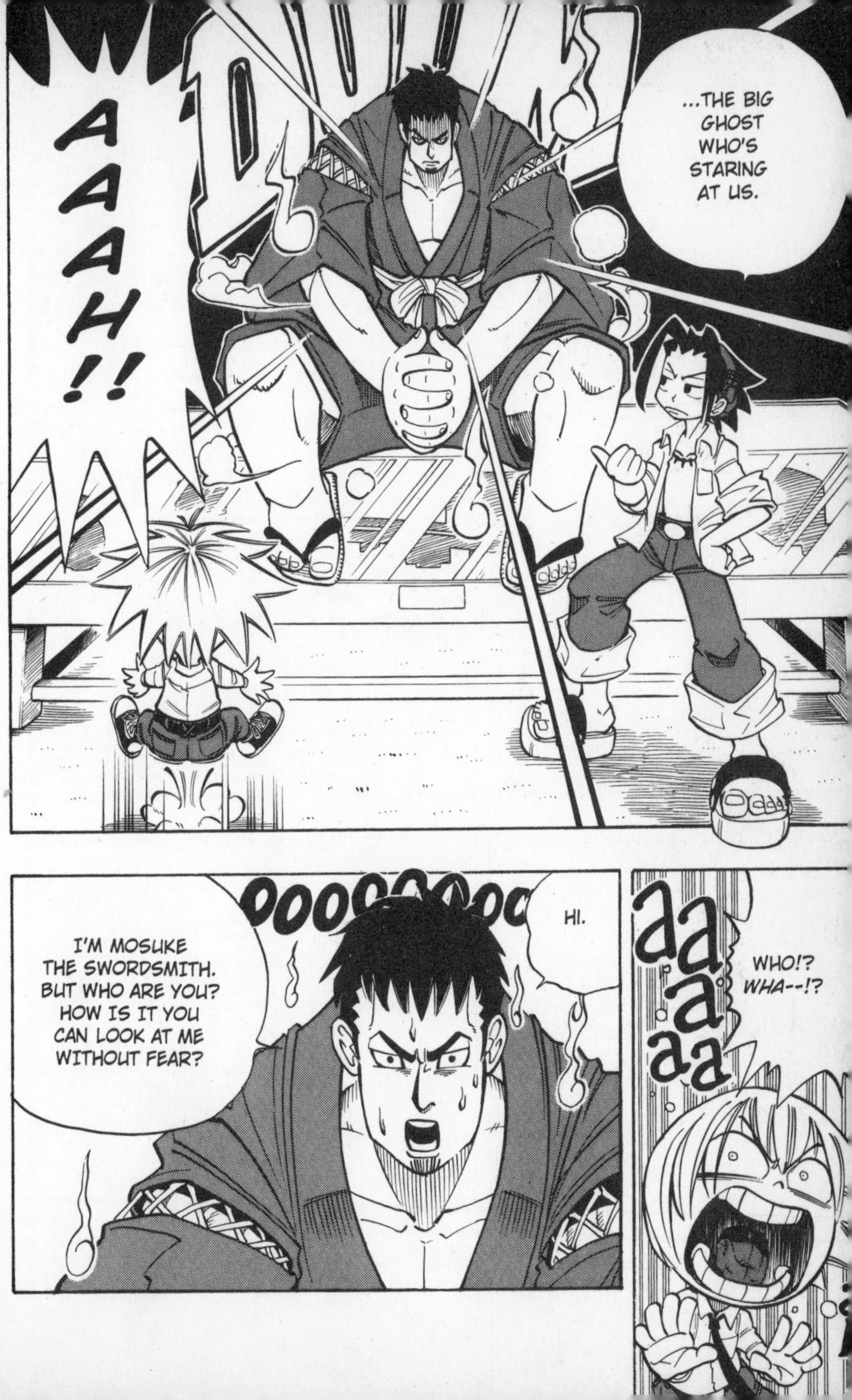
...THE BIG GHOST WHO'S STARING AT US.
WAAAAH!!
aaaaa
WHO!? WHA--!?
HI.
OOOOOOOO
I'M MOSUKE THE SWORDSMITH. BUT WHO ARE YOU? HOW IS IT YOU CAN LOOK AT ME WITHOUT FEAR?

READ THIS WAY

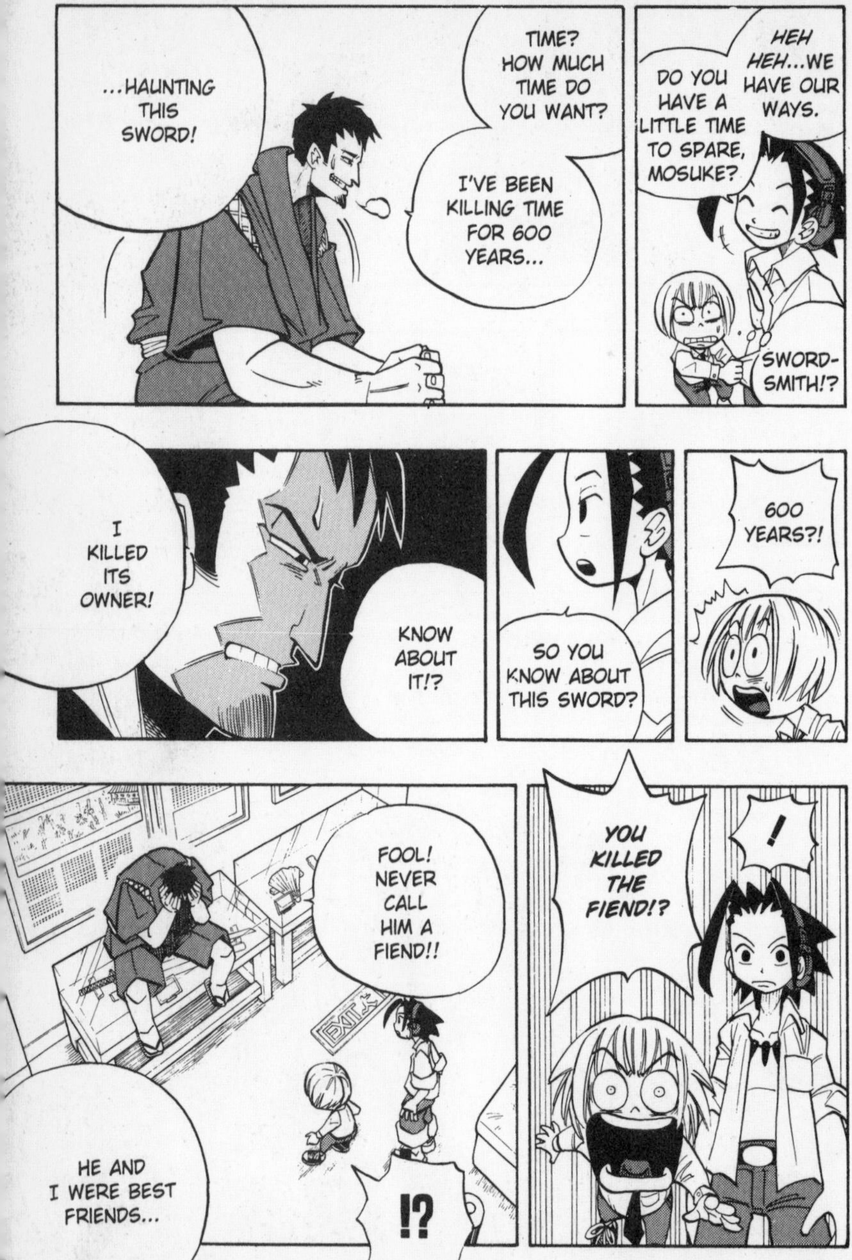
HEH HEH...WE HAVE OUR WAYS.
DO YOU HAVE A LITTLE TIME TO SPARE, MOSUKE?
SWORD-SMITH!?
TIME? HOW MUCH TIME DO YOU WANT?
I'VE BEEN KILLING TIME FOR 600 YEARS...
...HAUNTING THIS SWORD!
600 YEARS?!
SO YOU KNOW ABOUT THIS SWORD?
KNOW ABOUT IT!?
I KILLED ITS OWNER!
!
YOU KILLED THE FIEND!?
FOOL! NEVER CALL HIM A FIEND!!
EXIT
!?
HE AND I WERE BEST FRIENDS...

READ THIS WAY

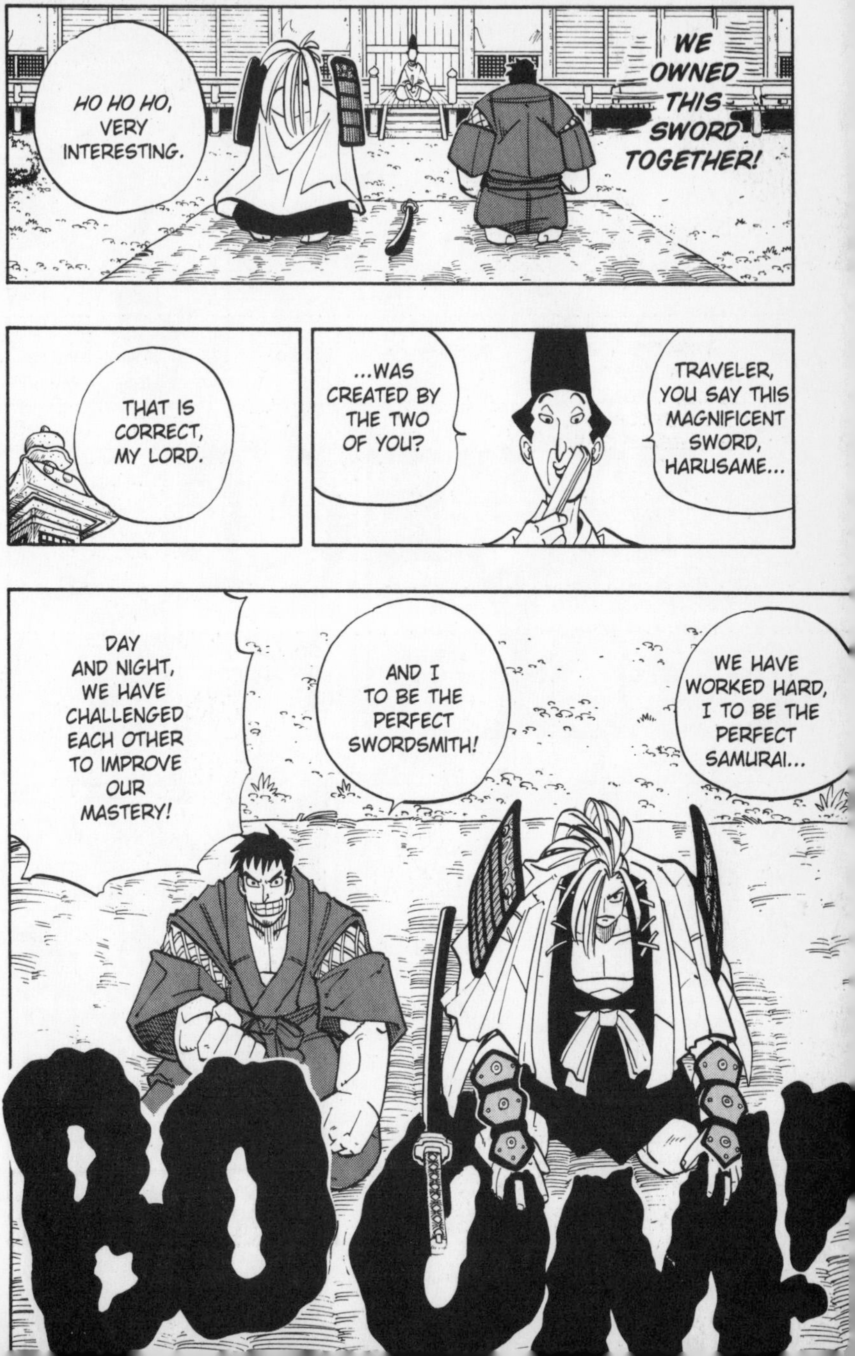
WE OWNED THIS SWORD TOGETHER!
HO HO HO, VERY INTERESTING.
TRAVELER, YOU SAY THIS MAGNIFICENT SWORD, HARUSAME...
...WAS CREATED BY THE TWO OF YOU?
THAT IS CORRECT, MY LORD.
WE HAVE WORKED HARD, I TO BE THE PERFECT SAMURAI...
AND I TO BE THE PERFECT SWORDSMITH!
DAY AND NIGHT, WE HAVE CHALLENGED EACH OTHER TO IMPROVE OUR MASTERY!
BOW!

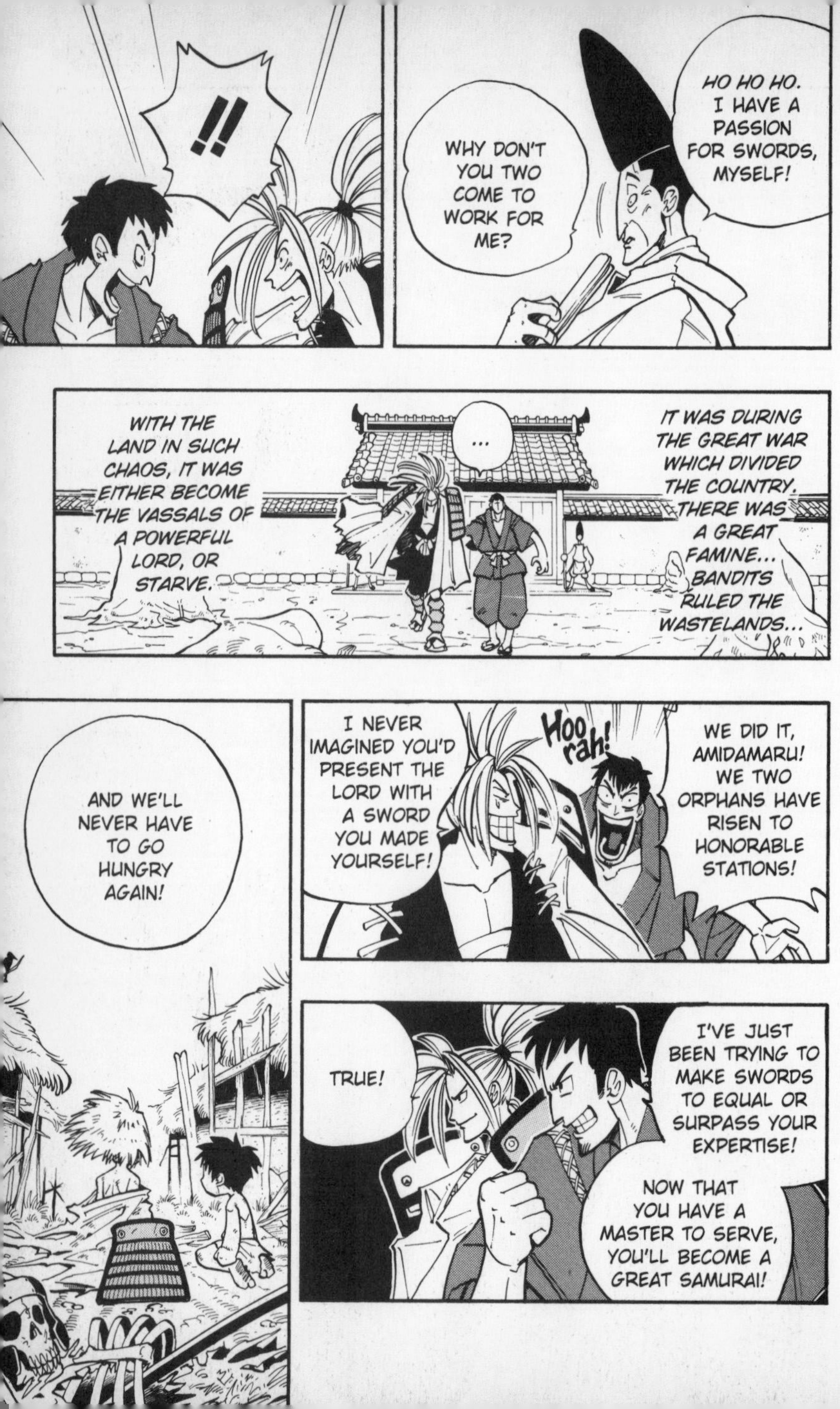
HO HO HO. I HAVE A PASSION FOR SWORDS, MYSELF!
WHY DON'T YOU TWO COME TO WORK FOR ME?
!!
IT WAS DURING THE GREAT WAR WHICH DIVIDED THE COUNTRY. THERE WAS A GREAT FAMINE... BANDITS RULED THE WASTELANDS...
...
WITH THE LAND IN SUCH CHAOS, IT WAS EITHER BECOME THE VASSALS OF A POWERFUL LORD, OR STARVE.
WE DID IT, AMIDAMARU! WE TWO ORPHANS HAVE RISEN TO HONORABLE STATIONS!
Hoo rah!
I NEVER IMAGINED YOU'D PRESENT THE LORD WITH A SWORD YOU MADE YOURSELF!
I'VE JUST BEEN TRYING TO MAKE SWORDS TO EQUAL OR SURPASS YOUR EXPERTISE!
NOW THAT YOU HAVE A MASTER TO SERVE, YOU'LL BECOME A GREAT SAMURAI!
TRUE!
AND WE'LL NEVER HAVE TO GO HUNGRY AGAIN!

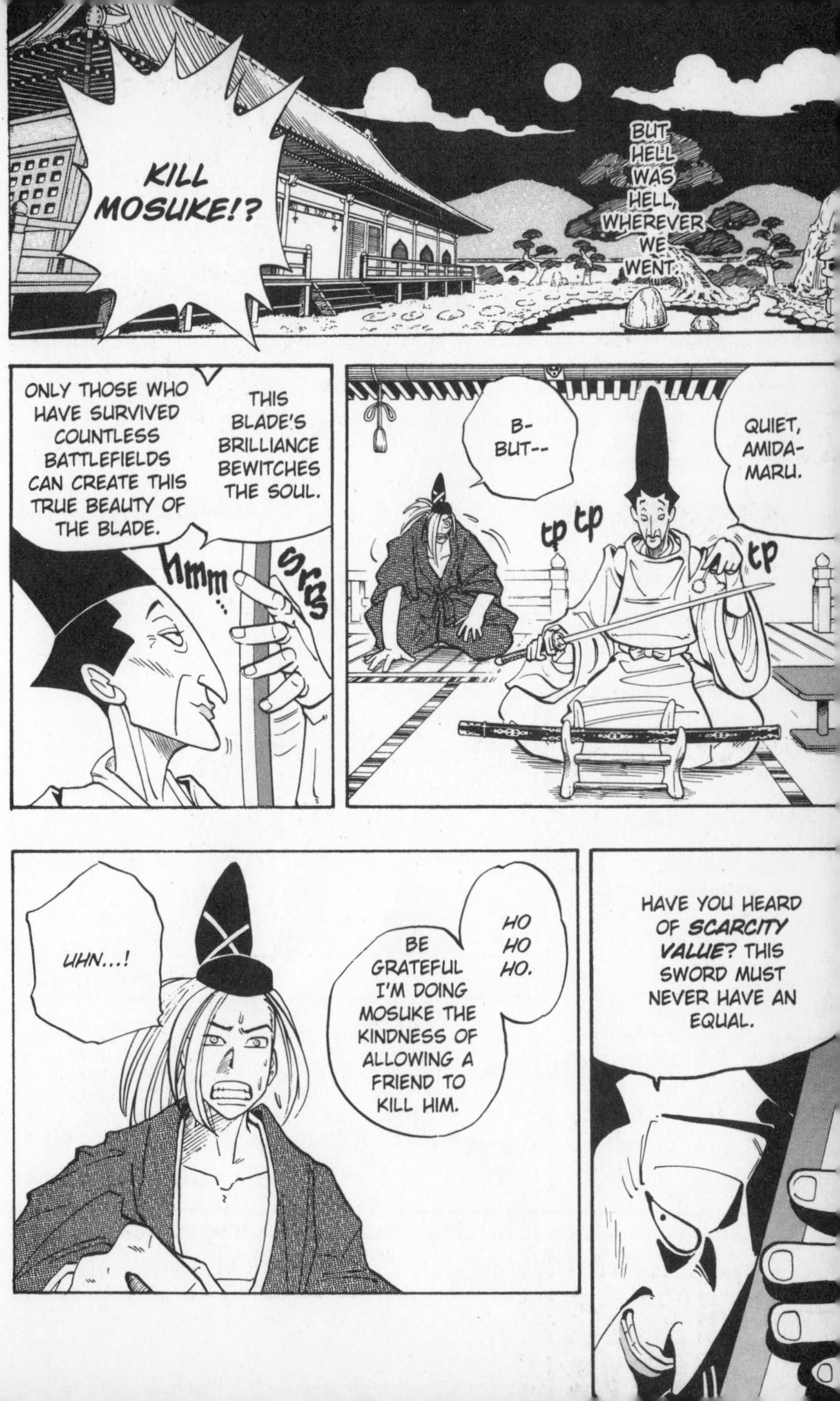
BUT HELL WAS HELL, WHEREVER WE WENT.
KILL MOSUKE!?
QUIET, AMIDA-MARU.
B-BUT--
tp tp
tp
THIS BLADE'S BRILLIANCE BEWITCHES THE SOUL.
ONLY THOSE WHO HAVE SURVIVED COUNTLESS BATTLEFIELDS CAN CREATE THIS TRUE BEAUTY OF THE BLADE.
hmm...
srrs
HAVE YOU HEARD OF *SCARCITY VALUE*? THIS SWORD MUST NEVER HAVE AN EQUAL.
HO HO HO.
BE GRATEFUL I'M DOING MOSUKE THE KINDNESS OF ALLOWING A FRIEND TO KILL HIM.
UHN...!

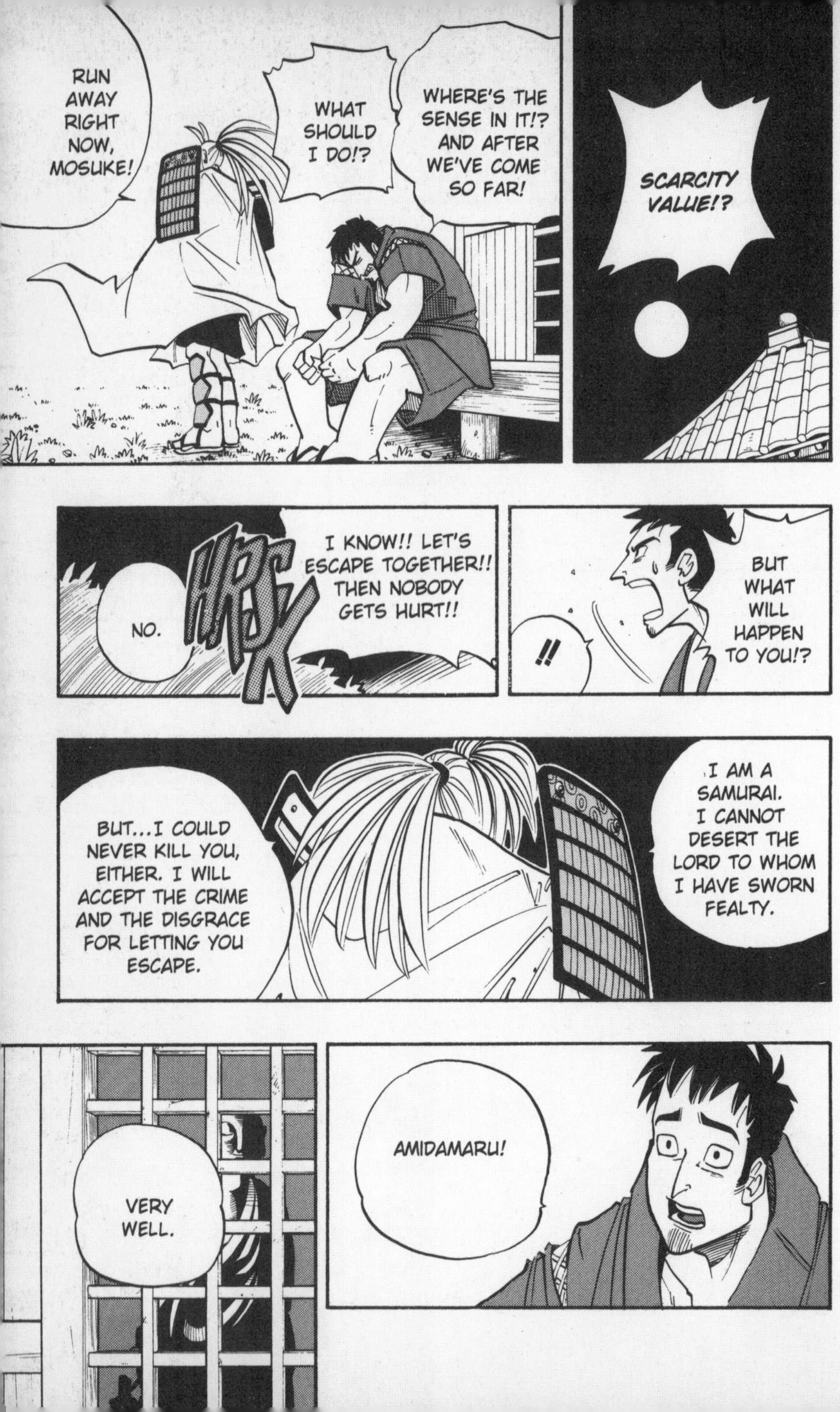
SCARCITY VALUE!?
WHERE'S THE SENSE IN IT!? AND AFTER WE'VE COME SO FAR!
WHAT SHOULD I DO!?
RUN AWAY RIGHT NOW, MOSUKE!
BUT WHAT WILL HAPPEN TO YOU!?
!!
I KNOW!! LET'S ESCAPE TOGETHER!! THEN NOBODY GETS HURT!!
HRSK
NO.
I AM A SAMURAI. I CANNOT DESERT THE LORD TO WHOM I HAVE SWORN FEALTY.
BUT...I COULD NEVER KILL YOU, EITHER. I WILL ACCEPT THE CRIME AND THE DISGRACE FOR LETTING YOU ESCAPE.
AMIDAMARU!
VERY WELL.

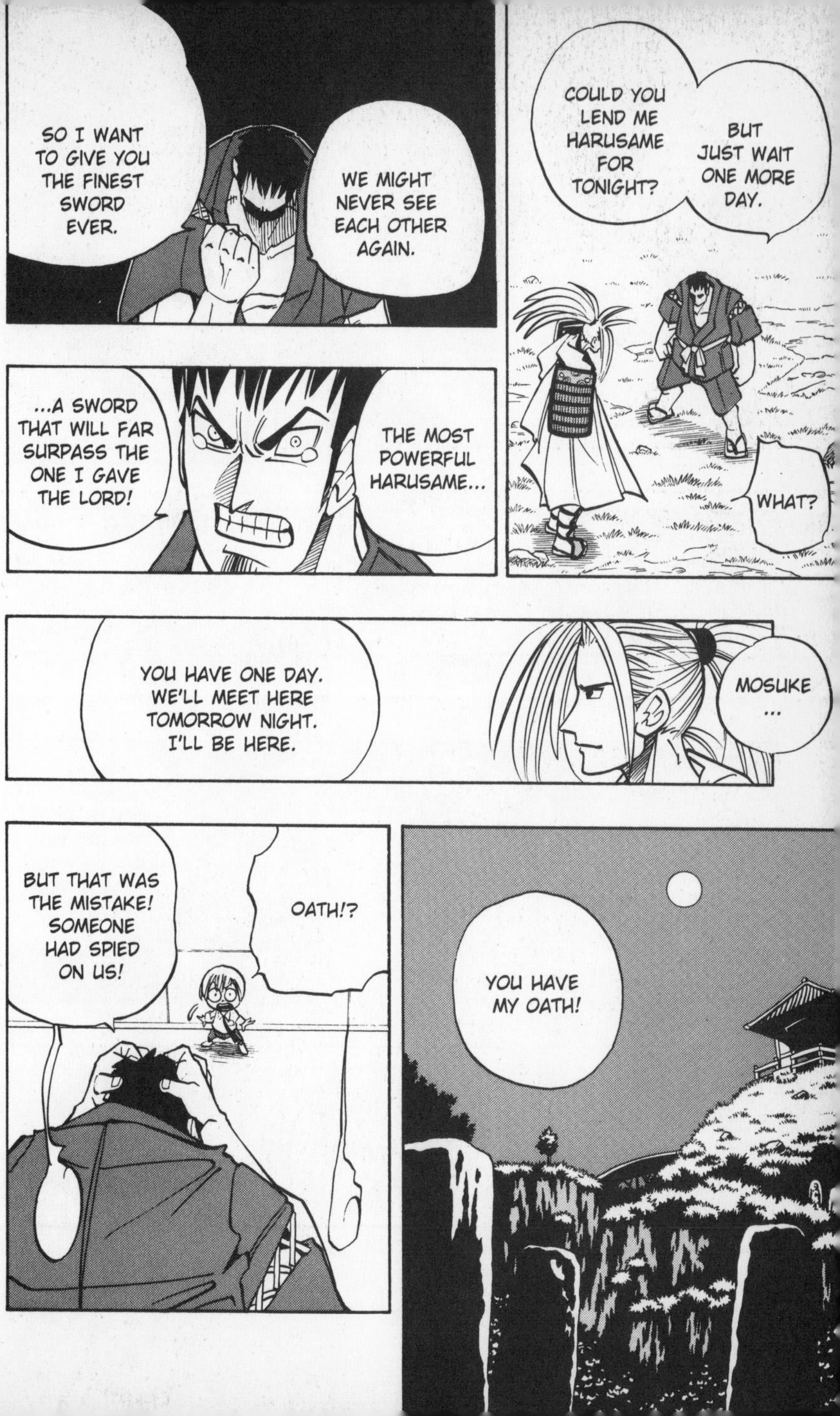
BUT JUST WAIT ONE MORE DAY.
COULD YOU LEND ME HARUSAME FOR TONIGHT?
WHAT?
WE MIGHT NEVER SEE EACH OTHER AGAIN.
SO I WANT TO GIVE YOU THE FINEST SWORD EVER.
THE MOST POWERFUL HARUSAME...
...A SWORD THAT WILL FAR SURPASS THE ONE I GAVE THE LORD!
MOSUKE ...
YOU HAVE ONE DAY. WE'LL MEET HERE TOMORROW NIGHT. I'LL BE HERE.
YOU HAVE MY OATH!
OATH!?
BUT THAT WAS THE MISTAKE! SOMEONE HAD SPIED ON US!

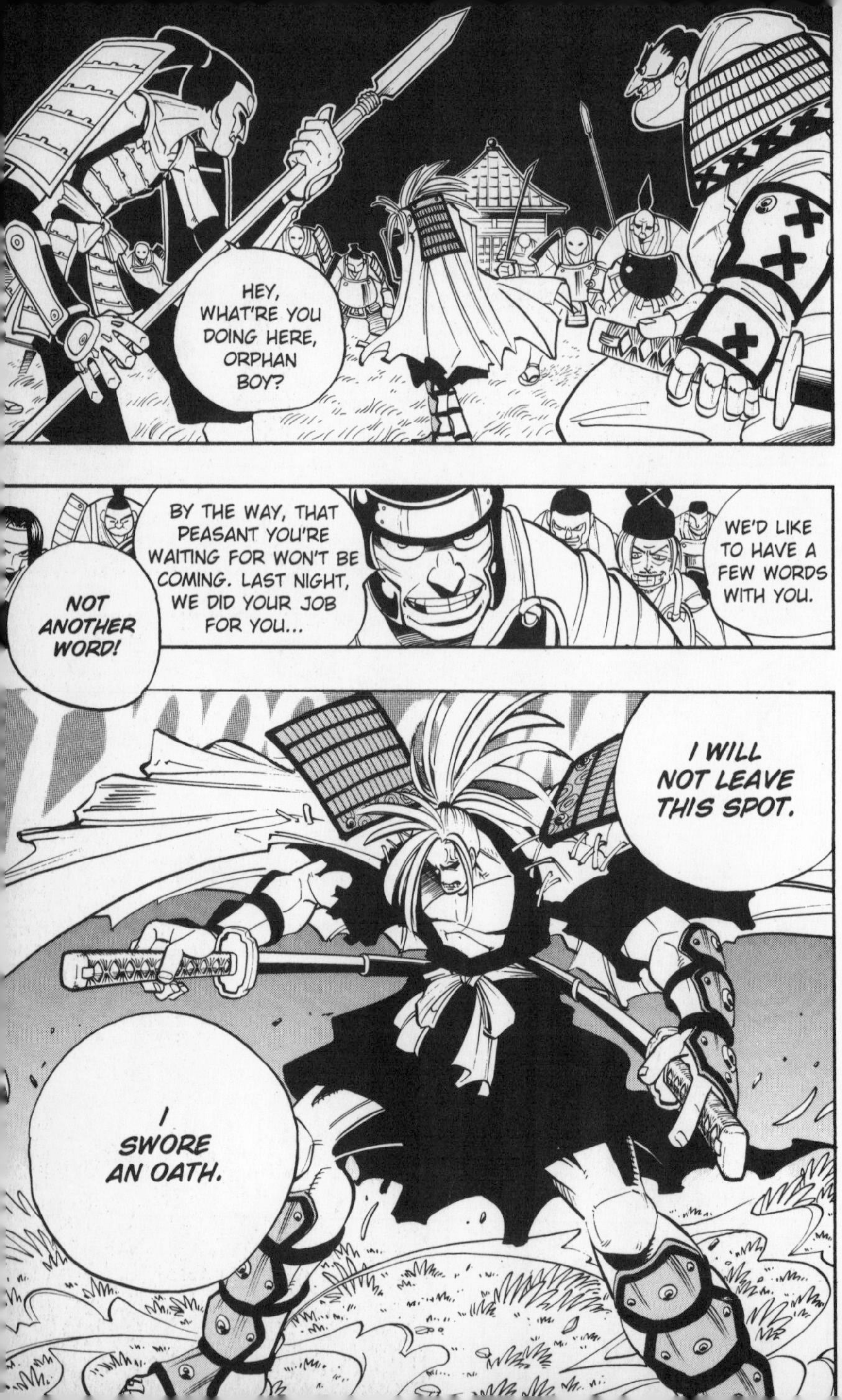
HEY, WHAT'RE YOU DOING HERE, ORPHAN BOY?
WE'D LIKE TO HAVE A FEW WORDS WITH YOU.
BY THE WAY, THAT PEASANT YOU'RE WAITING FOR WON'T BE COMING. LAST NIGHT, WE DID YOUR JOB FOR YOU...
NOT ANOTHER WORD!
I WILL NOT LEAVE THIS SPOT.
I SWORE AN OATH.

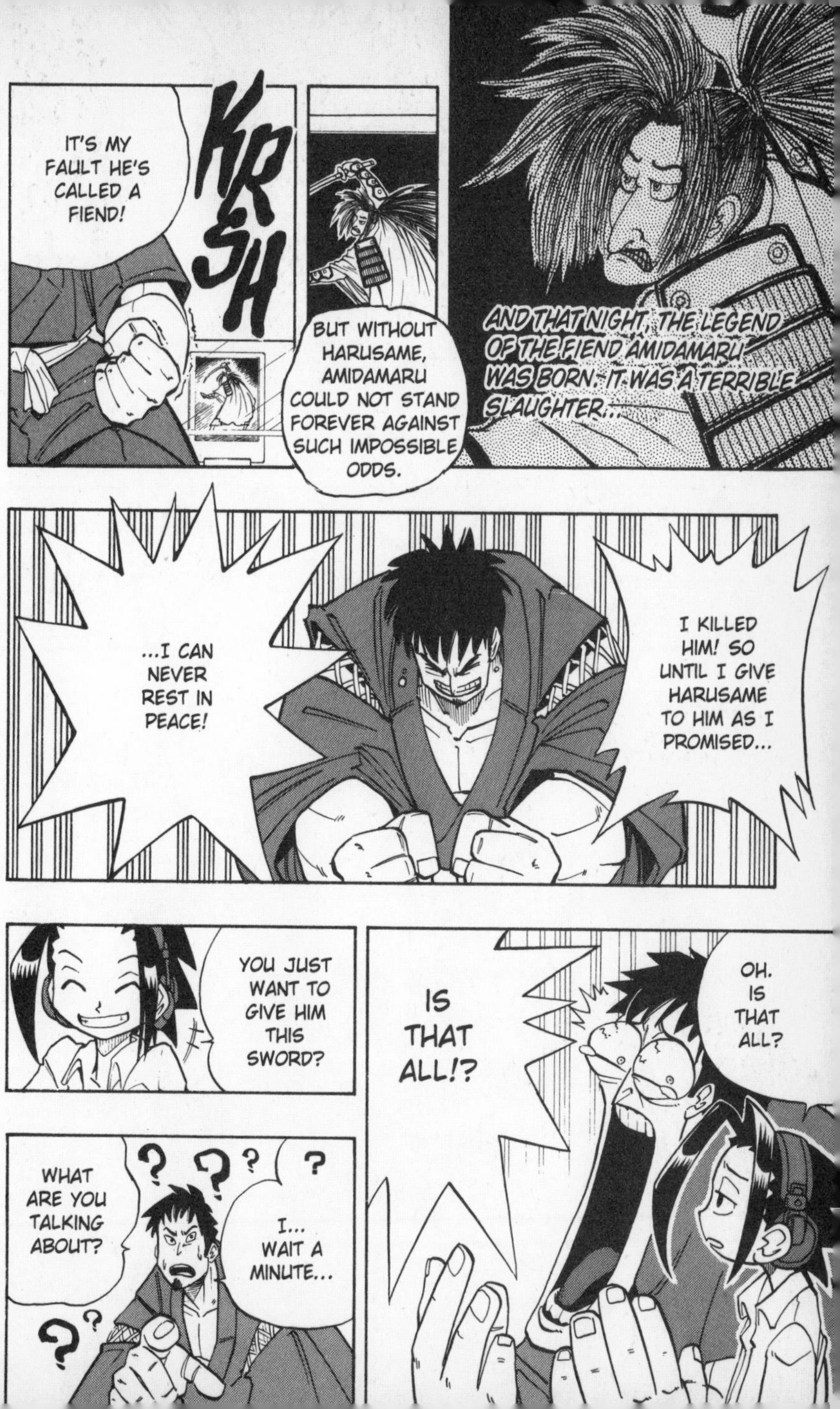
AND THAT NIGHT, THE LEGEND OF THE FIEND AMIDAMARU WAS BORN. IT WAS A TERRIBLE SLAUGHTER...
BUT WITHOUT HARUSAME, AMIDAMARU COULD NOT STAND FOREVER AGAINST SUCH IMPOSSIBLE ODDS.
KRSH
IT'S MY FAULT HE'S CALLED A FIEND!
I KILLED HIM! SO UNTIL I GIVE HARUSAME TO HIM AS I PROMISED...
...I CAN NEVER REST IN PEACE!
OH. IS THAT ALL?
IS THAT ALL!?
YOU JUST WANT TO GIVE HIM THIS SWORD?
I... WAIT A MINUTE...
WHAT ARE YOU TALKING ABOUT?

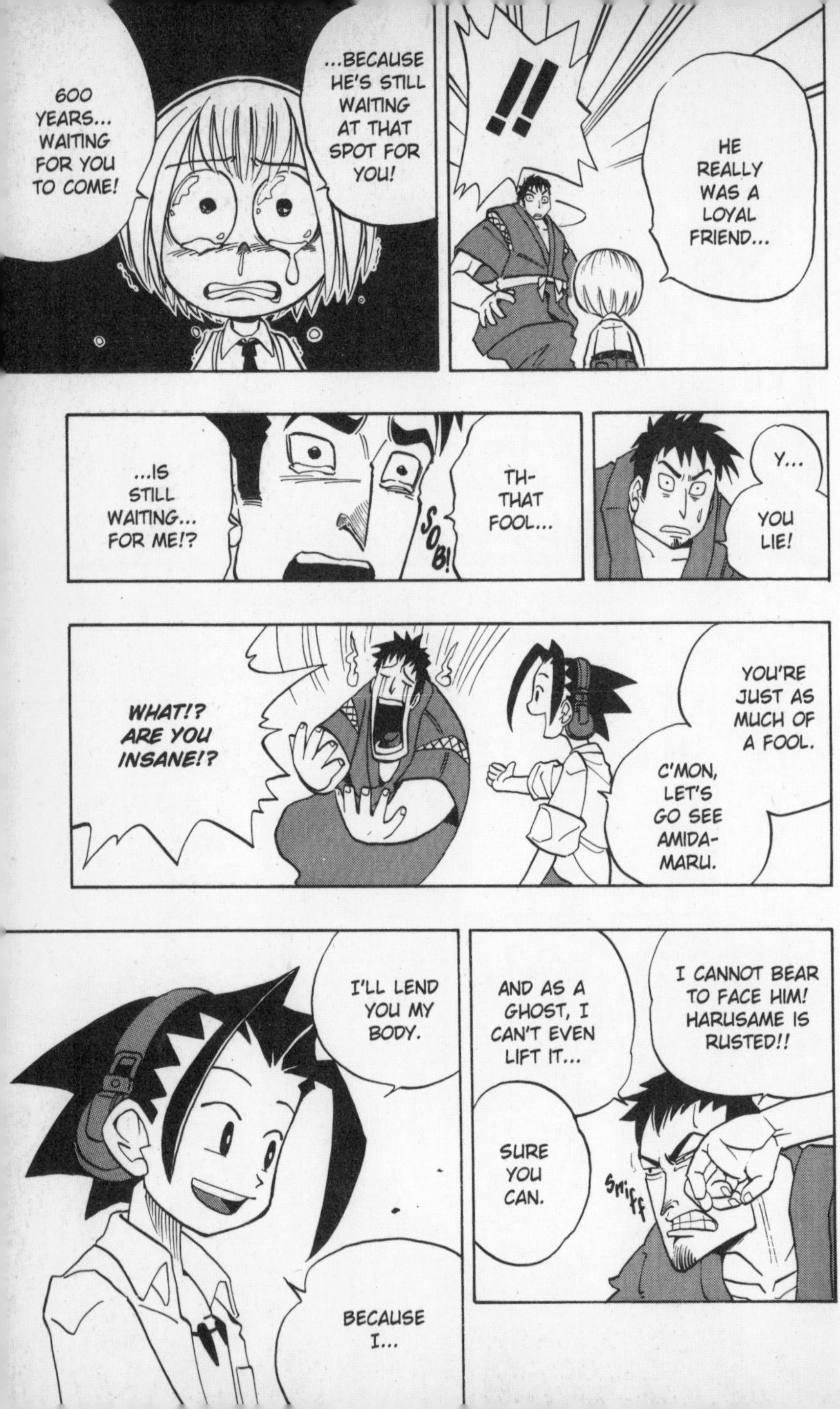
!!
HE REALLY WAS A LOYAL FRIEND...
...BECAUSE HE'S STILL WAITING AT THAT SPOT FOR YOU!
600 YEARS... WAITING FOR YOU TO COME!
Y... YOU LIE!
TH- THAT FOOL...
SOB!
...IS STILL WAITING... FOR ME!?
YOU'RE JUST AS MUCH OF A FOOL.
C'MON, LET'S GO SEE AMIDA-MARU.
WHAT!? ARE YOU INSANE!?
I CANNOT BEAR TO FACE HIM! HARUSAME IS RUSTED!!
AND AS A GHOST, I CAN'T EVEN LIFT IT...
SURE YOU CAN.
SNIFF
I'LL LEND YOU MY BODY.
BECAUSE I...

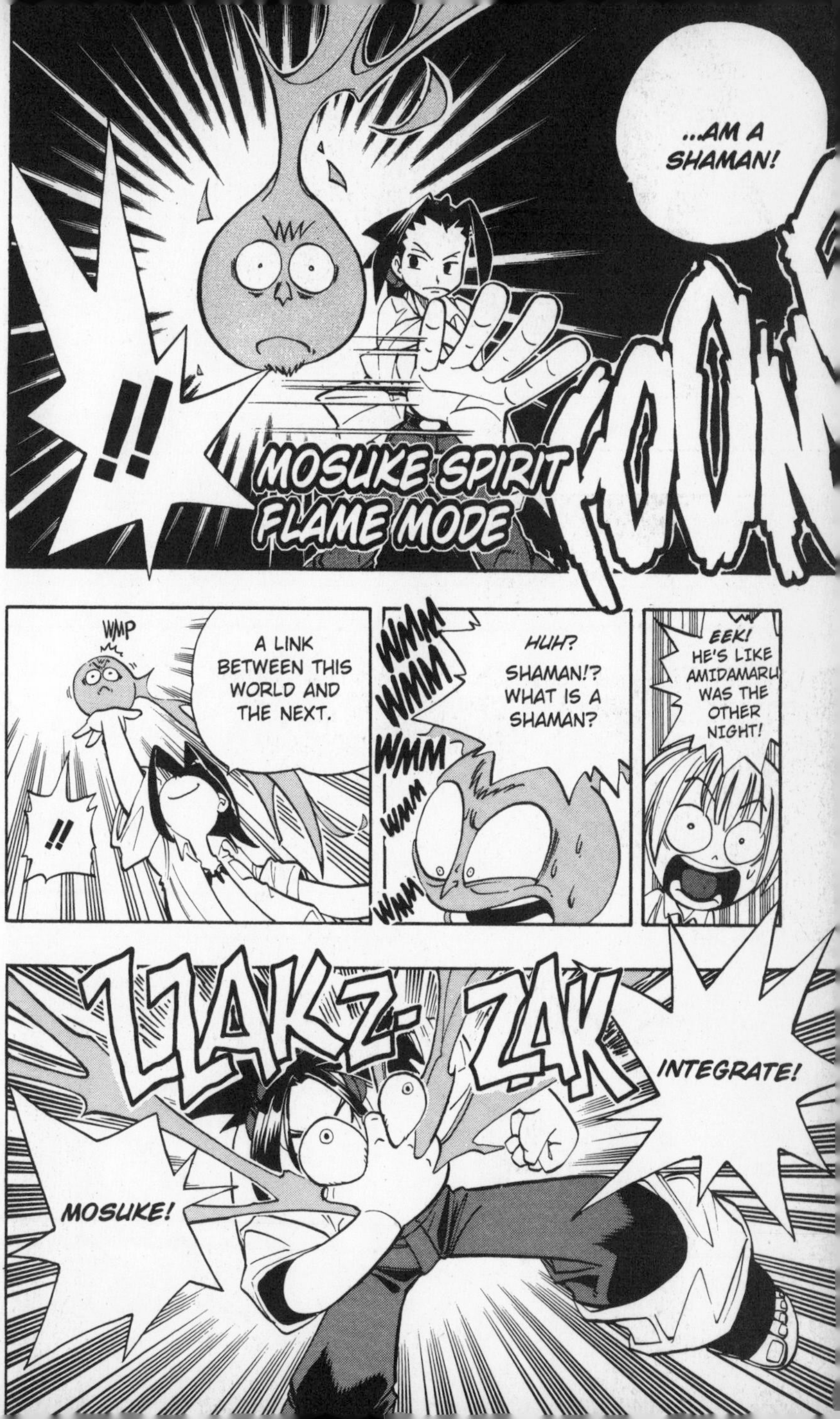
...AM A SHAMAN!
MOSUKE SPIRIT FLAME MODE
!!
EEK! HE'S LIKE AMIDAMARU WAS THE OTHER NIGHT!
HUH?
SHAMAN!? WHAT IS A SHAMAN?
WMM WMM
WMM
WMM
WMM
A LINK BETWEEN THIS WORLD AND THE NEXT.
WMP
!!
INTEGRATE!
ZZAK-ZAK
MOSUKE!

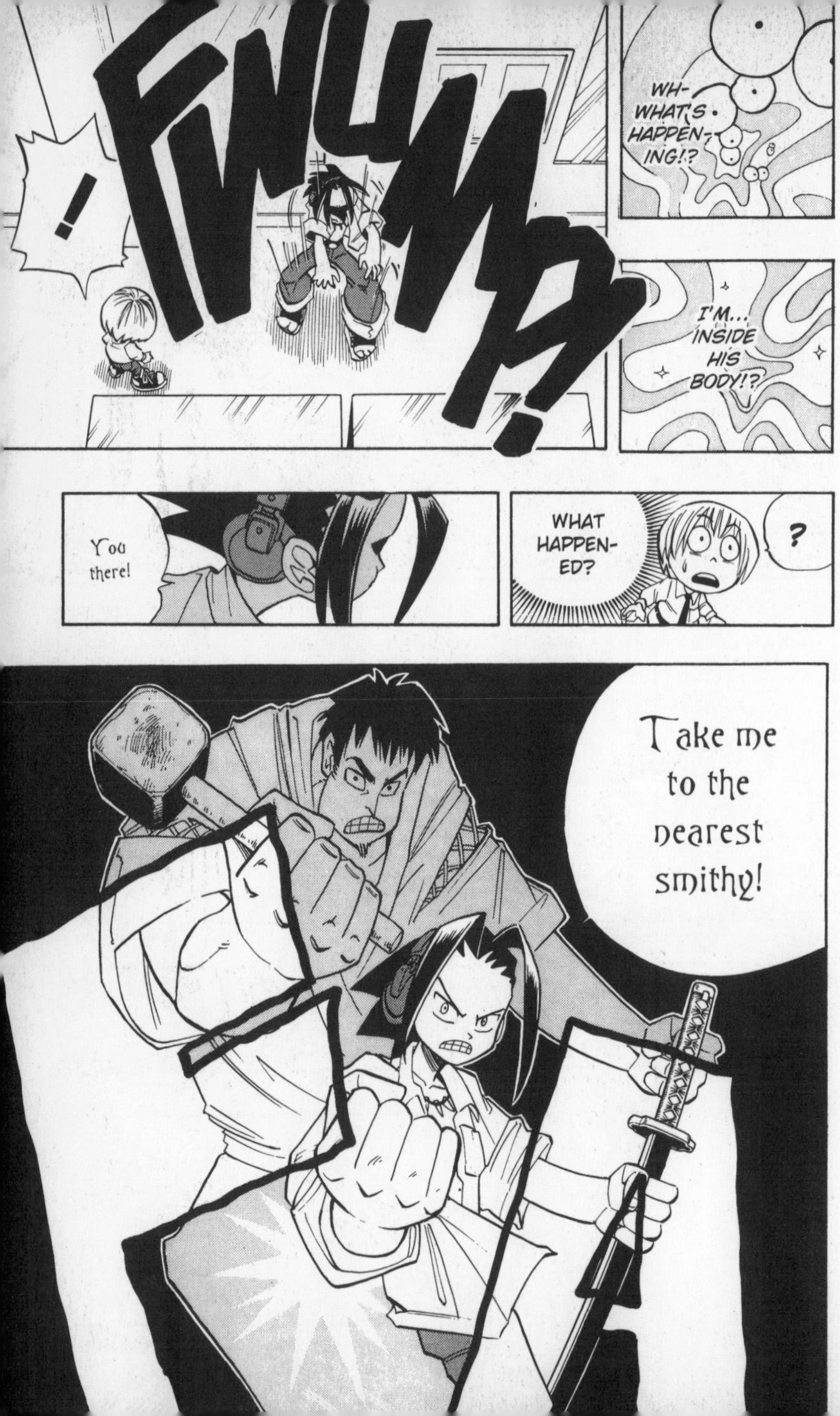
WH-WHAT'S HAPPENING!?
I'M... INSIDE HIS BODY!?
FWUMP!?
!
?
WHAT HAPPEN-ED?
You there!
Take me to the nearest smithy!

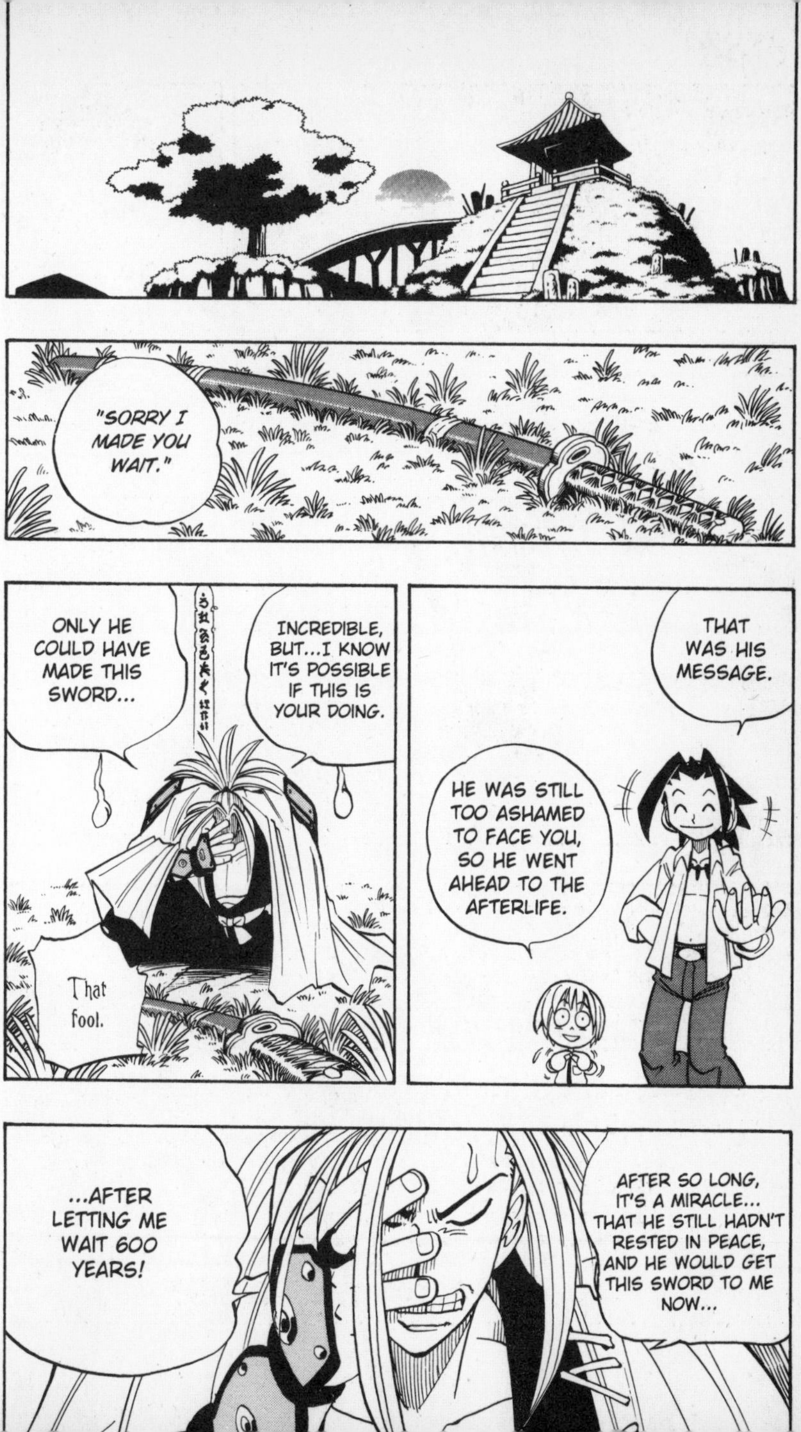
"SORRY I MADE YOU WAIT."
THAT WAS HIS MESSAGE.
HE WAS STILL TOO ASHAMED TO FACE YOU, SO HE WENT AHEAD TO THE AFTERLIFE.
INCREDIBLE, BUT...I KNOW IT'S POSSIBLE IF THIS IS YOUR DOING.
ONLY HE COULD HAVE MADE THIS SWORD...
That fool.
AFTER SO LONG, IT'S A MIRACLE... THAT HE STILL HADN'T RESTED IN PEACE, AND HE WOULD GET THIS SWORD TO ME NOW...
...AFTER LETTING ME WAIT 600 YEARS!

READ THIS WAY

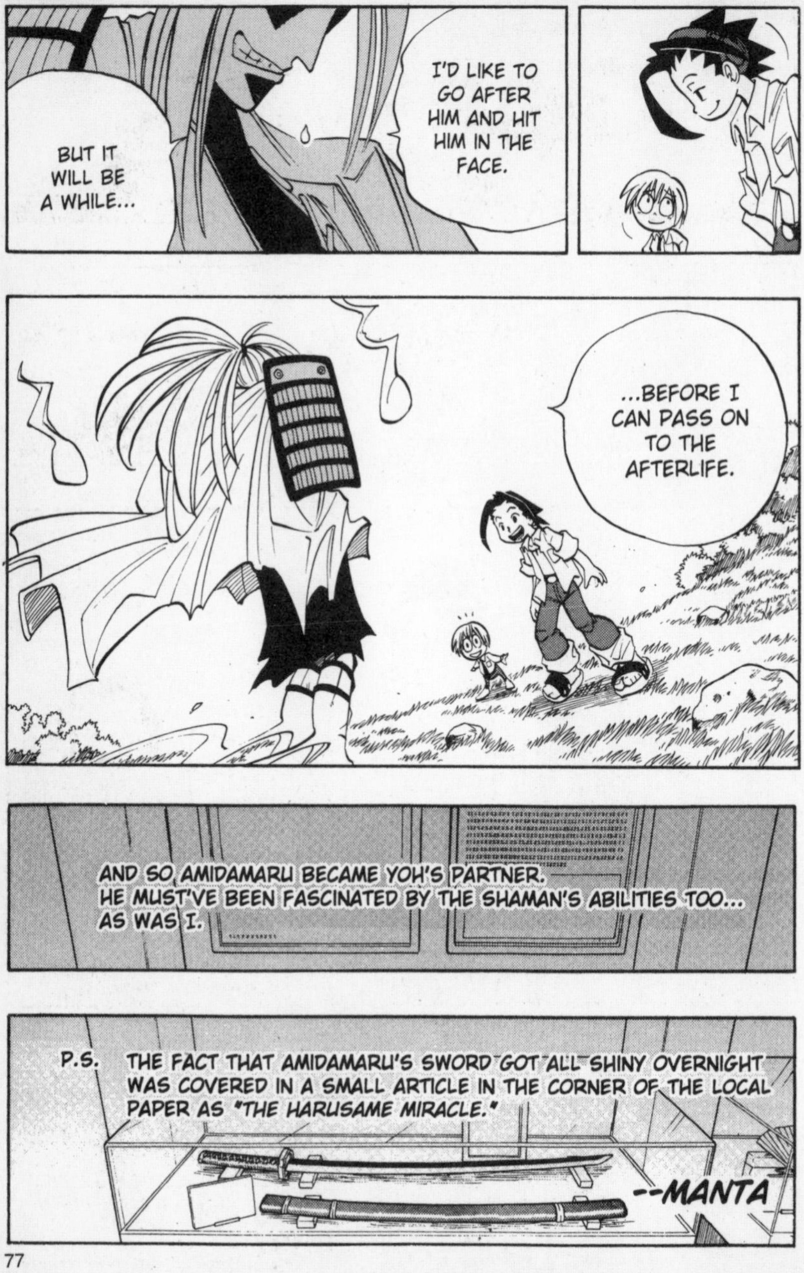
I'D LIKE TO GO AFTER HIM AND HIT HIM IN THE FACE.
BUT IT WILL BE A WHILE...
...BEFORE I CAN PASS ON TO THE AFTERLIFE.
AND SO AMIDAMARU BECAME YOH'S PARTNER. HE MUST'VE BEEN FASCINATED BY THE SHAMAN'S ABILITIES TOO... AS WAS I.
P.S. THE FACT THAT AMIDAMARU'S SWORD GOT ALL SHINY OVERNIGHT WAS COVERED IN A SMALL ARTICLE IN THE CORNER OF THE LOCAL PAPER AS "THE HARUSAME MIRACLE."
--MANTA

SHAMAN
KING

1

HEADPHONES

REINCARNATION 3: THE UNFINISHED BILLBOARD

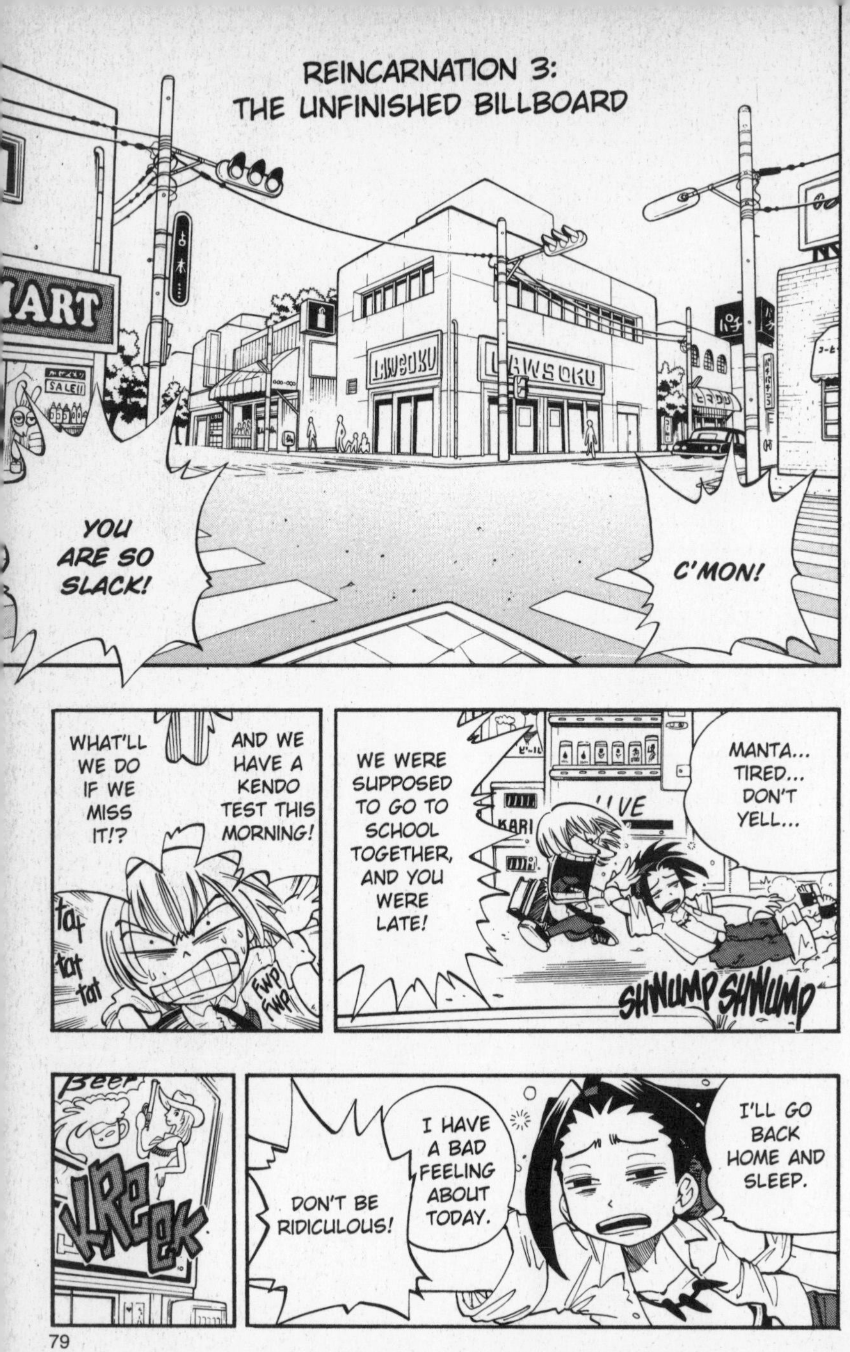

C'MON!
YOU ARE SO SLACK!
MART
SALE!!
LAWSOKU
LAWSOKU
MANTA... TIRED... DON'T YELL...
WE WERE SUPPOSED TO GO TO SCHOOL TOGETHER, AND YOU WERE LATE!
SHNUMP SHNUMP
AND WE HAVE A KENDO TEST THIS MORNING!
WHAT'LL WE DO IF WE MISS IT!?
tat tat tat
FWP FWP
I'LL GO BACK HOME AND SLEEP.
I HAVE A BAD FEELING ABOUT TODAY.
DON'T BE RIDICULOUS!
Beer

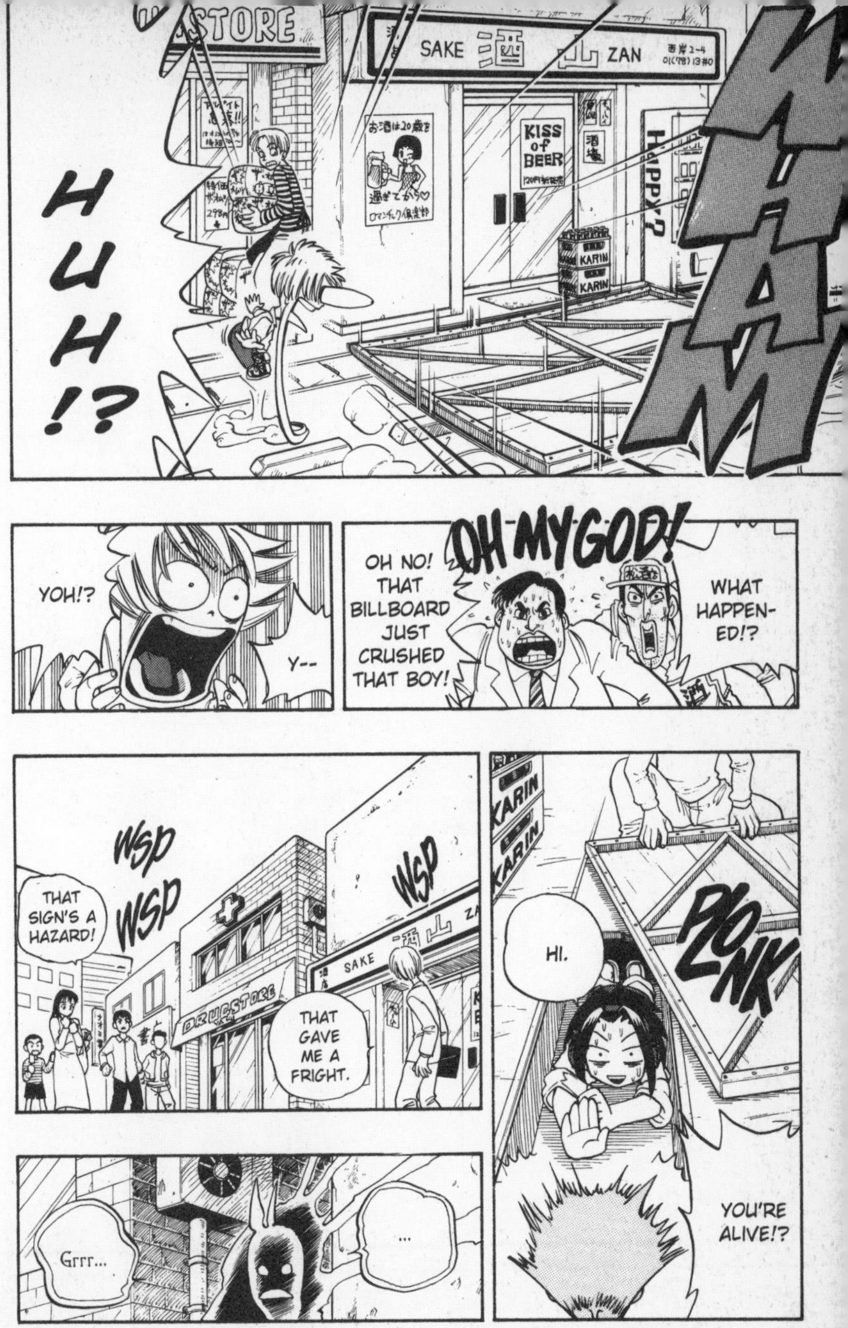
STORE
SAKE 酒山 ZAN
KISS of BEER
KARIN
KARIN
HUH!?
OH MY GOD!
WHAT HAPPENED!?
OH NO! THAT BILLBOARD JUST CRUSHED THAT BOY!
YOH!?
Y--
PLONK
HI.
YOU'RE ALIVE!?
WSP
WSP WSP
THAT SIGN'S A HAZARD!
THAT GAVE ME A FRIGHT.
...
Grrr...

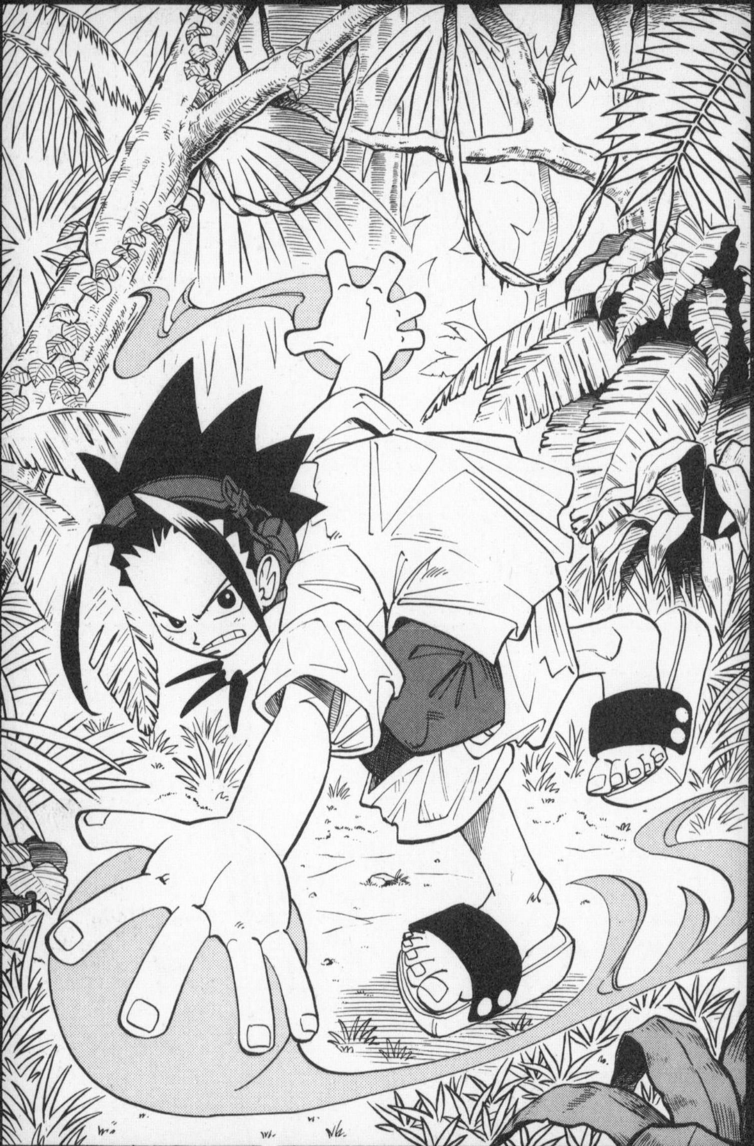

Reincarnation 3:
THE UNFINISHED BILLBOARD

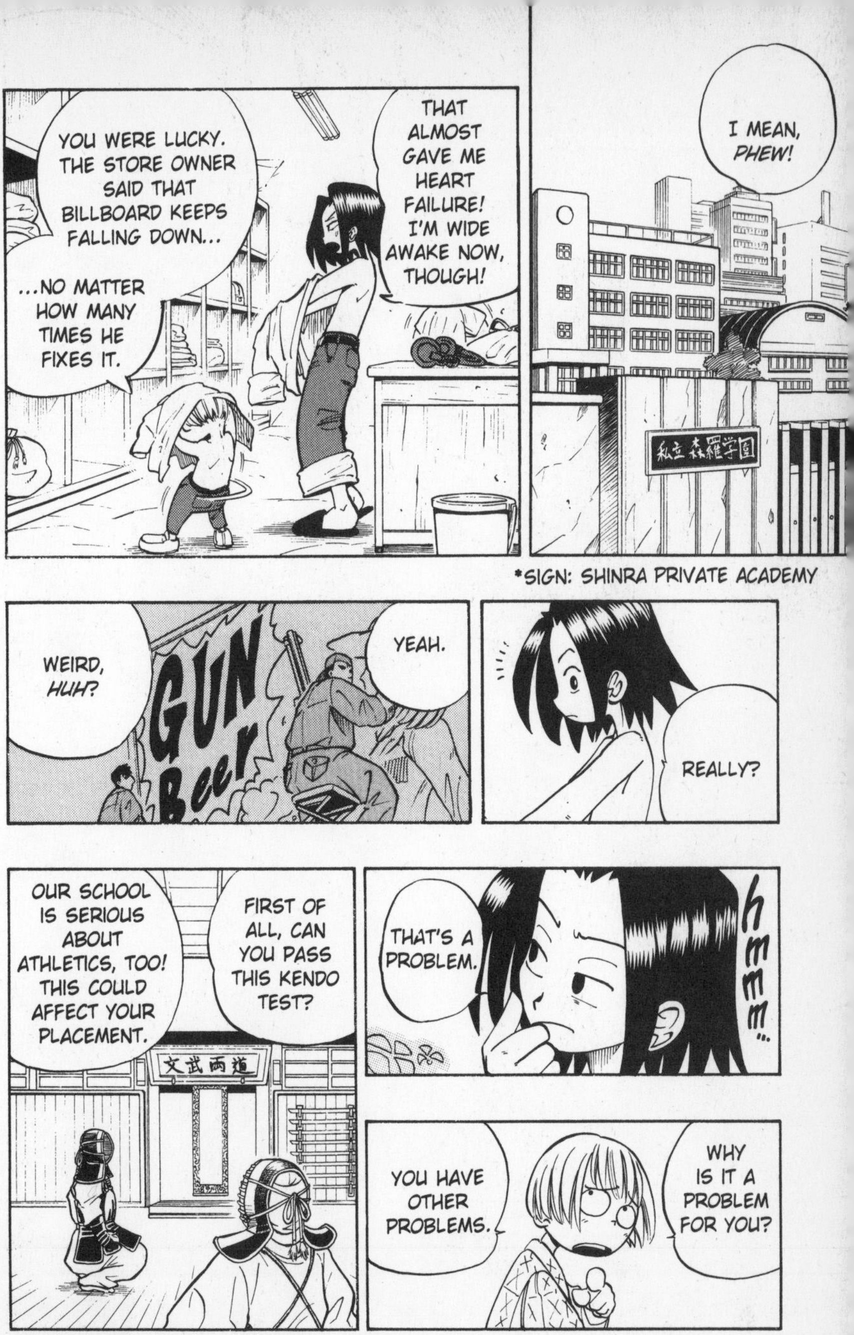
I MEAN, *PHEW!*
THAT ALMOST GAVE ME HEART FAILURE! I'M WIDE AWAKE NOW, THOUGH!
YOU WERE LUCKY. THE STORE OWNER SAID THAT BILLBOARD KEEPS FALLING DOWN...
...NO MATTER HOW MANY TIMES HE FIXES IT.
*SIGN: SHINRA PRIVATE ACADEMY
REALLY?
YEAH.
WEIRD, *HUH?*
GUN Beer
hmmm...
THAT'S A PROBLEM.
WHY IS IT A PROBLEM FOR YOU?
YOU HAVE OTHER PROBLEMS.
FIRST OF ALL, CAN YOU PASS THIS KENDO TEST?
OUR SCHOOL IS SERIOUS ABOUT ATHLETICS, TOO! THIS COULD AFFECT YOUR PLACEMENT.

* SIGN: SCHOLARSHIP AND SPORT

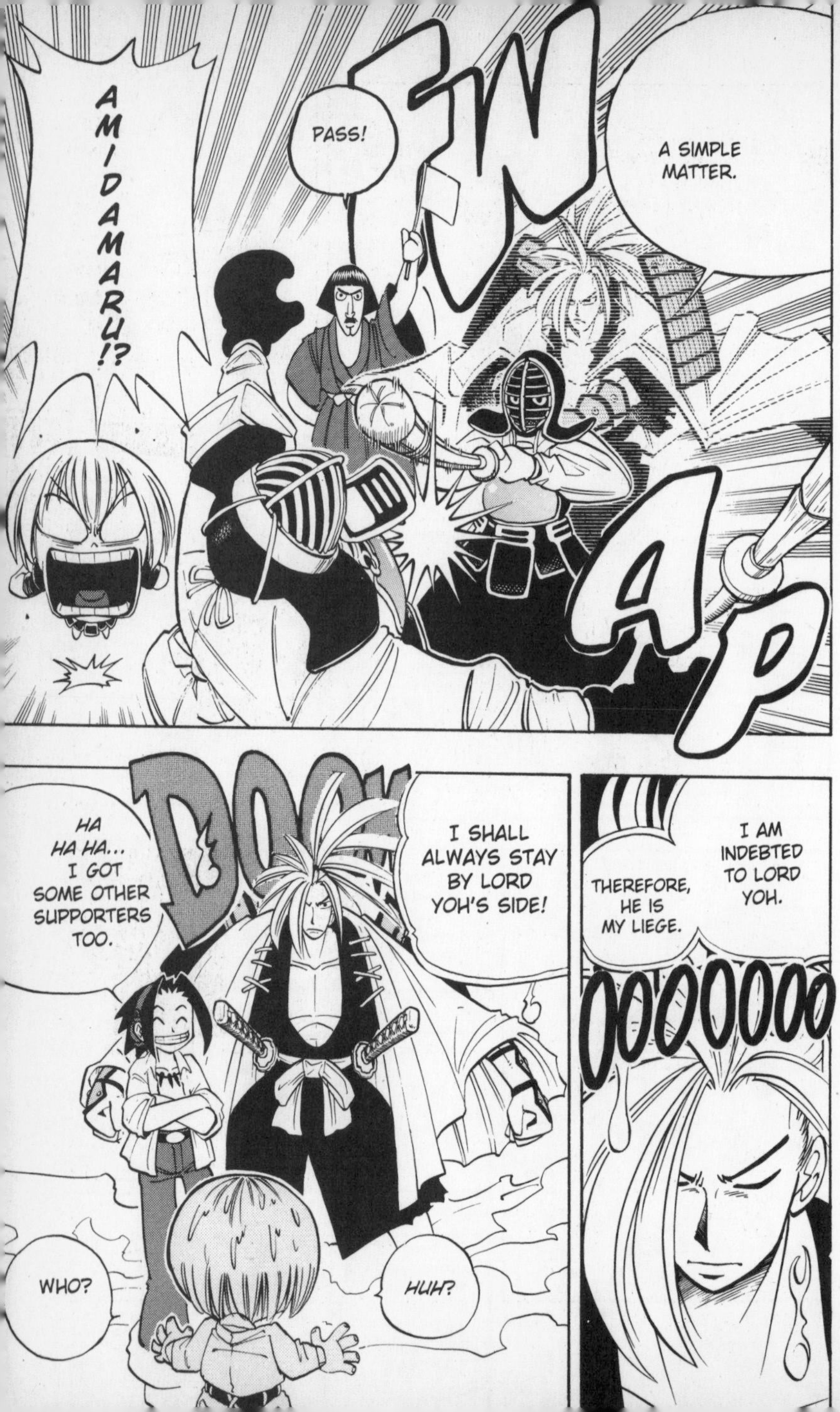
A SIMPLE MATTER.
FWAP
PASS!
AMIDAMARU!?
I AM INDEBTED TO LORD YOH.
THEREFORE, HE IS MY LIEGE.
OOOOOOO
I SHALL ALWAYS STAY BY LORD YOH'S SIDE!
HA HA HA... I GOT SOME OTHER SUPPORTERS TOO.
HUH?
WHO?

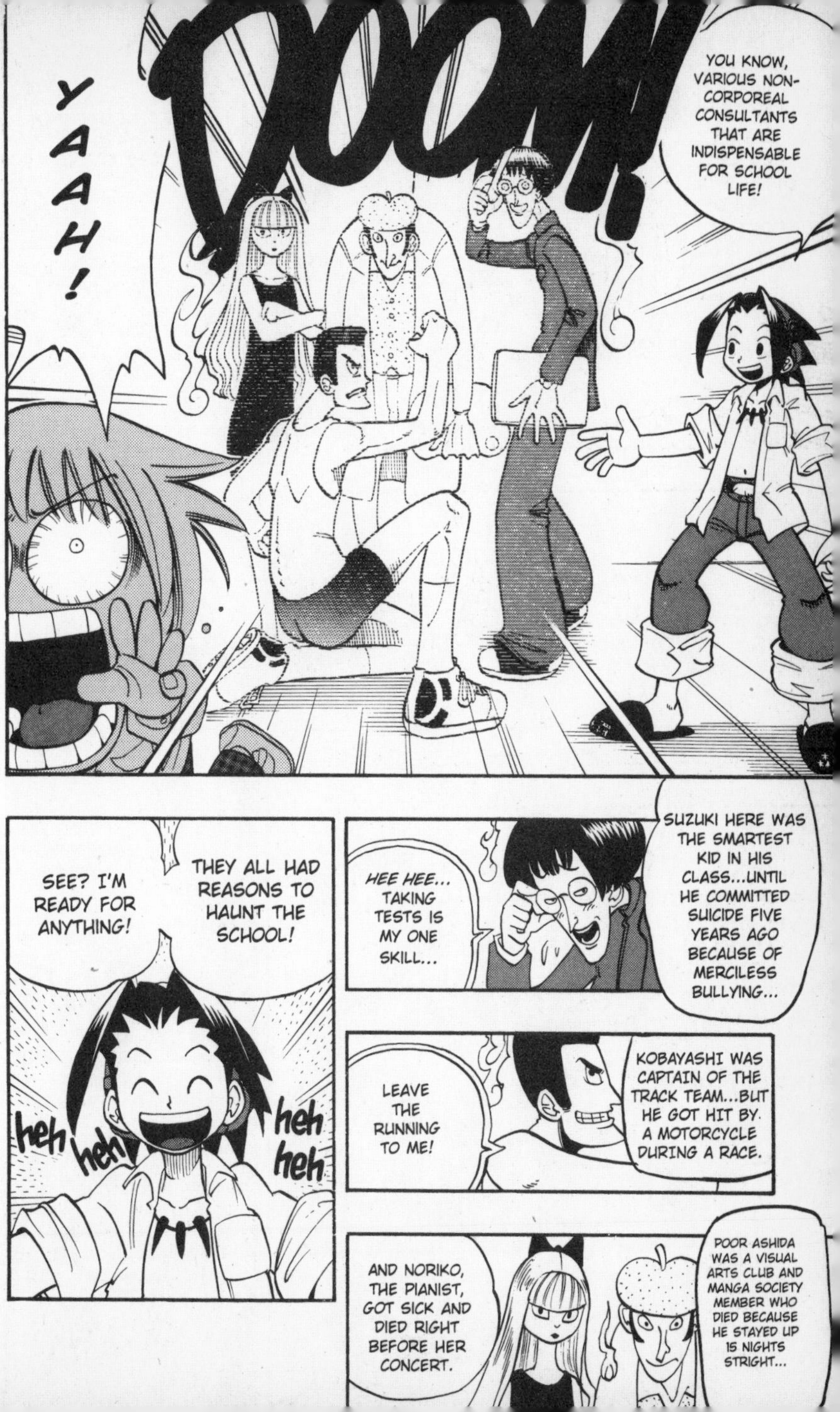
YOU KNOW, VARIOUS NON-CORPOREAL CONSULTANTS THAT ARE INDISPENSABLE FOR SCHOOL LIFE!
DOOM!
YAAAH!
SUZUKI HERE WAS THE SMARTEST KID IN HIS CLASS...UNTIL HE COMMITTED SUICIDE FIVE YEARS AGO BECAUSE OF MERCILESS BULLYING...
HEE HEE... TAKING TESTS IS MY ONE SKILL...
KOBAYASHI WAS CAPTAIN OF THE TRACK TEAM...BUT HE GOT HIT BY. A MOTORCYCLE DURING A RACE.
LEAVE THE RUNNING TO ME!
POOR ASHIDA WAS A VISUAL ARTS CLUB AND MANGA SOCIETY MEMBER WHO DIED BECAUSE HE STAYED UP 15 NIGHTS STRIGHT...
AND NORIKO, THE PIANIST, GOT SICK AND DIED RIGHT BEFORE HER CONCERT.
THEY ALL HAD REASONS TO HAUNT THE SCHOOL!
SEE? I'M READY FOR ANYTHING!
heh heh
heh heh

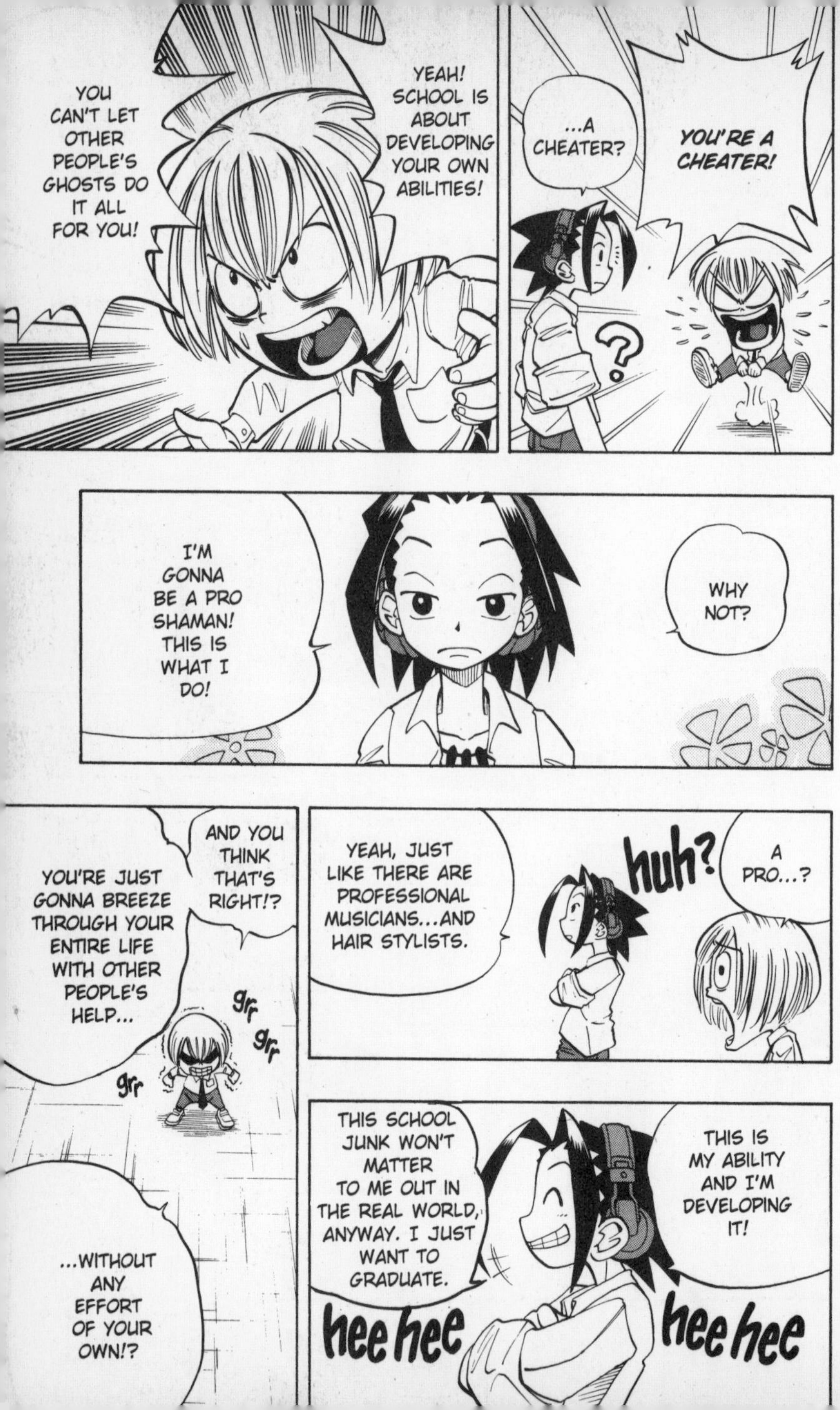
YOU'RE A CHEATER!
...A CHEATER?
YEAH! SCHOOL IS ABOUT DEVELOPING YOUR OWN ABILITIES!
YOU CAN'T LET OTHER PEOPLE'S GHOSTS DO IT ALL FOR YOU!
WHY NOT?
I'M GONNA BE A PRO SHAMAN! THIS IS WHAT I DO!
A PRO...?
huh?
YEAH, JUST LIKE THERE ARE PROFESSIONAL MUSICIANS...AND HAIR STYLISTS.
THIS IS MY ABILITY AND I'M DEVELOPING IT!
hee hee
THIS SCHOOL JUNK WON'T MATTER TO ME OUT IN THE REAL WORLD, ANYWAY. I JUST WANT TO GRADUATE.
hee hee
AND YOU THINK THAT'S RIGHT!?
YOU'RE JUST GONNA BREEZE THROUGH YOUR ENTIRE LIFE WITH OTHER PEOPLE'S HELP...
grr
grr
grr
...WITHOUT ANY EFFORT OF YOUR OWN!?

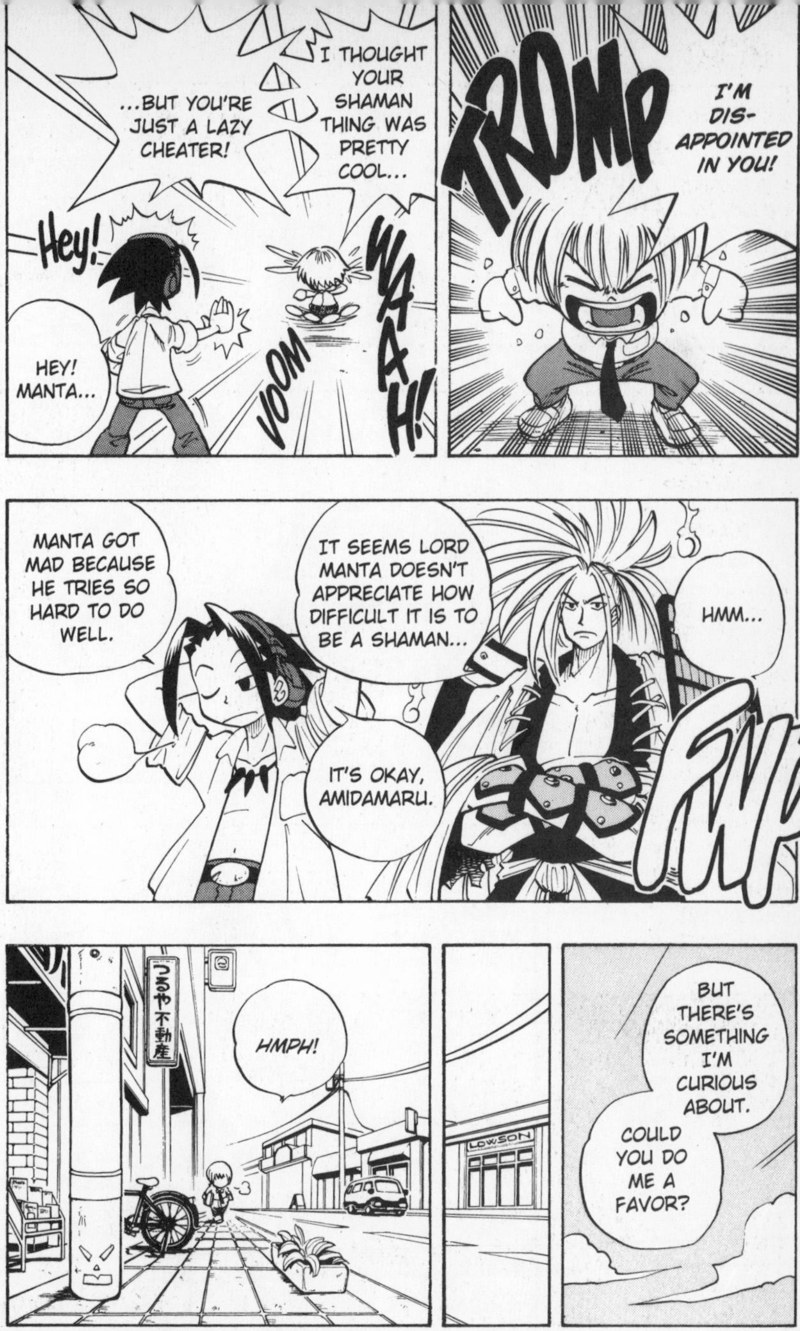
TROMP
I'M DIS-APPOINTED IN YOU!
I THOUGHT YOUR SHAMAN THING WAS PRETTY COOL...
...BUT YOU'RE JUST A LAZY CHEATER!
WAAH!
Hey!
VOOM
HEY! MANTA...
HMM...
FWP
IT SEEMS LORD MANTA DOESN'T APPRECIATE HOW DIFFICULT IT IS TO BE A SHAMAN...
MANTA GOT MAD BECAUSE HE TRIES SO HARD TO DO WELL.
IT'S OKAY, AMIDAMARU.
BUT THERE'S SOMETHING I'M CURIOUS ABOUT.
COULD YOU DO ME A FAVOR?
LOWSON
HMPH!
つるや不動産

READ THIS WAY

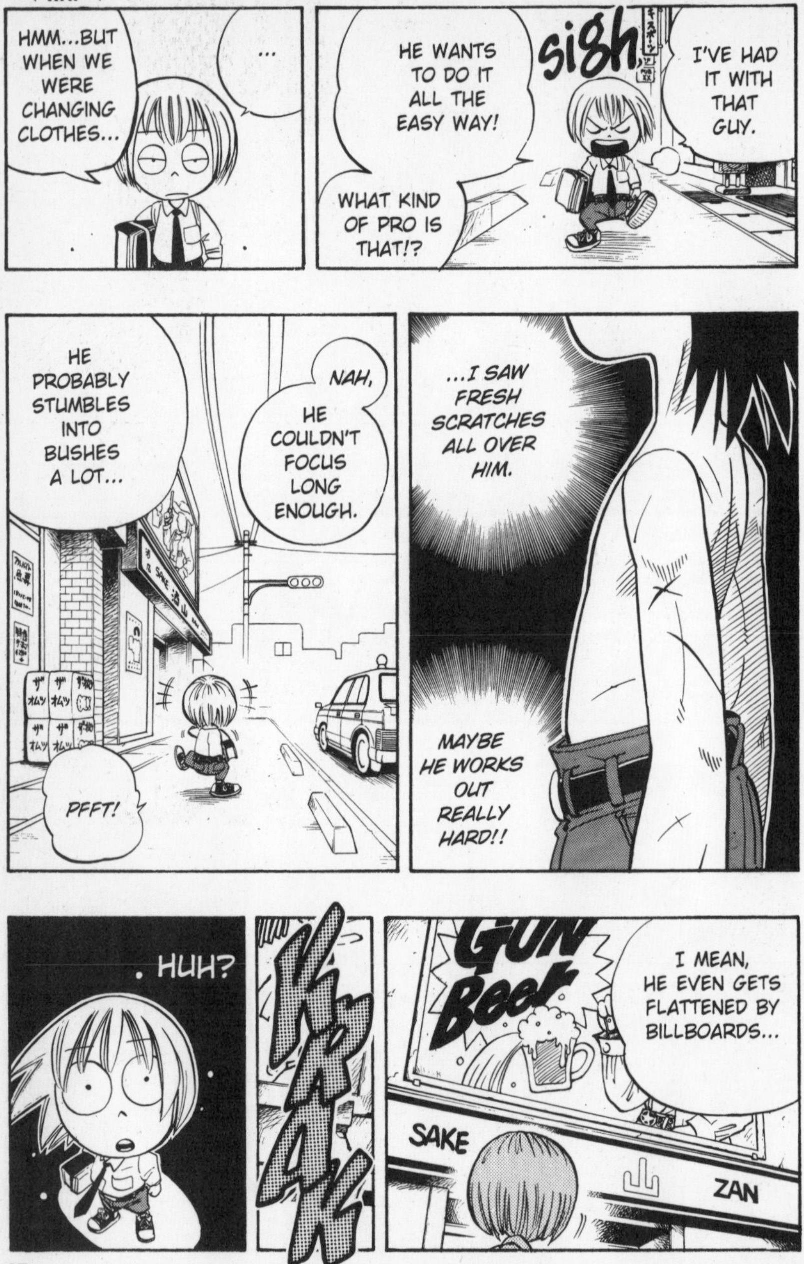
sigh
I'VE HAD IT WITH THAT GUY.
HE WANTS TO DO IT ALL THE EASY WAY!
WHAT KIND OF PRO IS THAT!?
...
HMM...BUT WHEN WE WERE CHANGING CLOTHES...
...I SAW FRESH SCRATCHES ALL OVER HIM.
MAYBE HE WORKS OUT REALLY HARD!!
NAH,
HE COULDN'T FOCUS LONG ENOUGH.
HE PROBABLY STUMBLES INTO BUSHES A LOT...
PFFT!
GUN Beer
I MEAN, HE EVEN GETS FLATTENED BY BILLBOARDS...
SAKE
ZAN
HUH?

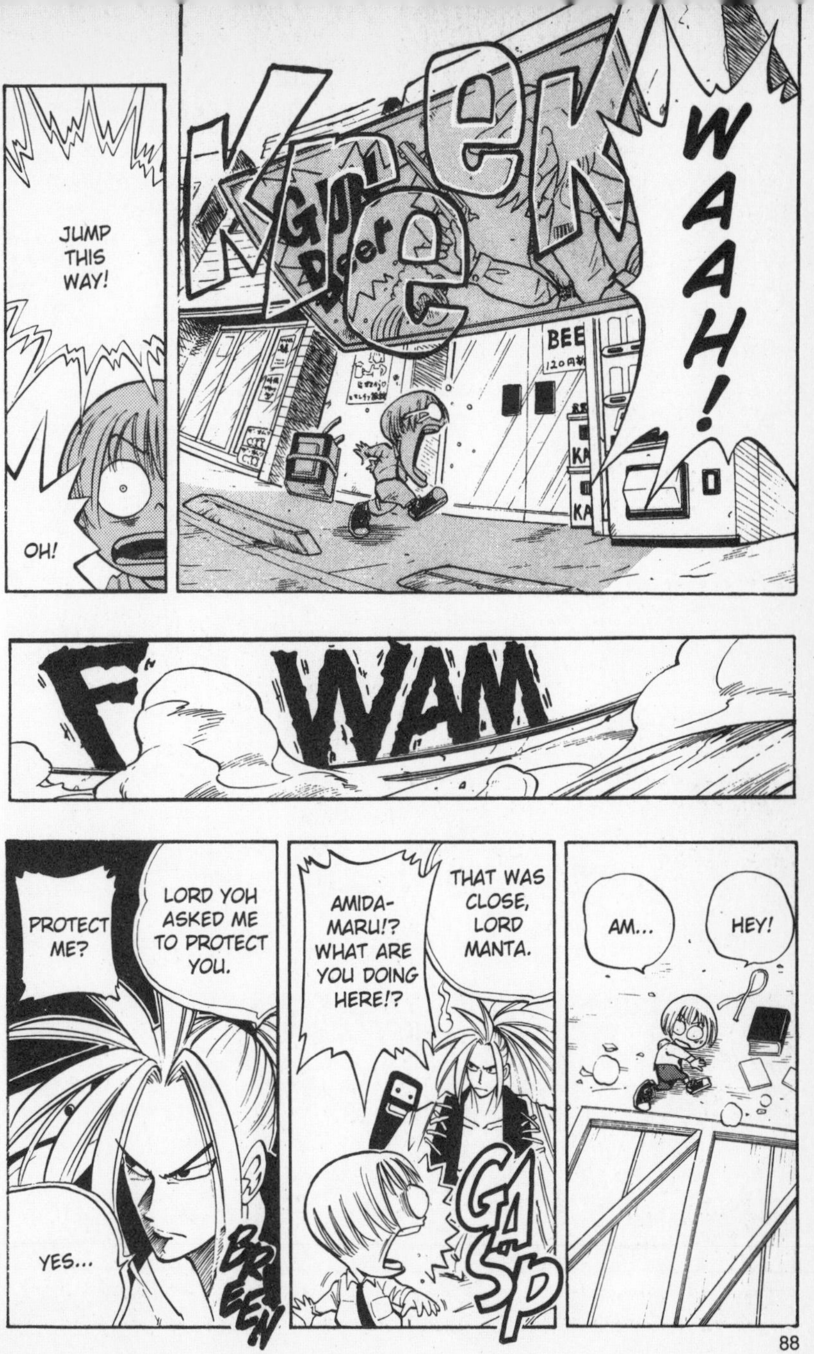
WAAAH!
JUMP THIS WAY!
OH!
FWAM
HEY!
AM...
THAT WAS CLOSE, LORD MANTA.
AMIDA-MARU!? WHAT ARE YOU DOING HERE!?
GASP
LORD YOH ASKED ME TO PROTECT YOU.
PROTECT ME?
YES...

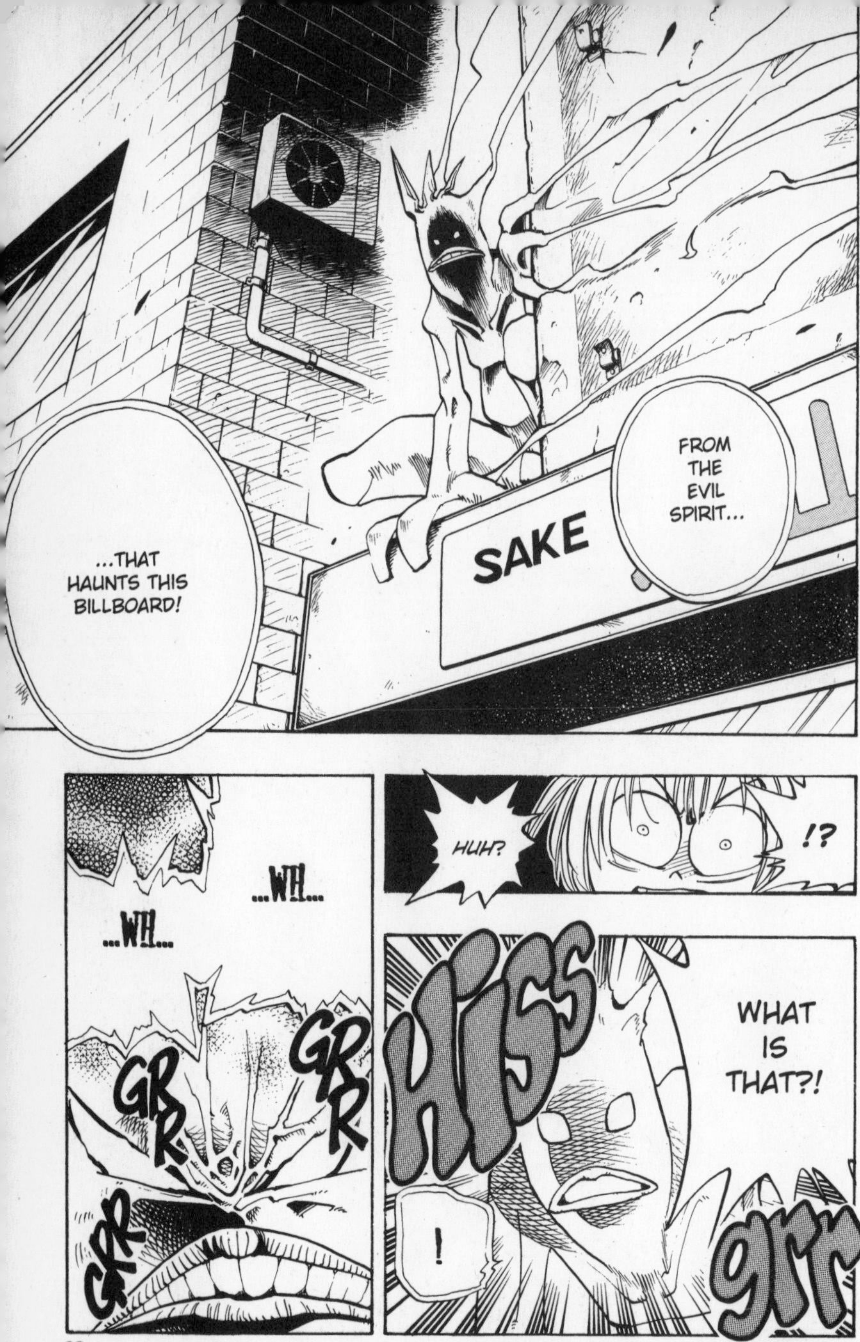

FROM THE EVIL SPIRIT...
SAKE
...THAT HAUNTS THIS BILLBOARD!
!?
HUH?
WHAT IS THAT?!
grr
HISS
!
...WH...
...WH...
GRR
GRR
GRR

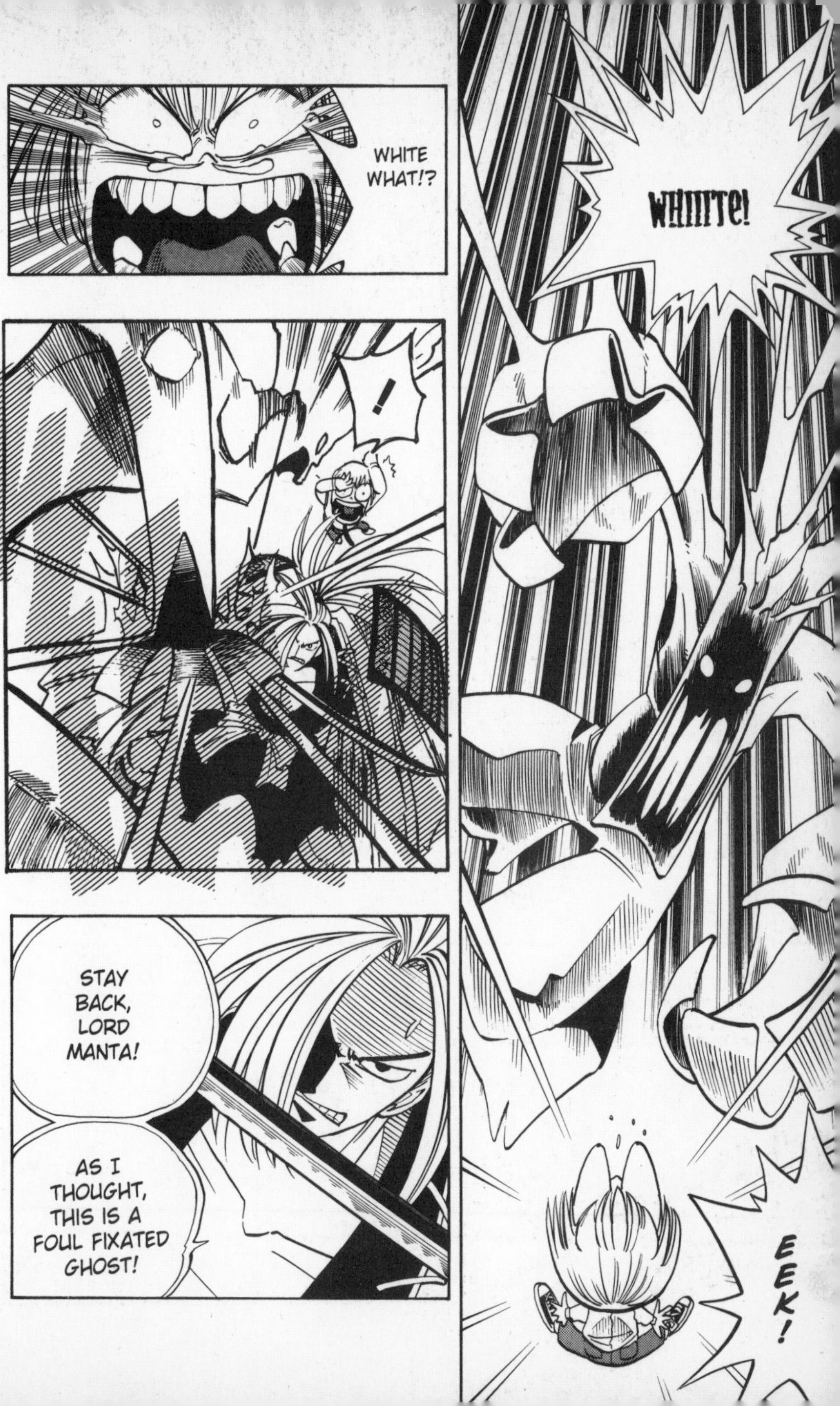
WHIIIITE!
EEK!
WHITE WHAT!?
!
STAY BACK, LORD MANTA!
AS I THOUGHT, THIS IS A FOUL FIXATED GHOST!

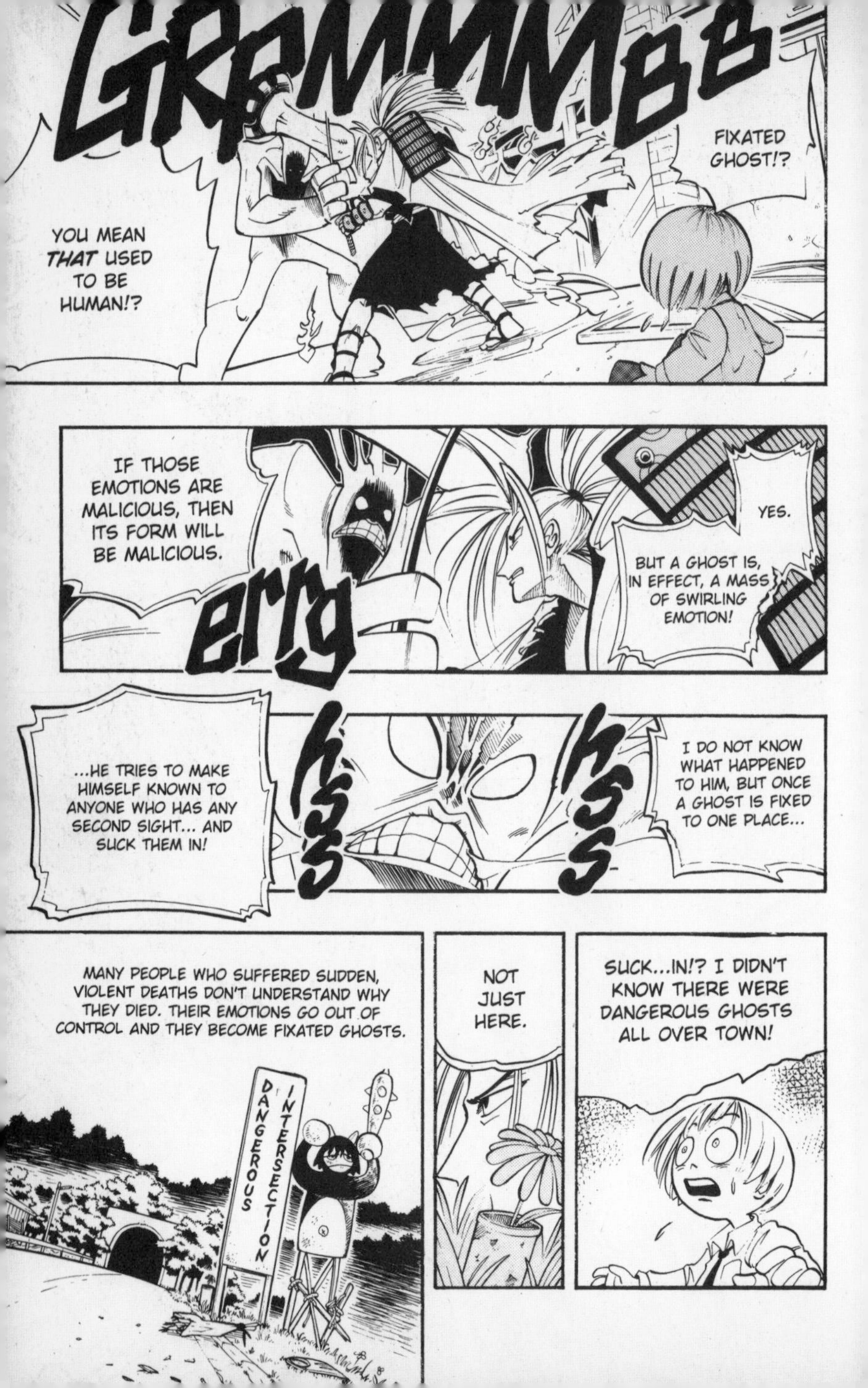
GRRMMMBB
FIXATED GHOST!?
YOU MEAN THAT USED TO BE HUMAN!?
YES.
BUT A GHOST IS, IN EFFECT, A MASS OF SWIRLING EMOTION!
IF THOSE EMOTIONS ARE MALICIOUS, THEN ITS FORM WILL BE MALICIOUS.
errg
I DO NOT KNOW WHAT HAPPENED TO HIM, BUT ONCE A GHOST IS FIXED TO ONE PLACE...
hss
hss
...HE TRIES TO MAKE HIMSELF KNOWN TO ANYONE WHO HAS ANY SECOND SIGHT... AND SUCK THEM IN!
SUCK...IN!? I DIDN'T KNOW THERE WERE DANGEROUS GHOSTS ALL OVER TOWN!
NOT JUST HERE.
MANY PEOPLE WHO SUFFERED SUDDEN, VIOLENT DEATHS DON'T UNDERSTAND WHY THEY DIED. THEIR EMOTIONS GO OUT OF CONTROL AND THEY BECOME FIXATED GHOSTS.
INTERSECTION
DANGEROUS

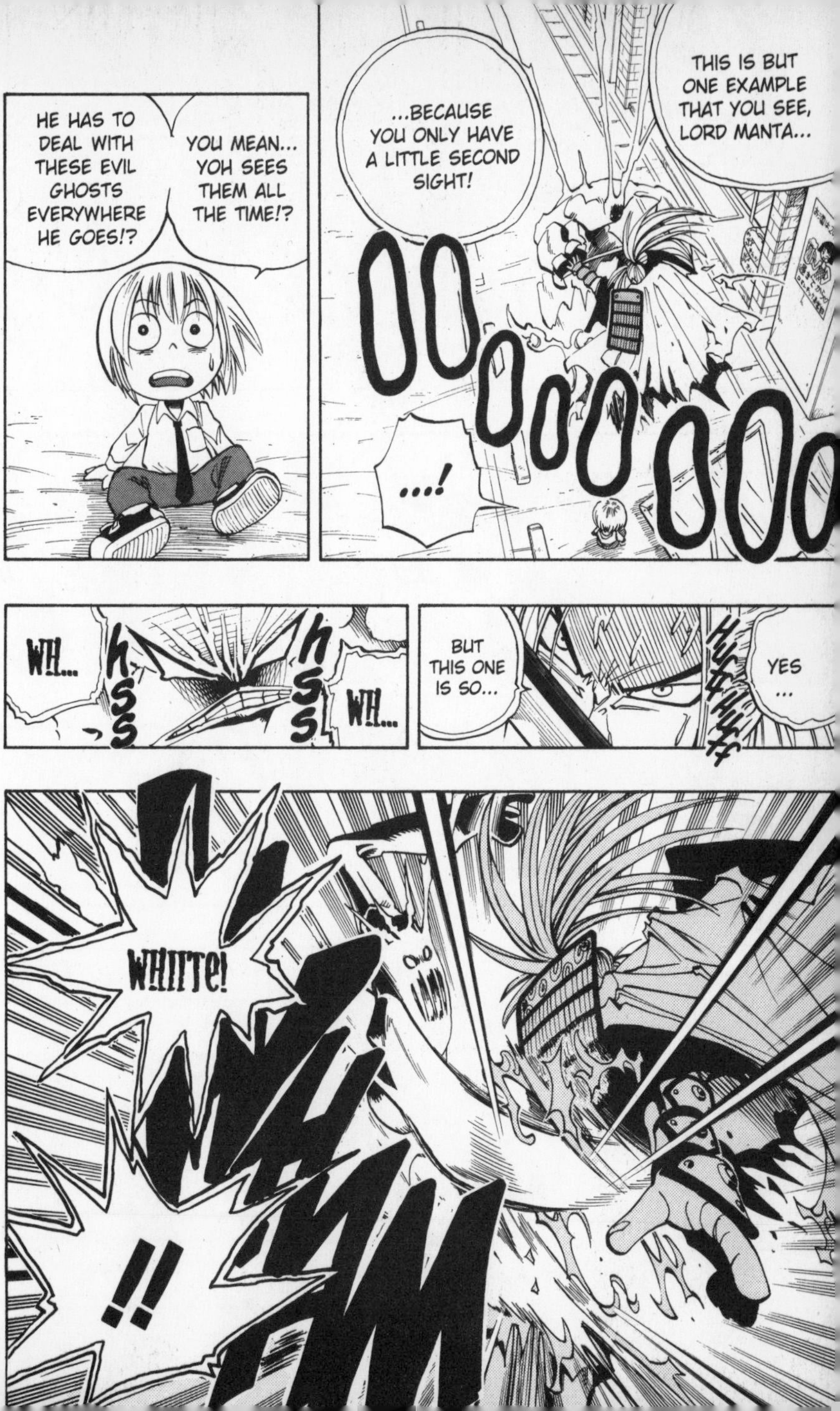
THIS IS BUT ONE EXAMPLE THAT YOU SEE, LORD MANTA...
...BECAUSE YOU ONLY HAVE A LITTLE SECOND SIGHT!
OOOOOOOOO
...!
YOU MEAN... YOH SEES THEM ALL THE TIME!?
HE HAS TO DEAL WITH THESE EVIL GHOSTS EVERYWHERE HE GOES!?
YES ...
HUFF HUFF
BUT THIS ONE IS SO...
WH...
hSS
hSS
WH...
WHITE!
!!

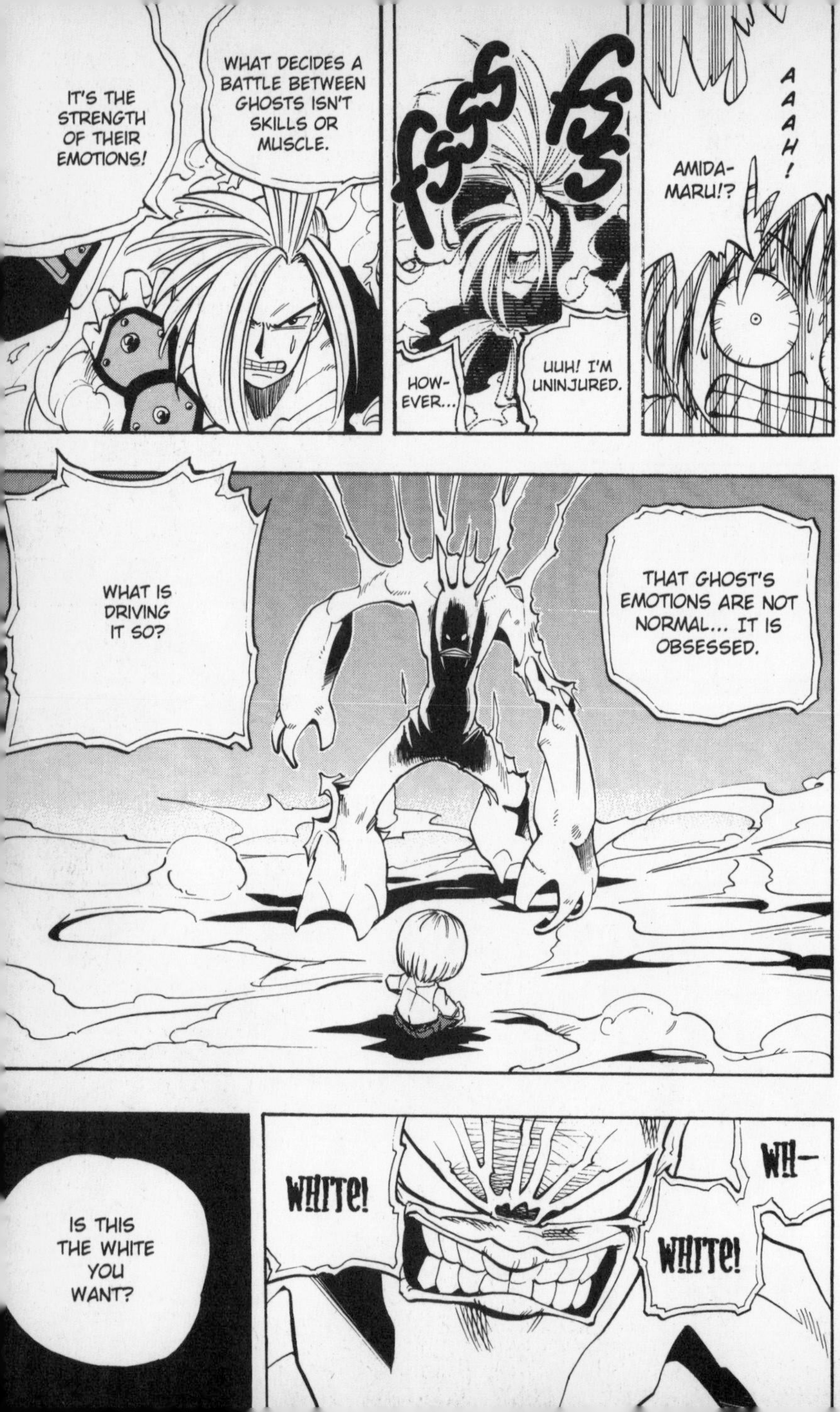
AAAH!
AMIDA-MARU!?
FSSS FSSS
UUH! I'M UNINJURED.
HOW-EVER...
WHAT DECIDES A BATTLE BETWEEN GHOSTS ISN'T SKILLS OR MUSCLE.
IT'S THE STRENGTH OF THEIR EMOTIONS!
THAT GHOST'S EMOTIONS ARE NOT NORMAL... IT IS OBSESSED.
WHAT IS DRIVING IT SO?
WH-
WHITE!
WHITE!
IS THIS THE WHITE YOU WANT?

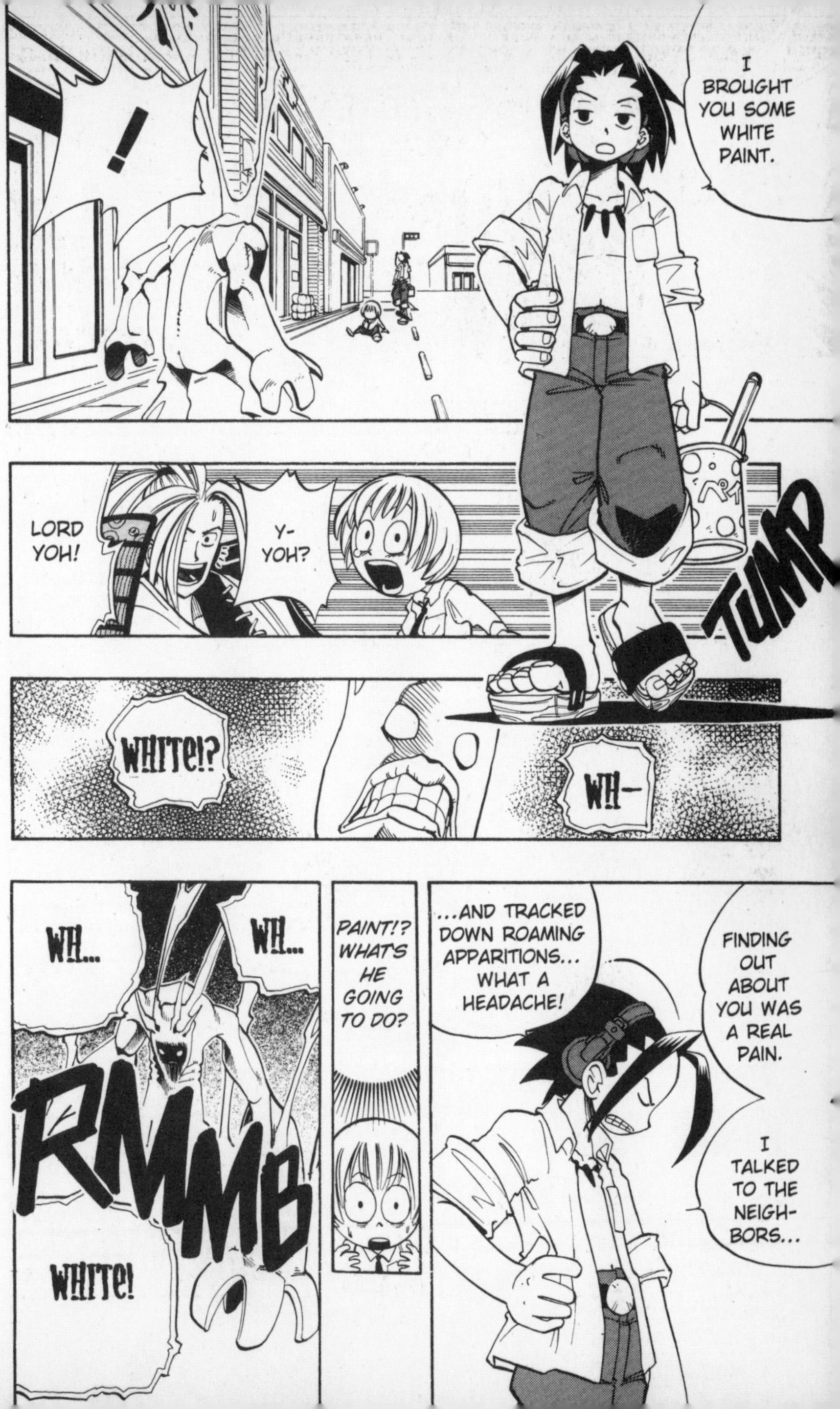

I BROUGHT YOU SOME WHITE PAINT.
TUMP
!
Y- YOH?
LORD YOH!
WH-
WHITE!?
FINDING OUT ABOUT YOU WAS A REAL PAIN.
I TALKED TO THE NEIGH- BORS...
...AND TRACKED DOWN ROAMING APPARITIONS... WHAT A HEADACHE!
PAINT!? WHAT'S HE GOING TO DO?
WH...
WH...
RMMMB
WHITE!

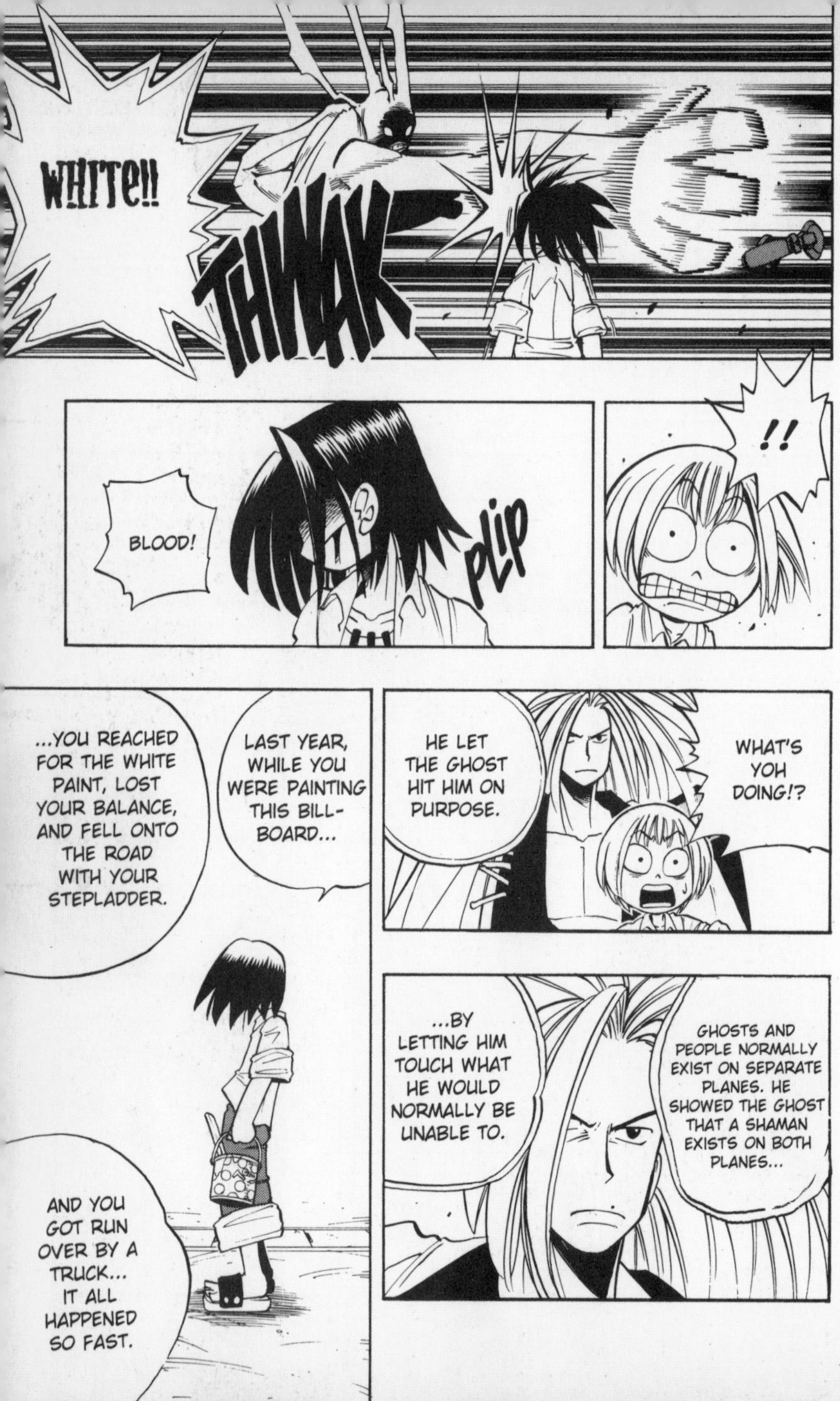
WHITE!!
THWAK
!!
BLOOD!
PLIP
WHAT'S YOH DOING!?
HE LET THE GHOST HIT HIM ON PURPOSE.
GHOSTS AND PEOPLE NORMALLY EXIST ON SEPARATE PLANES. HE SHOWED THE GHOST THAT A SHAMAN EXISTS ON BOTH PLANES...
...BY LETTING HIM TOUCH WHAT HE WOULD NORMALLY BE UNABLE TO.
LAST YEAR, WHILE YOU WERE PAINTING THIS BILL-BOARD...
...YOU REACHED FOR THE WHITE PAINT, LOST YOUR BALANCE, AND FELL ONTO THE ROAD WITH YOUR STEPLADDER.
AND YOU GOT RUN OVER BY A TRUCK... IT ALL HAPPENED SO FAST.

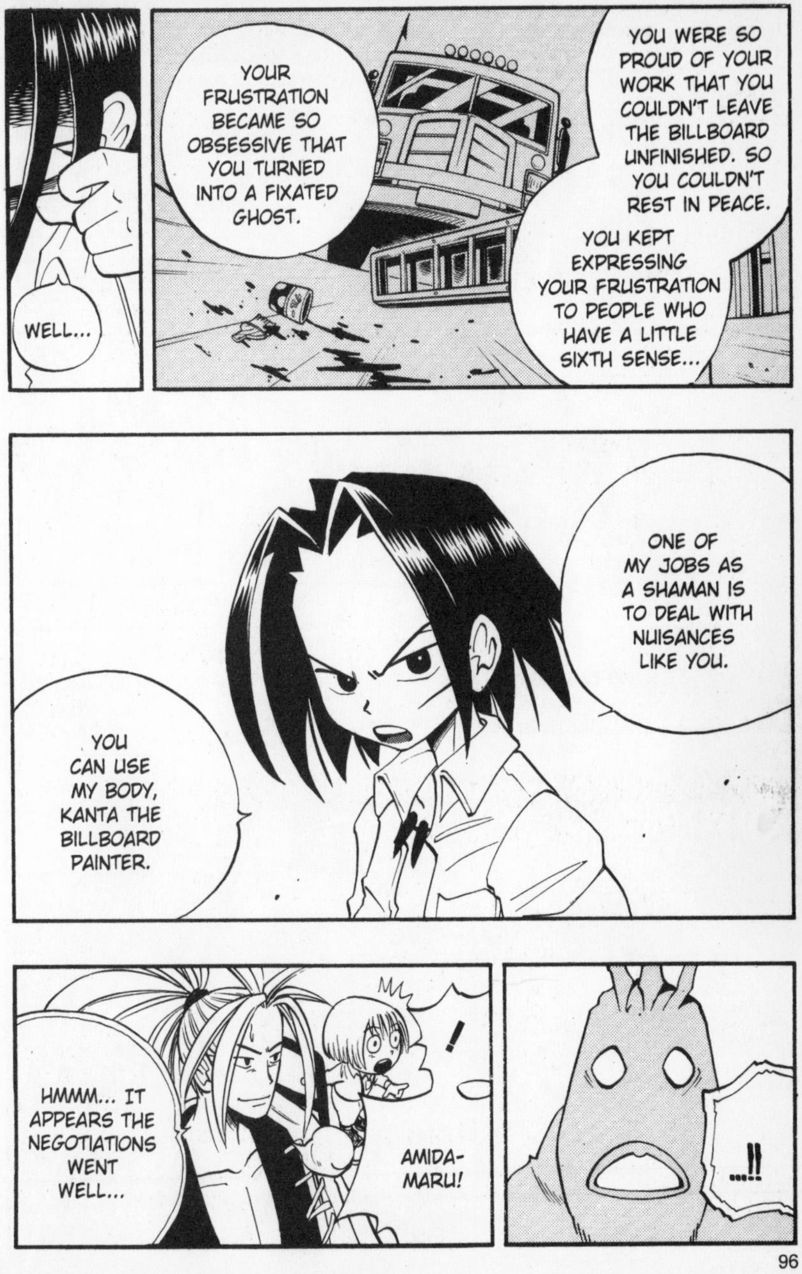
YOU WERE SO PROUD OF YOUR WORK THAT YOU COULDN'T LEAVE THE BILLBOARD UNFINISHED. SO YOU COULDN'T REST IN PEACE.
YOUR FRUSTRATION BECAME SO OBSESSIVE THAT YOU TURNED INTO A FIXATED GHOST.
YOU KEPT EXPRESSING YOUR FRUSTRATION TO PEOPLE WHO HAVE A LITTLE SIXTH SENSE...
WELL...
ONE OF MY JOBS AS A SHAMAN IS TO DEAL WITH NUISANCES LIKE YOU.
YOU CAN USE MY BODY, KANTA THE BILLBOARD PAINTER.
...!!
!
AMIDA-MARU!
HMMM... IT APPEARS THE NEGOTIATIONS WENT WELL...

READ THIS WAY

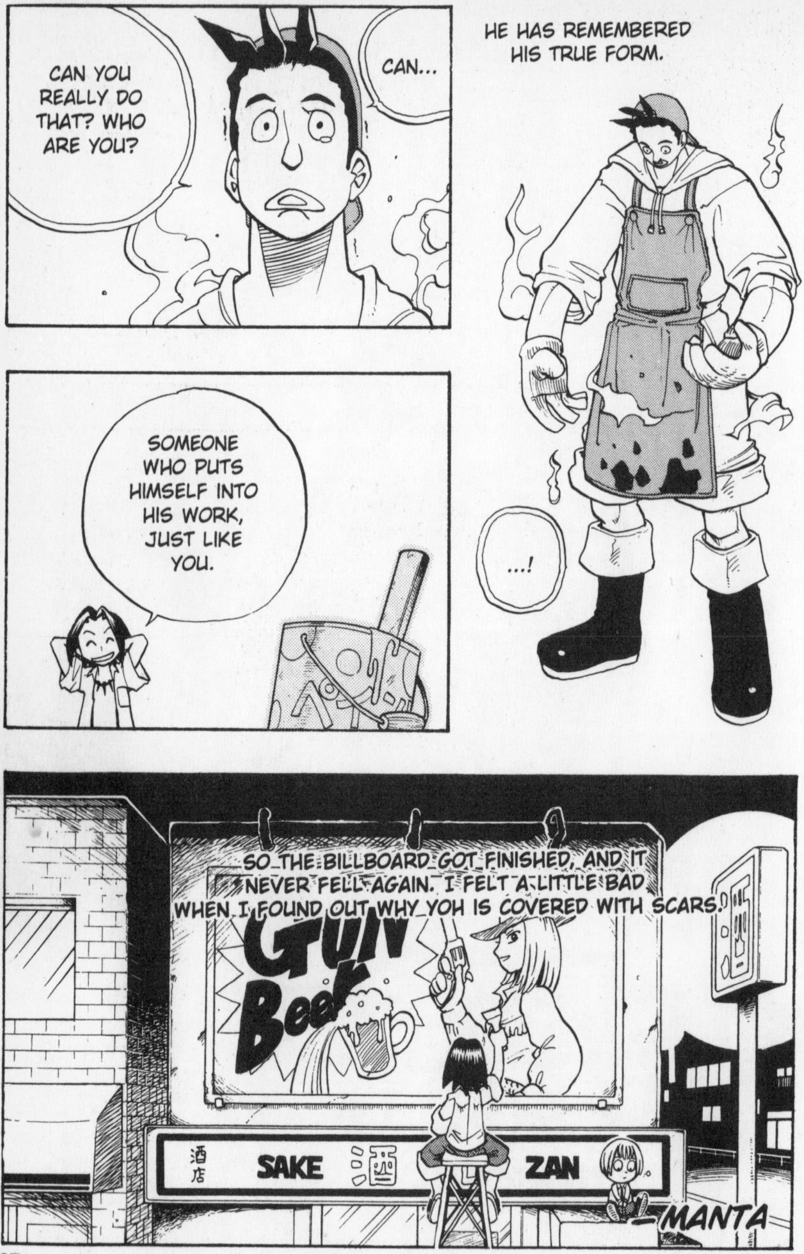
HE HAS REMEMBERED HIS TRUE FORM.
...!
CAN...
CAN YOU REALLY DO THAT? WHO ARE YOU?
SOMEONE WHO PUTS HIMSELF INTO HIS WORK, JUST LIKE YOU.
SO THE BILLBOARD GOT FINISHED, AND IT NEVER FELL AGAIN. I FELT A LITTLE BAD WHEN I FOUND OUT WHY YOH IS COVERED WITH SCARS.
—MANTA
GUN Beer
酒店 SAKE 酒 ZAN

SHAMAN KING CHARACTER FILE No.2

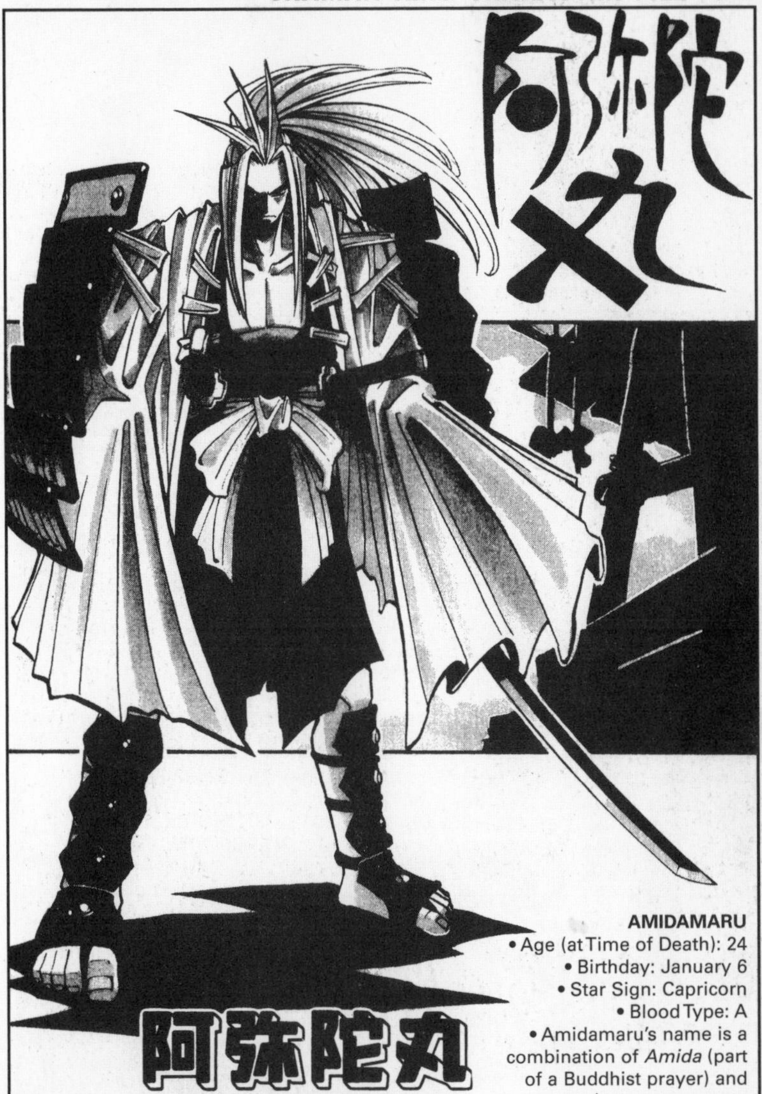

阿弥陀丸
阿弥陀丸
AMIDAMARU

AMIDAMARU

- Age (at Time of Death): 24
- Birthday: January 6
- Star Sign: Capricorn
- Blood Type: A
- Amidamaru's name is a combination of *Amida* (part of a Buddhist prayer) and *maru* (a common name ending for samurai).

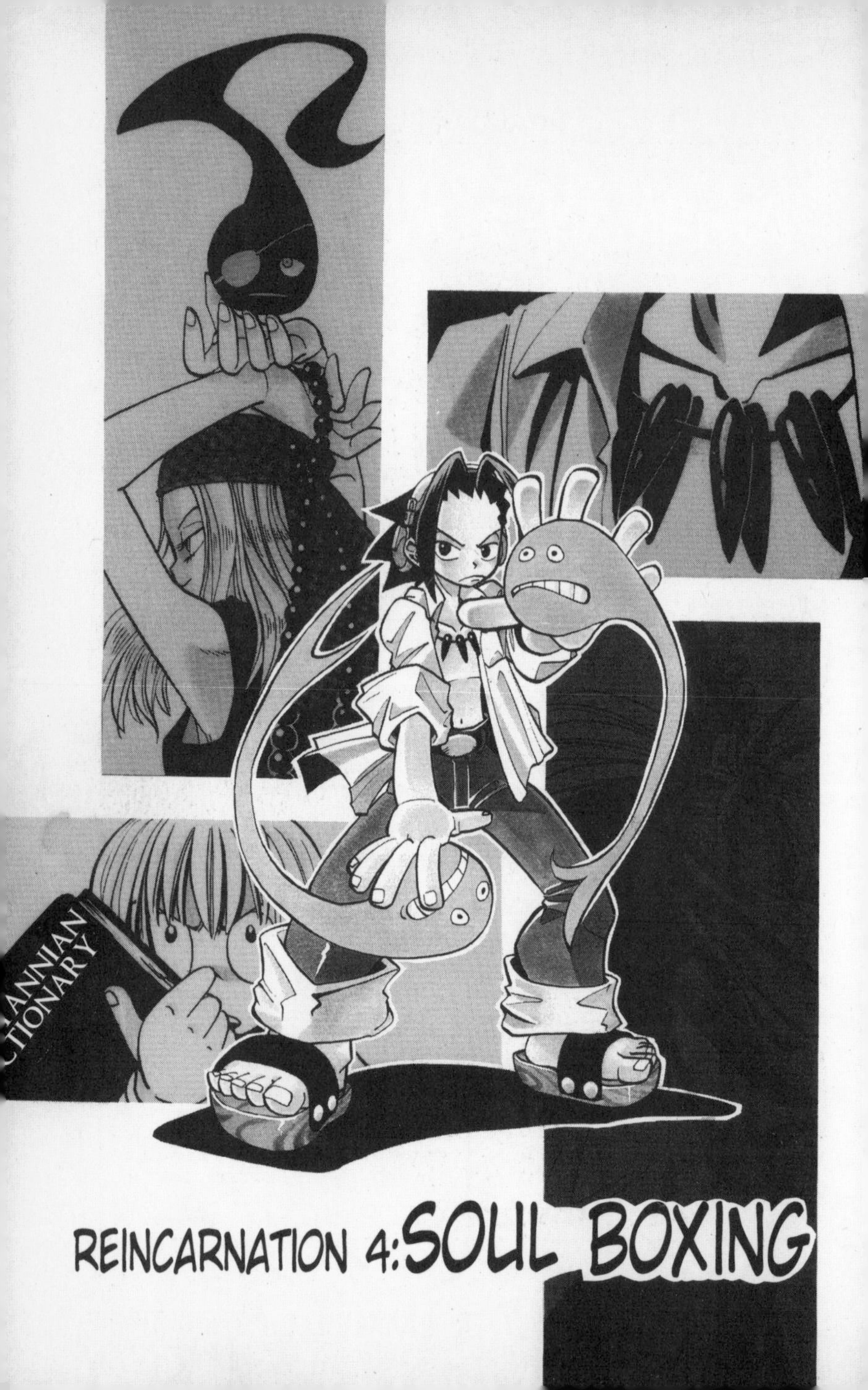
REINCARNATION 4: SOUL BOXING

MANTA OYAMANDA'S SHAMAN SYMPOSIUM

PAY ATTENTION, THERE WILL BE A TEST!

WHAT IS A "SHAMAN"?

A SHAMAN IS A PERSON WHO CAN INTERFACE WITH THE WORLD OF GODS AND SPIRITS, WHICH ALLOWS THEM TO DO AMAZING THINGS. THEY CAN ASK THE GODS FOR WISDOM, BORROW THE POWER OF THE SPIRITS TO HEAL THE SICK, AND SUMMON THE GHOSTS OF THE DEAD INTO THIS WORLD. OF COURSE, BY CONTACTING THE DEAD, THEY CAN ALSO SPEAK WITH THE GREAT FIGURES OF HISTORY (THIS IS YOH'S ABILITY).

BECAUSE NOT EVERYONE CAN TALK WITH SPIRITS, SHAMANS HAVE BEEN REVERED SINCE THE EARLIEST TIMES, AND THEY STILL EXIST ALL OVER THE WORLD. THE MOST WELL-KNOWN SHAMANS ARE FOUND IN NATIVE AMERICAN TRIBES, CHINA, AND PAPUA NEW GUINEA. IN JAPAN THERE ARE SPIRIT-SUMMONING SHAMANS CALLED **ITAKO** IN THE NORTHEAST REGIONS, AND THE **YUTA** IN THE AMAMI ISLANDS NORTH OF OKINAWA WHO TELL FORTUNES AND HEAL THE SICK WITH SPIRITUAL POWERS. BOTH WORK FOR THE PEOPLE'S GOOD AND ARE WELL RESPECTED.

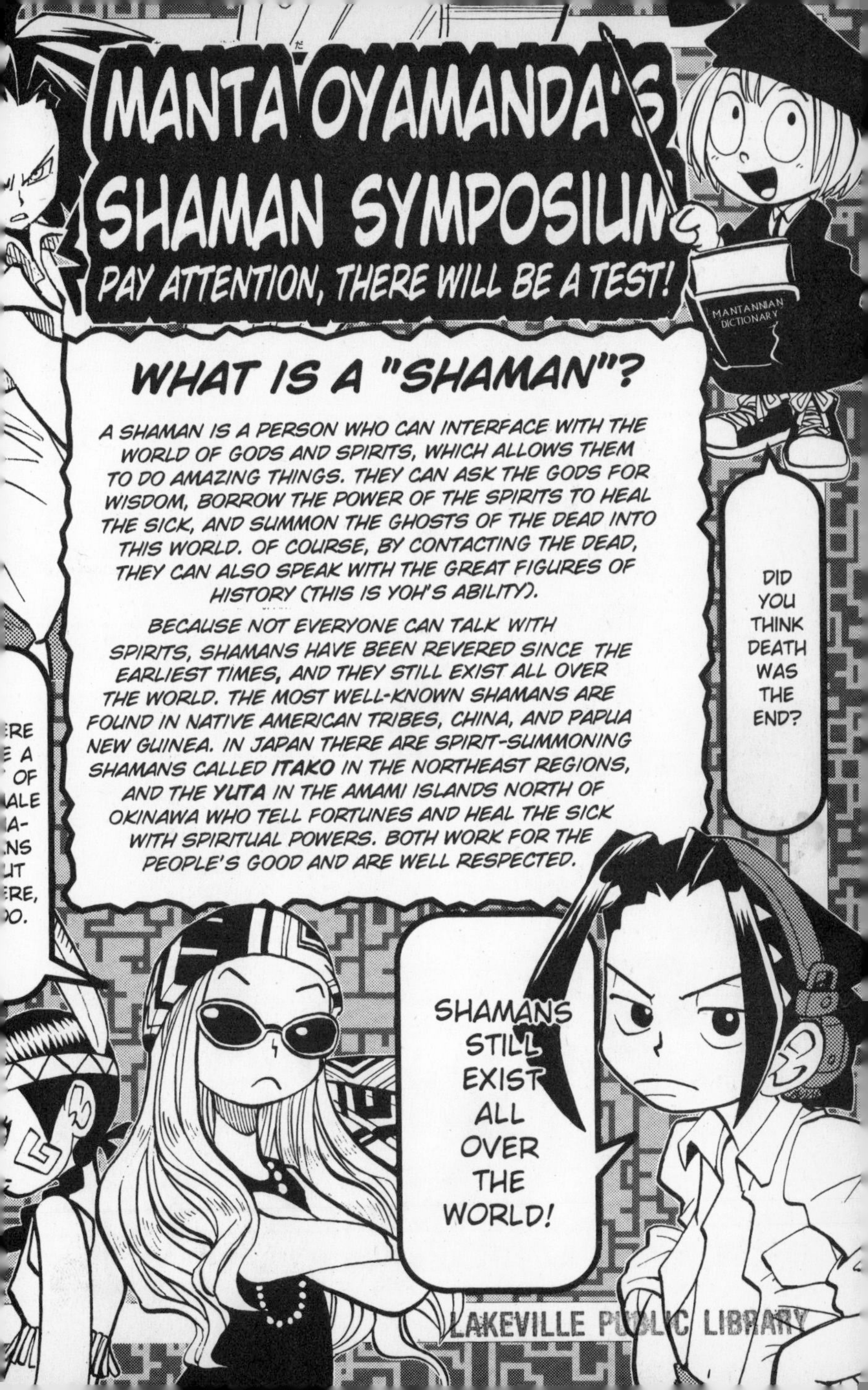
MANTANNIAN DICTIONARY
DID YOU THINK DEATH WAS THE END?
SHAMANS STILL EXIST ALL OVER THE WORLD!

READ THIS WAY

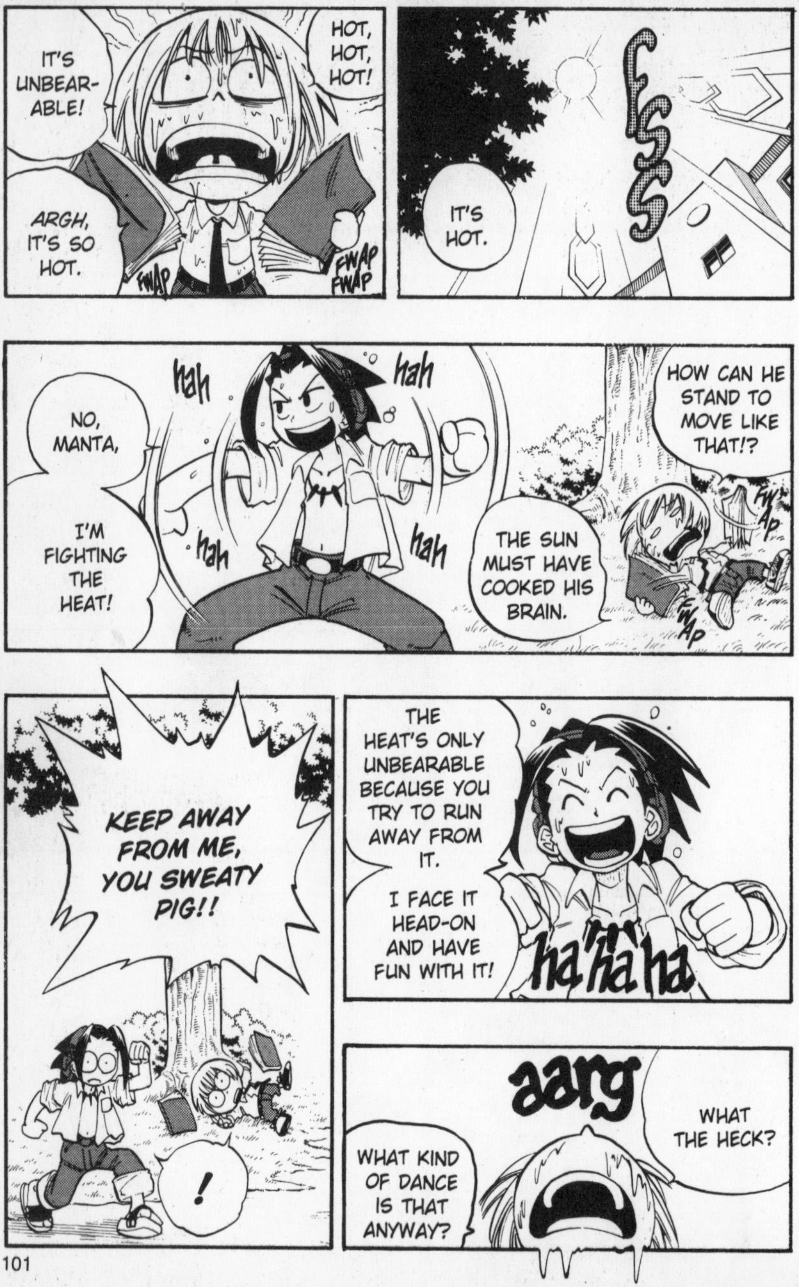
FSS
IT'S HOT.
HOT, HOT, HOT!
IT'S UNBEAR-ABLE!
ARGH, IT'S SO HOT.
FWAP FWAP
FWAP
HOW CAN HE STAND TO MOVE LIKE THAT!?
FWAP
hah
hah
THE SUN MUST HAVE COOKED HIS BRAIN.
FWAP
hah
hah
NO, MANTA,
I'M FIGHTING THE HEAT!
THE HEAT'S ONLY UNBEARABLE BECAUSE YOU TRY TO RUN AWAY FROM IT.
I FACE IT HEAD-ON AND HAVE FUN WITH IT!
ha ha ha ha
WHAT THE HECK?
aarg
WHAT KIND OF DANCE IS THAT ANYWAY?
KEEP AWAY FROM ME, YOU SWEATY PIG!!
!

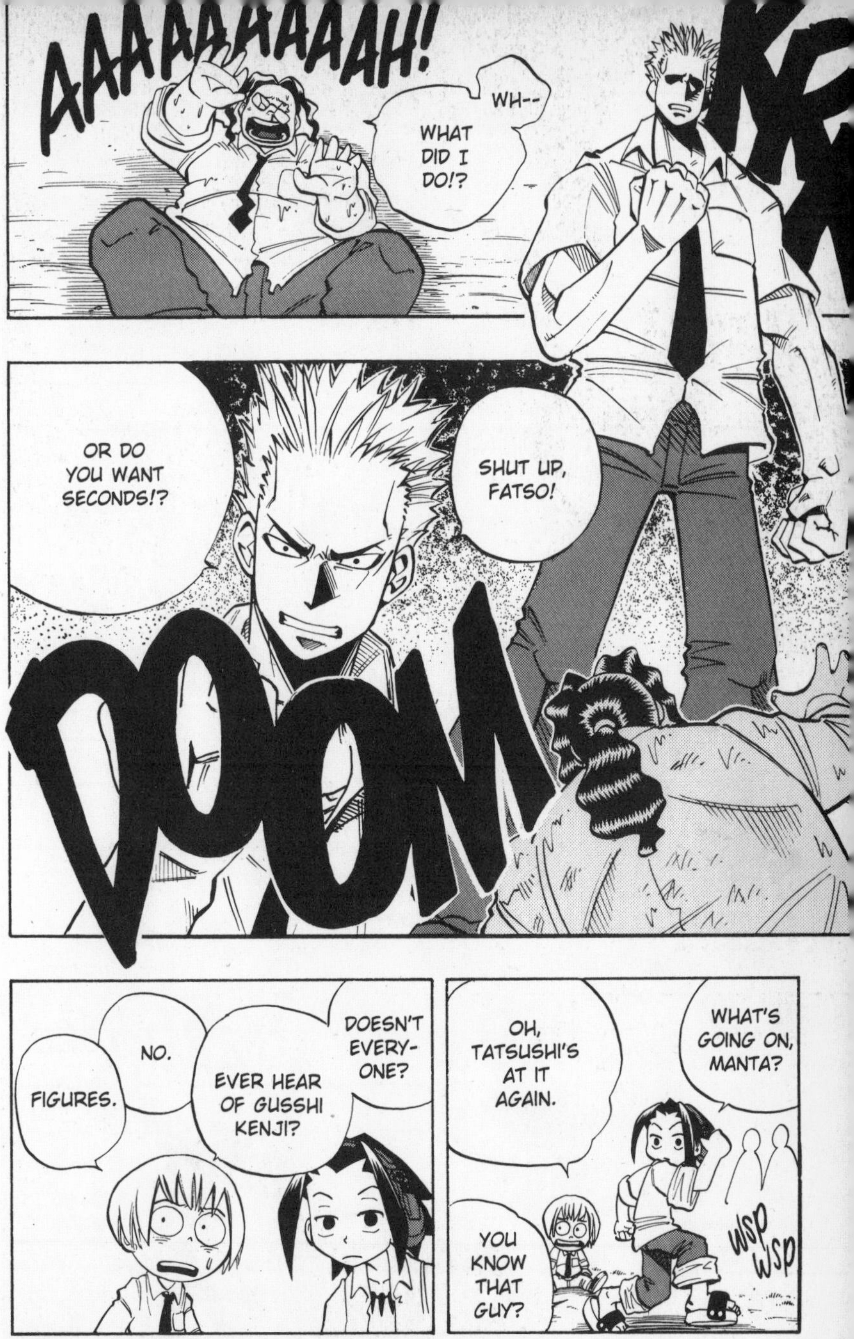
WH--
WHAT DID I DO!?
AAAAAAAAAH!
SHUT UP, FATSO!
OR DO YOU WANT SECONDS!?
DOOM
WHAT'S GOING ON, MANTA?
OH, TATSUSHI'S AT IT AGAIN.
YOU KNOW THAT GUY?
WSP WSP
DOESN'T EVERY-ONE?
EVER HEAR OF GUSSHI KENJI?
NO.
FIGURES.

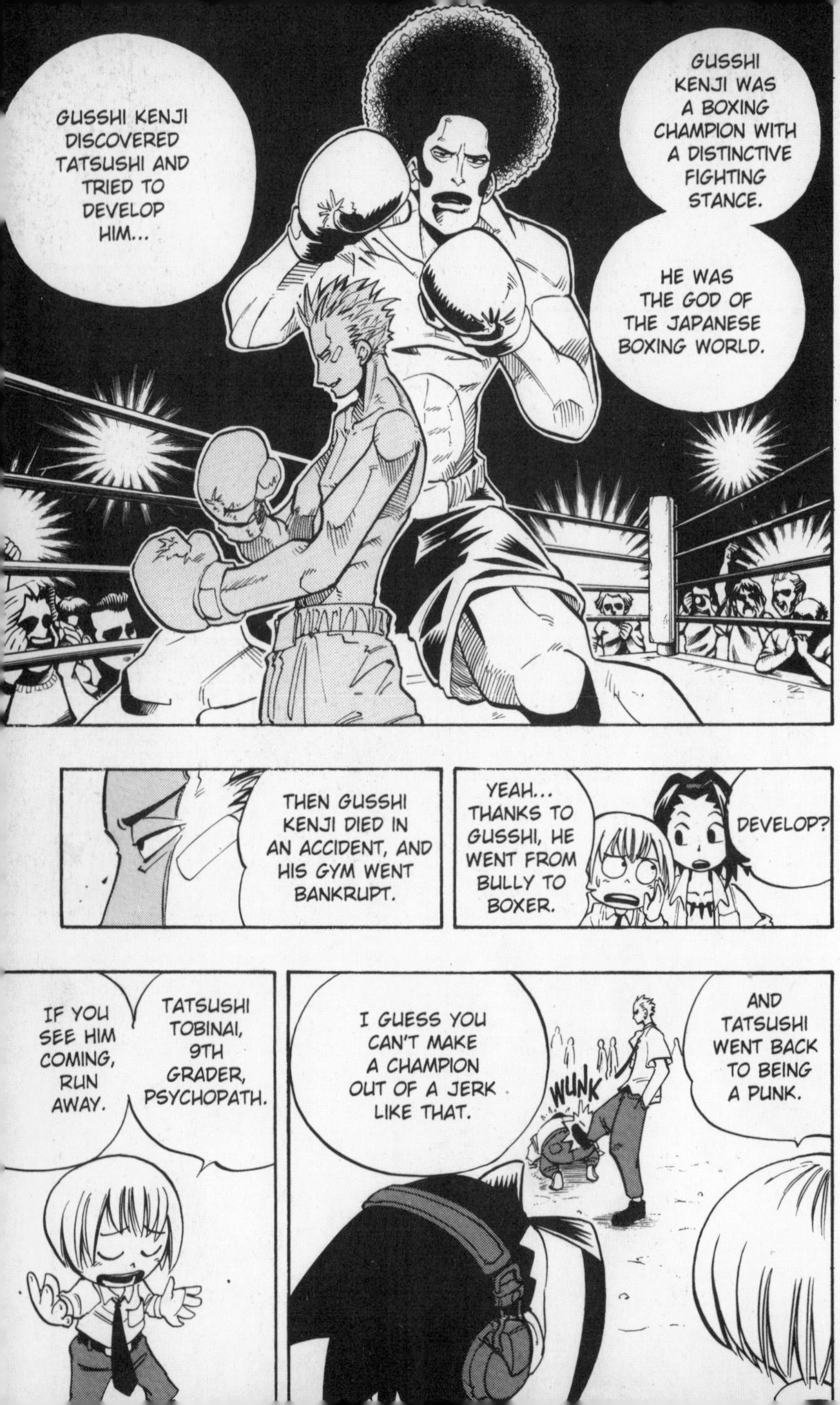
GUSSHI KENJI WAS A BOXING CHAMPION WITH A DISTINCTIVE FIGHTING STANCE.
HE WAS THE GOD OF THE JAPANESE BOXING WORLD.
GUSSHI KENJI DISCOVERED TATSUSHI AND TRIED TO DEVELOP HIM...
DEVELOP?
YEAH... THANKS TO GUSSHI, HE WENT FROM BULLY TO BOXER.
THEN GUSSHI KENJI DIED IN AN ACCIDENT, AND HIS GYM WENT BANKRUPT.
AND TATSUSHI WENT BACK TO BEING A PUNK.
WUNK
I GUESS YOU CAN'T MAKE A CHAMPION OUT OF A JERK LIKE THAT.
TATSUSHI TOBINAI, 9TH GRADER, PSYCHOPATH.
IF YOU SEE HIM COMING, RUN AWAY.

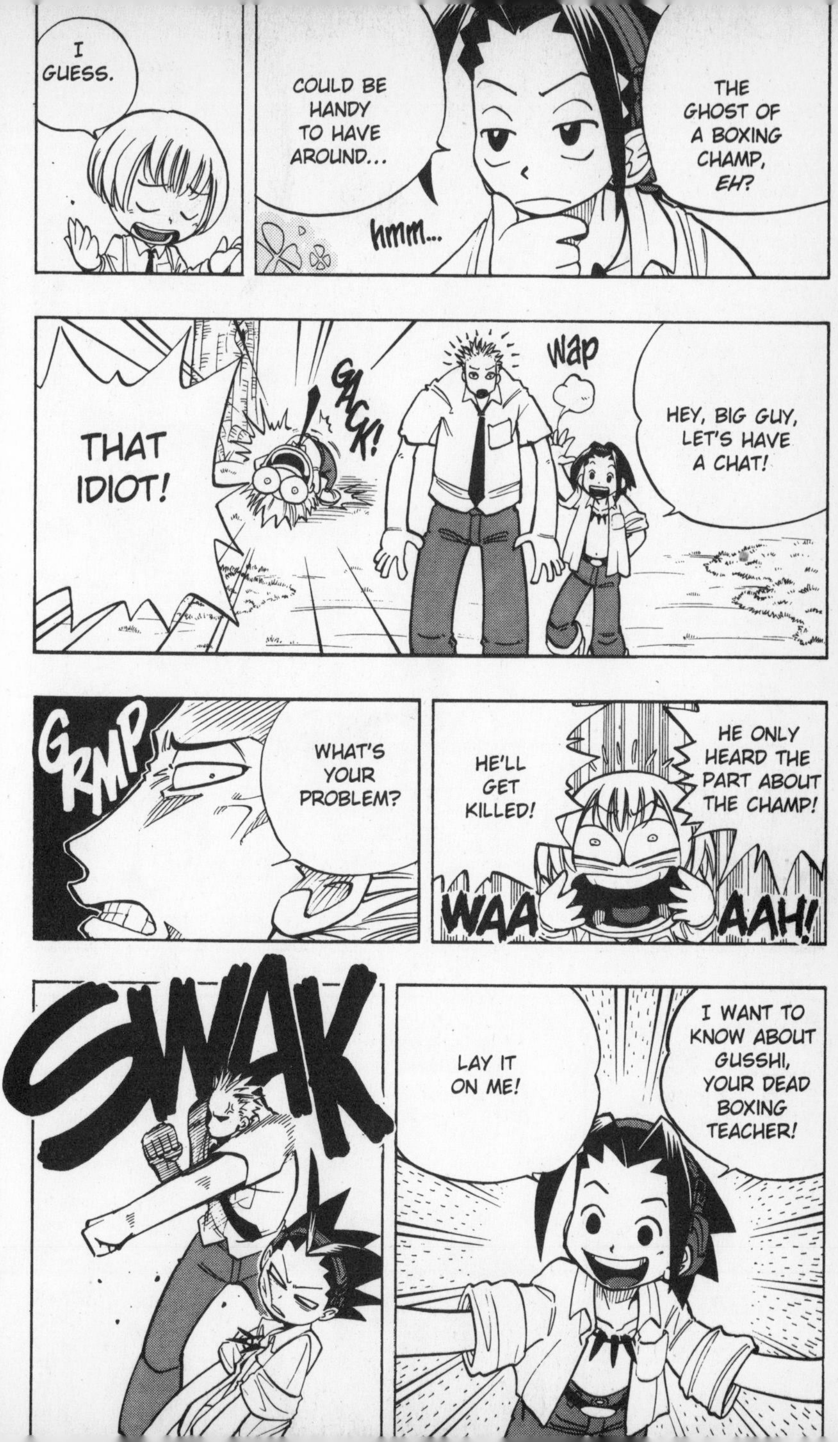
THE GHOST OF A BOXING CHAMP, EH?
COULD BE HANDY TO HAVE AROUND...
hmm...
I GUESS.
HEY, BIG GUY, LET'S HAVE A CHAT!
wap
GACK!
THAT IDIOT!
HE ONLY HEARD THE PART ABOUT THE CHAMP!
HE'LL GET KILLED!
WAA AAH!
WHAT'S YOUR PROBLEM?
GRMP
I WANT TO KNOW ABOUT GUSSHI, YOUR DEAD BOXING TEACHER!
LAY IT ON ME!
SWAK

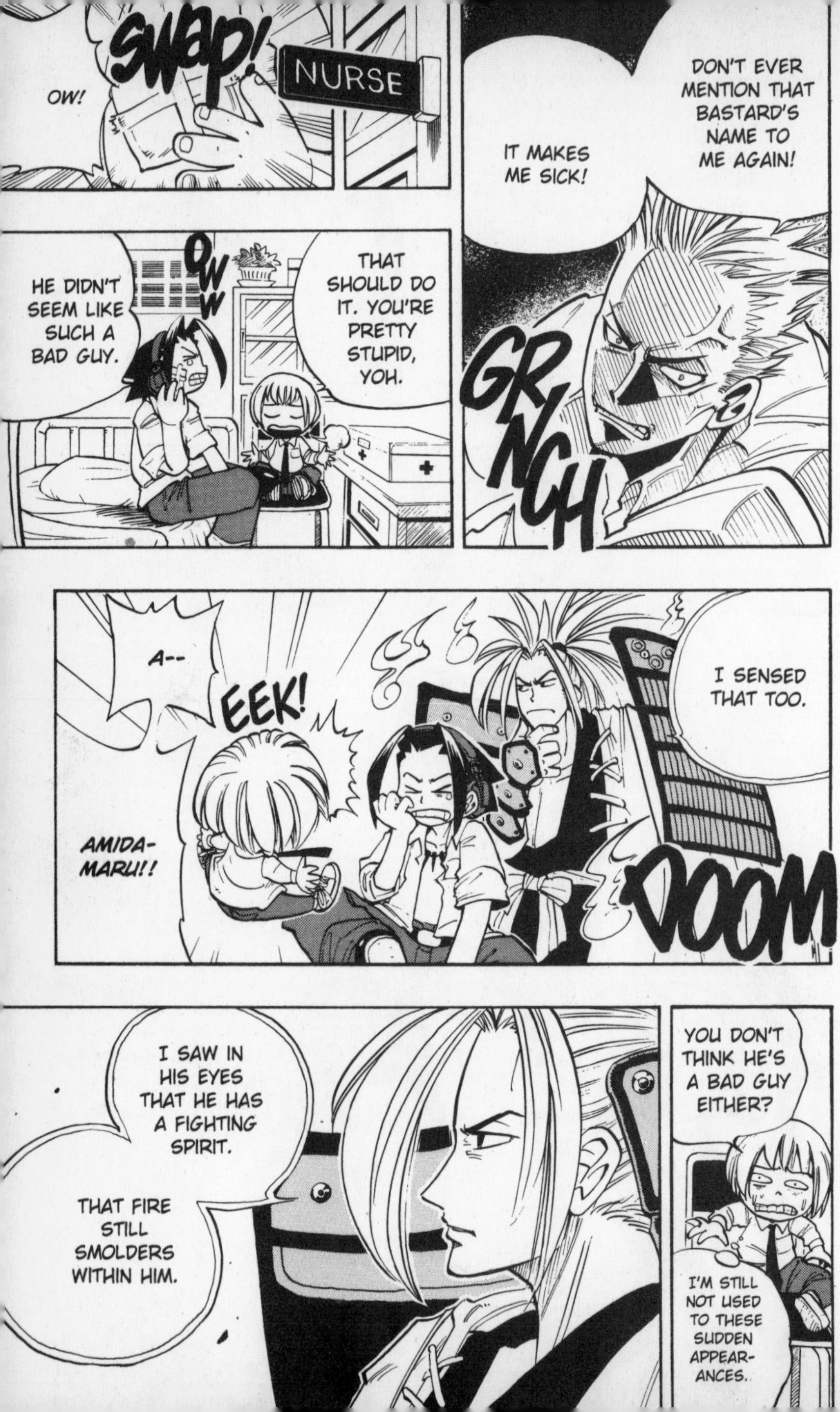
DON'T EVER MENTION THAT BASTARD'S NAME TO ME AGAIN!
IT MAKES ME SICK!
GRNCH
SWAP!
NURSE
OW!
THAT SHOULD DO IT. YOU'RE PRETTY STUPID, YOH.
OWW
HE DIDN'T SEEM LIKE SUCH A BAD GUY.
I SENSED THAT TOO.
DOOM
EEK!
A--
AMIDA-MARU!!
YOU DON'T THINK HE'S A BAD GUY EITHER?
I'M STILL NOT USED TO THESE SUDDEN APPEAR-ANCES.
I SAW IN HIS EYES THAT HE HAS A FIGHTING SPIRIT.
THAT FIRE STILL SMOLDERS WITHIN HIM.

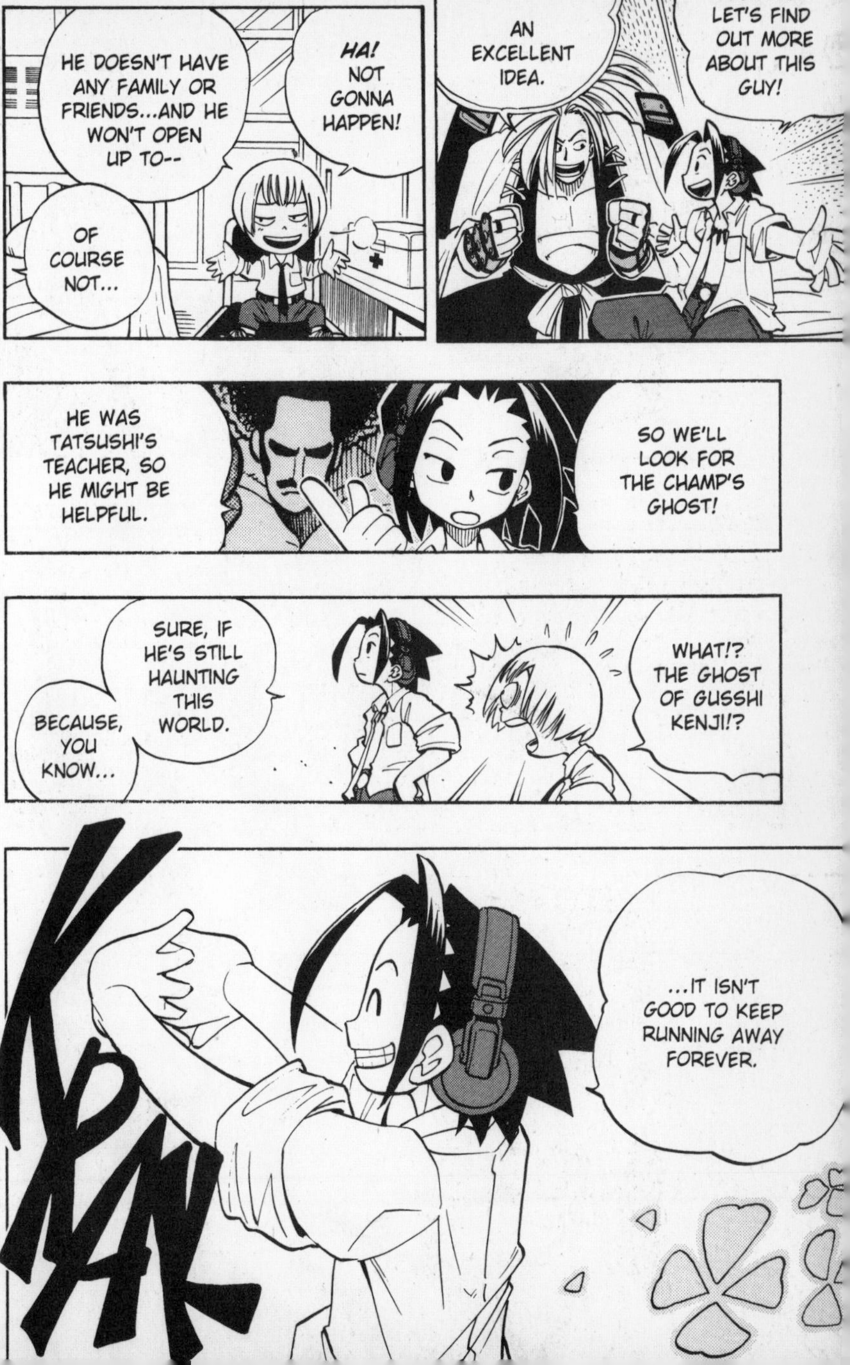
EXACTLY! LET'S FIND OUT MORE ABOUT THIS GUY!
AN EXCELLENT IDEA.
HE DOESN'T HAVE ANY FAMILY OR FRIENDS...AND HE WON'T OPEN UP TO--
HA! NOT GONNA HAPPEN!
OF COURSE NOT...
SO WE'LL LOOK FOR THE CHAMP'S GHOST!
HE WAS TATSUSHI'S TEACHER, SO HE MIGHT BE HELPFUL.
WHAT!? THE GHOST OF GUSSHI KENJI!?
SURE, IF HE'S STILL HAUNTING THIS WORLD.
BECAUSE, YOU KNOW...
...IT ISN'T GOOD TO KEEP RUNNING AWAY FOREVER.
KPAK

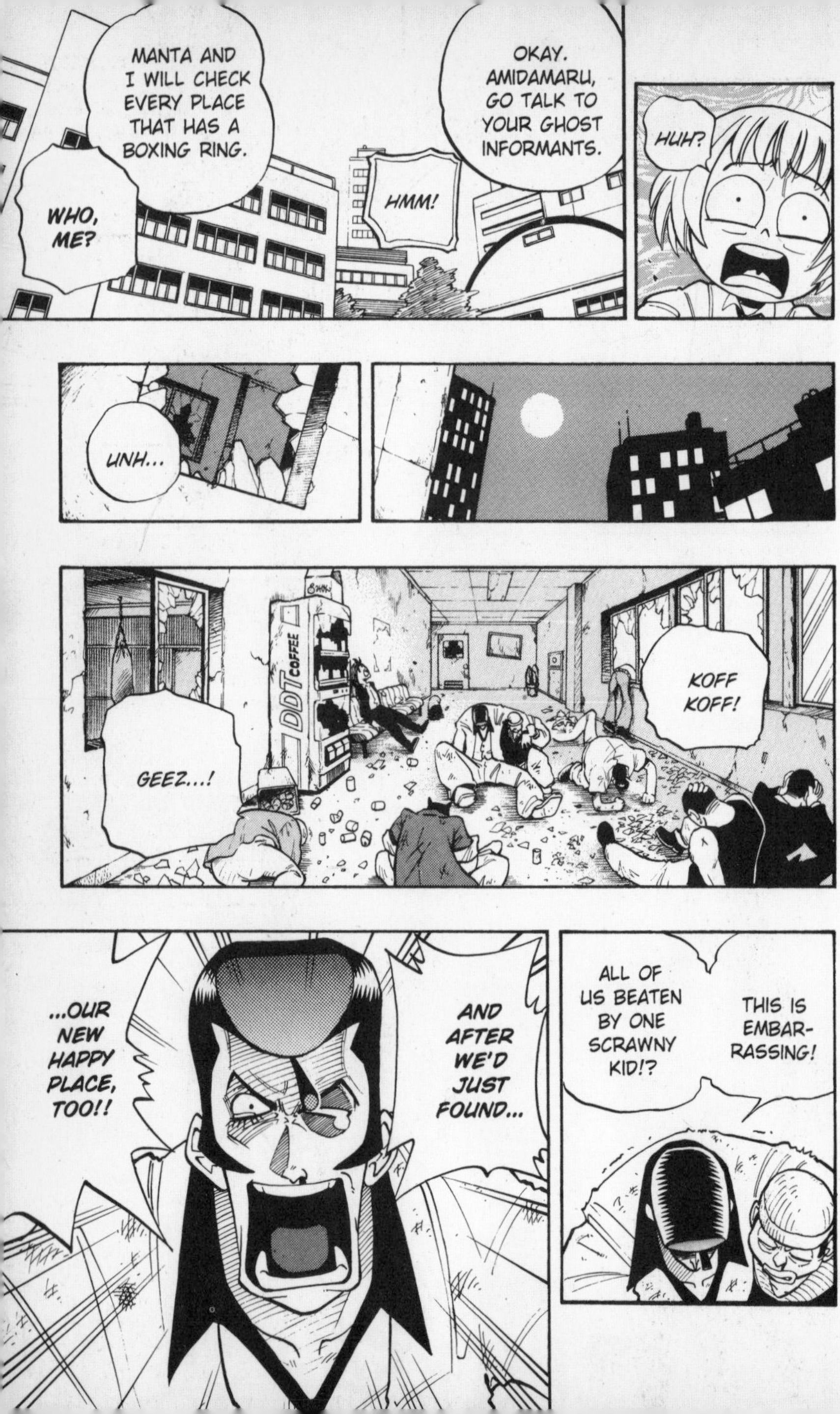
HUH?
OKAY. AMIDAMARU, GO TALK TO YOUR GHOST INFORMANTS.
HMM!
MANTA AND I WILL CHECK EVERY PLACE THAT HAS A BOXING RING.
WHO, ME?
UNH...
KOFF KOFF!
GEEZ...!
THIS IS EMBAR-RASSING!
ALL OF US BEATEN BY ONE SCRAWNY KID!?
AND AFTER WE'D JUST FOUND...
...OUR NEW HAPPY PLACE, TOO!!

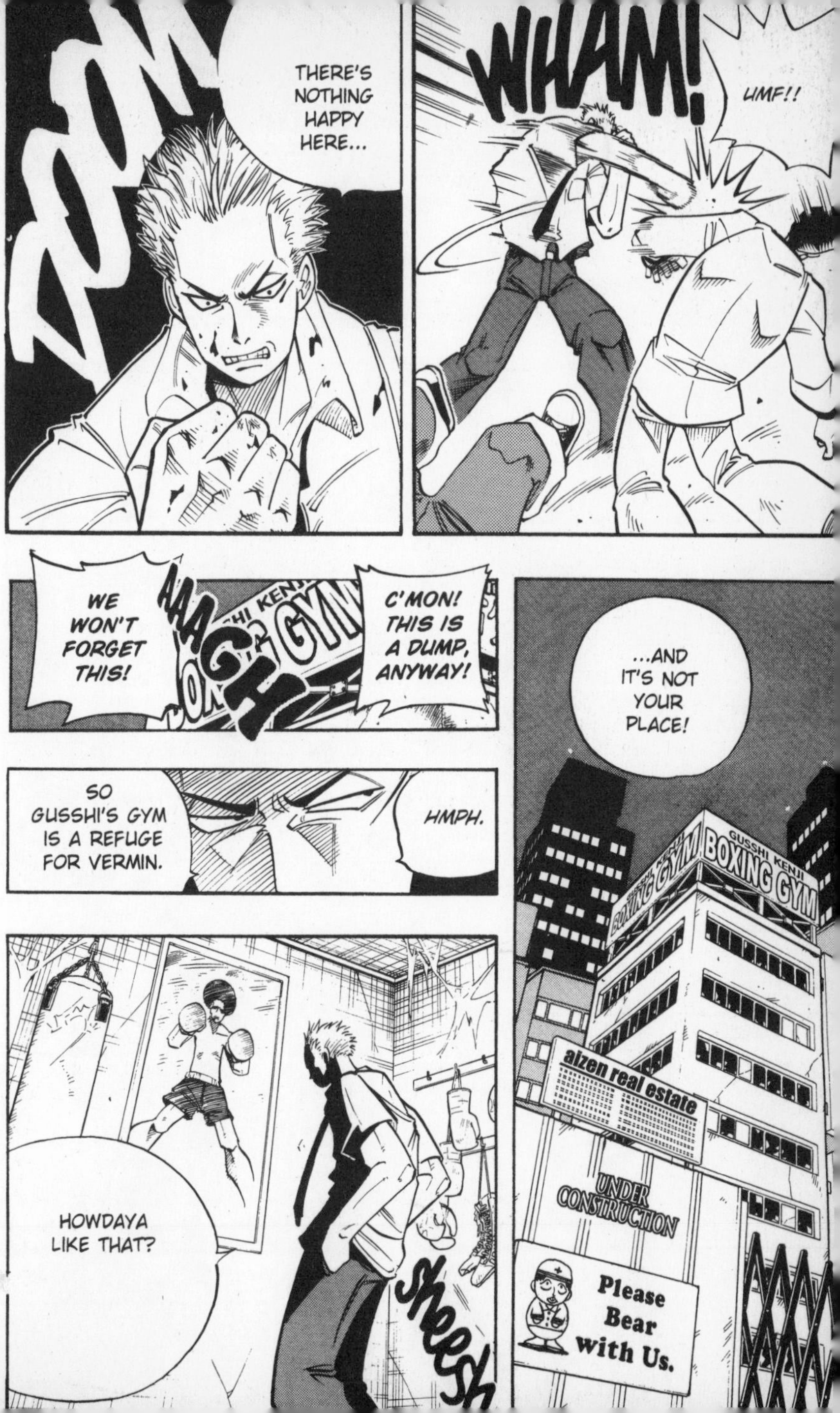
WHAM!
UMF!!
THERE'S NOTHING HAPPY HERE...
...AND IT'S NOT YOUR PLACE!
GUSSHI KENJI BOXING GYM
aizen real estate
UNDER CONSTRUCTION
Please Bear with Us.
C'MON! THIS IS A DUMP, ANYWAY!
AAAGH
WE WON'T FORGET THIS!
HMPH.
SO GUSSHI'S GYM IS A REFUGE FOR VERMIN.
HOWDAYA LIKE THAT?
SHEESH

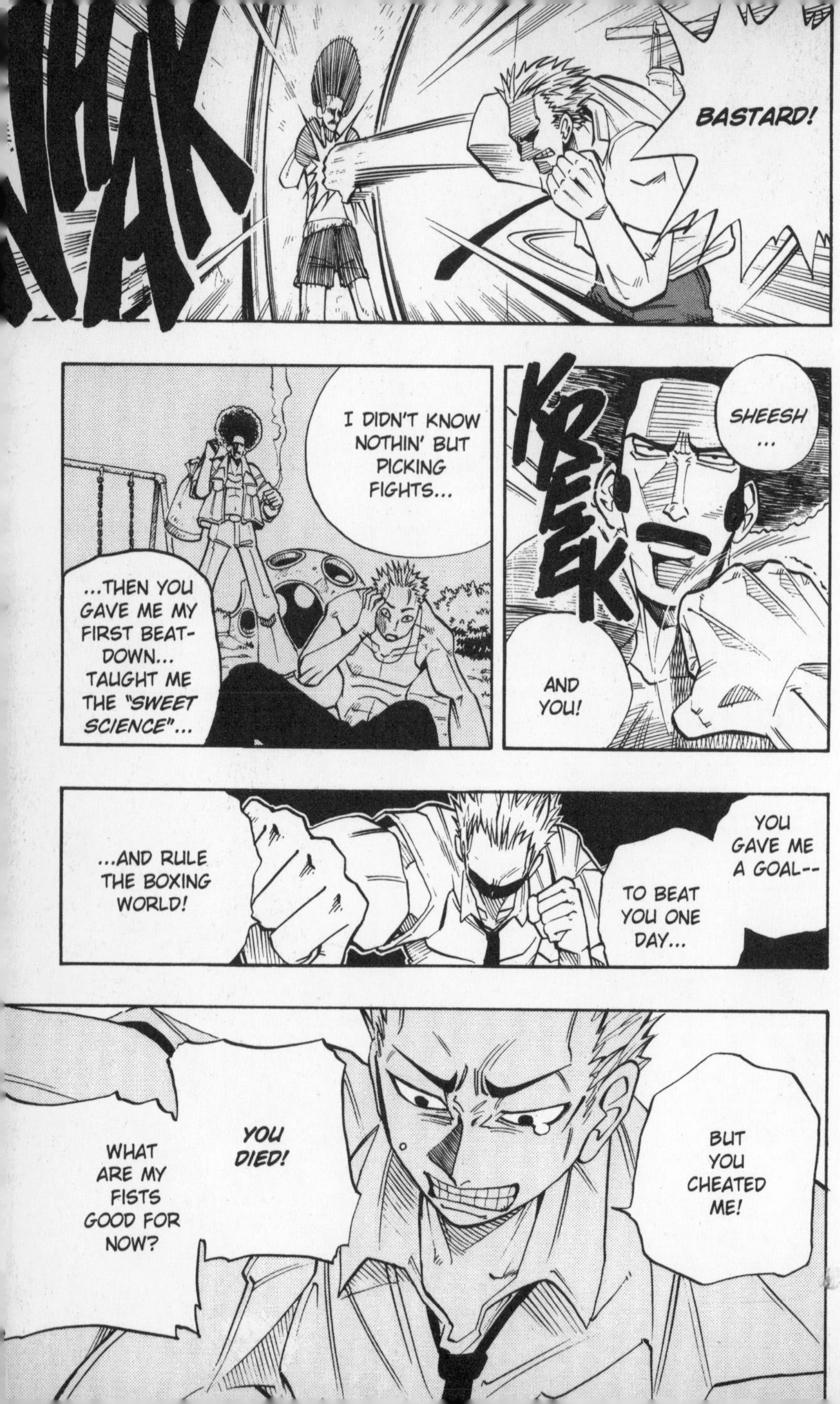
WHAK
BASTARD!
SHEESH ...
KREEK
AND YOU!
I DIDN'T KNOW NOTHIN' BUT PICKING FIGHTS...
...THEN YOU GAVE ME MY FIRST BEAT-DOWN... TAUGHT ME THE "SWEET SCIENCE"...
YOU GAVE ME A GOAL--
TO BEAT YOU ONE DAY...
...AND RULE THE BOXING WORLD!
BUT YOU CHEATED ME!
YOU DIED!
WHAT ARE MY FISTS GOOD FOR NOW?

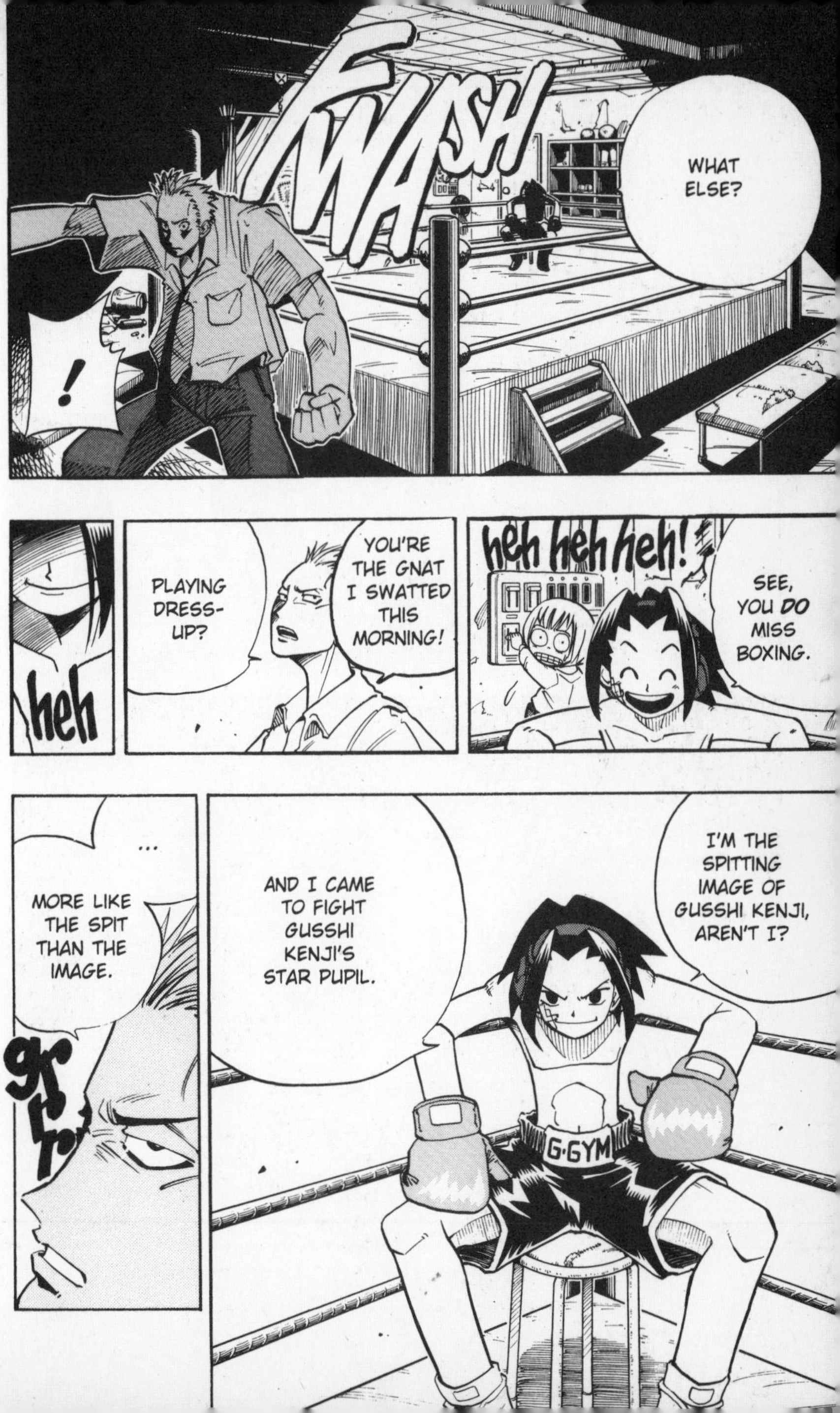
WHAT ELSE?
FWASH
!
SEE, YOU DO MISS BOXING.
heh heh heh!
YOU'RE THE GNAT I SWATTED THIS MORNING!
PLAYING DRESS-UP?
heh
I'M THE SPITTING IMAGE OF GUSSHI KENJI, AREN'T I?
AND I CAME TO FIGHT GUSSHI KENJI'S STAR PUPIL.
G·GYM
...
MORE LIKE THE SPIT THAN THE IMAGE.

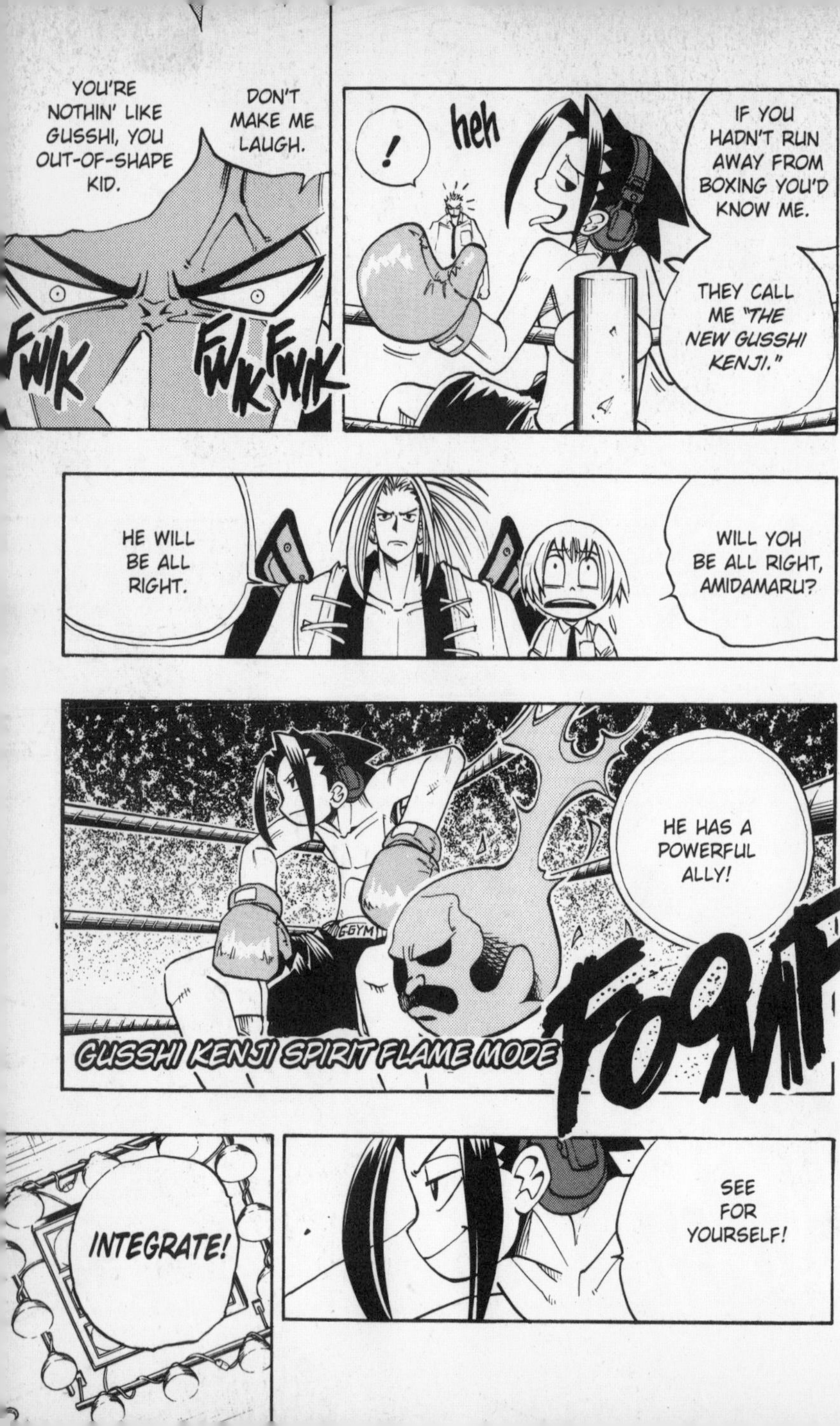

IF YOU HADN'T RUN AWAY FROM BOXING YOU'D KNOW ME.
heh
!
THEY CALL ME "THE NEW GUSSHI KENJI."
DON'T MAKE ME LAUGH.
YOU'RE NOTHIN' LIKE GUSSHI, YOU OUT-OF-SHAPE KID.
FWIK FWIK
FWIK
WILL YOH BE ALL RIGHT, AMIDAMARU?
HE WILL BE ALL RIGHT.
HE HAS A POWERFUL ALLY!
G-GYM
FOOM
GUSSHI KENJI SPIRIT FLAME MODE
SEE FOR YOURSELF!
INTEGRATE!

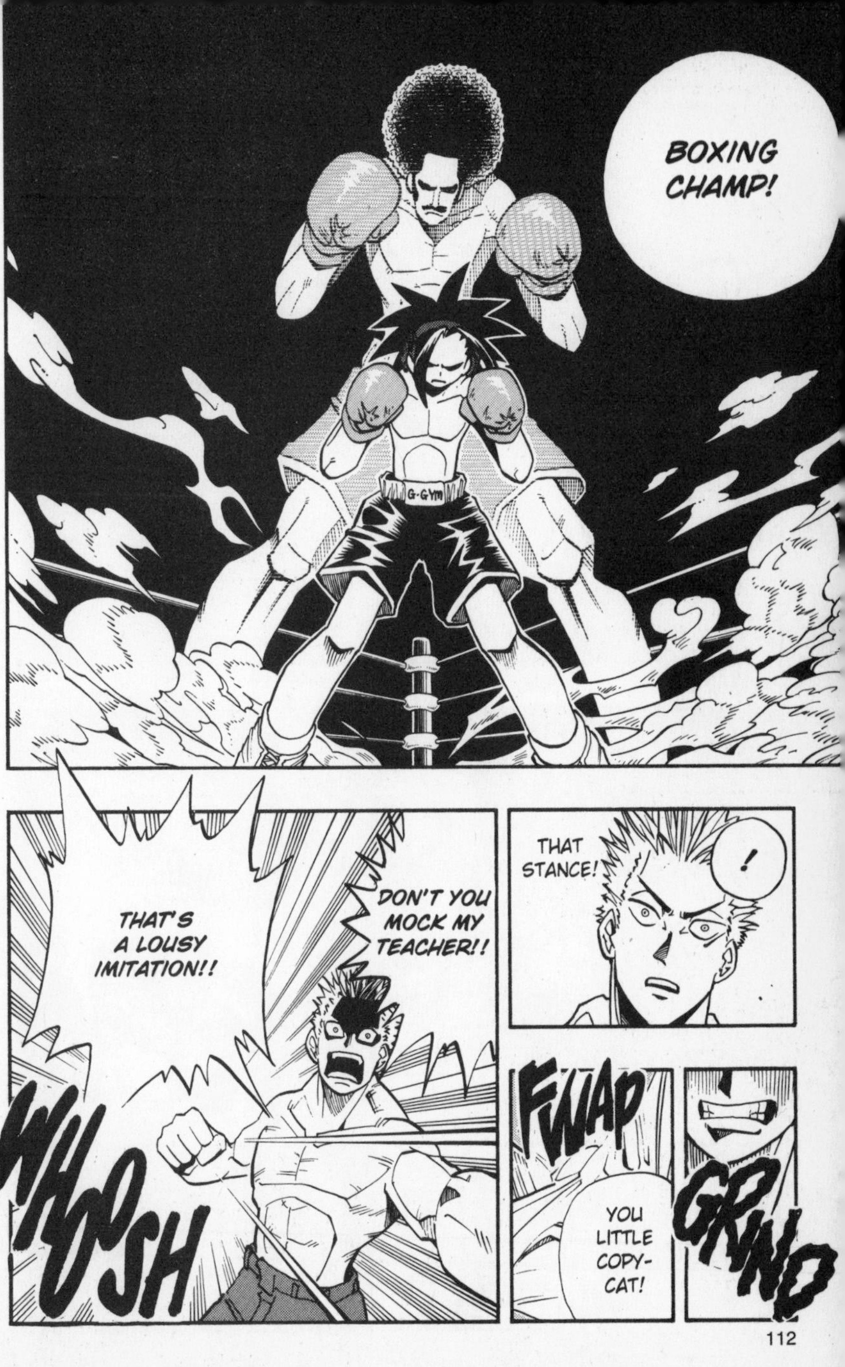
BOXING CHAMP!
THAT STANCE!
!
GRND
FWAP
YOU LITTLE COPY-CAT!
DON'T YOU MOCK MY TEACHER!!
THAT'S A LOUSY IMITATION!!
WHOOSH

READ THIS WAY

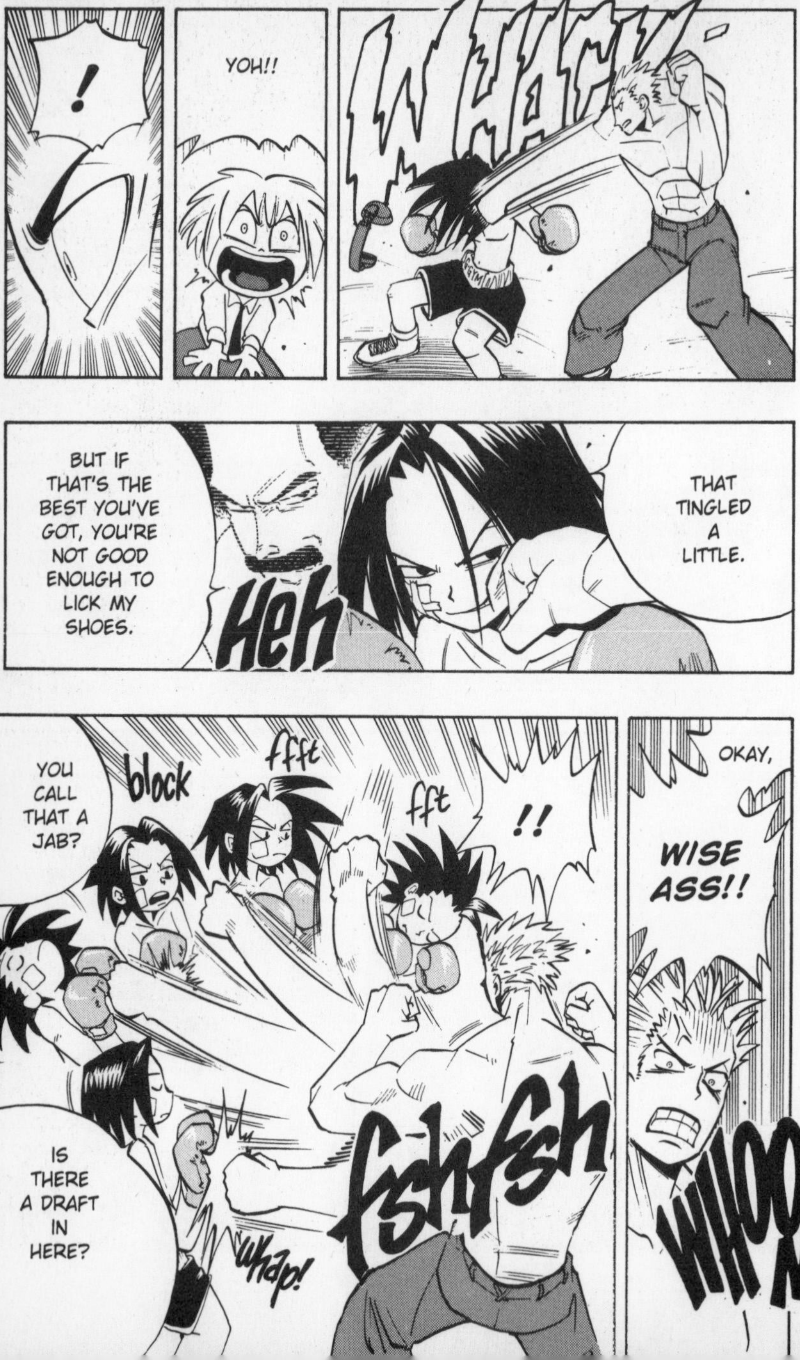
WHACK
YOH!!
!
THAT TINGLED A LITTLE.
Heh
BUT IF THAT'S THE BEST YOU'VE GOT, YOU'RE NOT GOOD ENOUGH TO LICK MY SHOES.
OKAY,
WISE ASS!!
WHOOA
!!
fft
ffft
block
YOU CALL THAT A JAB?
fshfsh
whap!
IS THERE A DRAFT IN HERE?

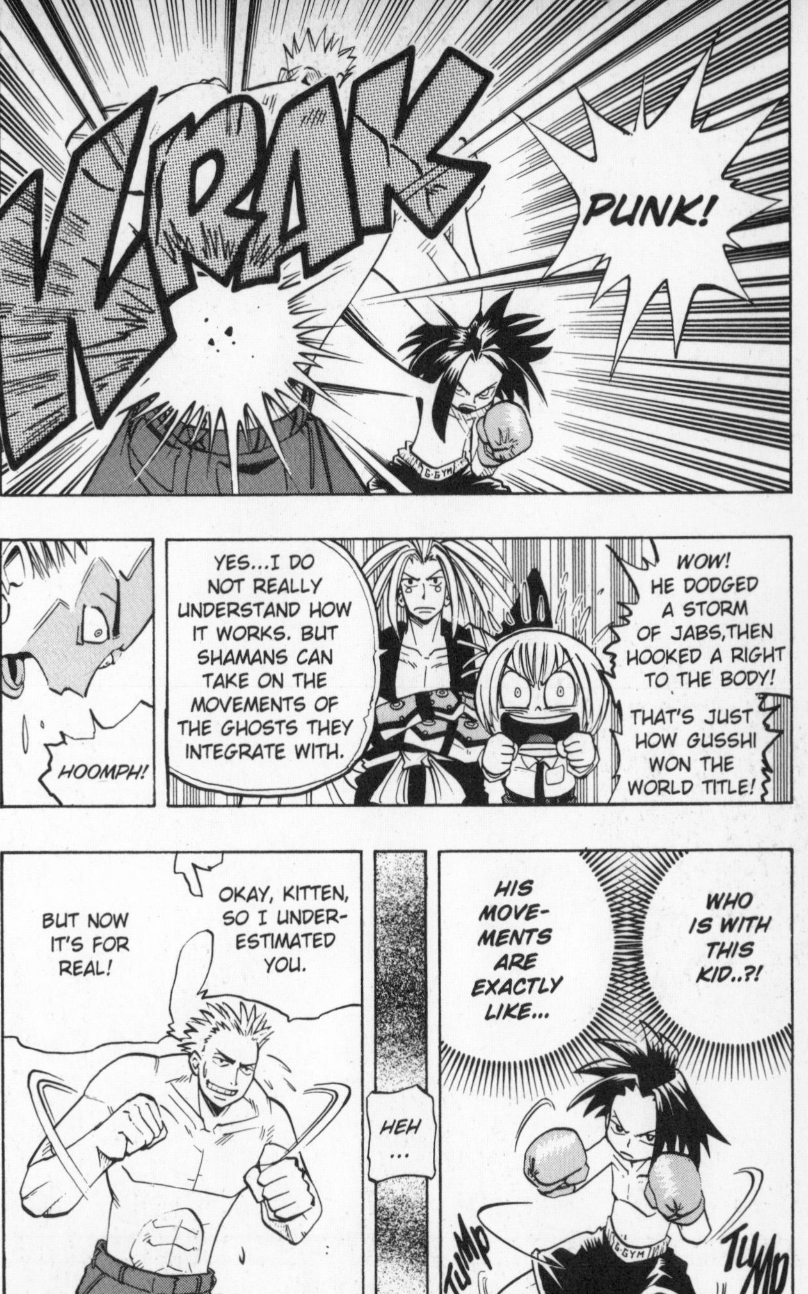
KRAK
PUNK!
WOW! HE DODGED A STORM OF JABS,THEN HOOKED A RIGHT TO THE BODY!
THAT'S JUST HOW GUSSHI WON THE WORLD TITLE!
YES...I DO NOT REALLY UNDERSTAND HOW IT WORKS. BUT SHAMANS CAN TAKE ON THE MOVEMENTS OF THE GHOSTS THEY INTEGRATE WITH.
HOOMPH!
HIS MOVEMENTS ARE EXACTLY LIKE...
WHO IS WITH THIS KID..?!
TUMP
TUMP
HEH ...
OKAY, KITTEN, SO I UNDER-ESTIMATED YOU.
BUT NOW IT'S FOR REAL!

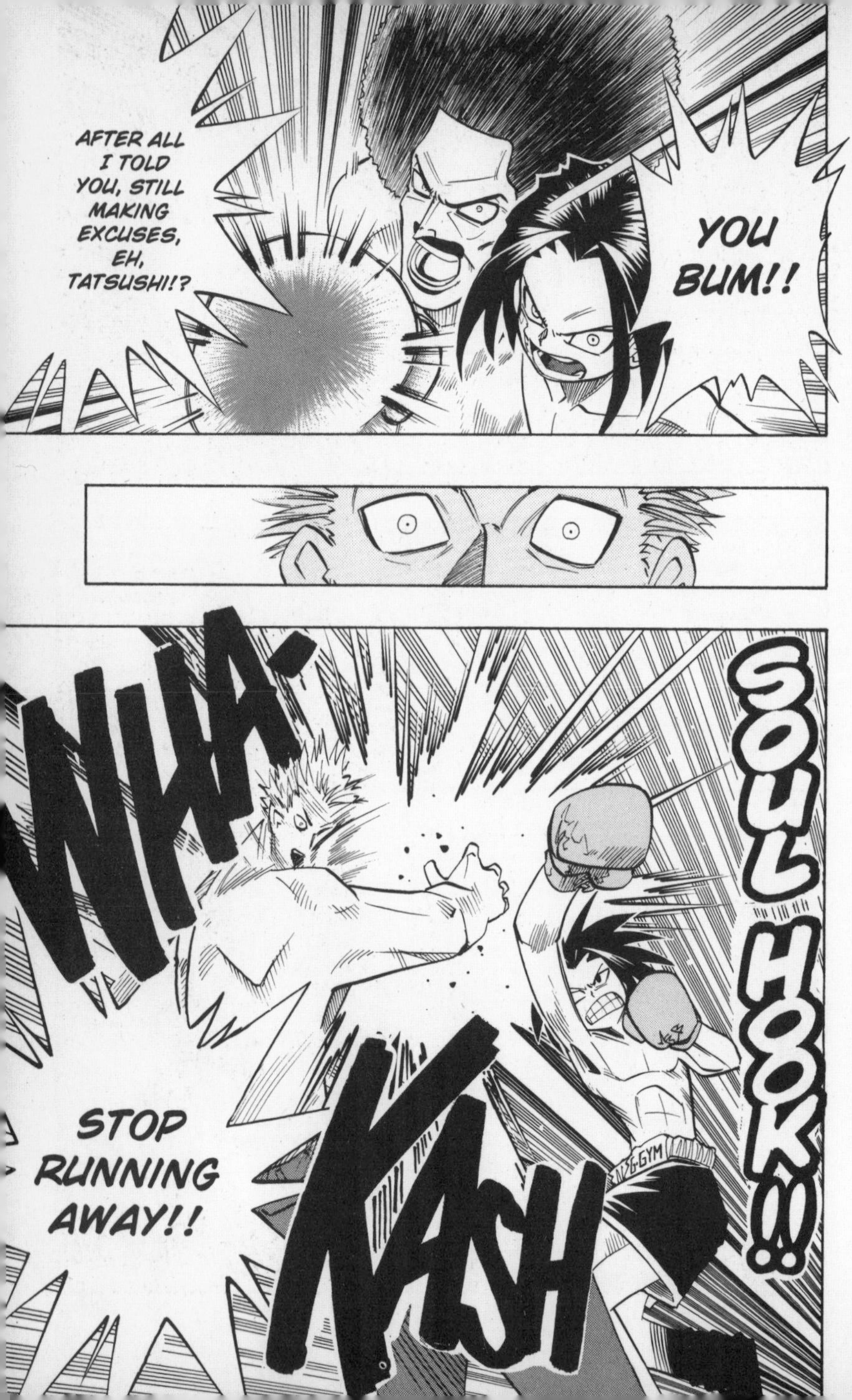
AFTER ALL I TOLD YOU, STILL MAKING EXCUSES, EH, TATSUSHI!?
YOU BUM!!
SOUL HOOK!!
WHA
KASH
STOP RUNNING AWAY!!

READ THIS WAY

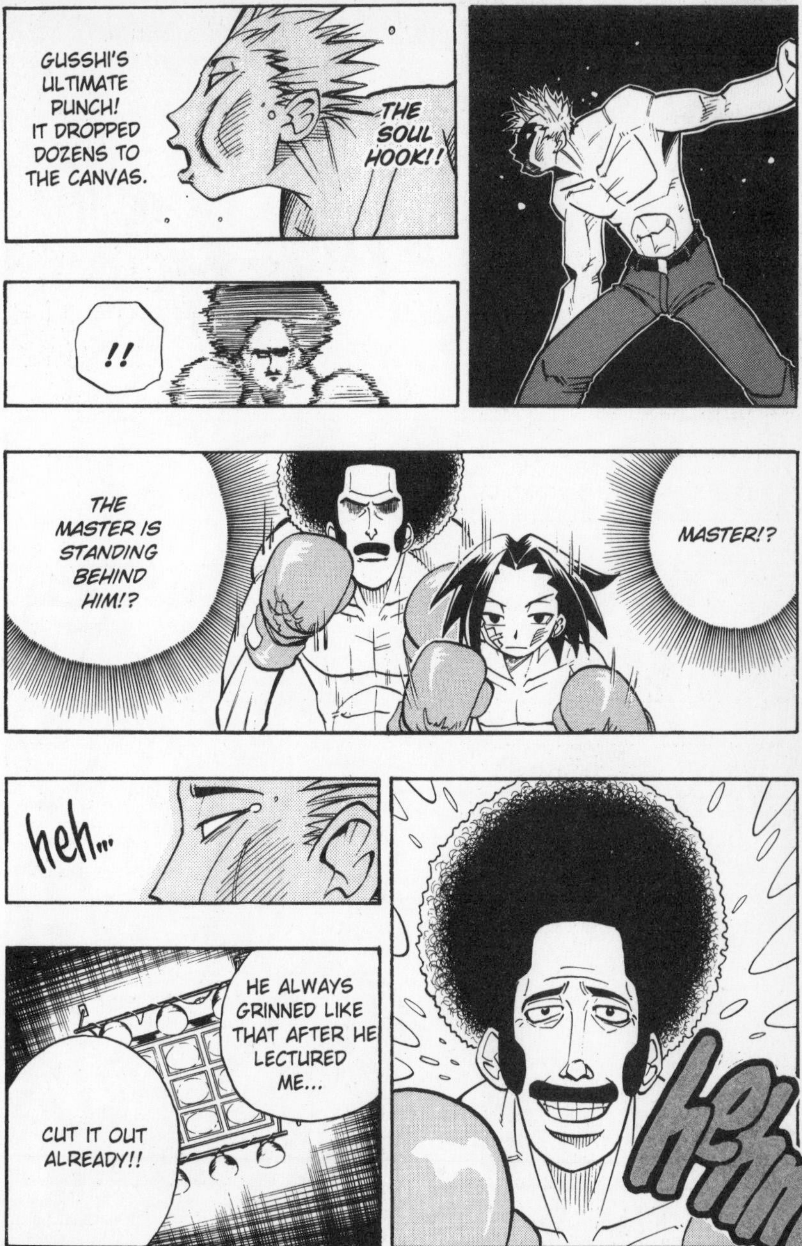
THE SOUL HOOK!!
GUSSHI'S ULTIMATE PUNCH! IT DROPPED DOZENS TO THE CANVAS.
!!
MASTER!?
THE MASTER IS STANDING BEHIND HIM!?
heh...
HE ALWAYS GRINNED LIKE THAT AFTER HE LECTURED ME...
CUT IT OUT ALREADY!!

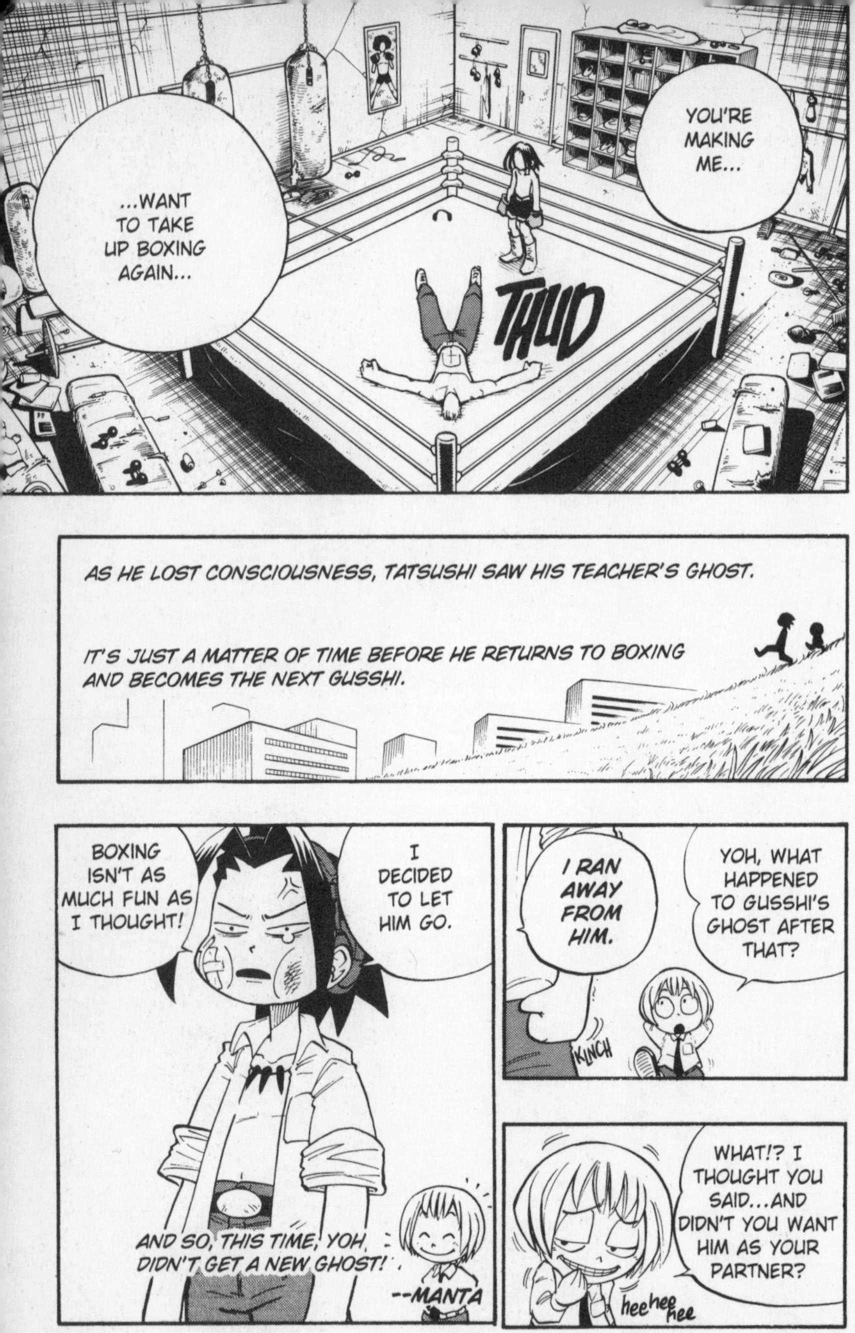
YOU'RE MAKING ME...
...WANT TO TAKE UP BOXING AGAIN...
THUD
AS HE LOST CONSCIOUSNESS, TATSUSHI SAW HIS TEACHER'S GHOST.
IT'S JUST A MATTER OF TIME BEFORE HE RETURNS TO BOXING AND BECOMES THE NEXT GUSSHI.
YOH, WHAT HAPPENED TO GUSSHI'S GHOST AFTER THAT?
I RAN AWAY FROM HIM.
KLINCH
WHAT!? I THOUGHT YOU SAID...AND DIDN'T YOU WANT HIM AS YOUR PARTNER?
heeheehee
I DECIDED TO LET HIM GO.
BOXING ISN'T AS MUCH FUN AS I THOUGHT!
AND SO, THIS TIME, YOH DIDN'T GET A NEW GHOST!
--MANTA

SHAMAN
KING
1

**BEAR-TALON
NECKLACE**

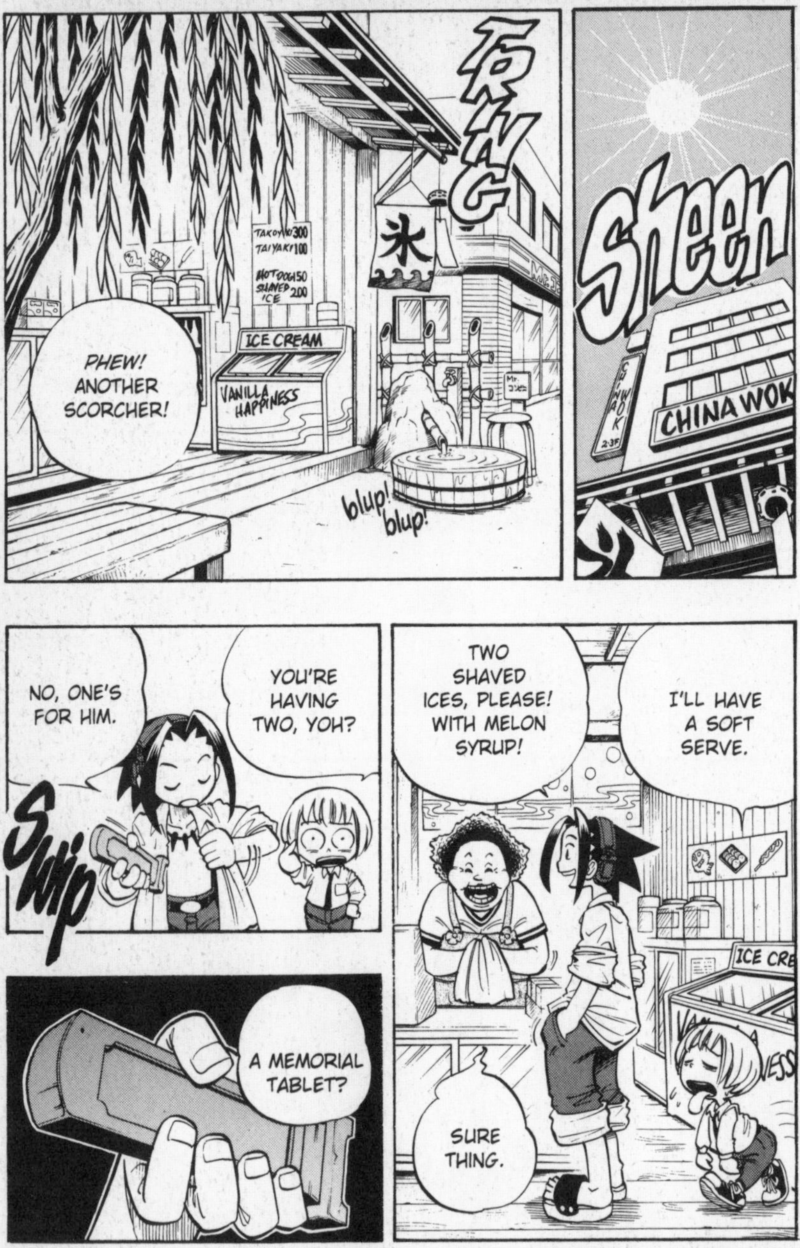
Sheen
CHINA WOK
CHINA WOK 2·3F
FRING
PHEW! ANOTHER SCORCHER!
TAKOYAKI 300
TAIYAKI 100
HOT DOG 150
SHAVED ICE 200
ICE CREAM
VANILLA HAPPINESS
blup! blup!
I'LL HAVE A SOFT SERVE.
TWO SHAVED ICES, PLEASE! WITH MELON SYRUP!
ICE CRE
SURE THING.
YOU'RE HAVING TWO, YOH?
NO, ONE'S FOR HIM.
Swip
A MEMORIAL TABLET?

READ THIS WAY

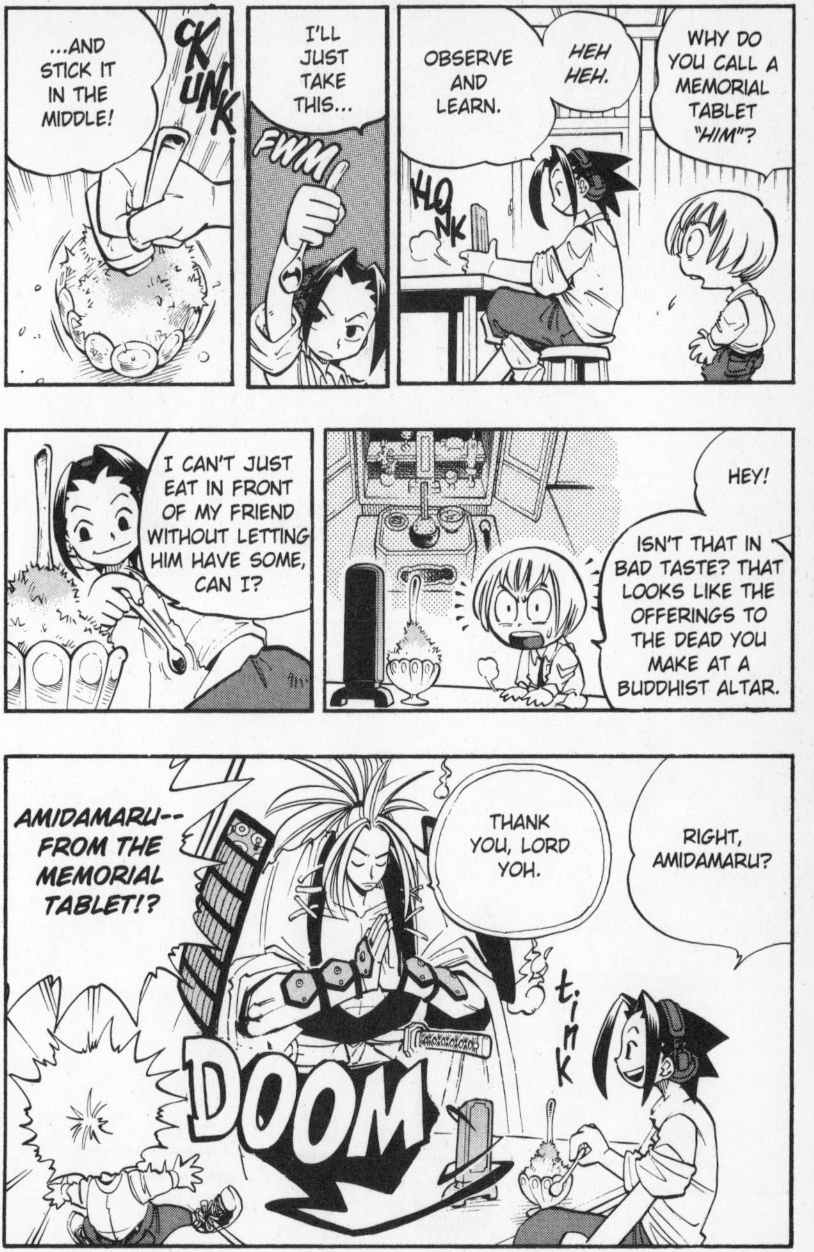

WHY DO YOU CALL A MEMORIAL TABLET "HIM"?
HEH HEH.
OBSERVE AND LEARN.
KLONK
I'LL JUST TAKE THIS...
FWM
...AND STICK IT IN THE MIDDLE!
CKUNK
HEY!
ISN'T THAT IN BAD TASTE? THAT LOOKS LIKE THE OFFERINGS TO THE DEAD YOU MAKE AT A BUDDHIST ALTAR.
I CAN'T JUST EAT IN FRONT OF MY FRIEND WITHOUT LETTING HIM HAVE SOME, CAN I?
RIGHT, AMIDAMARU?
THANK YOU, LORD YOH.
tink
DOOM
AMIDAMARU--FROM THE MEMORIAL TABLET!?

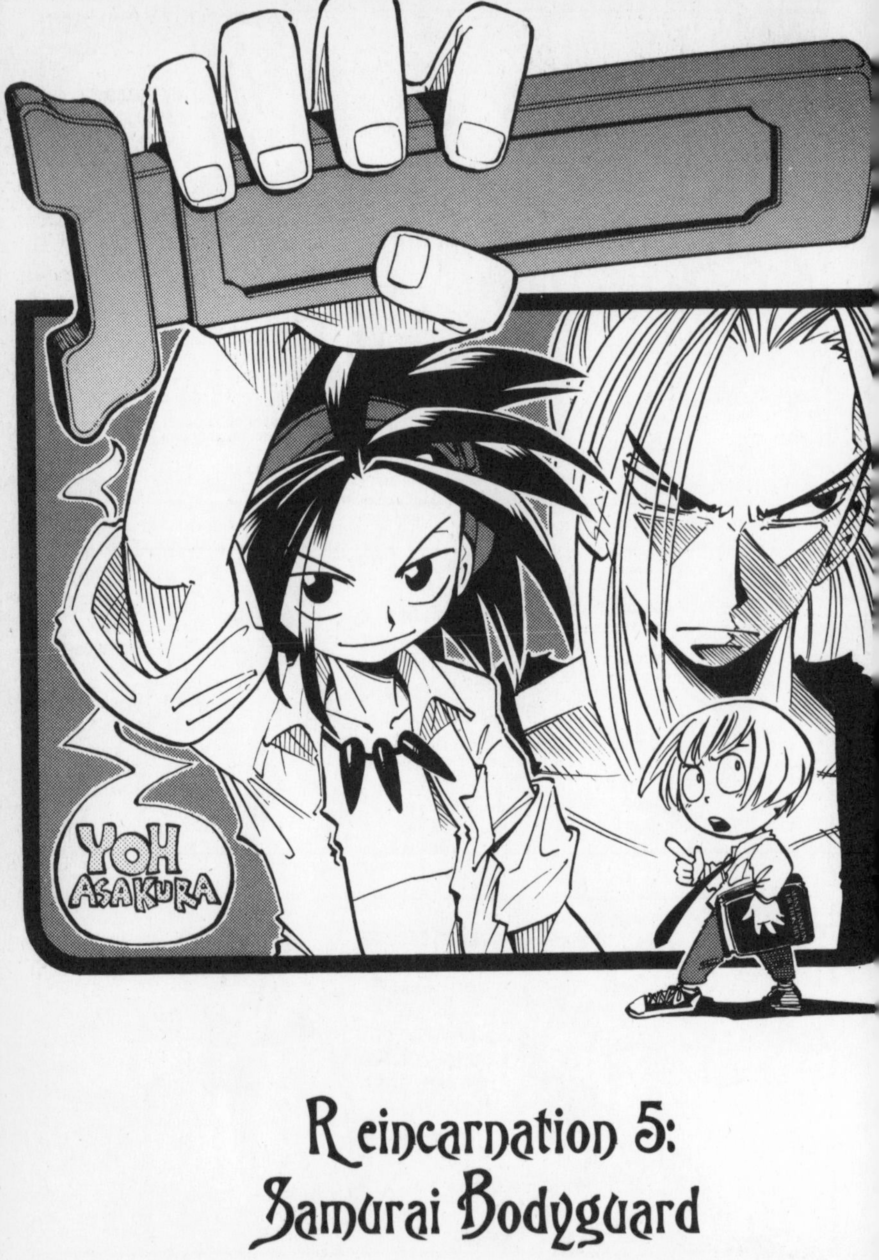
YOH ASAKURA

Reincarnation 5: Samurai Bodyguard

READ THIS WAY

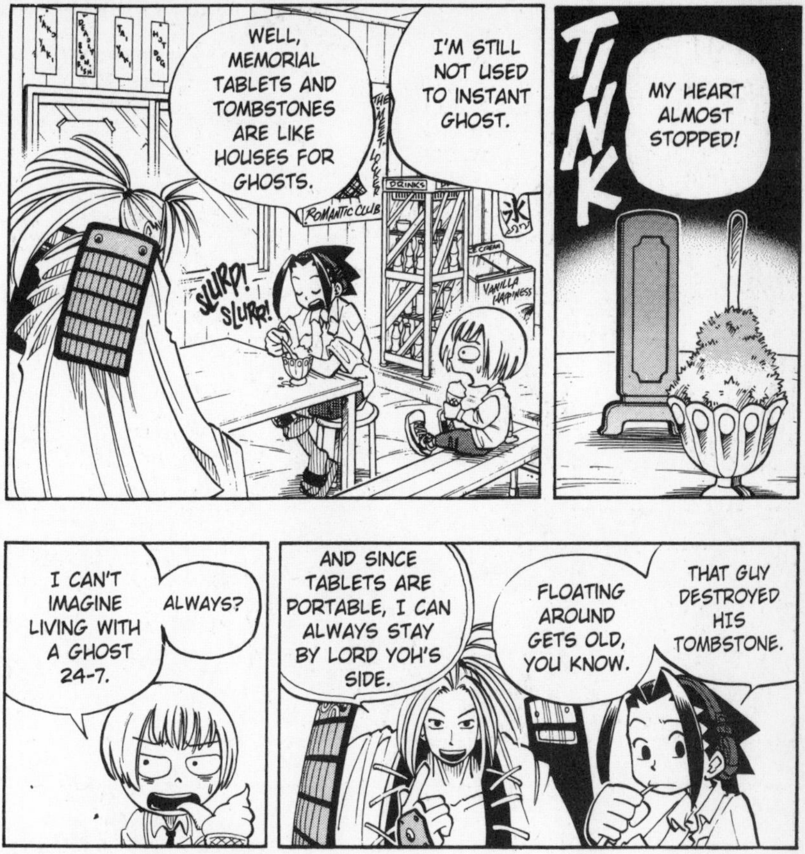
TINK
MY HEART ALMOST STOPPED!
I'M STILL NOT USED TO INSTANT GHOST.
WELL, MEMORIAL TABLETS AND TOMBSTONES ARE LIKE HOUSES FOR GHOSTS.
ROMANTIC CLUB
DRINKS
VANILLA HAPPINESS
SLURP! SLURP!
THAT GUY DESTROYED HIS TOMBSTONE.
FLOATING AROUND GETS OLD, YOU KNOW.
AND SINCE TABLETS ARE PORTABLE, I CAN ALWAYS STAY BY LORD YOH'S SIDE.
ALWAYS?
I CAN'T IMAGINE LIVING WITH A GHOST 24-7.
BUT THERE ARE A LOT OF ADVANTAGES.
IF I OVERSLEEP, HE WAKES ME WITH SLEEP PARALYSIS*--LIKE WHEN YOU KNOW YOU'RE AWAKE BUT CAN'T MOVE.
SLEEP PARALYSIS?!
SPHEW

*BELIEVED IN JAPAN TO BE CAUSED BY GHOSTS — EDITOR

READ THIS WAY

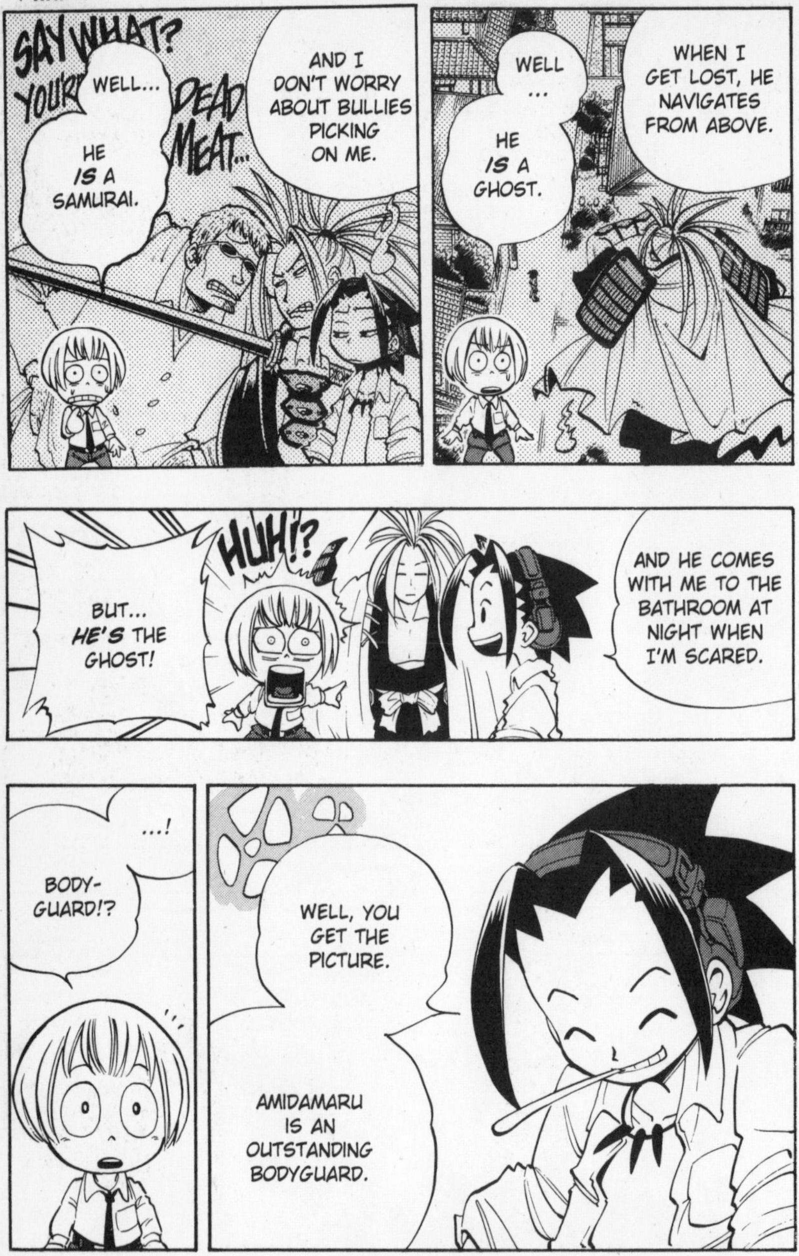

WHEN I GET LOST, HE NAVIGATES FROM ABOVE.
WELL ... HE *IS* A GHOST.
AND I DON'T WORRY ABOUT BULLIES PICKING ON ME.
SAY WHAT? YOU'R
DEAD MEAT...
WELL... HE *IS* A SAMURAI.
AND HE COMES WITH ME TO THE BATHROOM AT NIGHT WHEN I'M SCARED.
HUH!?
BUT... *HE'S* THE GHOST!
WELL, YOU GET THE PICTURE.
AMIDAMARU IS AN OUTSTANDING BODYGUARD.
...!
BODY-GUARD!?

READ THIS WAY

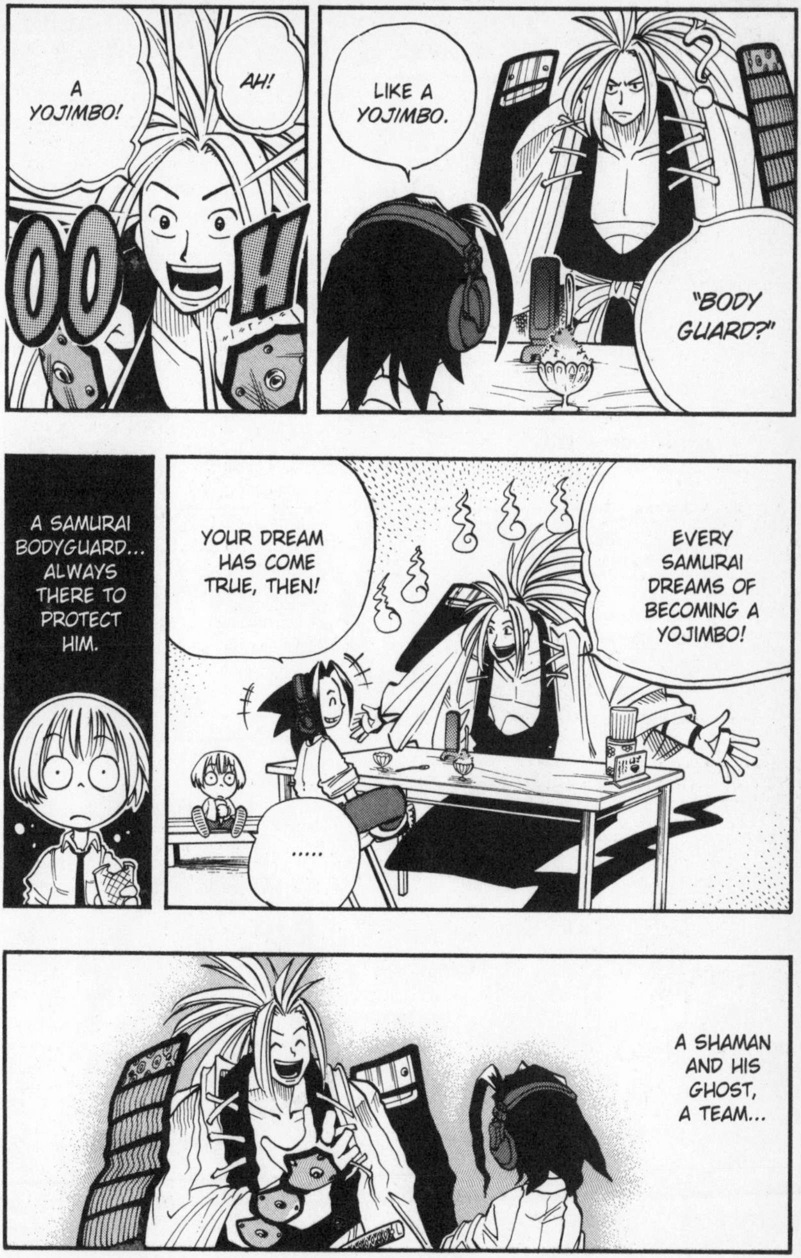
"BODY GUARD?"
LIKE A YOJIMBO.
AH!
A YOJIMBO!
OOH
EVERY SAMURAI DREAMS OF BECOMING A YOJIMBO!
YOUR DREAM HAS COME TRUE, THEN!
.....
A SAMURAI BODYGUARD... ALWAYS THERE TO PROTECT HIM.
A SHAMAN AND HIS GHOST, A TEAM...

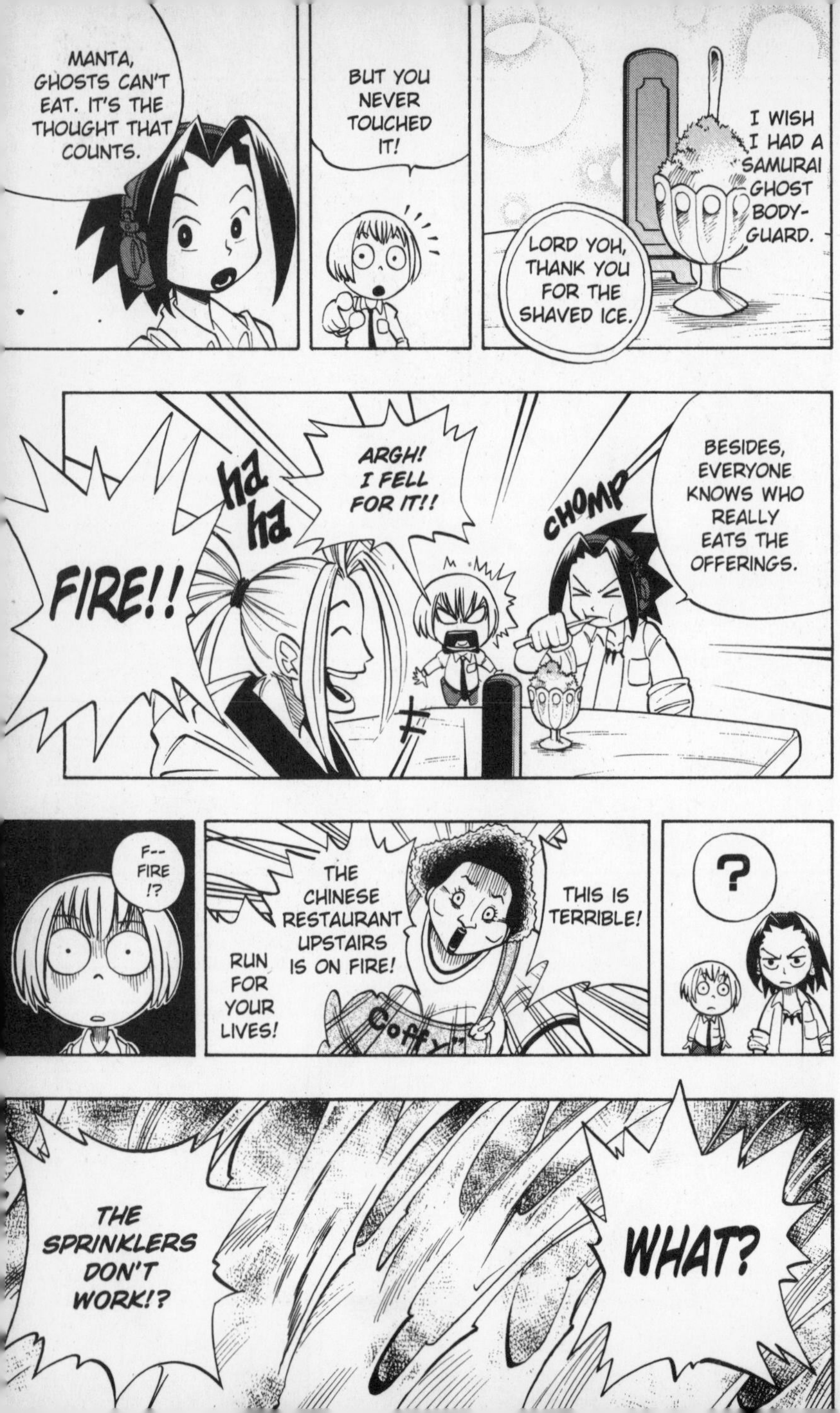
I WISH I HAD A SAMURAI GHOST BODY-GUARD.
LORD YOH, THANK YOU FOR THE SHAVED ICE.
BUT YOU NEVER TOUCHED IT!
MANTA, GHOSTS CAN'T EAT. IT'S THE THOUGHT THAT COUNTS.
BESIDES, EVERYONE KNOWS WHO REALLY EATS THE OFFERINGS.
CHOMP
ARGH! I FELL FOR IT!!
ha ha
FIRE!!
?
THIS IS TERRIBLE!
THE CHINESE RESTAURANT UPSTAIRS IS ON FIRE!
RUN FOR YOUR LIVES!
F-- FIRE !?
WHAT?
THE SPRINKLERS DON'T WORK!?

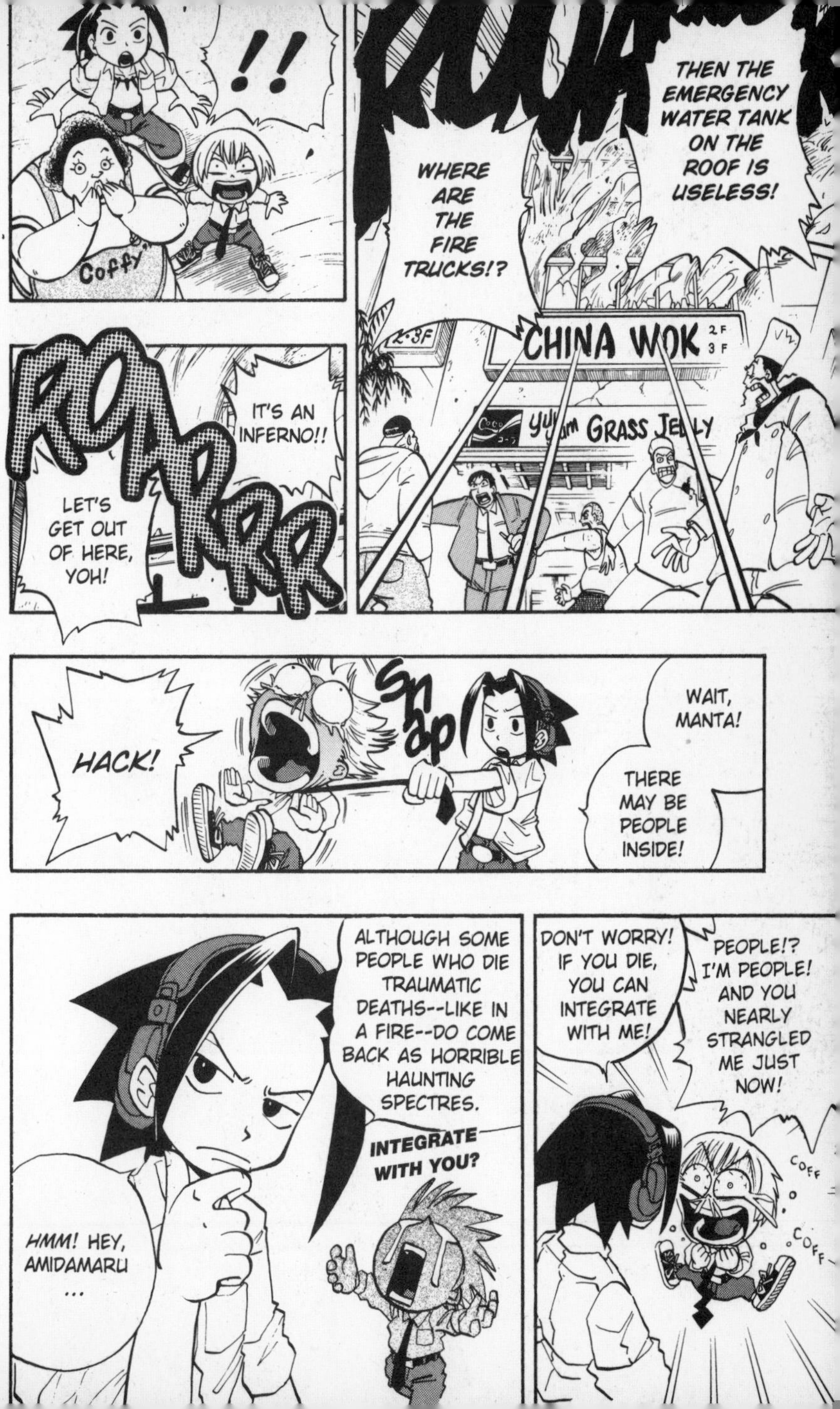
THEN THE EMERGENCY WATER TANK ON THE ROOF IS USELESS!
WHERE ARE THE FIRE TRUCKS!?
CHINA WOK 2F 3F
yum yum GRASS JELLY
!!
Coffy
IT'S AN INFERNO!!
LET'S GET OUT OF HERE, YOH!
WAIT, MANTA!
THERE MAY BE PEOPLE INSIDE!
Snap
HACK!
PEOPLE!? I'M PEOPLE! AND YOU NEARLY STRANGLED ME JUST NOW!
DON'T WORRY! IF YOU DIE, YOU CAN INTEGRATE WITH ME!
COFF
COFF
ALTHOUGH SOME PEOPLE WHO DIE TRAUMATIC DEATHS--LIKE IN A FIRE--DO COME BACK AS HORRIBLE HAUNTING SPECTRES.
INTEGRATE WITH YOU?
HMM! HEY, AMIDAMARU ...

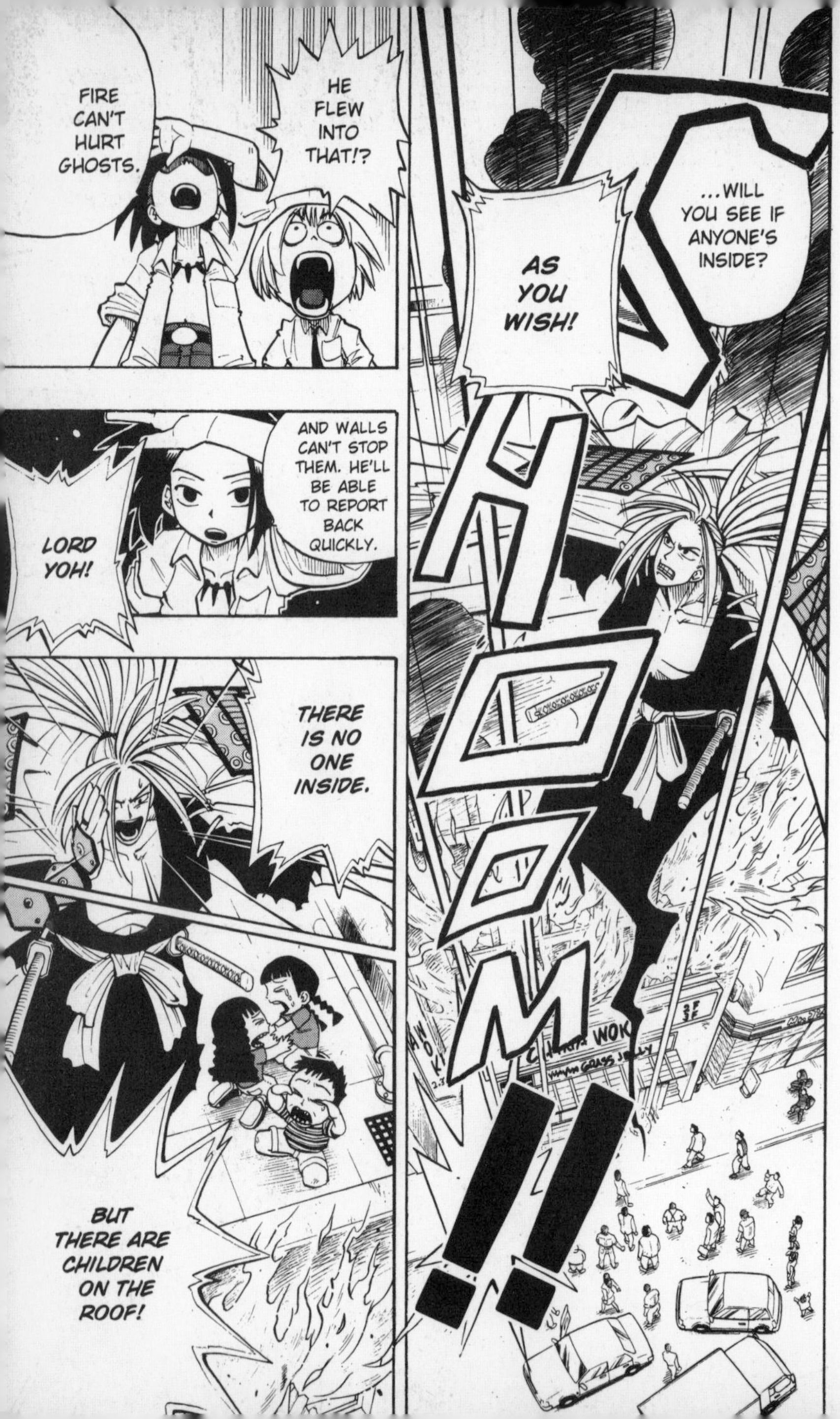
...WILL YOU SEE IF ANYONE'S INSIDE?
AS YOU WISH!
HOOM!!
HE FLEW INTO THAT!?
FIRE CAN'T HURT GHOSTS.
AND WALLS CAN'T STOP THEM. HE'LL BE ABLE TO REPORT BACK QUICKLY.
LORD YOH!
THERE IS NO ONE INSIDE.
BUT THERE ARE CHILDREN ON THE ROOF!

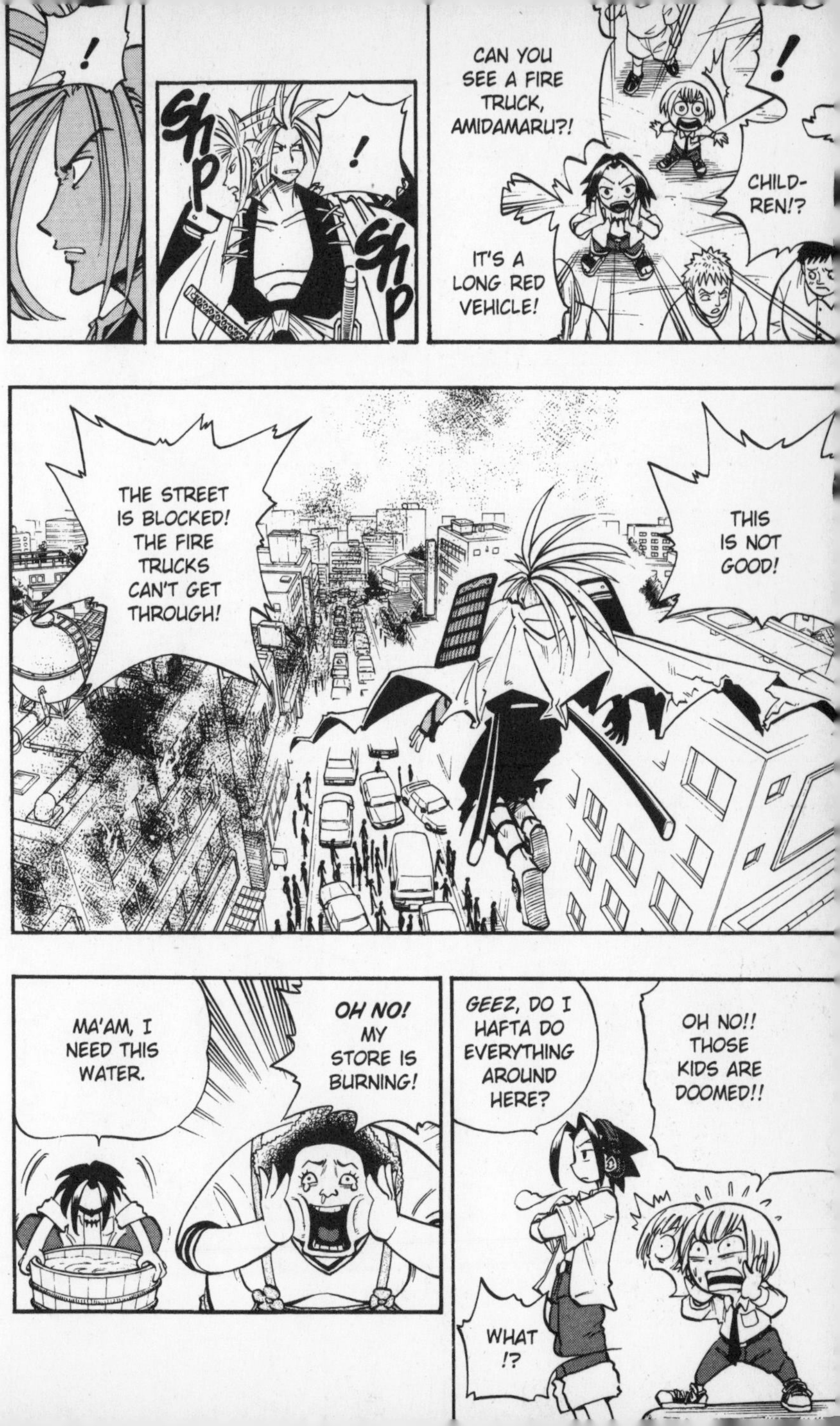
!
CAN YOU SEE A FIRE TRUCK, AMIDAMARU?!
CHILD-REN!?
IT'S A LONG RED VEHICLE!
SHP
!
SHP
!
THIS IS NOT GOOD!
THE STREET IS BLOCKED! THE FIRE TRUCKS CAN'T GET THROUGH!
OH NO!! THOSE KIDS ARE DOOMED!!
GEEZ, DO I HAFTA DO EVERYTHING AROUND HERE?
WHAT !?
OH NO! MY STORE IS BURNING!
MA'AM, I NEED THIS WATER.

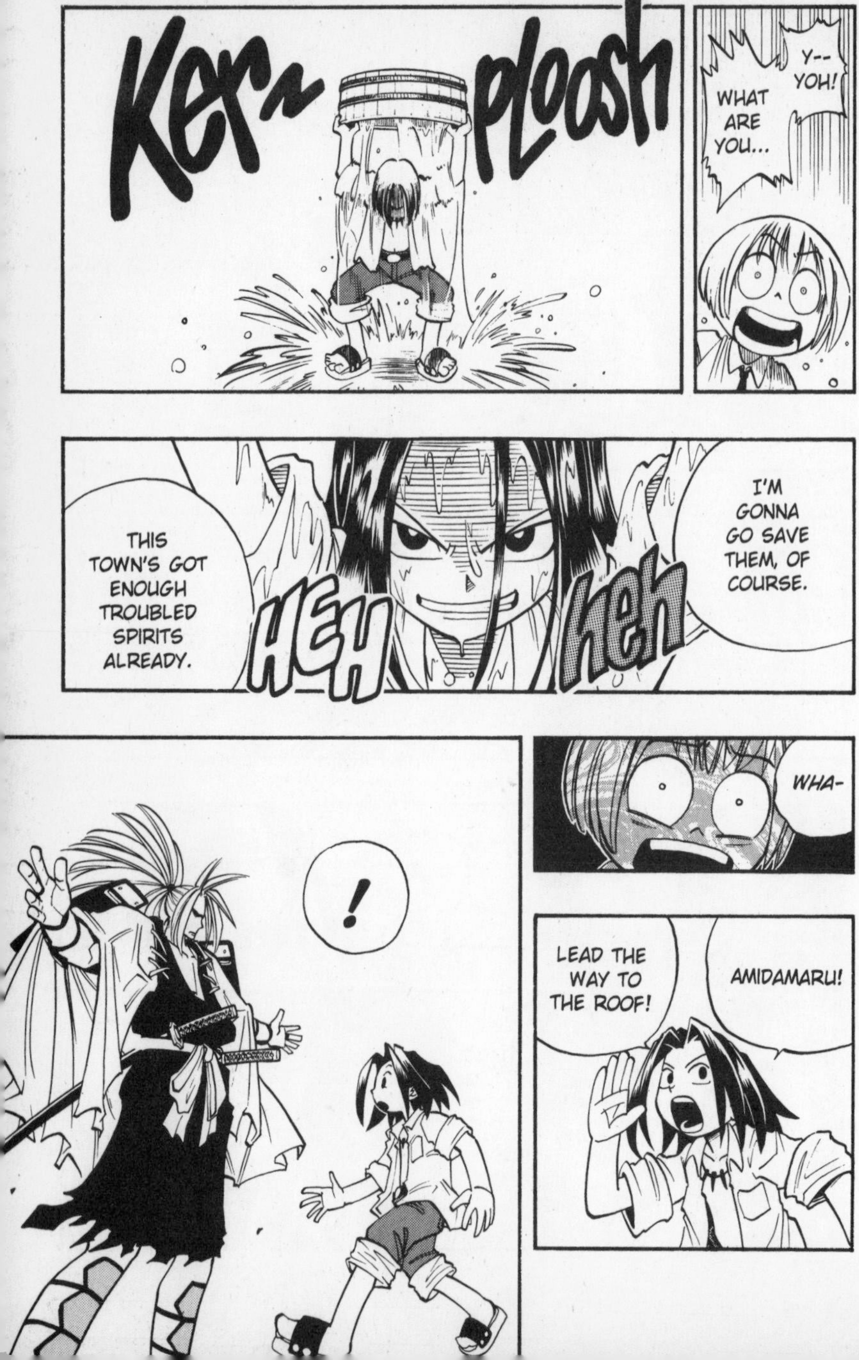
READ THIS WAY
Y-- YOH!
WHAT ARE YOU...
Ker-ploosh
I'M GONNA GO SAVE THEM, OF COURSE.
THIS TOWN'S GOT ENOUGH TROUBLED SPIRITS ALREADY.
HEH heh
WHA-
AMIDAMARU!
LEAD THE WAY TO THE ROOF!
!

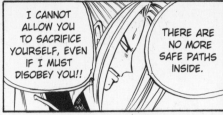

C'MON, AMIDAMARU!
YOU MUST NOT ENTER.
THERE ARE NO MORE SAFE PATHS INSIDE.
I CANNOT ALLOW YOU TO SACRIFICE YOURSELF, EVEN IF I MUST DISOBEY YOU!!
WE CAN'T JUST LET THOSE KIDS BURN.
WON'T YOU FEEL BAD IF YOU LET THEM DIE?
OF... COURSE... BUT...
BUT I WOULD FEEL WORSE IF YOU WERE TO DIE!!
!
...
THAT MAKES TWO OF US.
heh
?

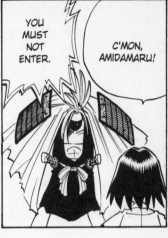

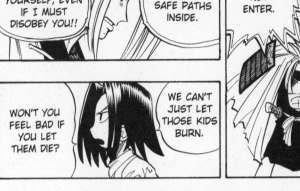

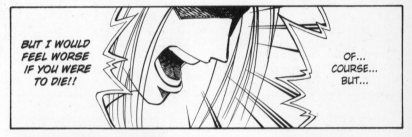

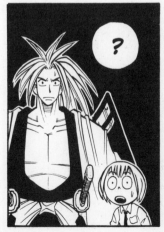

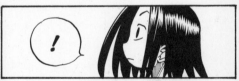

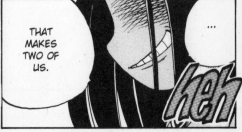

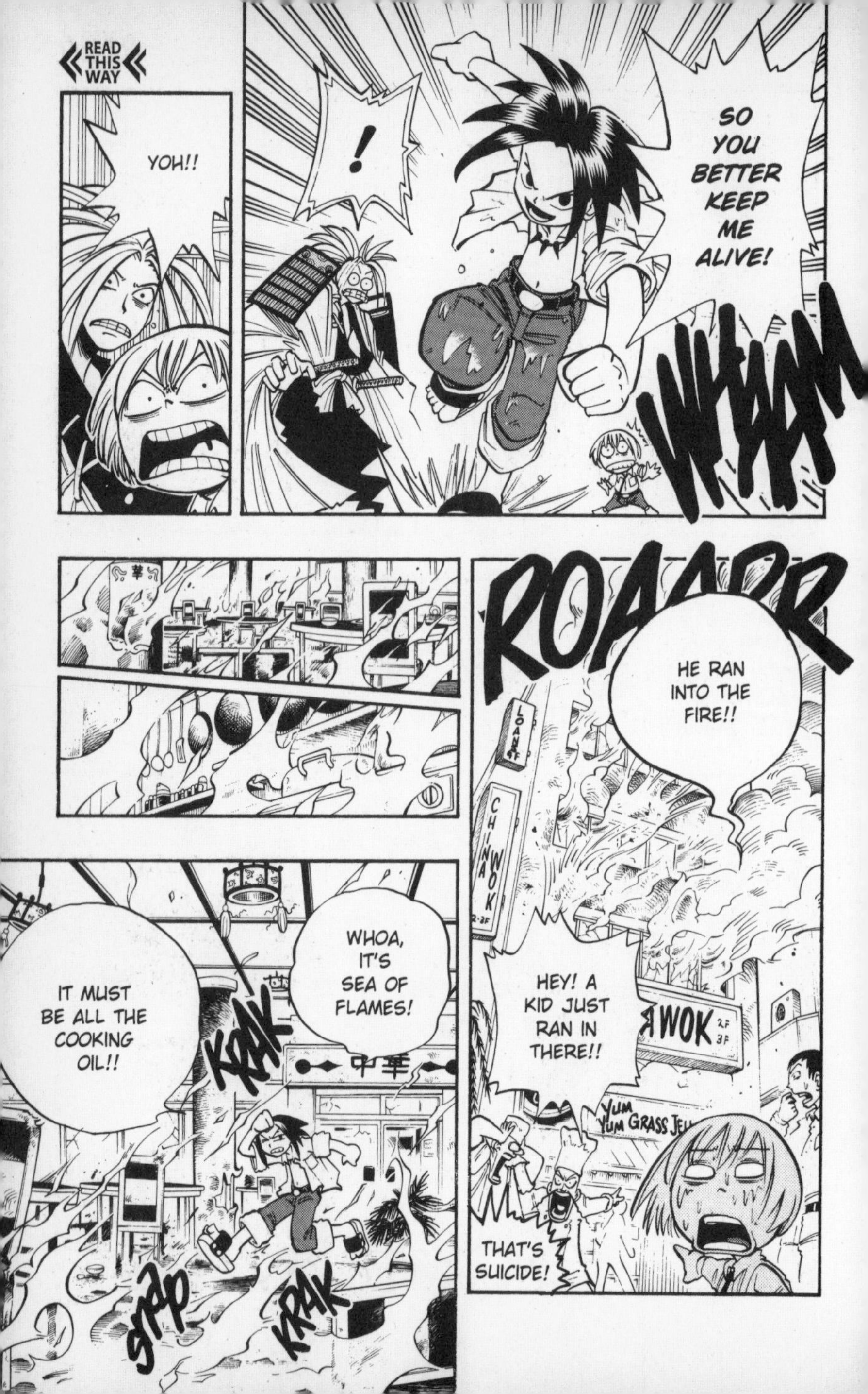
READ THIS WAY
SO YOU BETTER KEEP ME ALIVE!
!
WHAM
YOH!!
ROAARR
HE RAN INTO THE FIRE!!
CHINA WOK 2·3F
WOK 2F 3F
HEY! A KID JUST RAN IN THERE!!
THAT'S SUICIDE!
WHOA, IT'S SEA OF FLAMES!
KRAK
IT MUST BE ALL THE COOKING OIL!!
中華
SNAP
KRAK

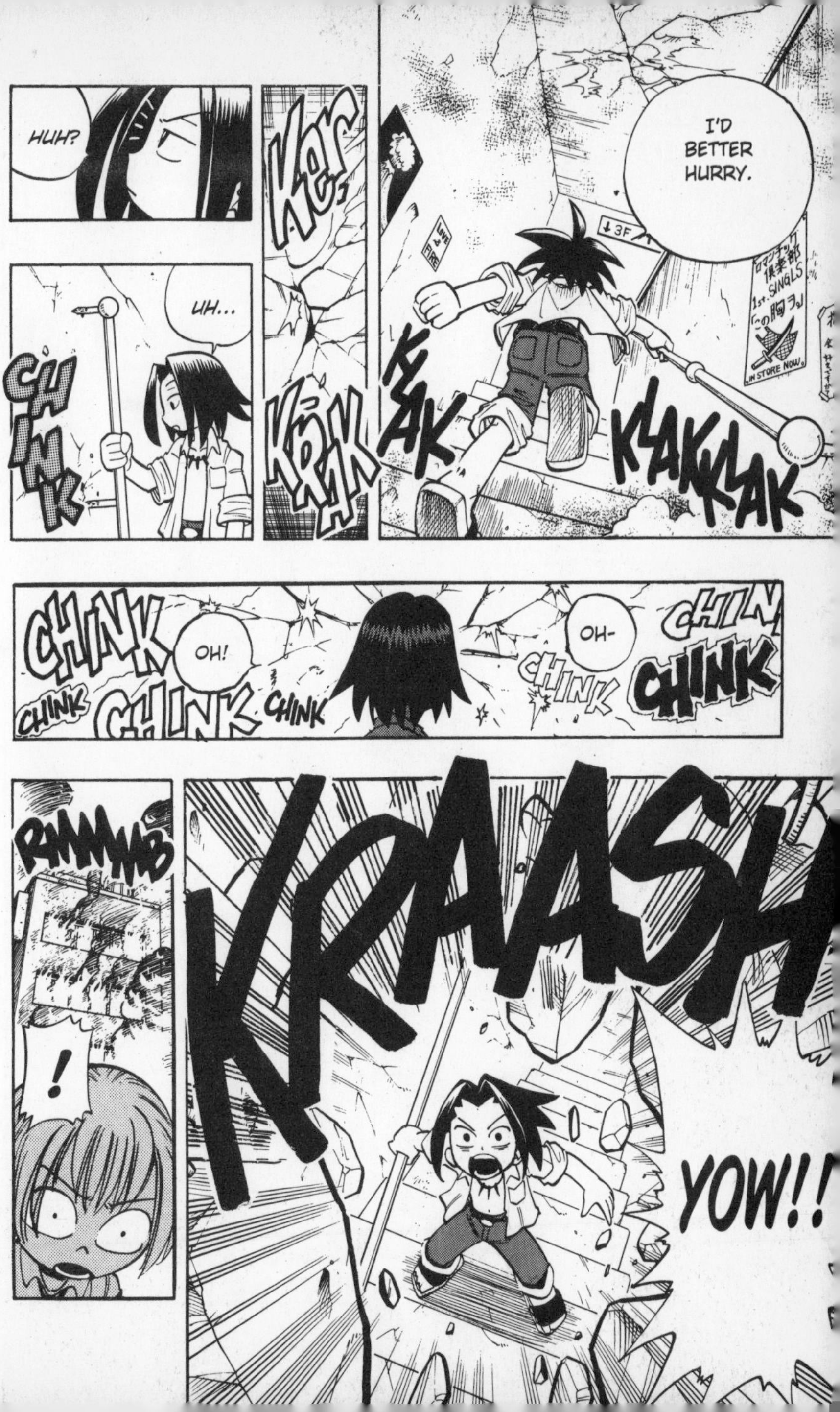

I'D BETTER HURRY.
↓3F
LOVE & FIRE
ロマンチック倶楽部
1st. SINGLS
「この胸ヲ」
IN STORE NOW.
KLAK
KLAKKLAK
Ker
HUH?
UH...
CHINK
CHIN
CHINK
OH-
CHINK
CHINK
OH!
CHINK
CHINK
CHINK
KRAASH
YOW!!
RMMMB
!

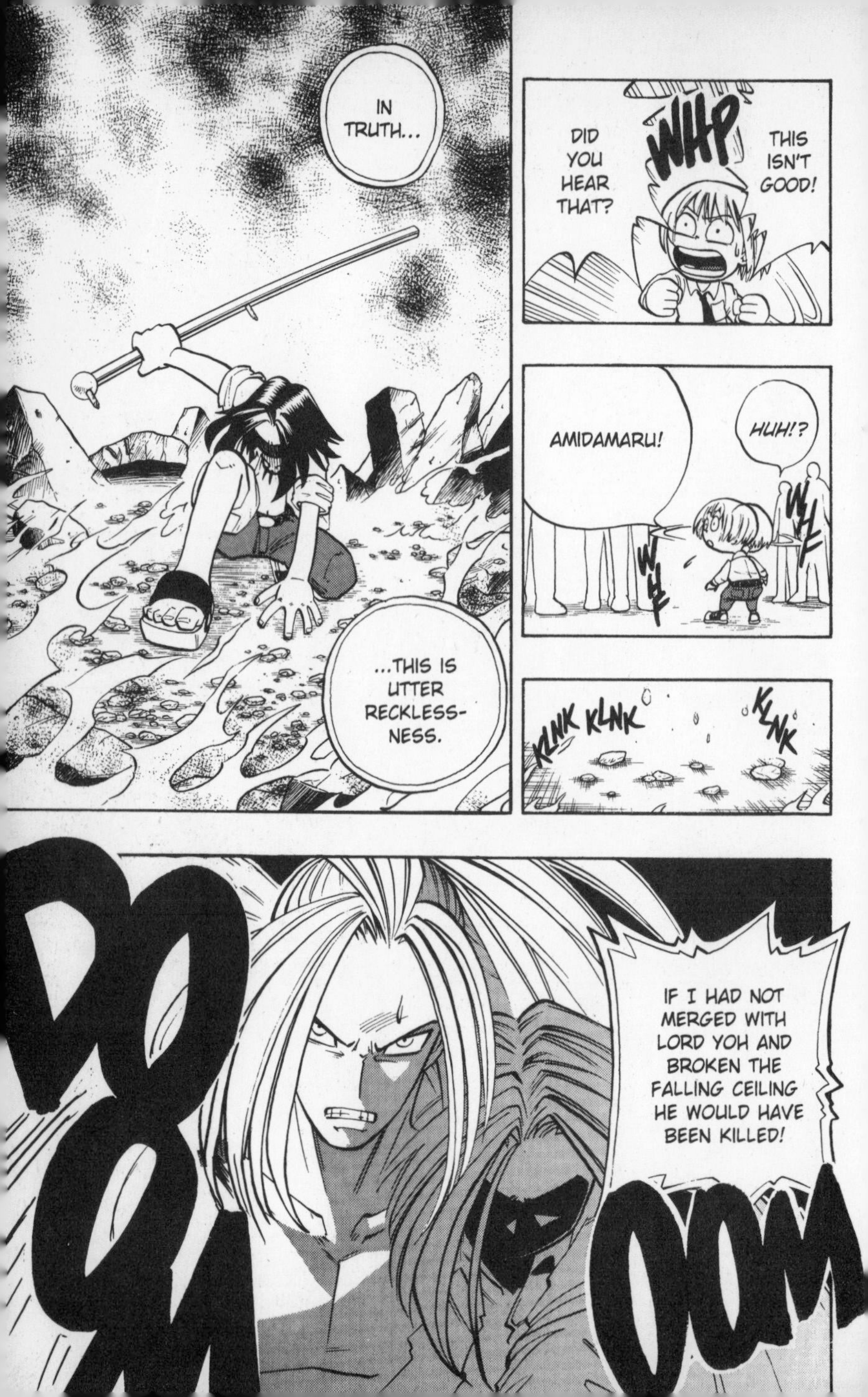
THIS ISN'T GOOD!
WHP
DID YOU HEAR THAT?
HUH!?
WHP
AMIDAMARU!
WHP
KLNK
KLNK
KLNK
IN TRUTH...
...THIS IS UTTER RECKLESS-NESS.
IF I HAD NOT MERGED WITH LORD YOH AND BROKEN THE FALLING CEILING HE WOULD HAVE BEEN KILLED!
DOOOOM

READ THIS WAY

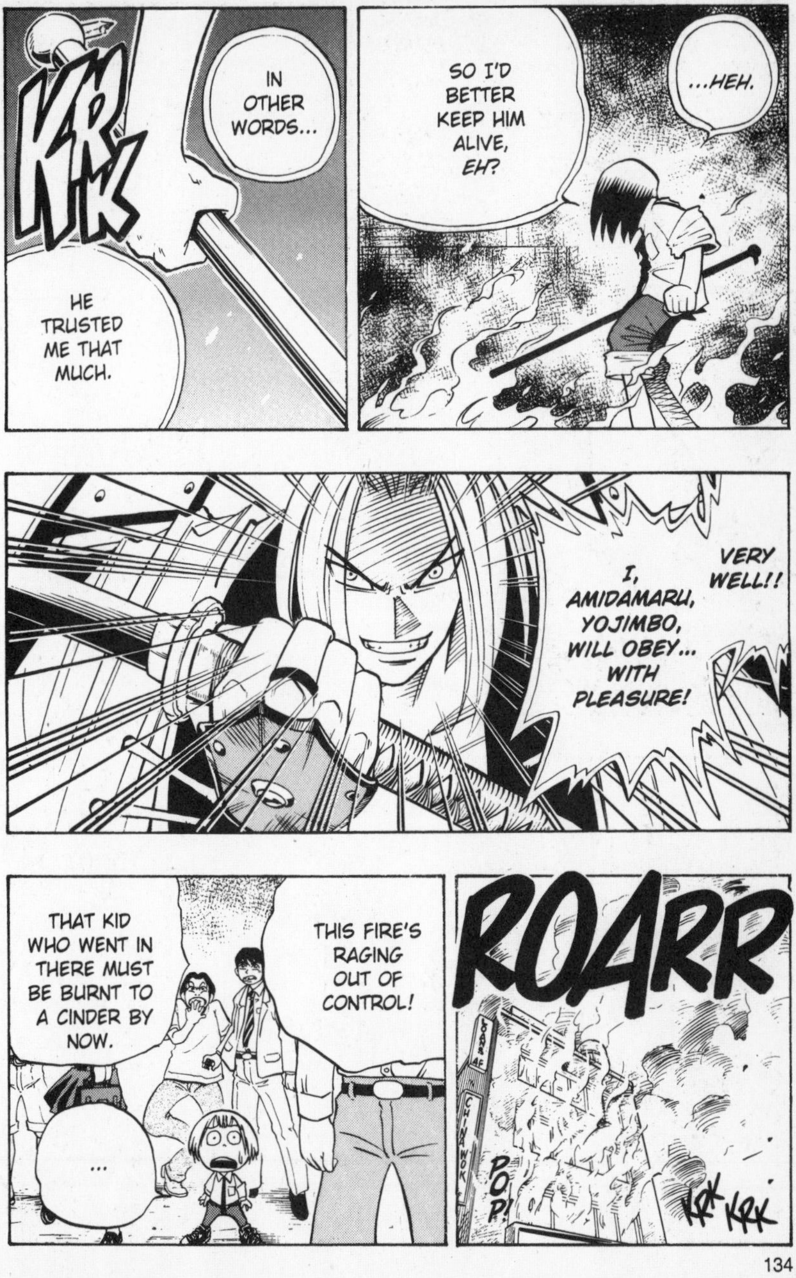
...HEH.
SO I'D BETTER KEEP HIM ALIVE, EH?
IN OTHER WORDS...
KRK
HE TRUSTED ME THAT MUCH.
VERY WELL!!
I, AMIDAMARU, YOJIMBO, WILL OBEY... WITH PLEASURE!
ROARR
LOANS 4F
CHINA WOK
POP!
KRK KRK
THIS FIRE'S RAGING OUT OF CONTROL!
THAT KID WHO WENT IN THERE MUST BE BURNT TO A CINDER BY NOW.
...

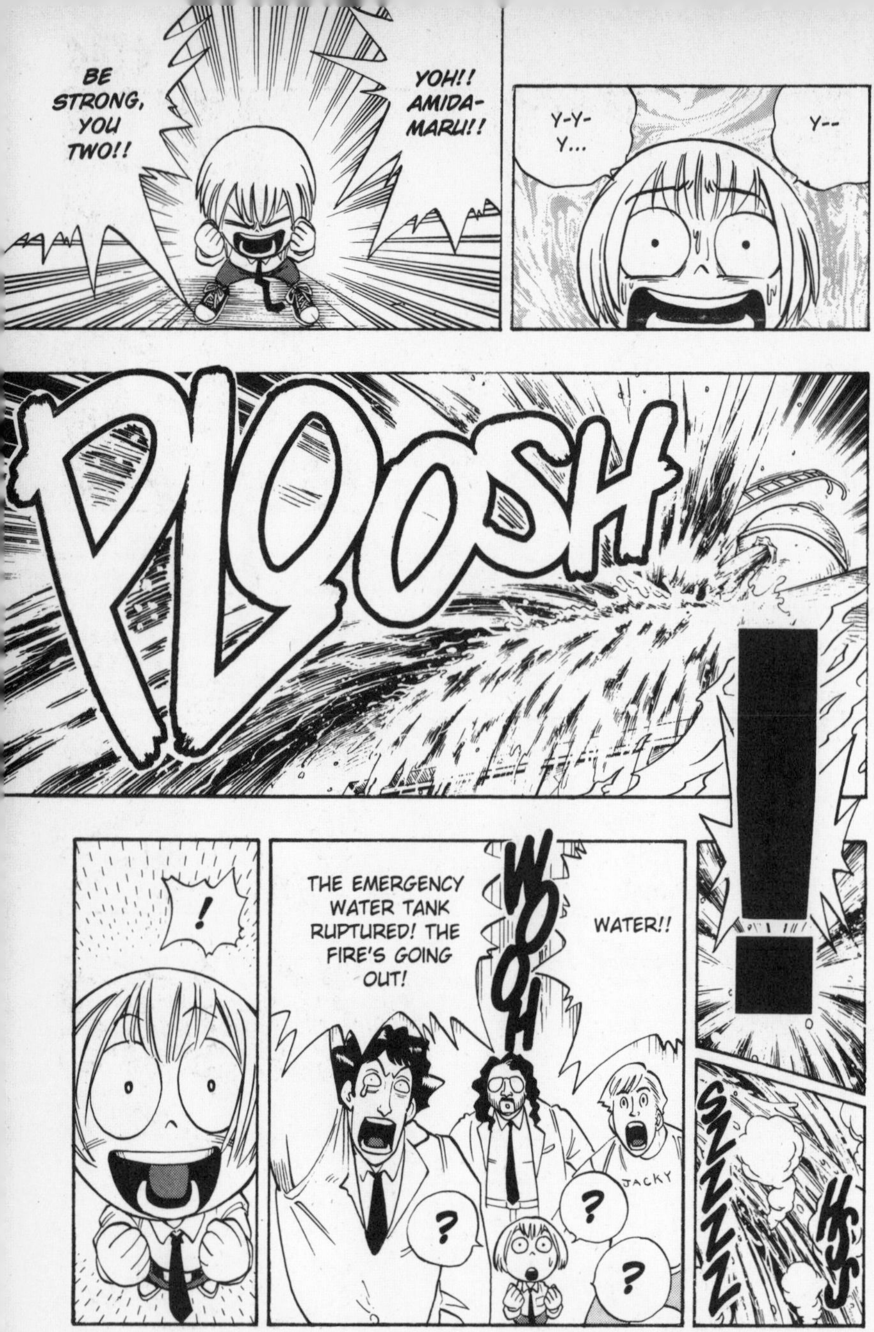
Y--
Y-Y-Y...
YOH!! AMIDA-MARU!!
BE STRONG, YOU TWO!!
PLOOSH
!
SZZZZ
WATER!!
WOOOH
THE EMERGENCY WATER TANK RUPTURED! THE FIRE'S GOING OUT!
JACKY
?
?
?
!

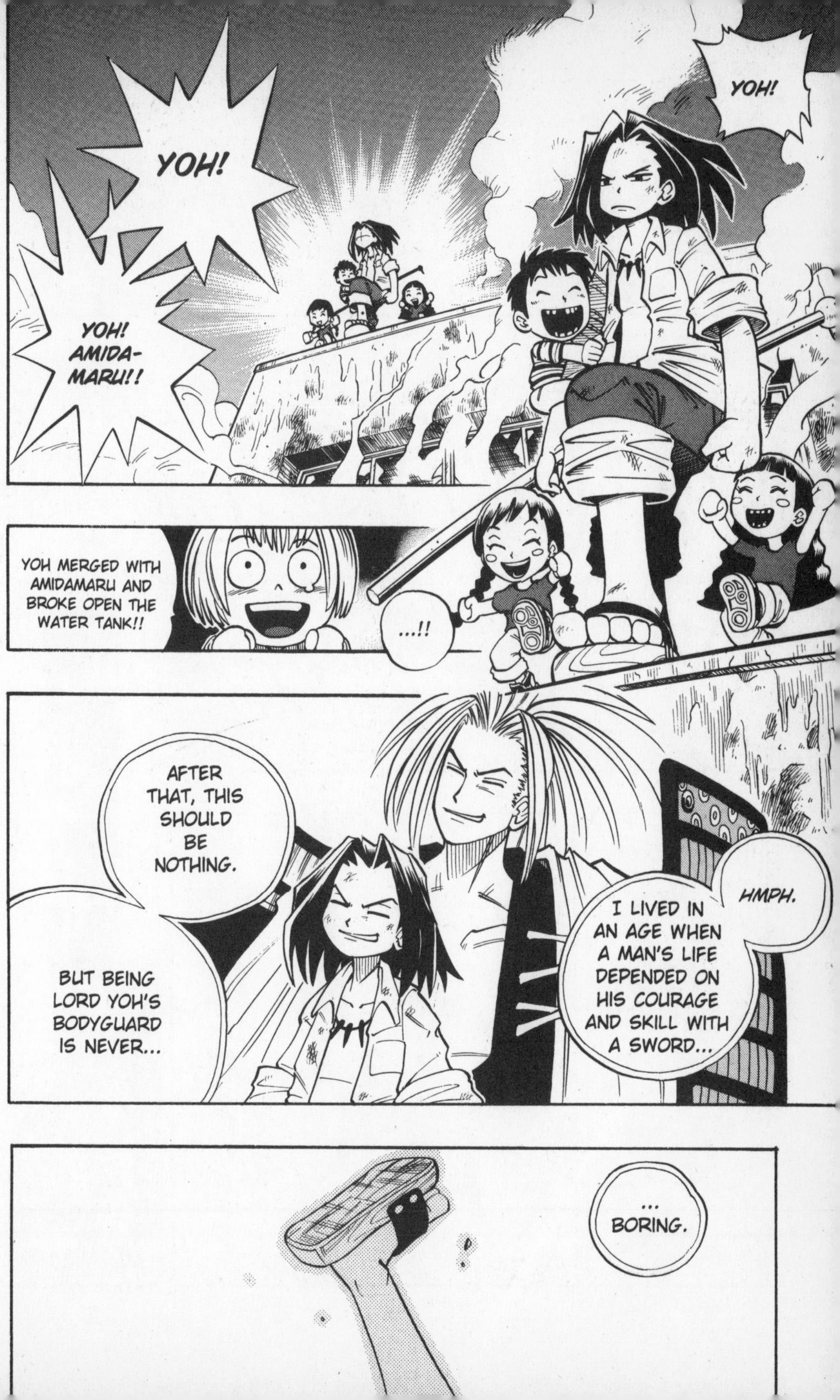
YOH!
YOH!
YOH! AMIDA-MARU!!
...!!
YOH MERGED WITH AMIDAMARU AND BROKE OPEN THE WATER TANK!!
AFTER THAT, THIS SHOULD BE NOTHING.
HMPH.
I LIVED IN AN AGE WHEN A MAN'S LIFE DEPENDED ON HIS COURAGE AND SKILL WITH A SWORD...
BUT BEING LORD YOH'S BODYGUARD IS NEVER...
... BORING.

READ THIS WAY

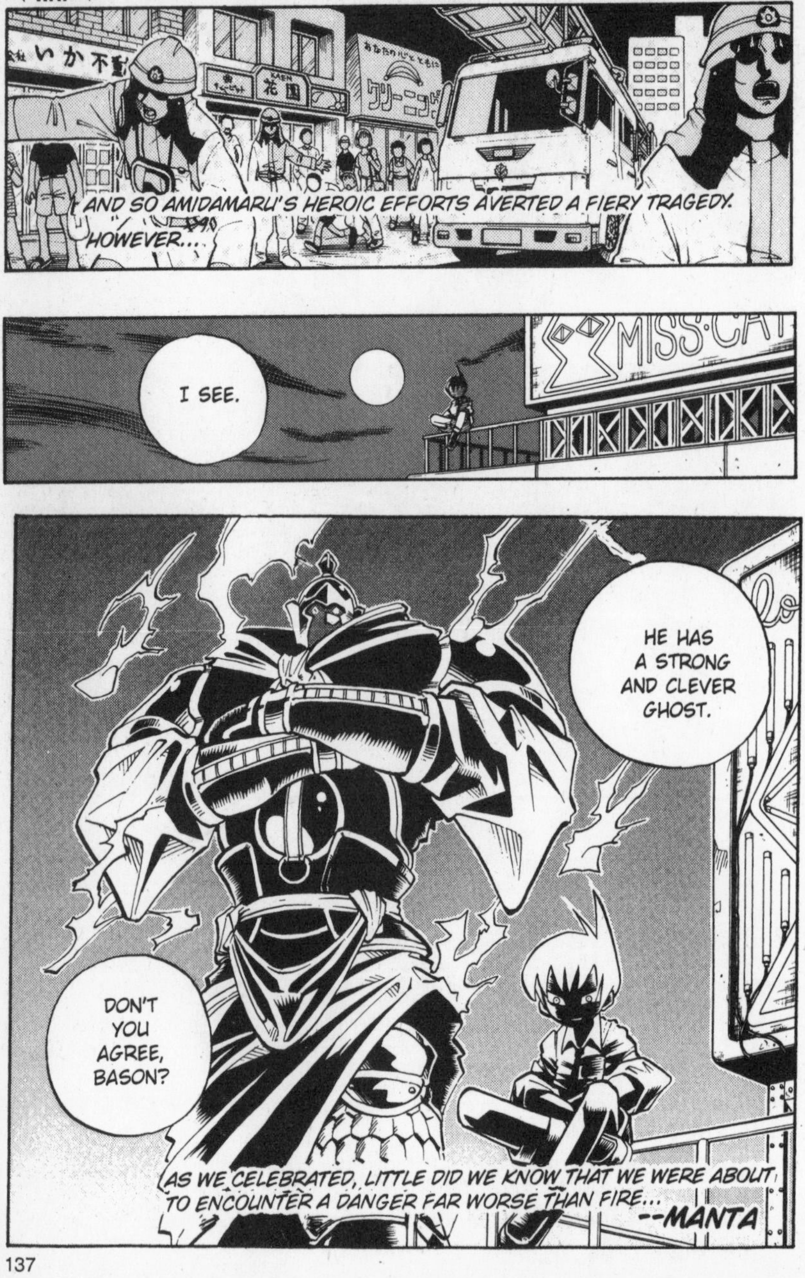
AND SO AMIDAMARU'S HEROIC EFFORTS AVERTED A FIERY TRAGEDY.
HOWEVER...
I SEE.
HE HAS A STRONG AND CLEVER GHOST.
DON'T YOU AGREE, BASON?
AS WE CELEBRATED, LITTLE DID WE KNOW THAT WE WERE ABOUT TO ENCOUNTER A DANGER FAR WORSE THAN FIRE... --MANTA

SHAMAN KING CHARACTER FILE No.3

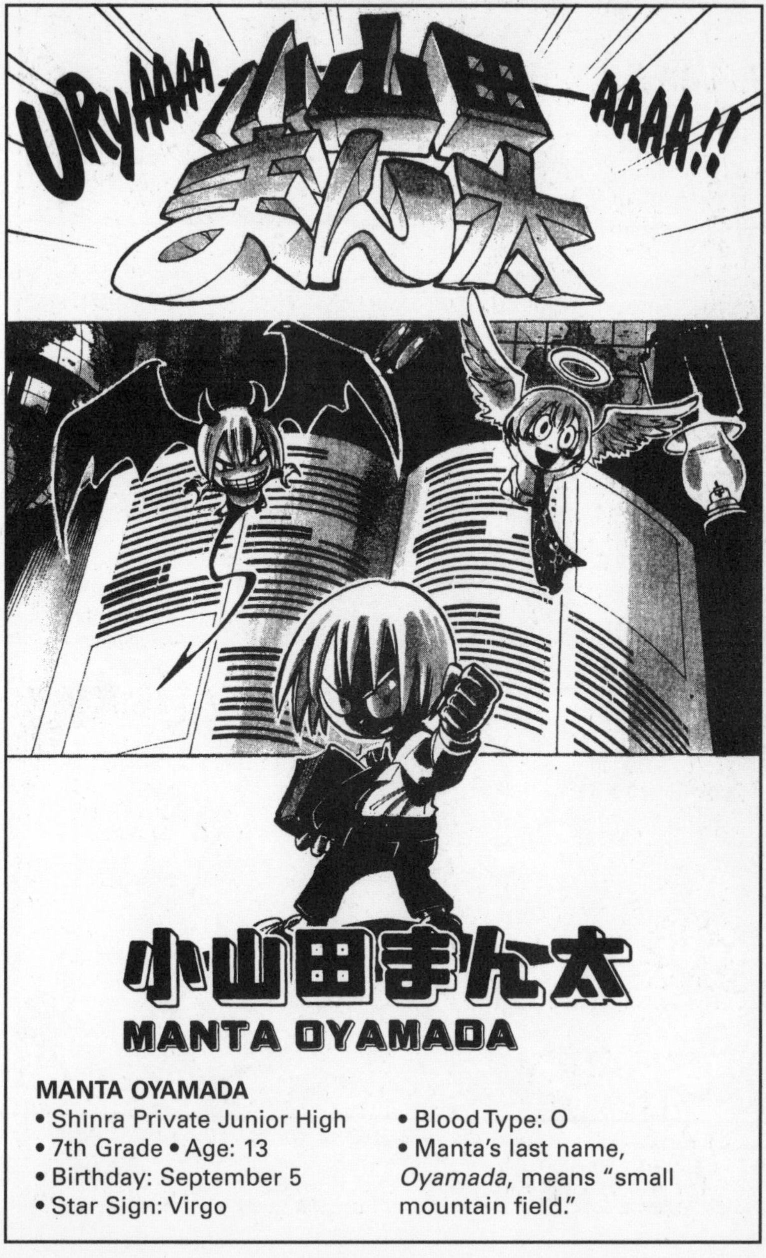
URYAAAA—
小山田まん太
—AAAA!!

小山田まん太
MANTA OYAMADA

MANTA OYAMADA

- Shinra Private Junior High
- 7th Grade • Age: 13
- Birthday: September 5
- Star Sign: Virgo
- Blood Type: O
- Manta's last name, *Oyamada*, means "small mountain field."

REINCARNATION 6: ANOTHER SHAMAN

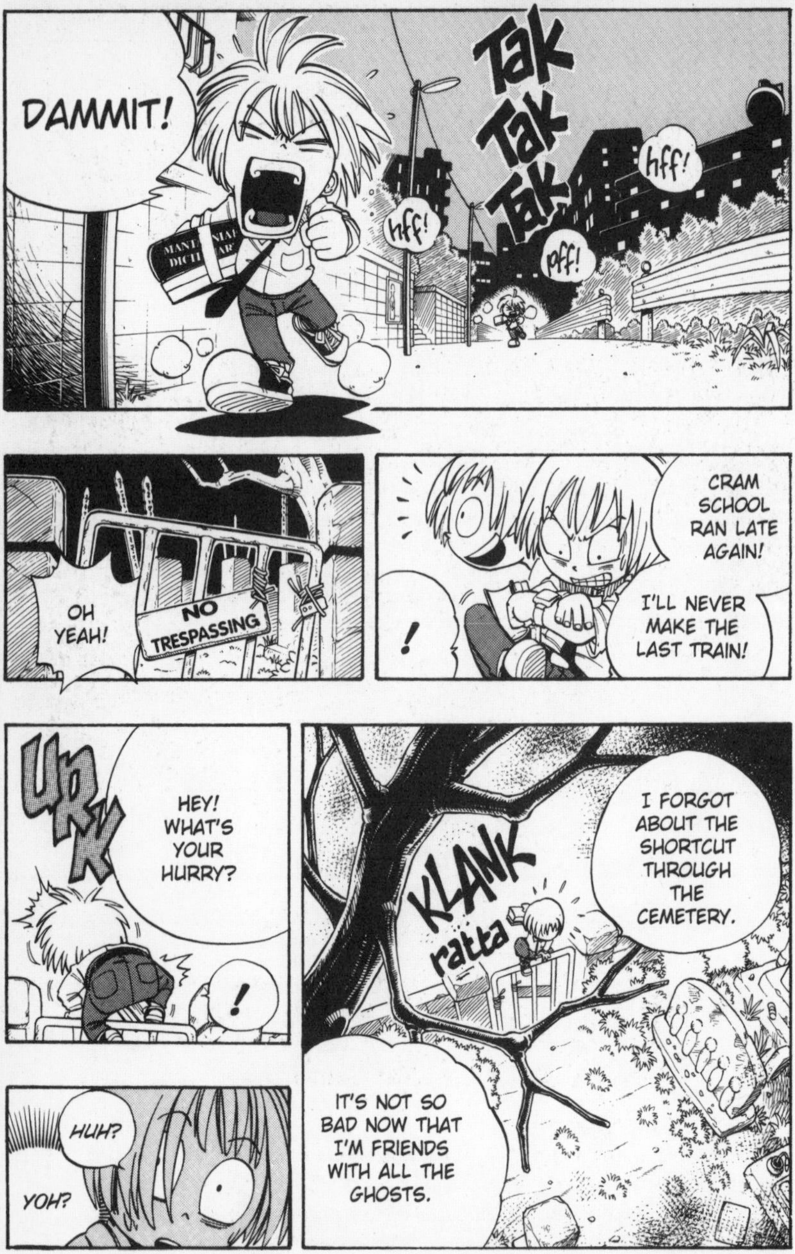
Tak
Tak
Tak
hff!
pff!
hff!
DAMMIT!
CRAM SCHOOL RAN LATE AGAIN!
I'LL NEVER MAKE THE LAST TRAIN!
!
OH YEAH!
NO TRESPASSING
I FORGOT ABOUT THE SHORTCUT THROUGH THE CEMETERY.
KLANK
ratta
IT'S NOT SO BAD NOW THAT I'M FRIENDS WITH ALL THE GHOSTS.
URK
HEY! WHAT'S YOUR HURRY?
!
HUH?
YOH?

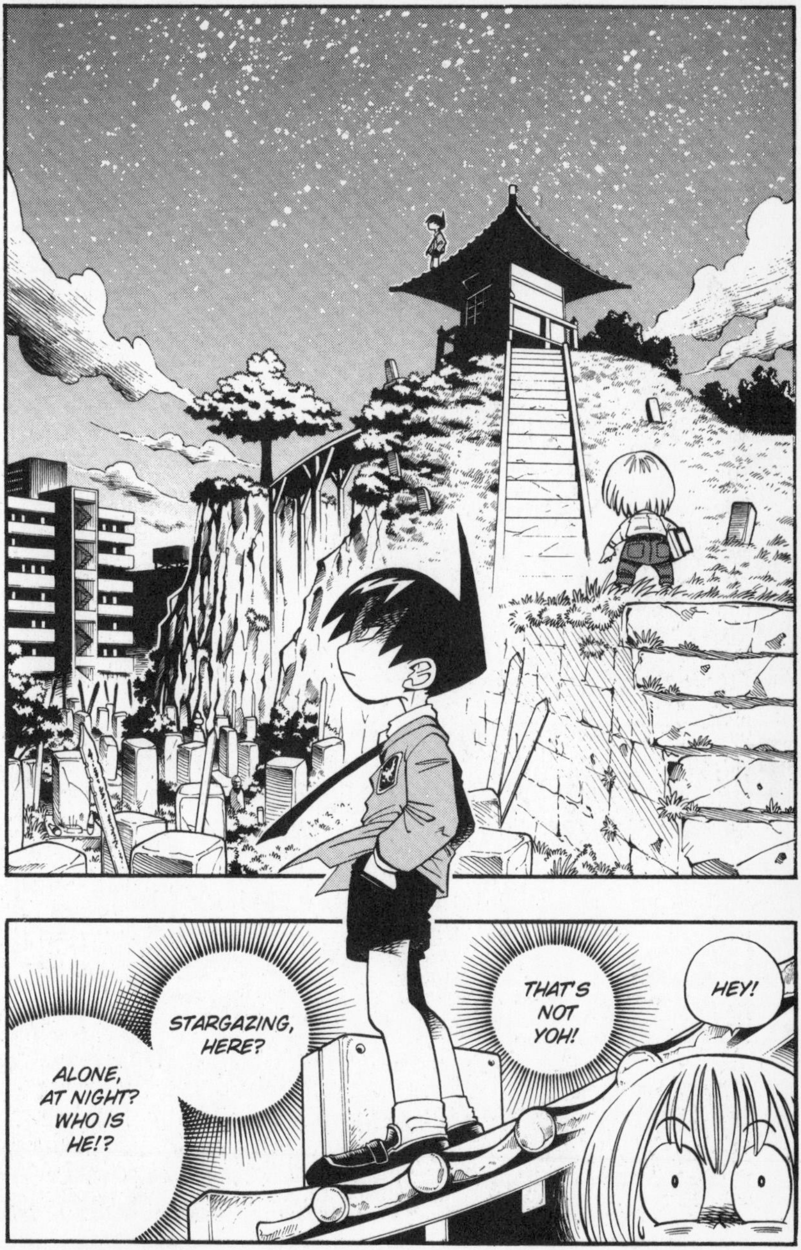
HEY!
THAT'S NOT YOH!
STARGAZING, HERE?
ALONE, AT NIGHT? WHO IS HE!?

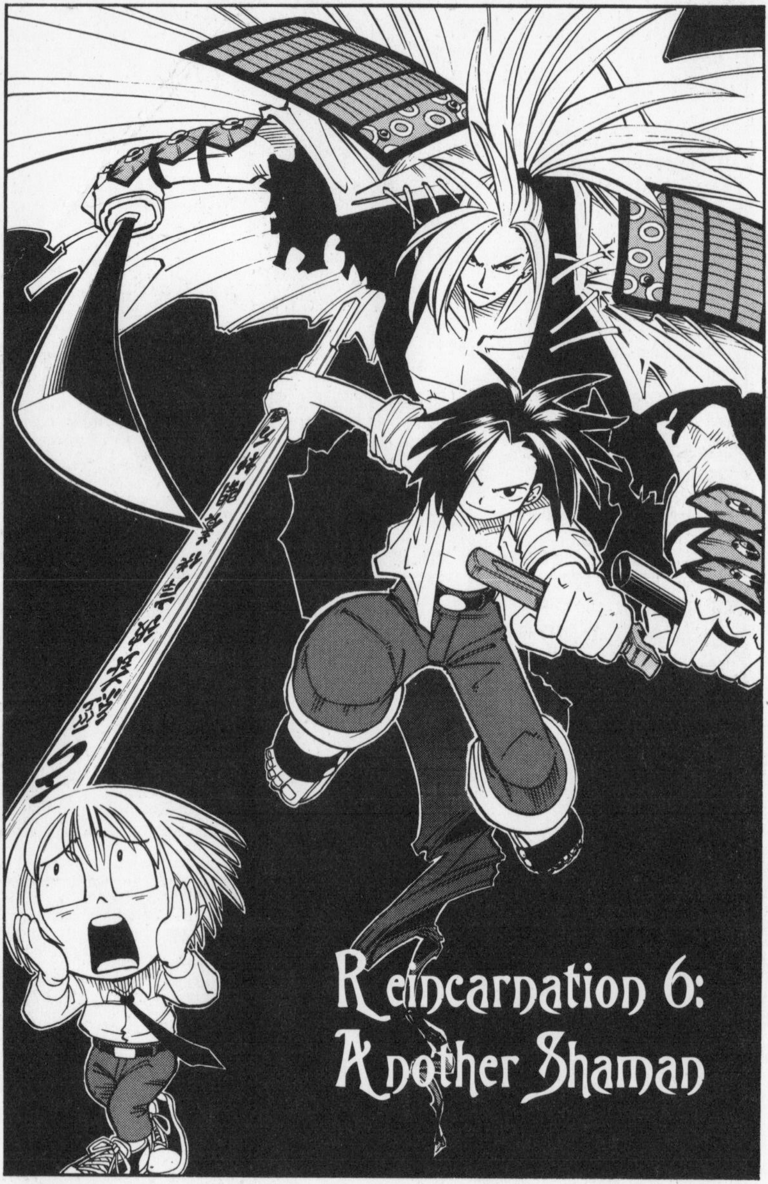
Reincarnation 6:
Another Shaman

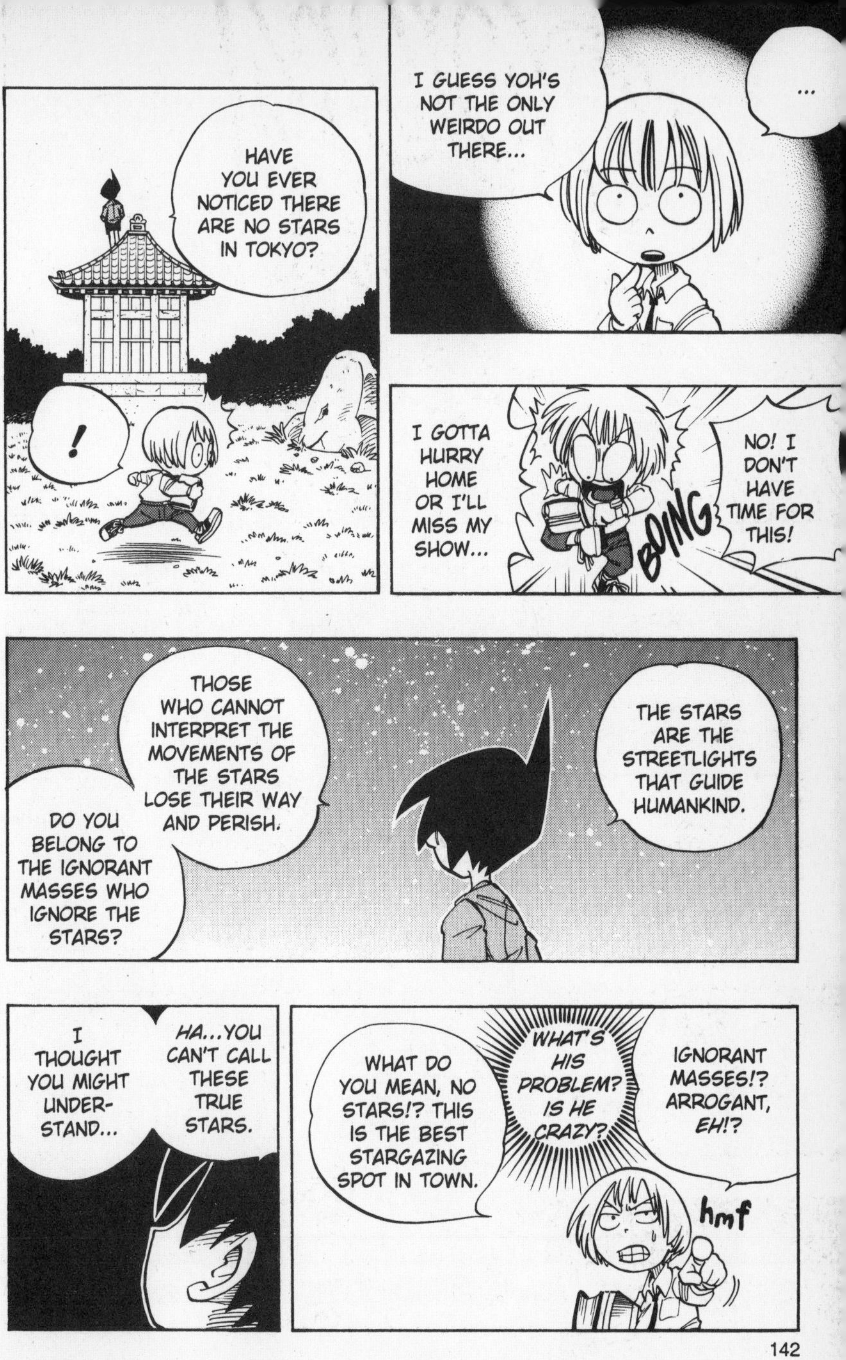
...
I GUESS YOH'S NOT THE ONLY WEIRDO OUT THERE...
NO! I DON'T HAVE TIME FOR THIS!
BOING
I GOTTA HURRY HOME OR I'LL MISS MY SHOW...
HAVE YOU EVER NOTICED THERE ARE NO STARS IN TOKYO?
!
THE STARS ARE THE STREETLIGHTS THAT GUIDE HUMANKIND.
THOSE WHO CANNOT INTERPRET THE MOVEMENTS OF THE STARS LOSE THEIR WAY AND PERISH.
DO YOU BELONG TO THE IGNORANT MASSES WHO IGNORE THE STARS?
IGNORANT MASSES!? ARROGANT, EH!?
WHAT'S HIS PROBLEM? IS HE CRAZY?
WHAT DO YOU MEAN, NO STARS!? THIS IS THE BEST STARGAZING SPOT IN TOWN.
hmf
HA...YOU CAN'T CALL THESE TRUE STARS.
I THOUGHT YOU MIGHT UNDER-STAND...

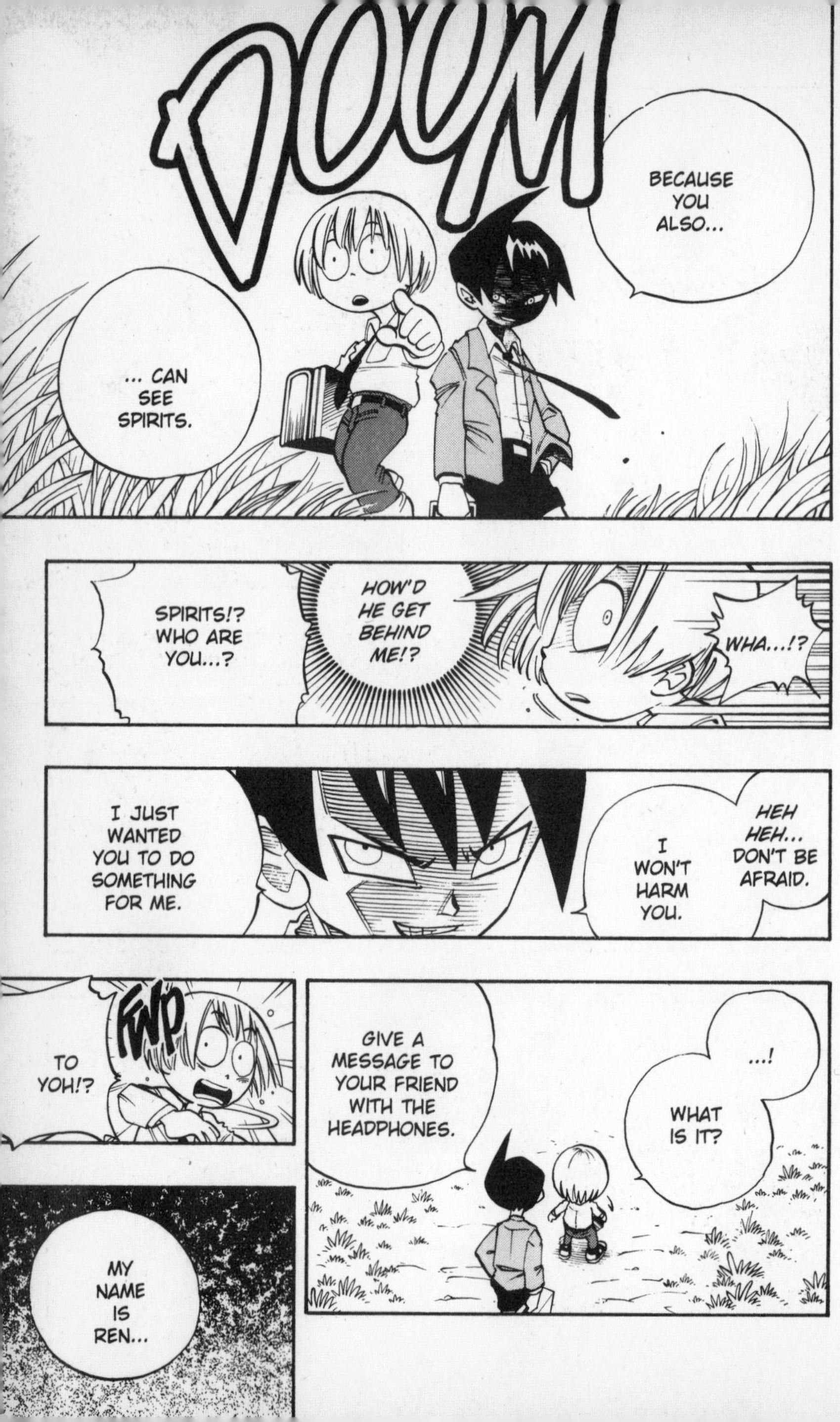
BECAUSE YOU ALSO...
DOOM
... CAN SEE SPIRITS.
WHA...!?
HOW'D HE GET BEHIND ME!?
SPIRITS!? WHO ARE YOU...?
HEH HEH... DON'T BE AFRAID.
I WON'T HARM YOU.
I JUST WANTED YOU TO DO SOMETHING FOR ME.
...!
WHAT IS IT?
GIVE A MESSAGE TO YOUR FRIEND WITH THE HEADPHONES.
FWP
TO YOH!?
MY NAME IS REN...

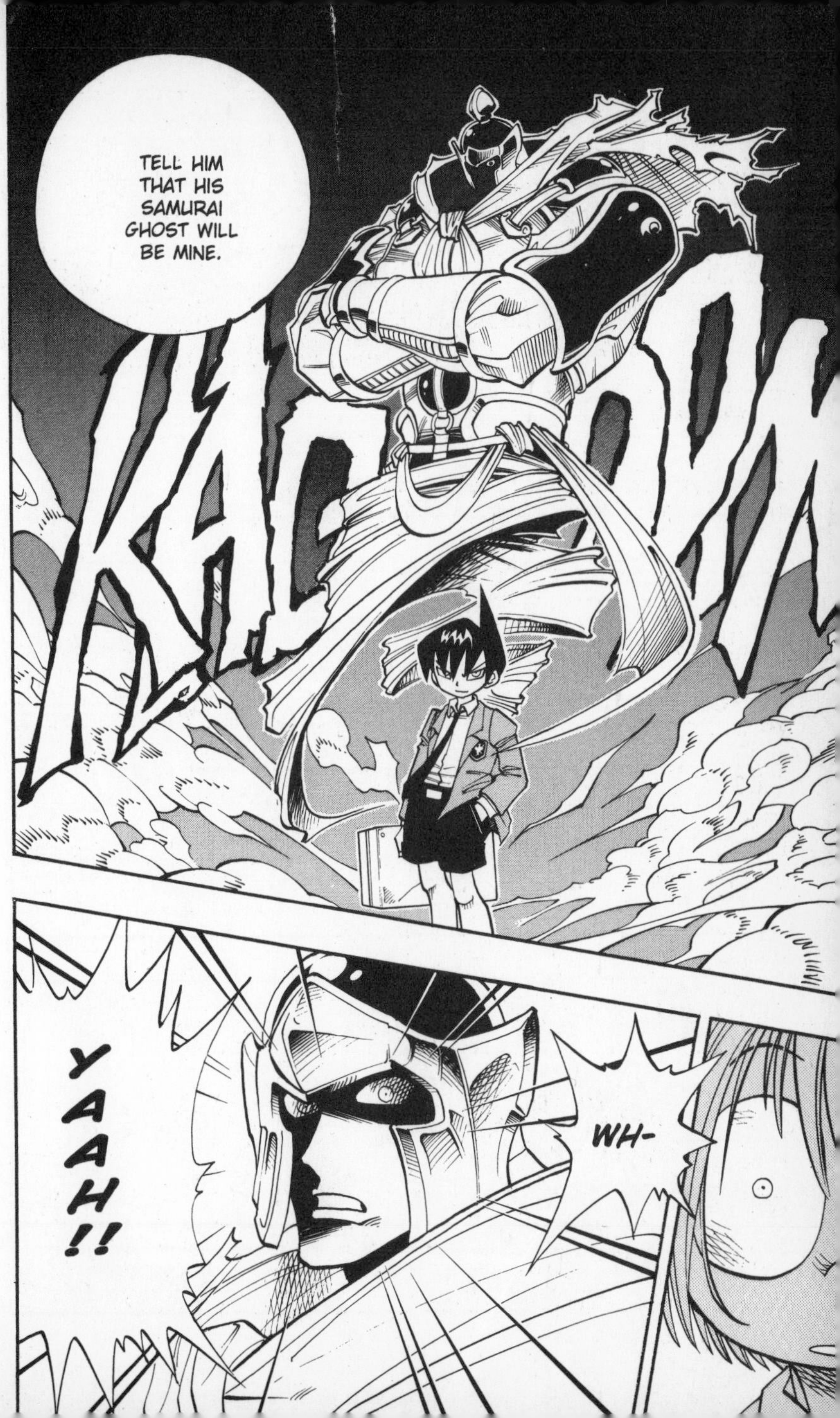
TELL HIM THAT HIS SAMURAI GHOST WILL BE MINE.
WH-
YAAAH!!

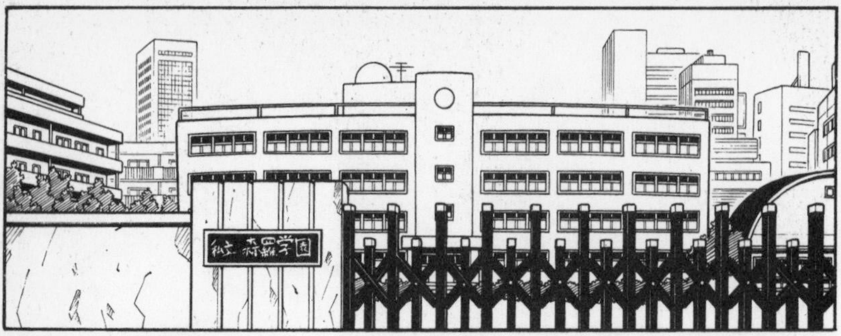

*SHINRA PRIVATE ACADEMY

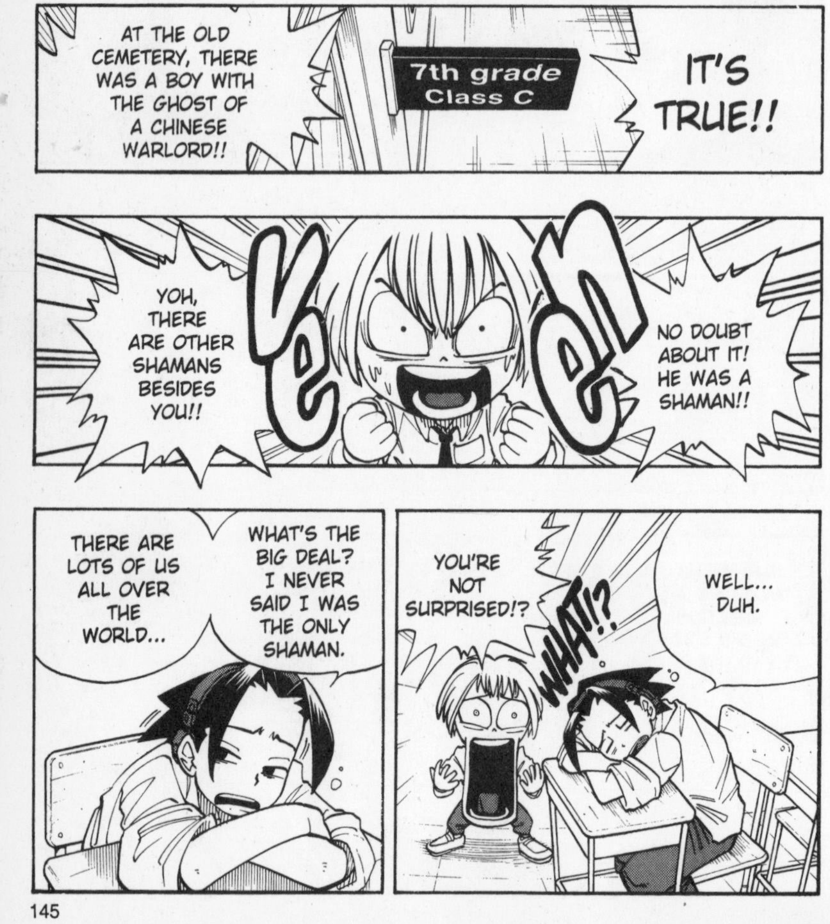
IT'S TRUE!!
7th grade Class C
AT THE OLD CEMETERY, THERE WAS A BOY WITH THE GHOST OF A CHINESE WARLORD!!
NO DOUBT ABOUT IT! HE WAS A SHAMAN!!
Yeah
YOH, THERE ARE OTHER SHAMANS BESIDES YOU!!
WELL... DUH.
WHAT!?
YOU'RE NOT SURPRISED!?
WHAT'S THE BIG DEAL? I NEVER SAID I WAS THE ONLY SHAMAN.
THERE ARE LOTS OF US ALL OVER THE WORLD...

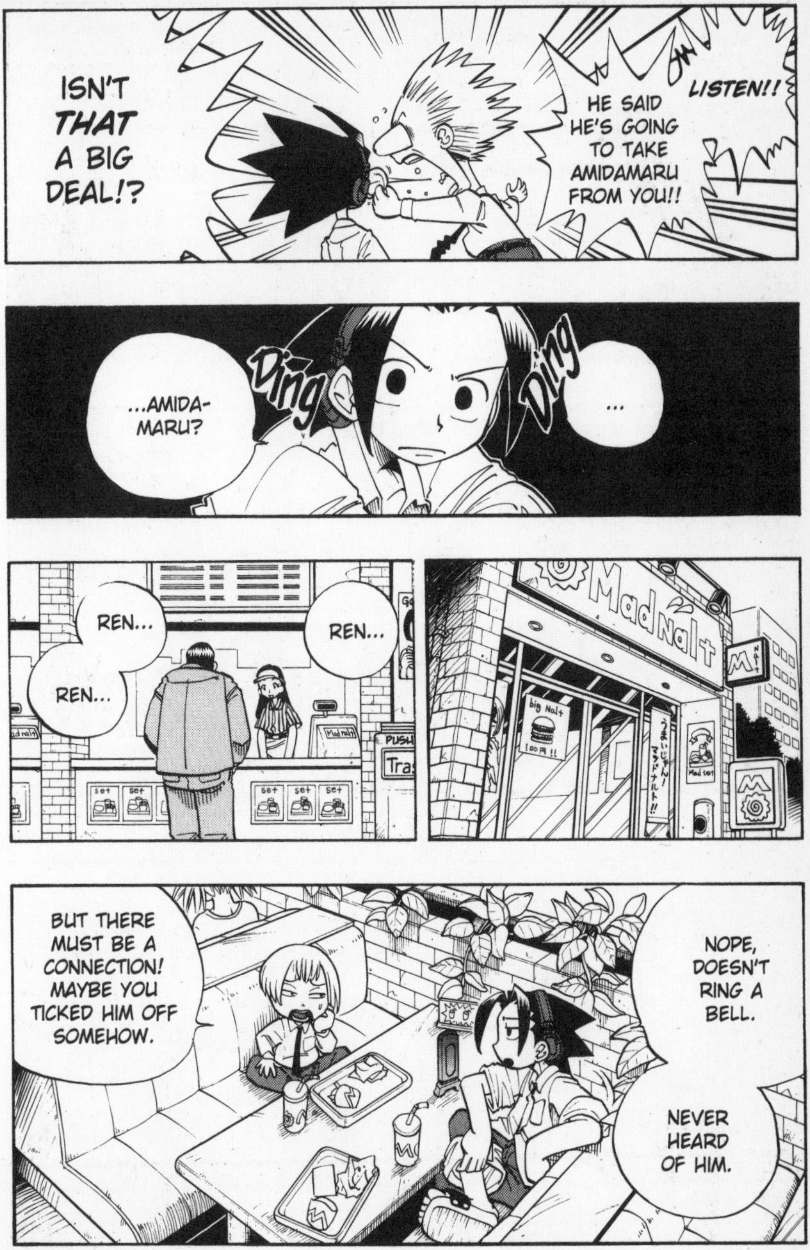
LISTEN!!
HE SAID HE'S GOING TO TAKE AMIDAMARU FROM YOU!!
ISN'T THAT A BIG DEAL!?
...
Ding
Ding
...AMIDA-MARU?
Mad Nalt
big Nalt 100円!!
うまいじゃん! マッドナルト!!
Mad set
REN...
REN...
REN...
PUSH
Tras
NOPE, DOESN'T RING A BELL.
NEVER HEARD OF HIM.
BUT THERE MUST BE A CONNECTION! MAYBE YOU TICKED HIM OFF SOMEHOW.

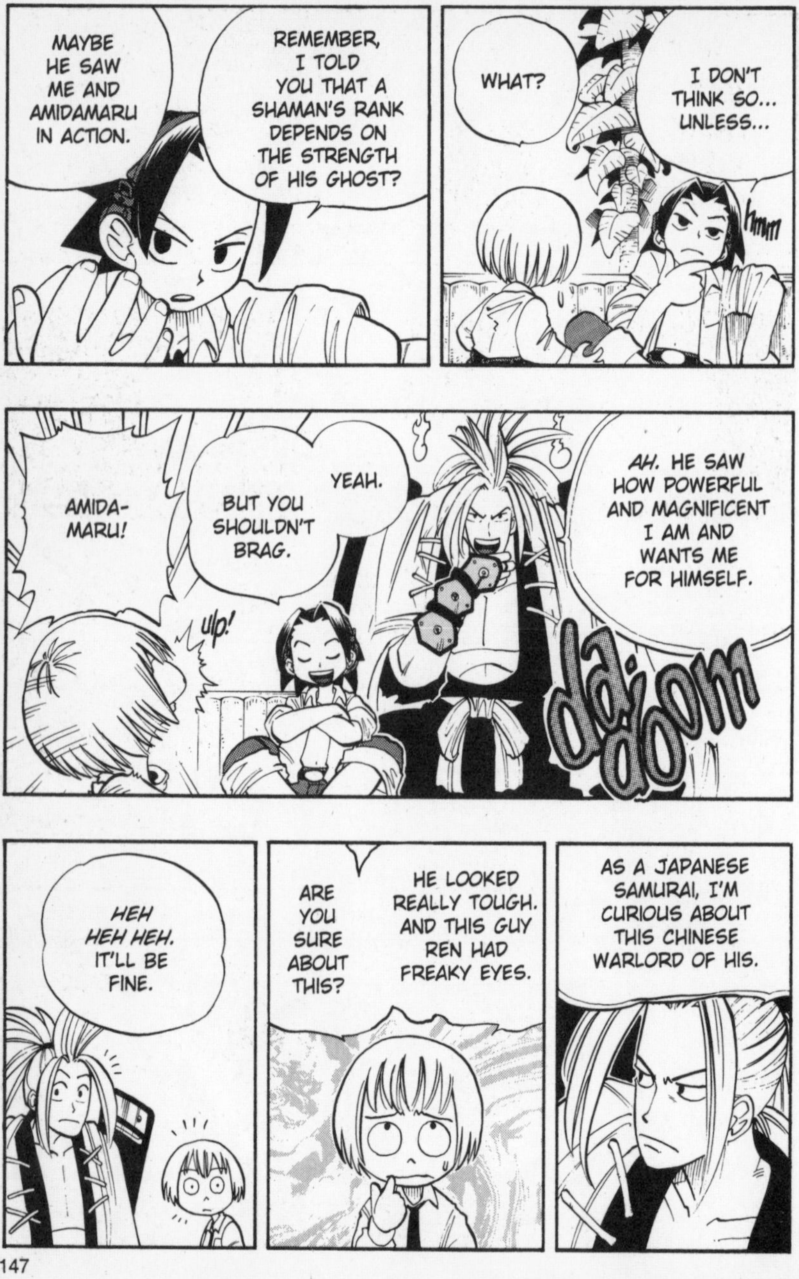
MAYBE HE SAW ME AND AMIDAMARU IN ACTION.
REMEMBER, I TOLD YOU THAT A SHAMAN'S RANK DEPENDS ON THE STRENGTH OF HIS GHOST?
WHAT?
I DON'T THINK SO... UNLESS...
hmm
AMIDA-MARU!
ulp!
YEAH.
BUT YOU SHOULDN'T BRAG.
AH. HE SAW HOW POWERFUL AND MAGNIFICENT I AM AND WANTS ME FOR HIMSELF.
da doom
HEH HEH HEH. IT'LL BE FINE.
ARE YOU SURE ABOUT THIS?
HE LOOKED REALLY TOUGH. AND THIS GUY REN HAD FREAKY EYES.
AS A JAPANESE SAMURAI, I'M CURIOUS ABOUT THIS CHINESE WARLORD OF HIS.

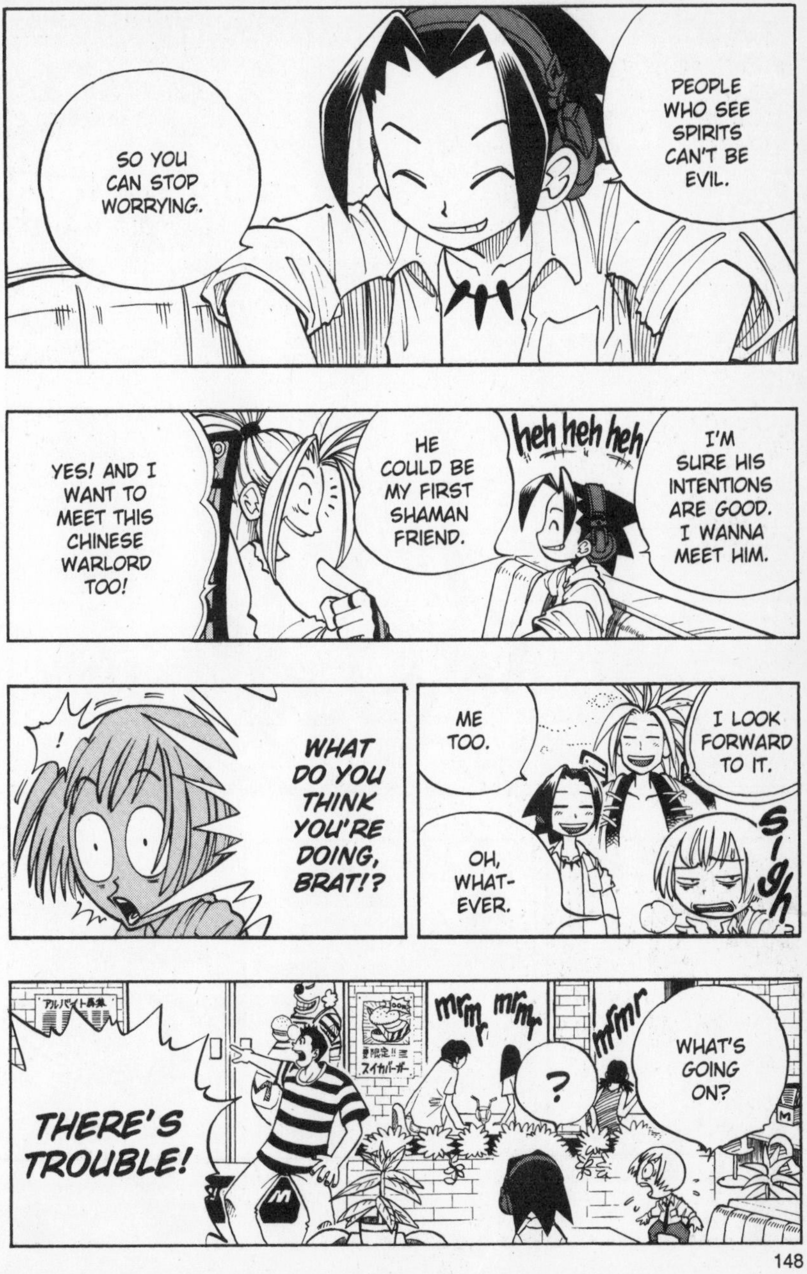
PEOPLE WHO SEE SPIRITS CAN'T BE EVIL.
SO YOU CAN STOP WORRYING.
I'M SURE HIS INTENTIONS ARE GOOD. I WANNA MEET HIM.
heh heh heh
HE COULD BE MY FIRST SHAMAN FRIEND.
YES! AND I WANT TO MEET THIS CHINESE WARLORD TOO!
I LOOK FORWARD TO IT.
ME TOO.
sigh
OH, WHAT-EVER.
!
WHAT DO YOU THINK YOU'RE DOING, BRAT!?
WHAT'S GOING ON?
mfmr
mrmr mrmr
?
アルバイト募集
スイカバーガー
THERE'S TROUBLE!

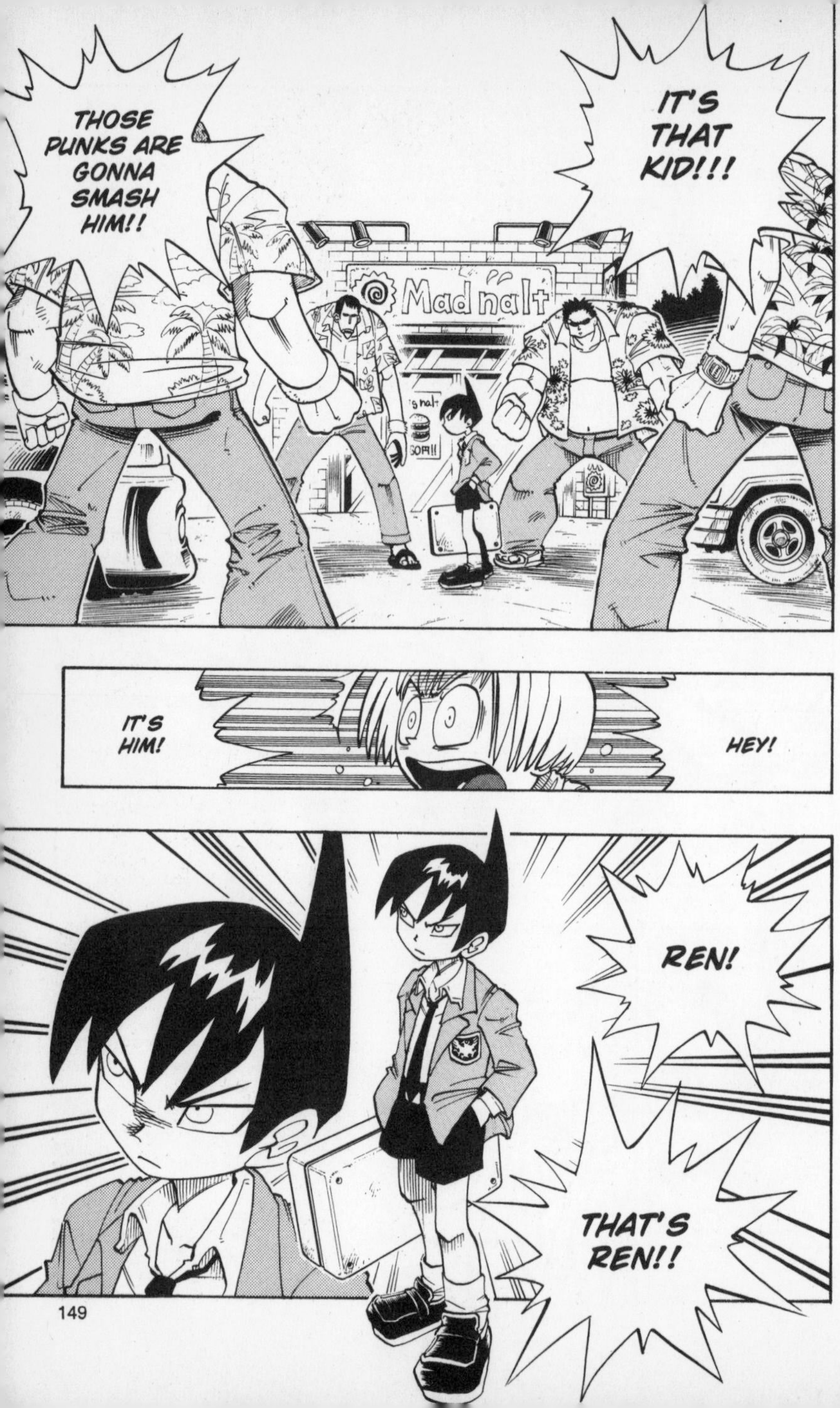
IT'S THAT KID!!!
THOSE PUNKS ARE GONNA SMASH HIM!!
Mad nalt
HEY!
IT'S HIM!
REN!
THAT'S REN!!

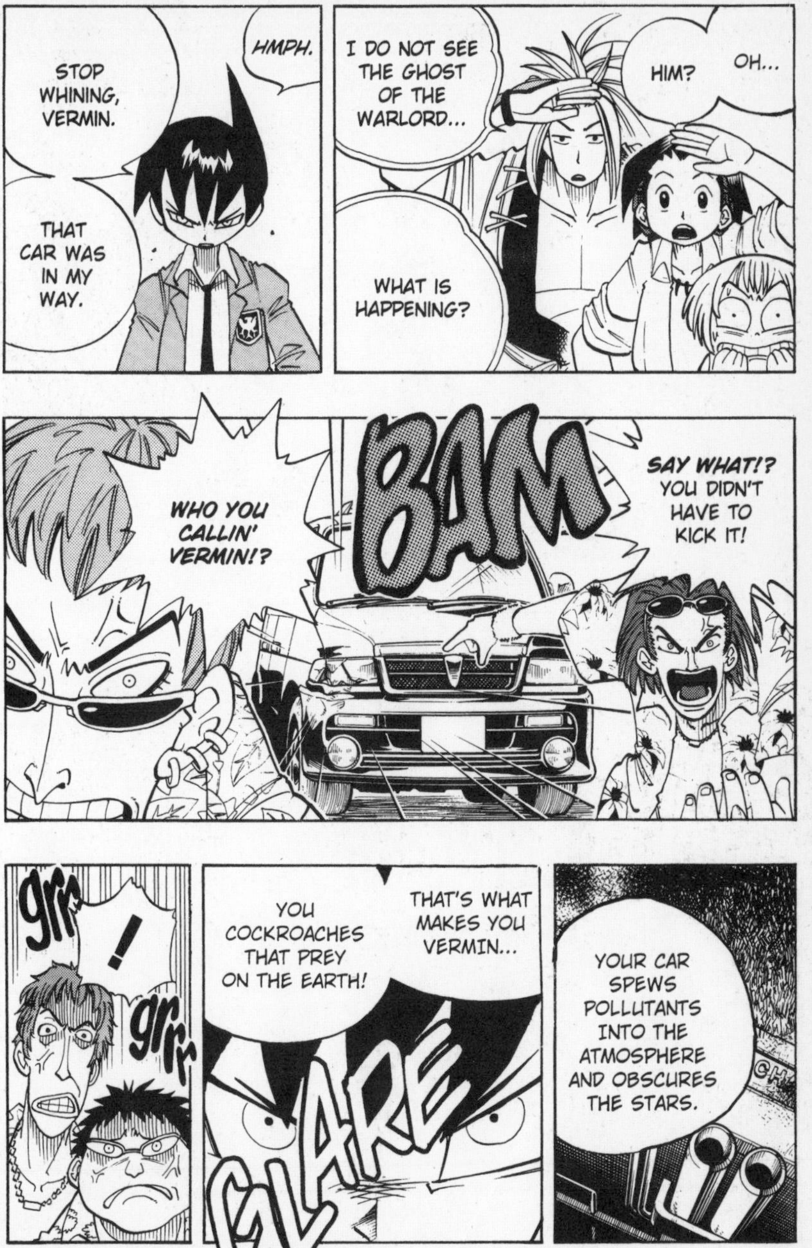
OH...
HIM?
I DO NOT SEE THE GHOST OF THE WARLORD...
WHAT IS HAPPENING?
HMPH.
STOP WHINING, VERMIN.
THAT CAR WAS IN MY WAY.
SAY WHAT!? YOU DIDN'T HAVE TO KICK IT!
BAM
WHO YOU CALLIN' VERMIN!?
YOUR CAR SPEWS POLLUTANTS INTO THE ATMOSPHERE AND OBSCURES THE STARS.
THAT'S WHAT MAKES YOU VERMIN...
YOU COCKROACHES THAT PREY ON THE EARTH!
GLARE
grr
!
grrr

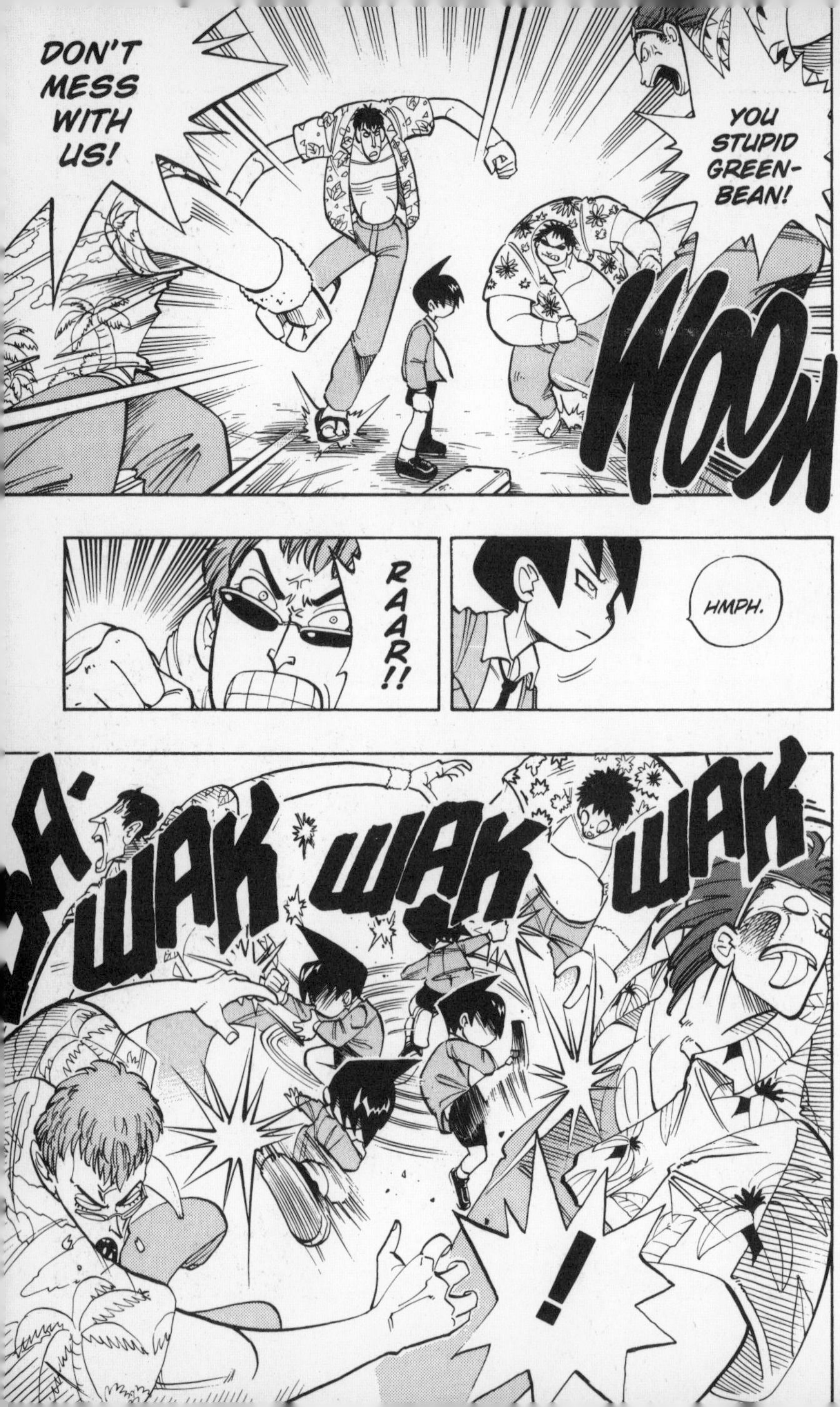

YOU STUPID GREEN-BEAN!
DON'T MESS WITH US!
WOOM
HMPH.
RAAAR!!
WAK
WAK
WAK
!

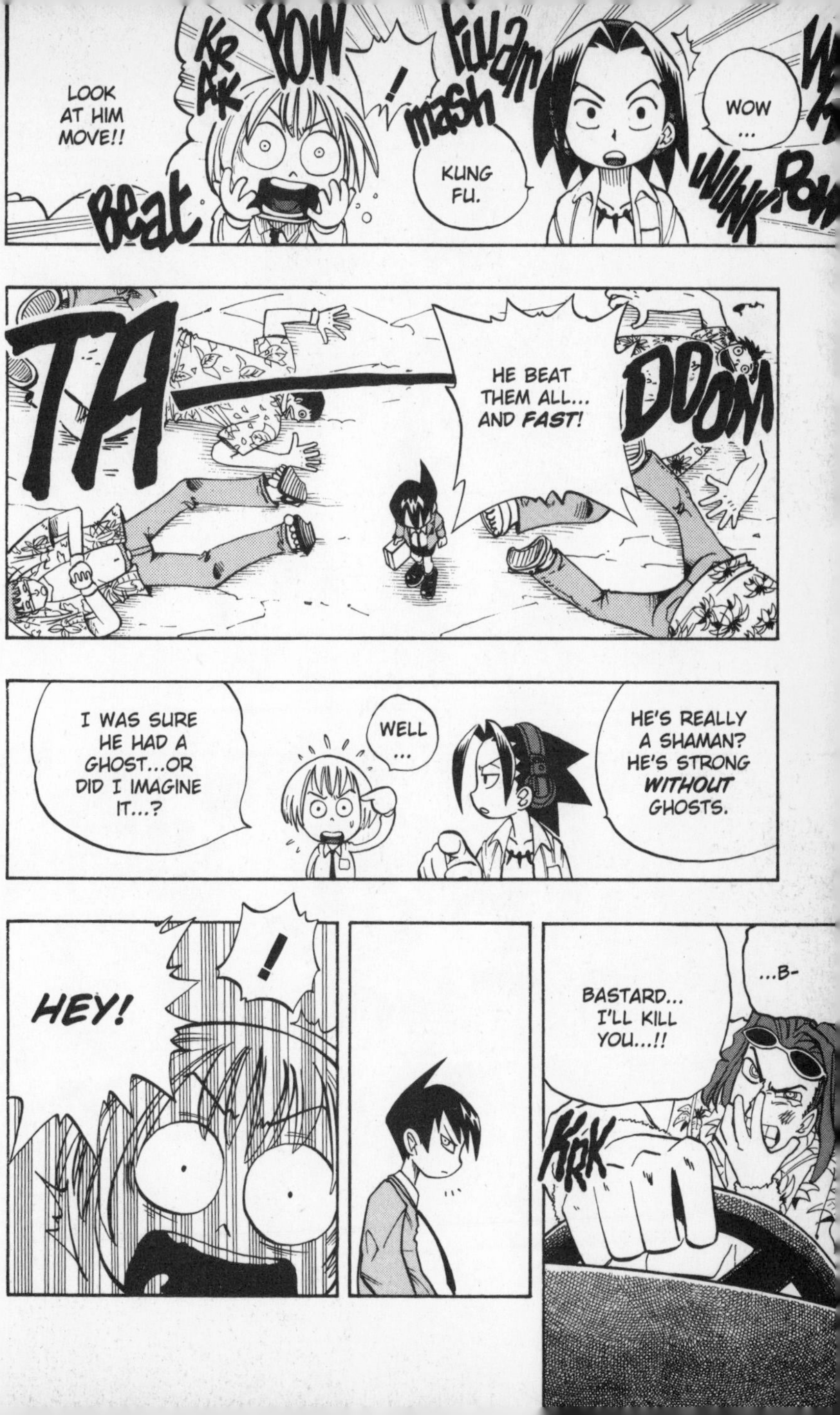
WOW ...
KUNG FU.
mash
POW
KRAK
LOOK AT HIM MOVE!!
Beat
DOOM
HE BEAT THEM ALL... AND *FAST*!
TA—
HE'S REALLY A SHAMAN? HE'S STRONG *WITHOUT* GHOSTS.
WELL ...
I WAS SURE HE HAD A GHOST...OR DID I IMAGINE IT...?
...B-
BASTARD... I'LL KILL YOU...!!
KRK
!
HEY!

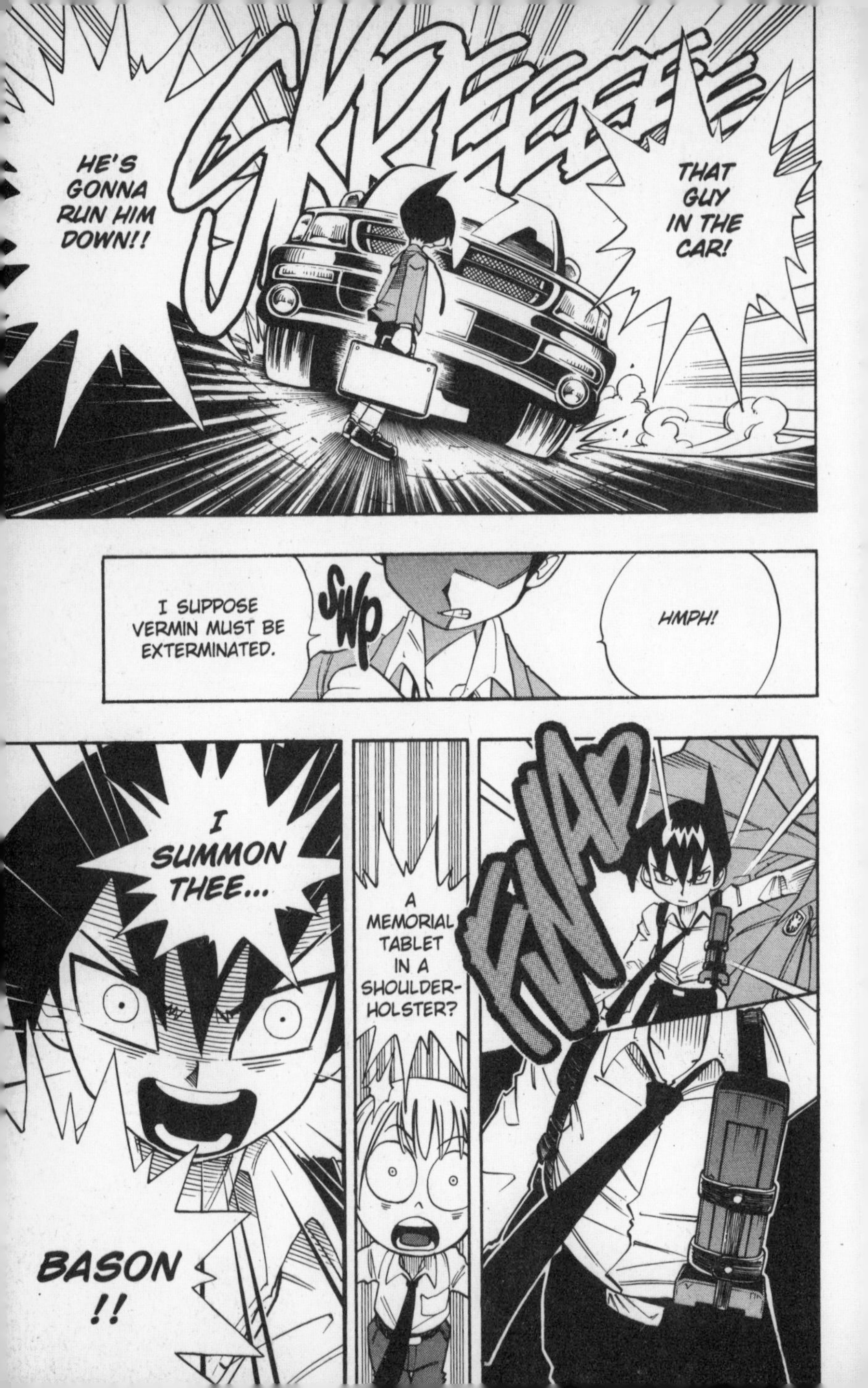
THAT GUY IN THE CAR!
HE'S GONNA RUN HIM DOWN!!
HMPH!
SWP
I SUPPOSE VERMIN MUST BE EXTERMINATED.
A MEMORIAL TABLET IN A SHOULDER-HOLSTER?
I SUMMON THEE...
BASON !!

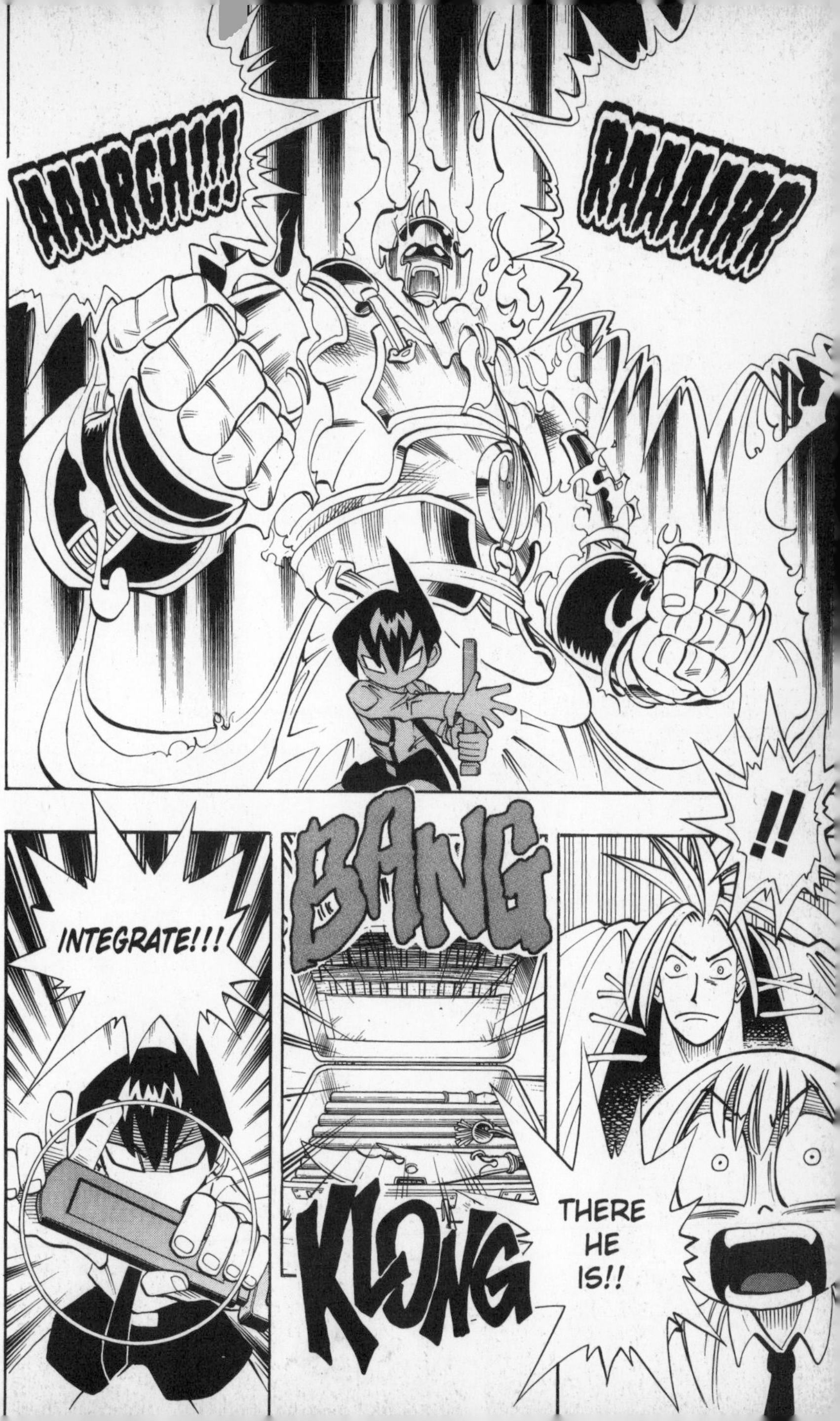
RAAAARR
AAARGH!!!!
!!
THERE HE IS!!
BANG
KLONG
INTEGRATE!!!

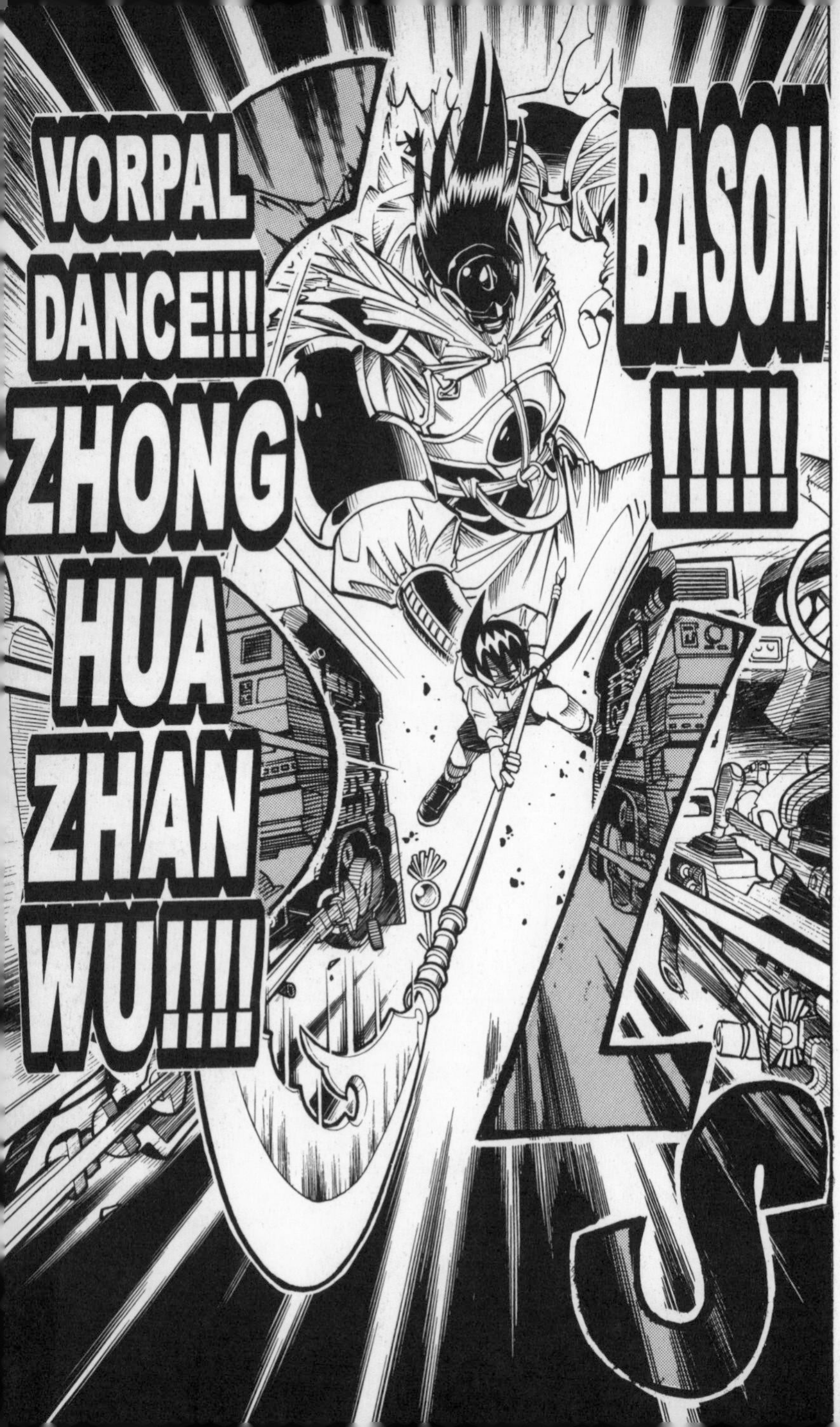
BASON!!!!!
VORPAL DANCE!!! ZHONG HUA ZHAN WU!!!!

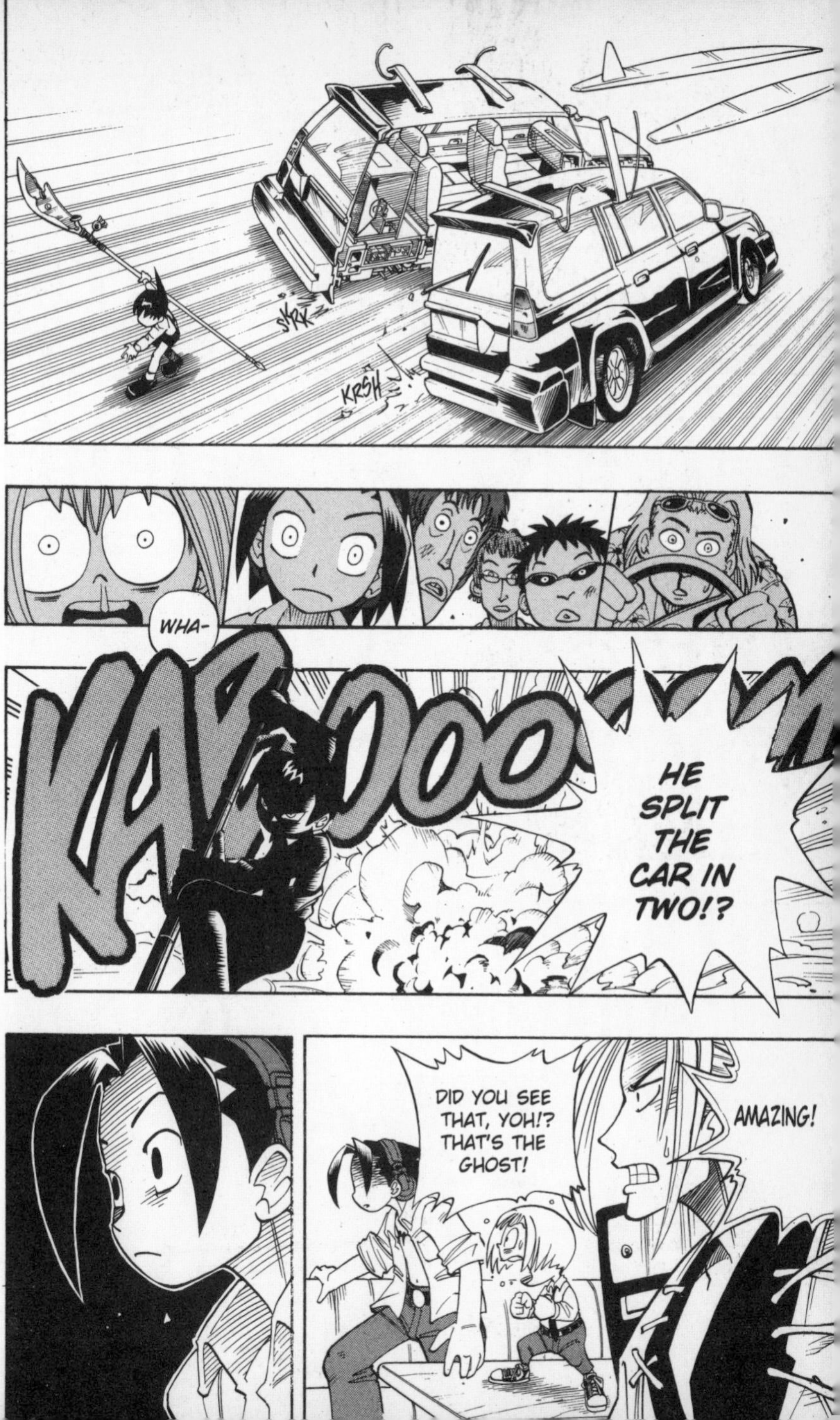
SKRK
KRSH
WHA-
HE SPLIT THE CAR IN TWO!?
AMAZING!
DID YOU SEE THAT, YOH!? THAT'S THE GHOST!

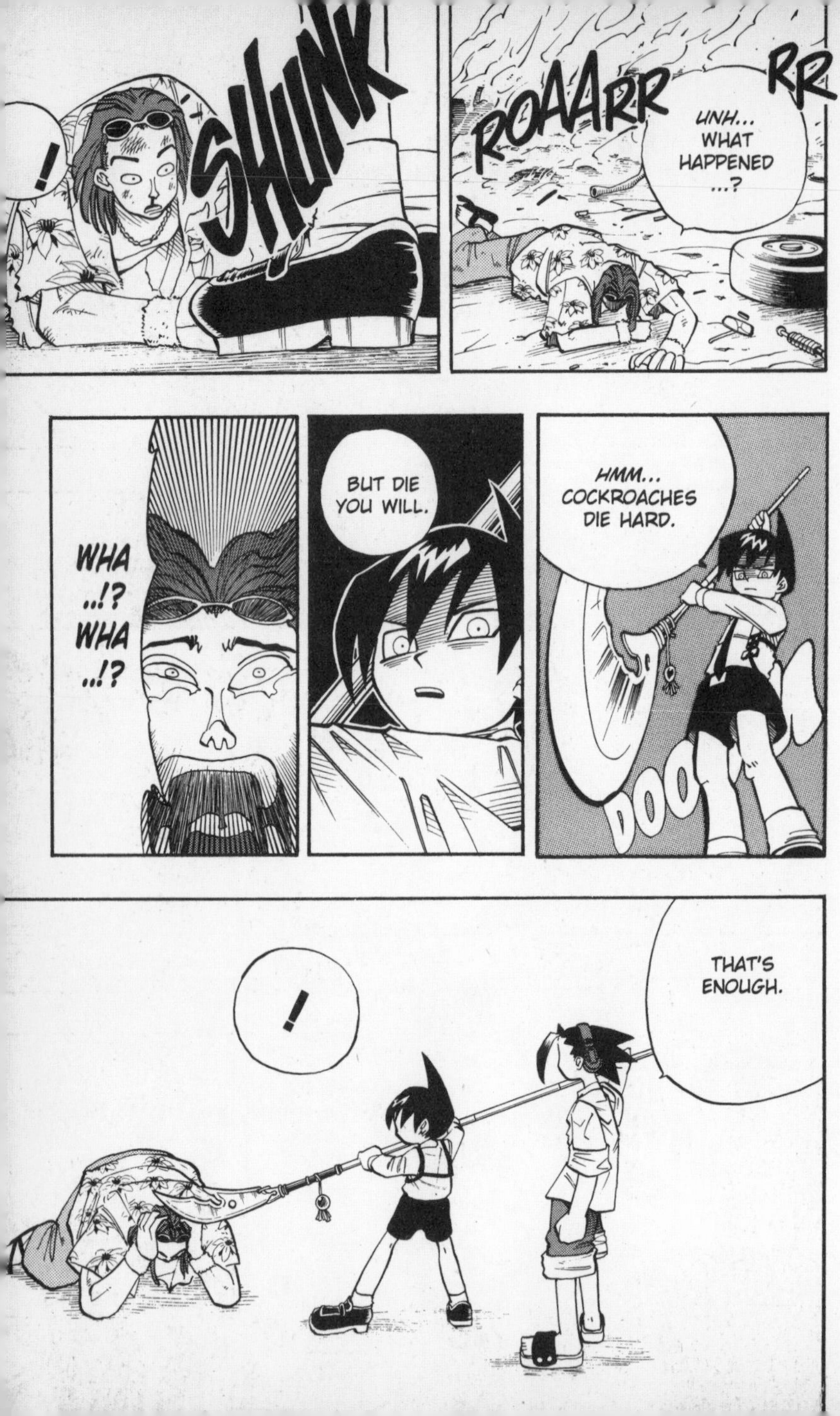
ROAAARR RR
UNH... WHAT HAPPENED ...?
SHUNK
!
HMM... COCKROACHES DIE HARD.
DOO
BUT DIE YOU WILL.
WHA ..!? WHA ..!?
THAT'S ENOUGH.
!

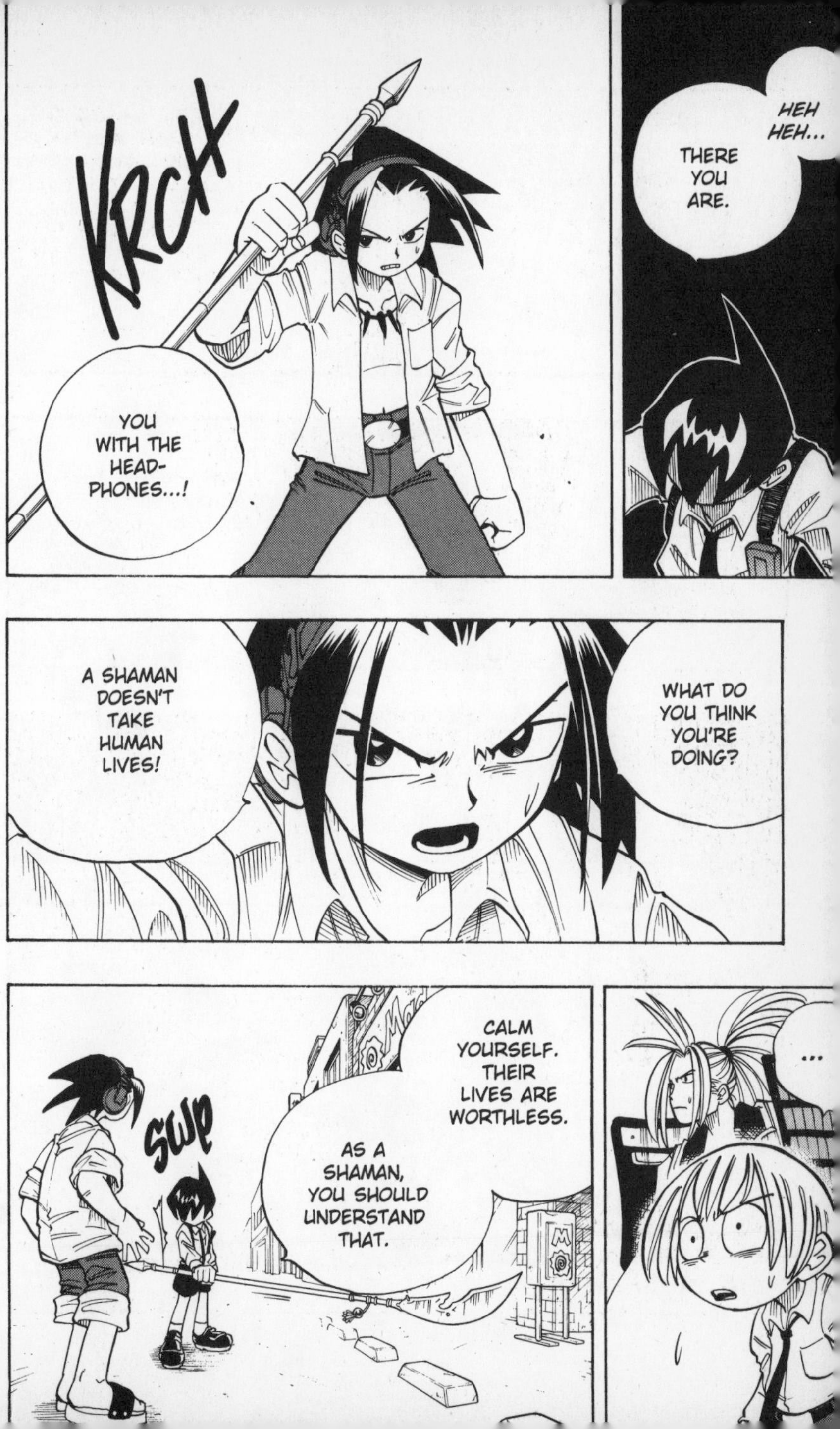
HEH HEH...
THERE YOU ARE.
KRCH
YOU WITH THE HEAD-PHONES...!
WHAT DO YOU THINK YOU'RE DOING?
A SHAMAN DOESN'T TAKE HUMAN LIVES!
...
CALM YOURSELF. THEIR LIVES ARE WORTHLESS.
SWP
AS A SHAMAN, YOU SHOULD UNDERSTAND THAT.

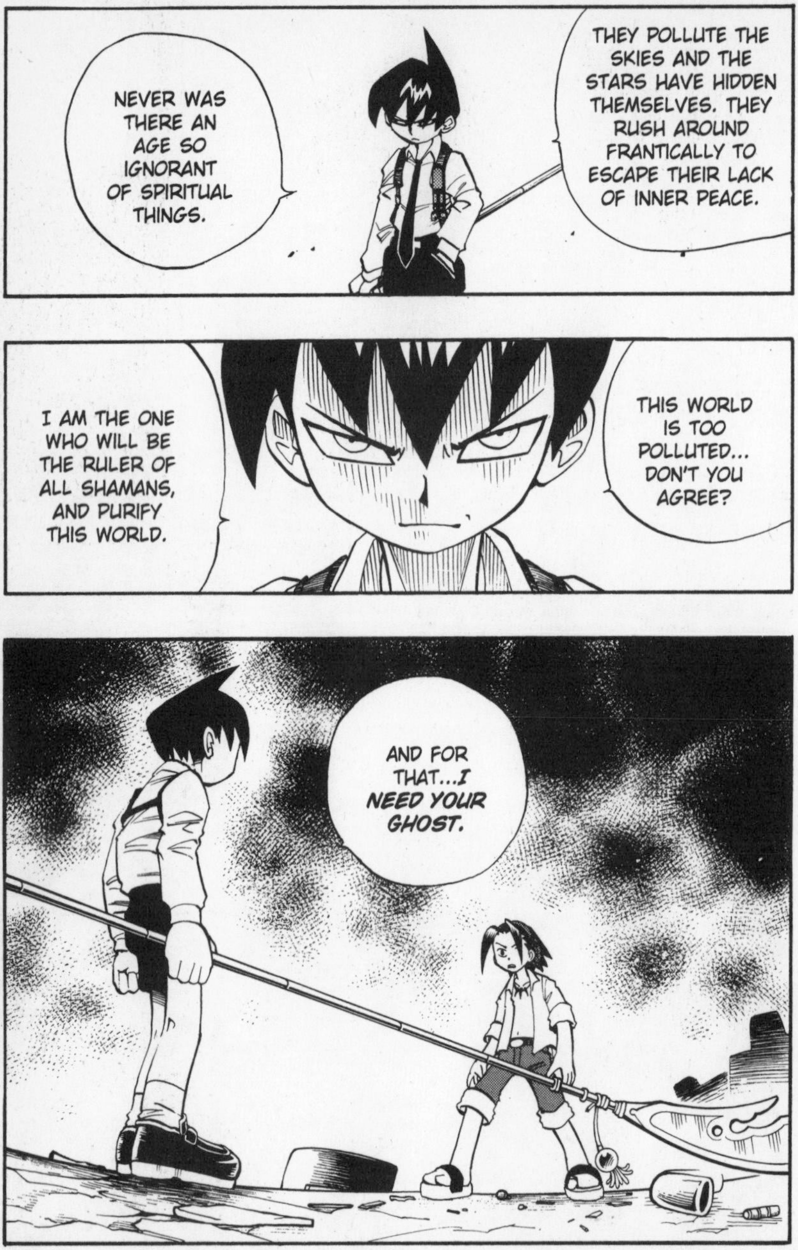
THEY POLLUTE THE SKIES AND THE STARS HAVE HIDDEN THEMSELVES. THEY RUSH AROUND FRANTICALLY TO ESCAPE THEIR LACK OF INNER PEACE.
NEVER WAS THERE AN AGE SO IGNORANT OF SPIRITUAL THINGS.
THIS WORLD IS TOO POLLUTED... DON'T YOU AGREE?
I AM THE ONE WHO WILL BE THE RULER OF ALL SHAMANS, AND PURIFY THIS WORLD.
AND FOR THAT...*I NEED YOUR GHOST.*

SHAMAN
KING
1

**MEMORIAL
TABLET**

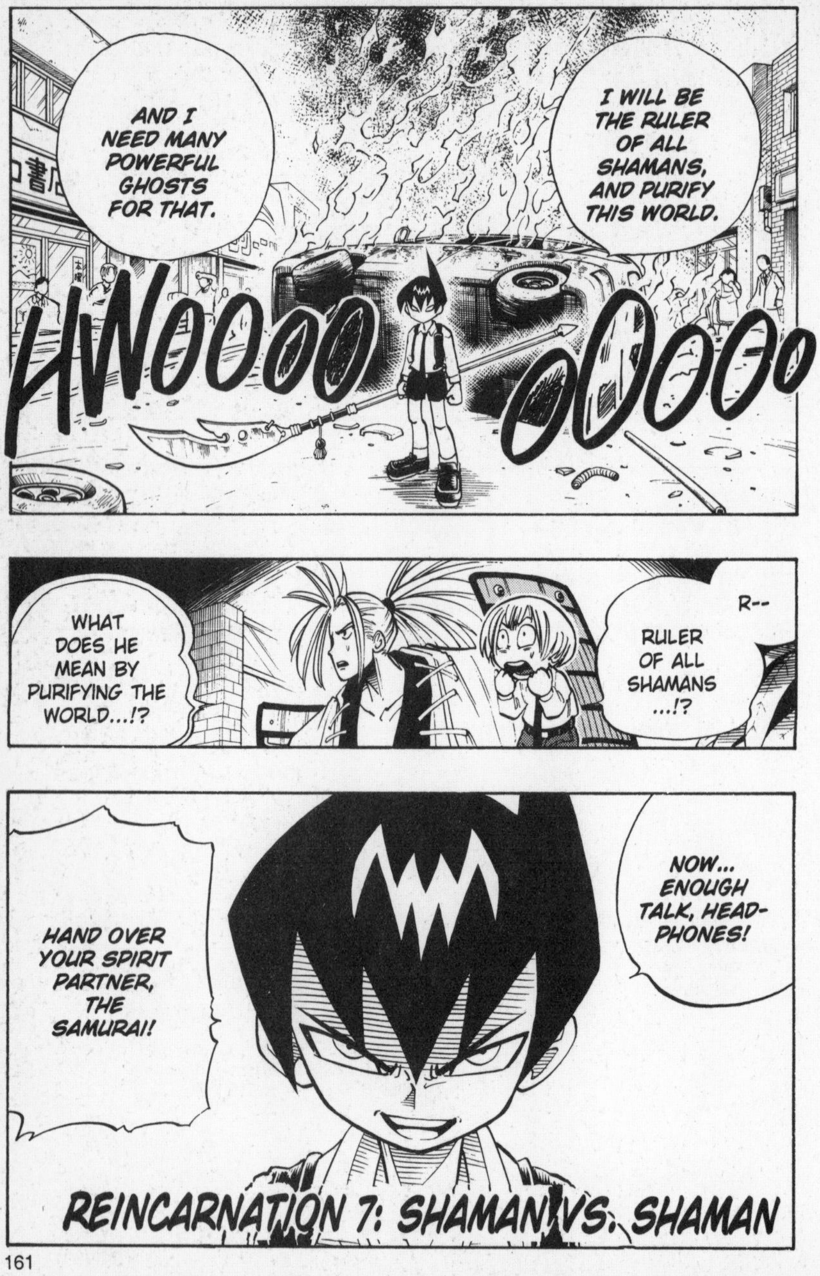
I WILL BE THE RULER OF ALL SHAMANS, AND PURIFY THIS WORLD.
AND I NEED MANY POWERFUL GHOSTS FOR THAT.
HWOOOOOOOOOO
R--
RULER OF ALL SHAMANS ...!?
WHAT DOES HE MEAN BY PURIFYING THE WORLD...!?
NOW... ENOUGH TALK, HEAD-PHONES!
HAND OVER YOUR SPIRIT PARTNER, THE SAMURAI!
REINCARNATION 7: SHAMAN VS. SHAMAN

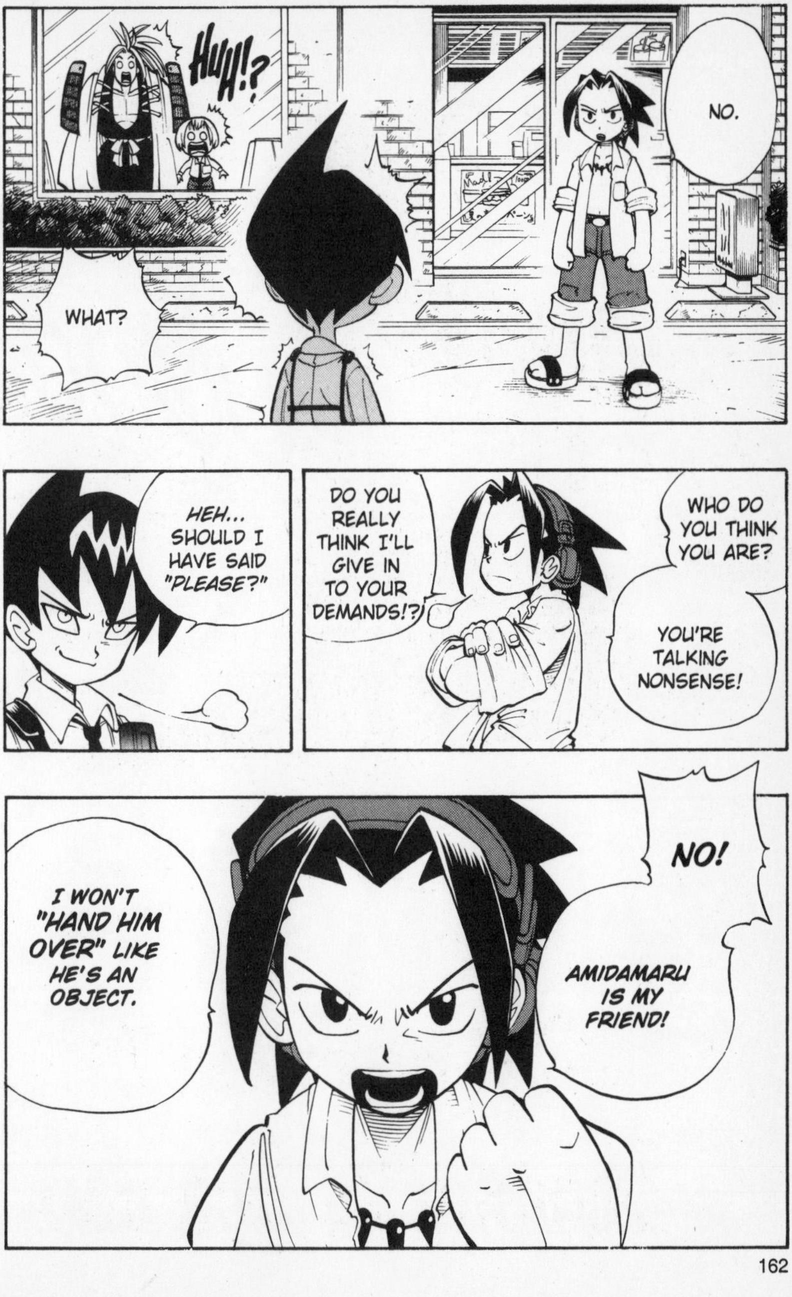
NO.
HUH!?
WHAT?
WHO DO YOU THINK YOU ARE?
YOU'RE TALKING NONSENSE!
DO YOU REALLY THINK I'LL GIVE IN TO YOUR DEMANDS!?
HEH... SHOULD I HAVE SAID "PLEASE?"
NO!
AMIDAMARU IS MY FRIEND!
I WON'T "HAND HIM OVER" LIKE HE'S AN OBJECT.

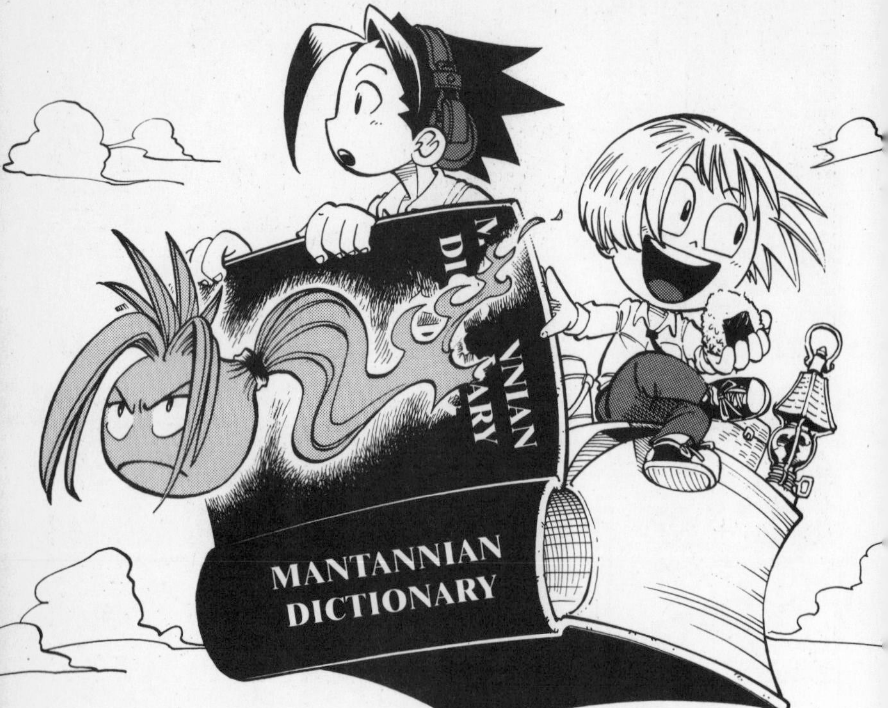
MANTANNIAN
DICTIONARY
MANTANNIAN
DICTIONARY

Reincarnation 7:
Shaman vs Shaman

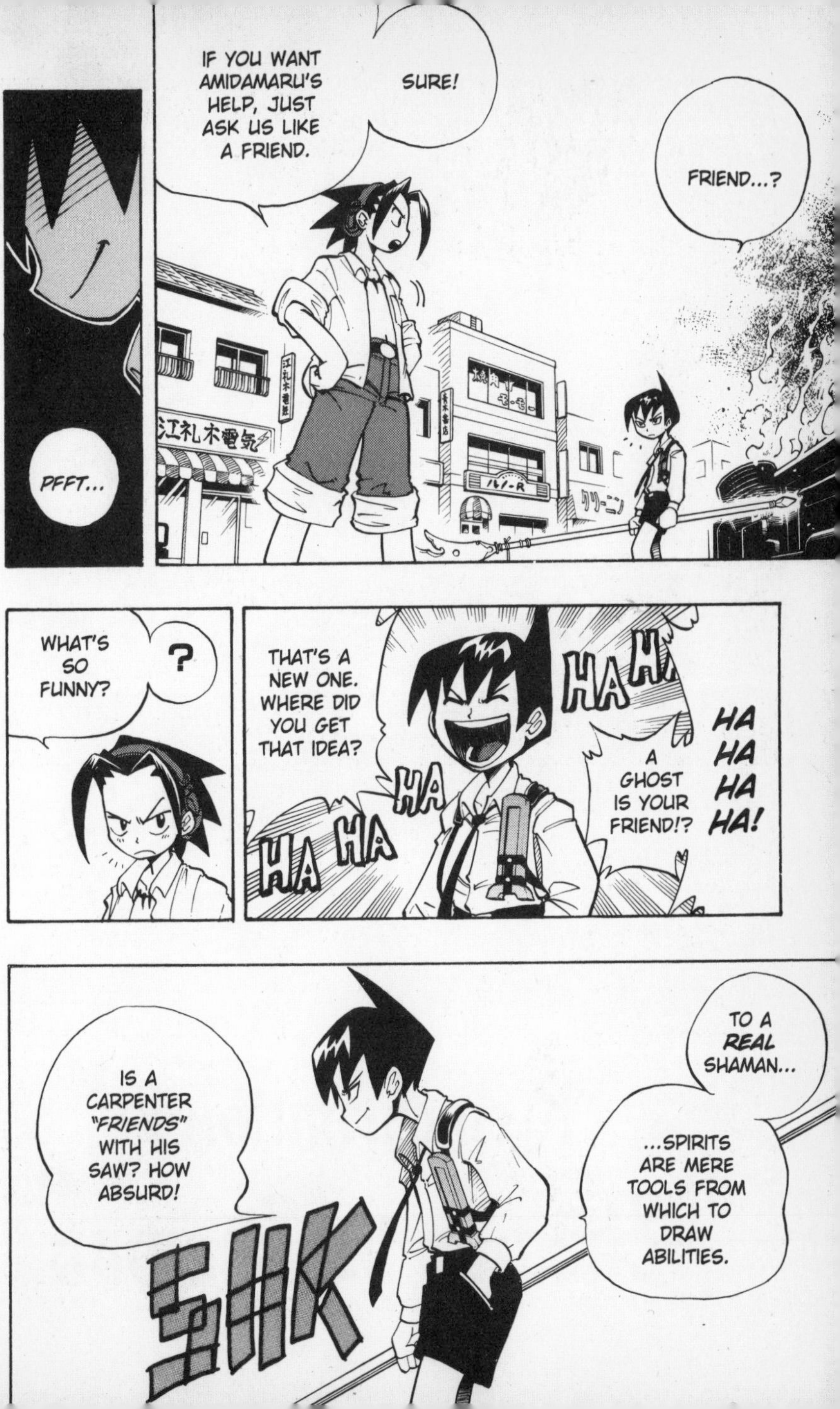
SURE!
IF YOU WANT AMIDAMARU'S HELP, JUST ASK US LIKE A FRIEND.
FRIEND...?
江礼木電気
PFFT...
HA HA
THAT'S A NEW ONE. WHERE DID YOU GET THAT IDEA?
HA HA HA HA!
A GHOST IS YOUR FRIEND!?
HA
HA HA
WHAT'S SO FUNNY?
?
TO A *REAL* SHAMAN...
...SPIRITS ARE MERE TOOLS FROM WHICH TO DRAW ABILITIES.
IS A CARPENTER *"FRIENDS"* WITH HIS SAW? HOW ABSURD!
SHK

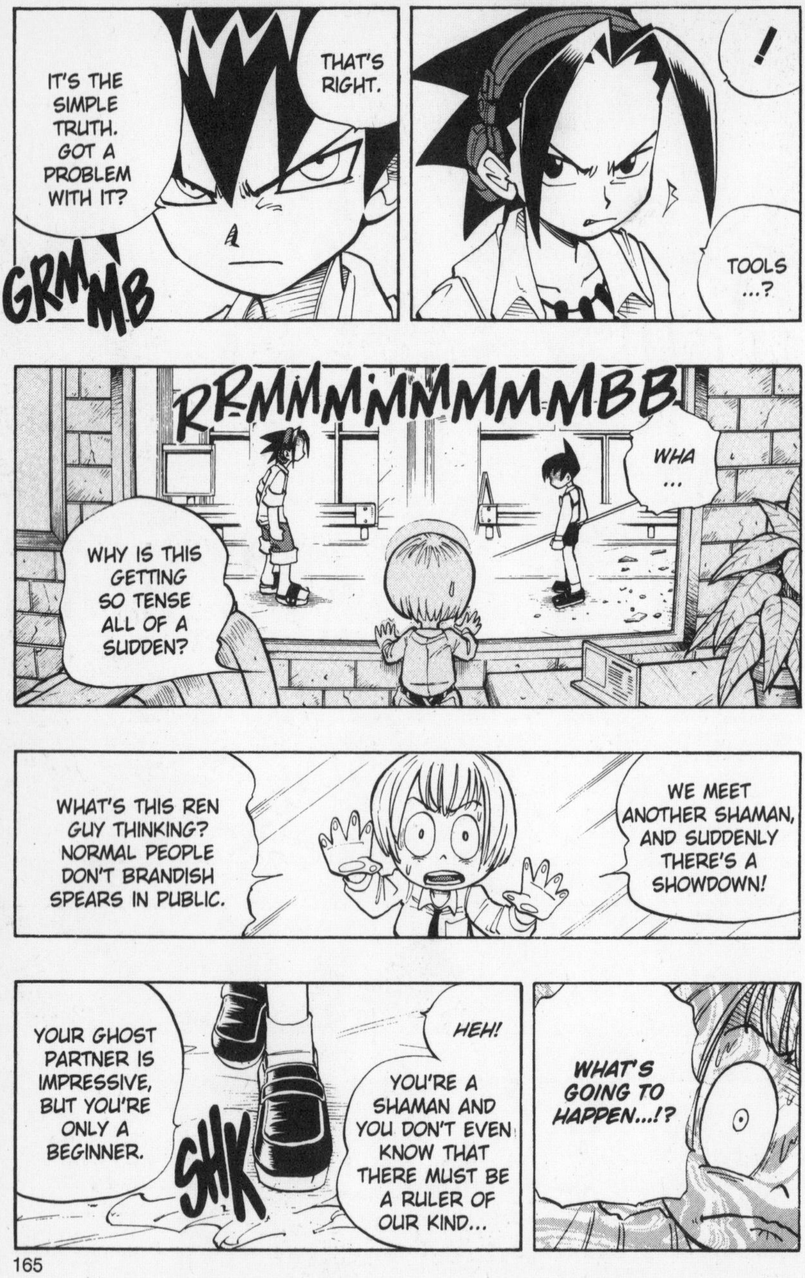

!
TOOLS ...?
THAT'S RIGHT.
IT'S THE SIMPLE TRUTH. GOT A PROBLEM WITH IT?
GRMMB
RRMMMMMMMMMBB
WHA ...
WHY IS THIS GETTING SO TENSE ALL OF A SUDDEN?
WE MEET ANOTHER SHAMAN, AND SUDDENLY THERE'S A SHOWDOWN!
WHAT'S THIS REN GUY THINKING? NORMAL PEOPLE DON'T BRANDISH SPEARS IN PUBLIC.
WHAT'S GOING TO HAPPEN...!?
HEH!
YOU'RE A SHAMAN AND YOU DON'T EVEN KNOW THAT THERE MUST BE A RULER OF OUR KIND...
SHK
YOUR GHOST PARTNER IS IMPRESSIVE, BUT YOU'RE ONLY A BEGINNER.

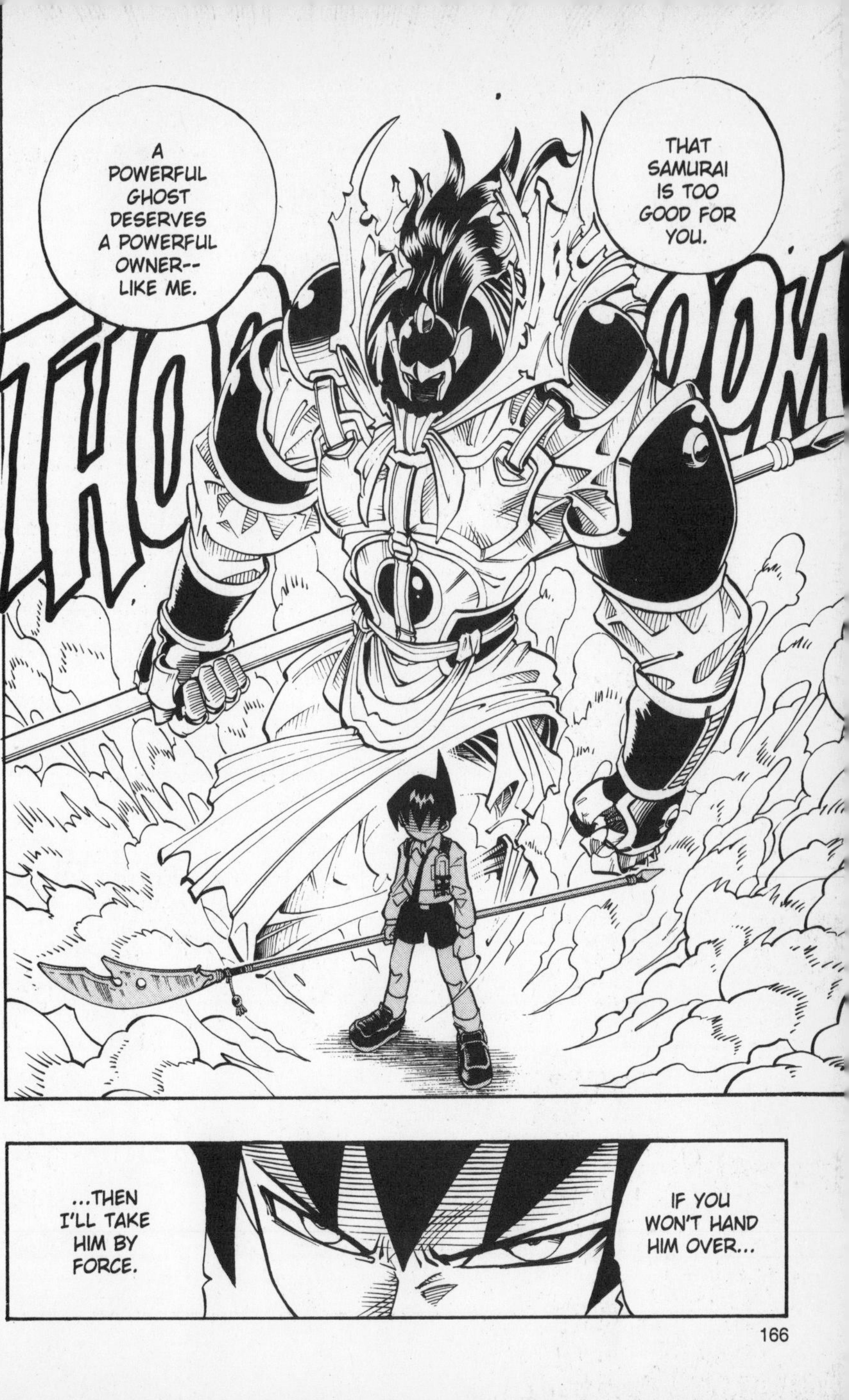
THAT SAMURAI IS TOO GOOD FOR YOU.
A POWERFUL GHOST DESERVES A POWERFUL OWNER-- LIKE ME.
THO
OOM
IF YOU WON'T HAND HIM OVER...
...THEN I'LL TAKE HIM BY FORCE.

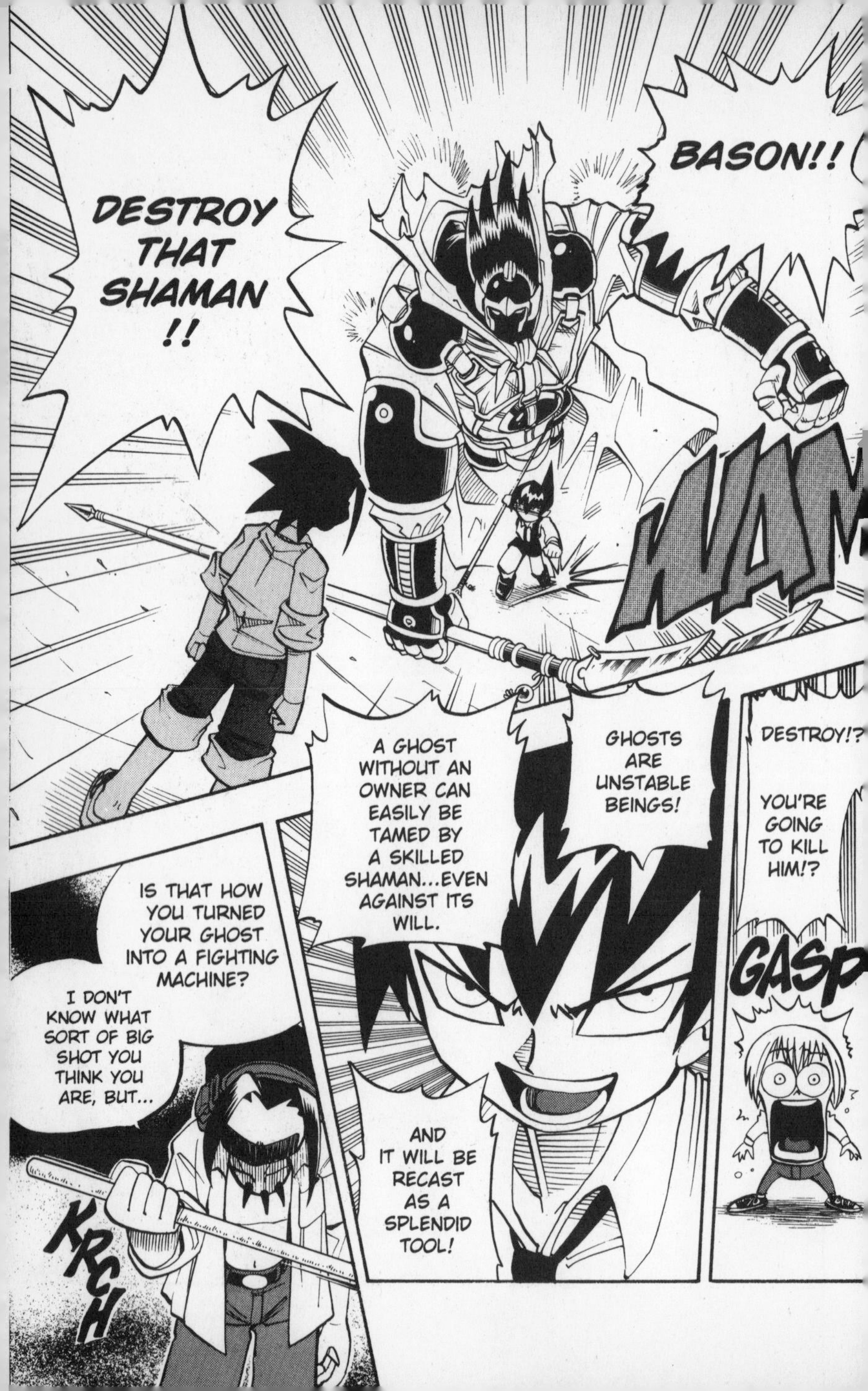
BASON!!
WAM
DESTROY THAT SHAMAN!!
DESTROY!?
YOU'RE GOING TO KILL HIM!?
GASP
GHOSTS ARE UNSTABLE BEINGS!
A GHOST WITHOUT AN OWNER CAN EASILY BE TAMED BY A SKILLED SHAMAN...EVEN AGAINST ITS WILL.
AND IT WILL BE RECAST AS A SPLENDID TOOL!
IS THAT HOW YOU TURNED YOUR GHOST INTO A FIGHTING MACHINE?
I DON'T KNOW WHAT SORT OF BIG SHOT YOU THINK YOU ARE, BUT...
KRCH

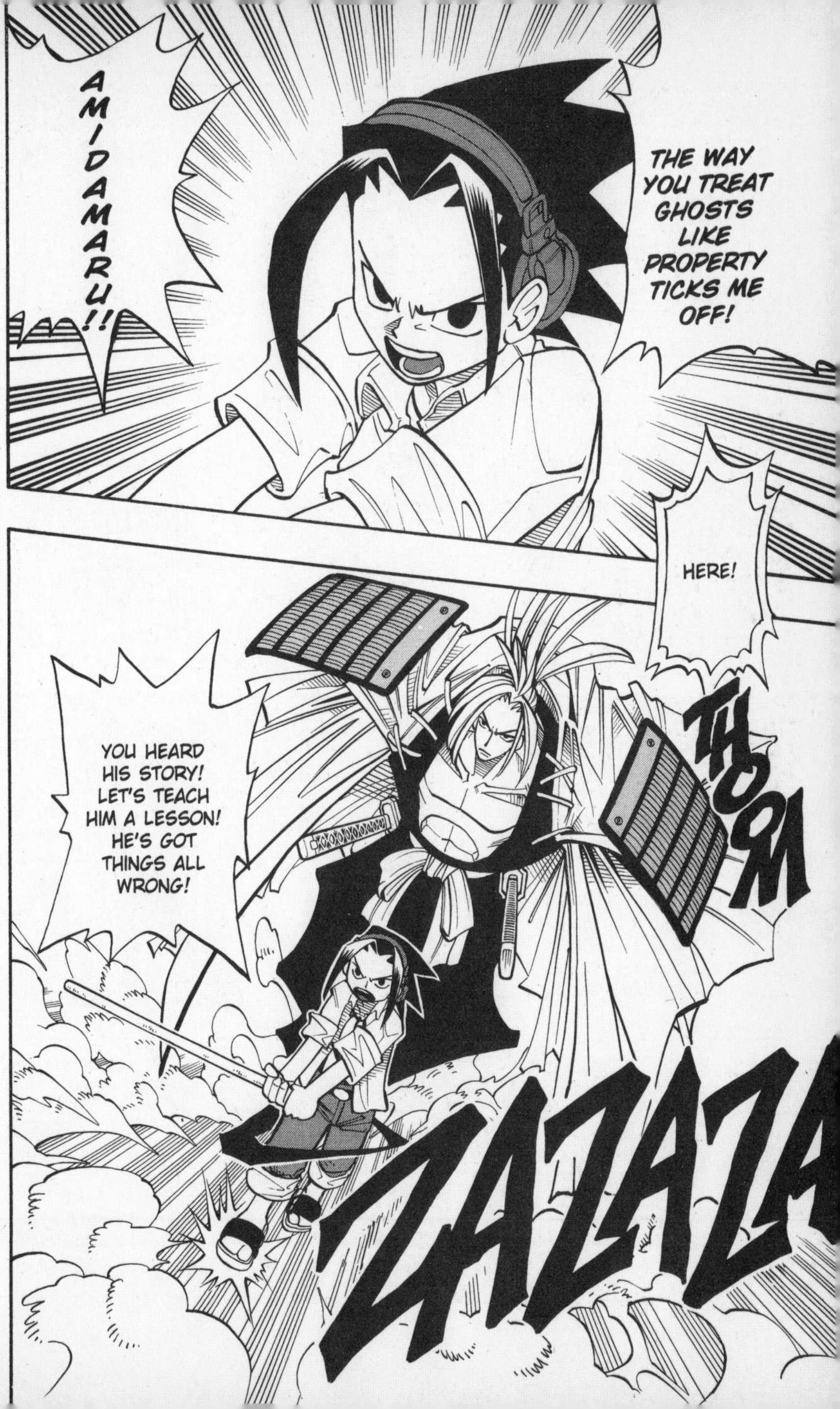
THE WAY YOU TREAT GHOSTS LIKE PROPERTY TICKS ME OFF!
AMIDAMARU!!
HERE!
THOOM
YOU HEARD HIS STORY! LET'S TEACH HIM A LESSON! HE'S GOT THINGS ALL WRONG!
ZAZAZA

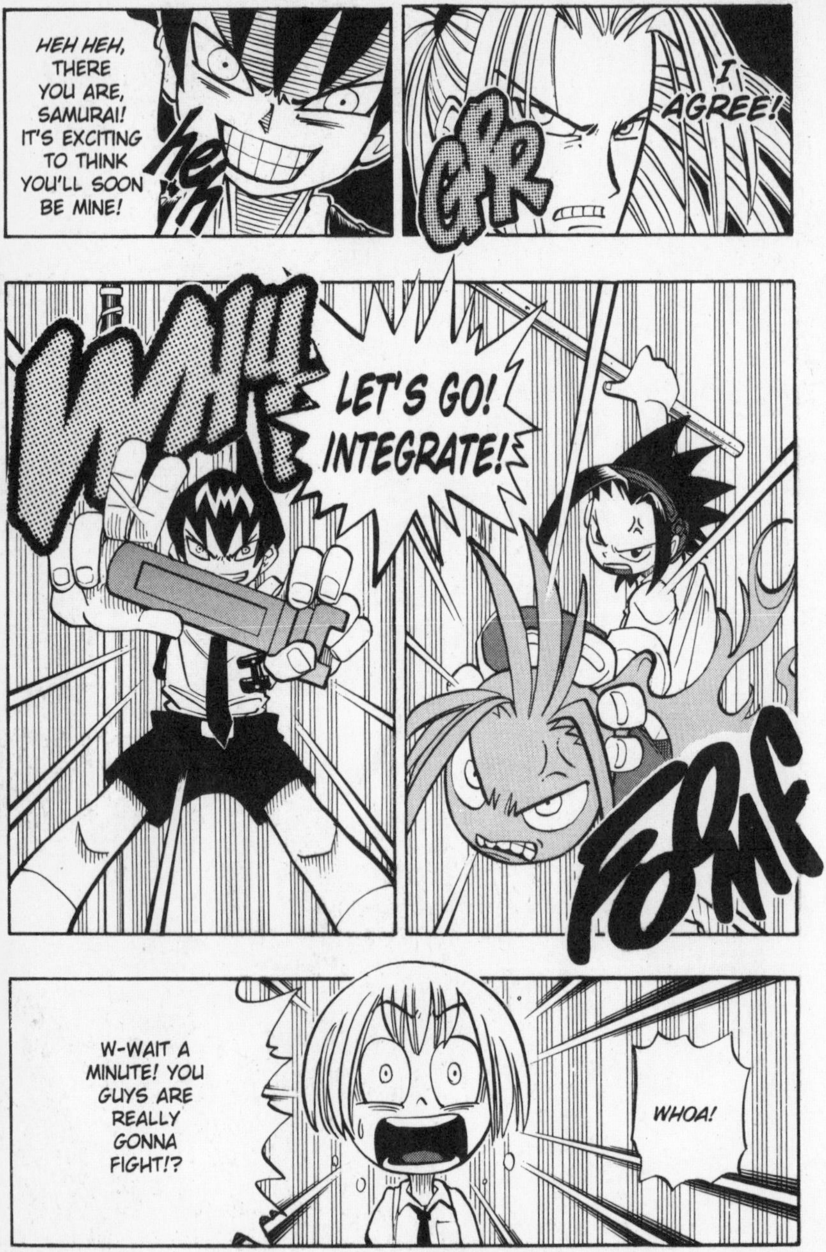
I AGREE!
GRR
HEH HEH, THERE YOU ARE, SAMURAI! IT'S EXCITING TO THINK YOU'LL SOON BE MINE!
heh heh
LET'S GO! INTEGRATE!
WHOA!
W-WAIT A MINUTE! YOU GUYS ARE REALLY GONNA FIGHT!?

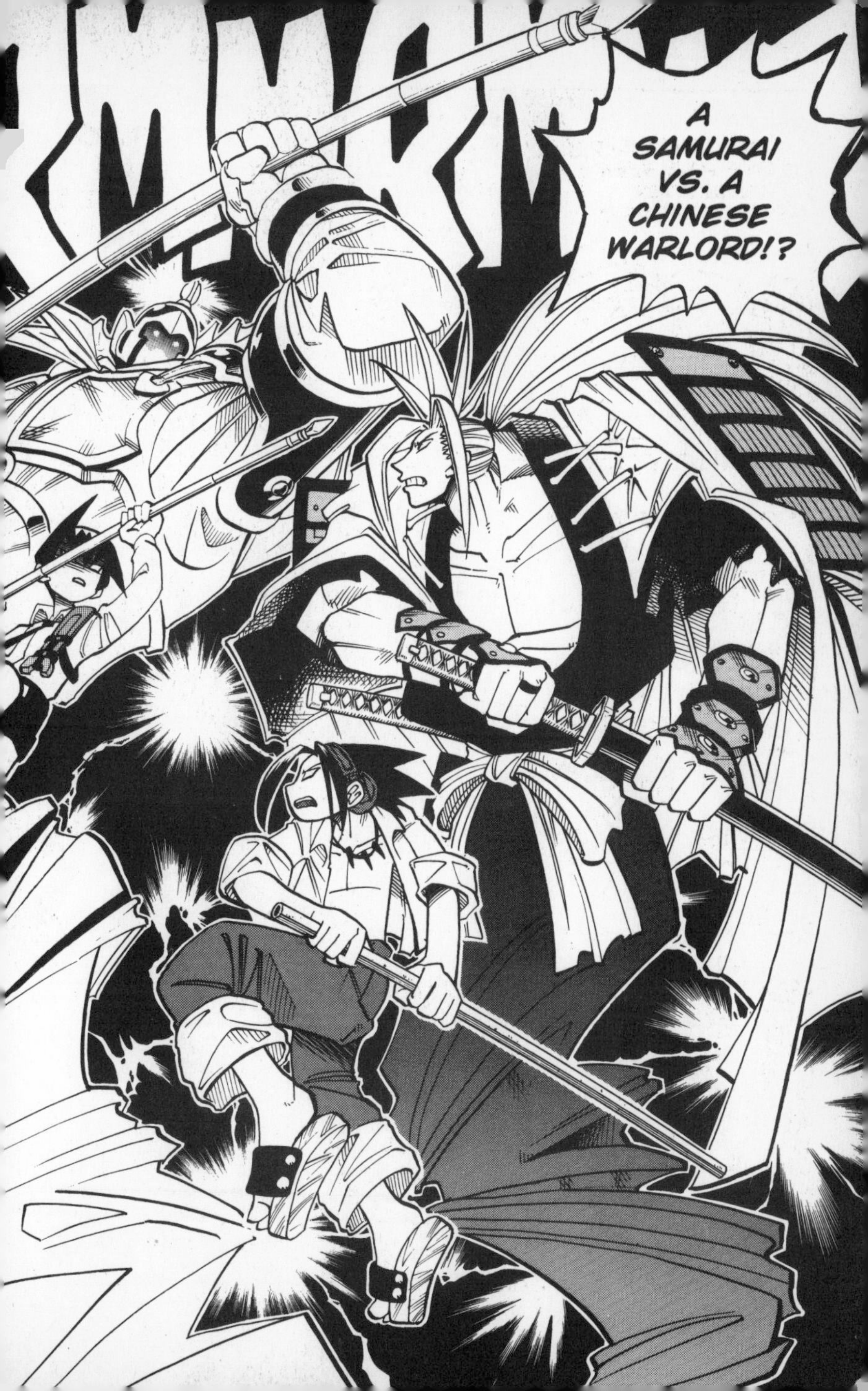
A SAMURAI VS. A CHINESE WARLORD!?

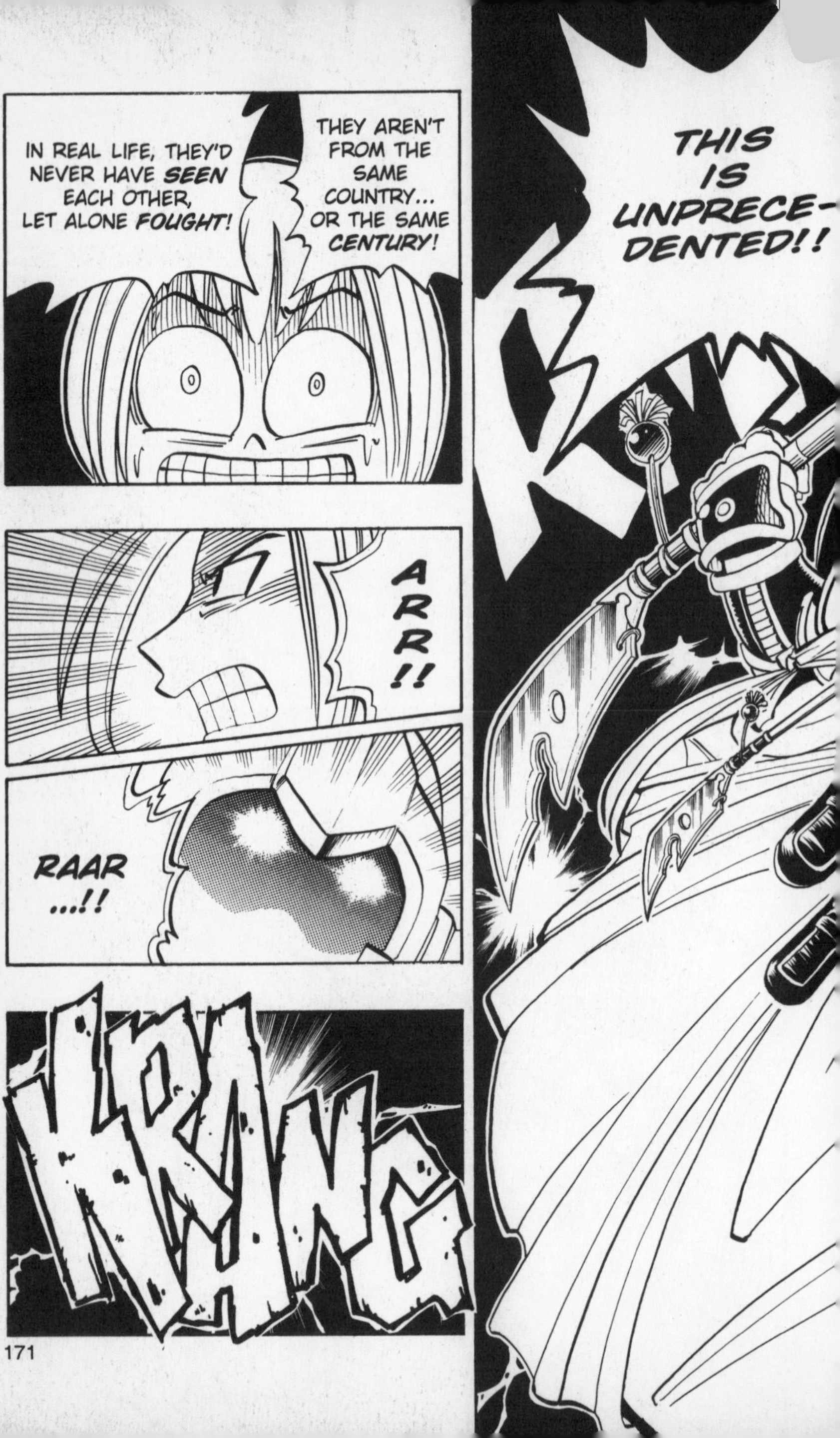
THIS IS UNPRECE-DENTED!!
THEY AREN'T FROM THE SAME COUNTRY... OR THE SAME CENTURY!
IN REAL LIFE, THEY'D NEVER HAVE SEEN EACH OTHER, LET ALONE FOUGHT!
ARR!!
RAAR ...!!
KRANG

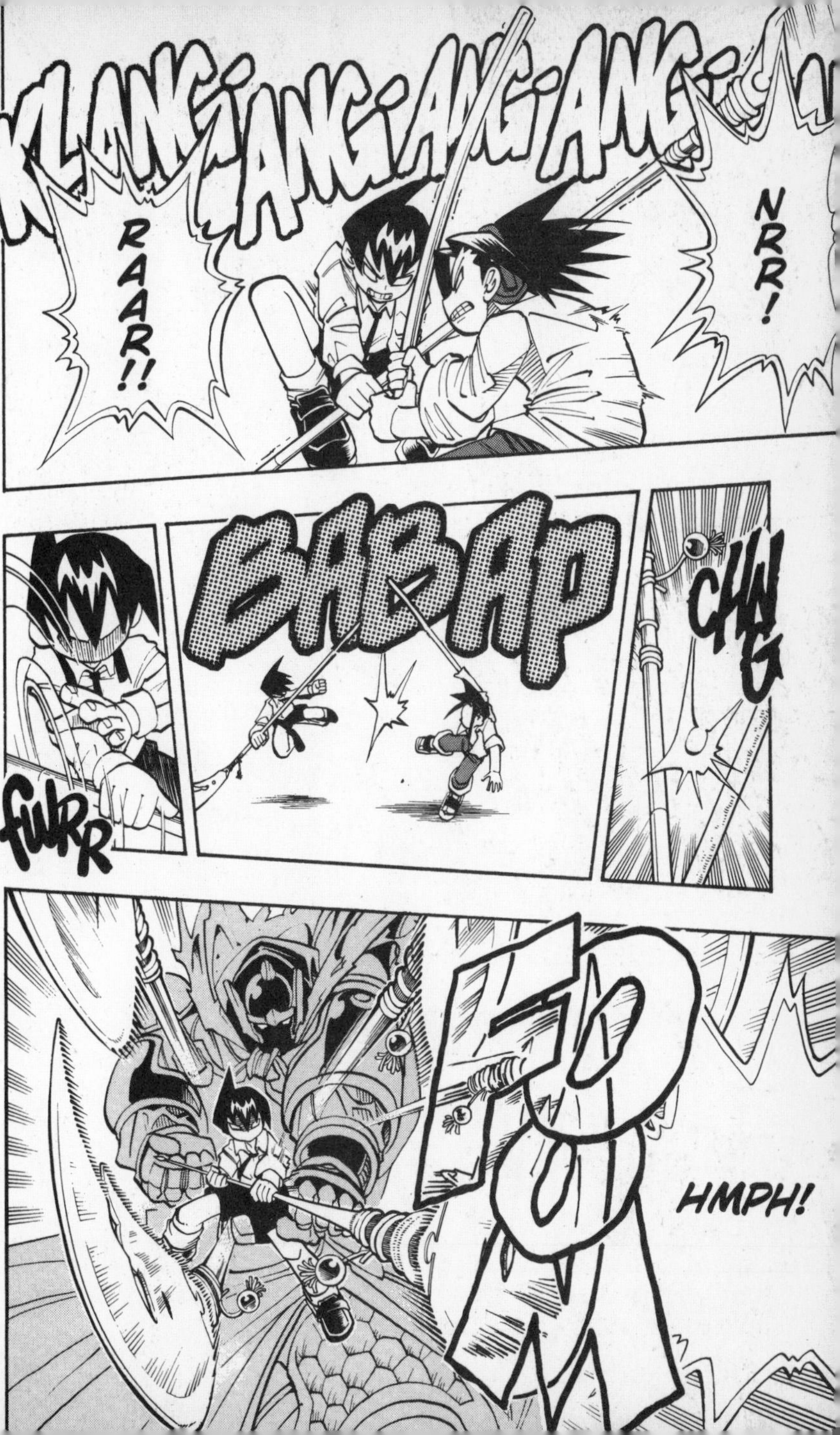
KLANG-ANG-ANG-ANG-AN
NRR!
RAAR!!
CHANG
BABAP
FWRR
HMPH!

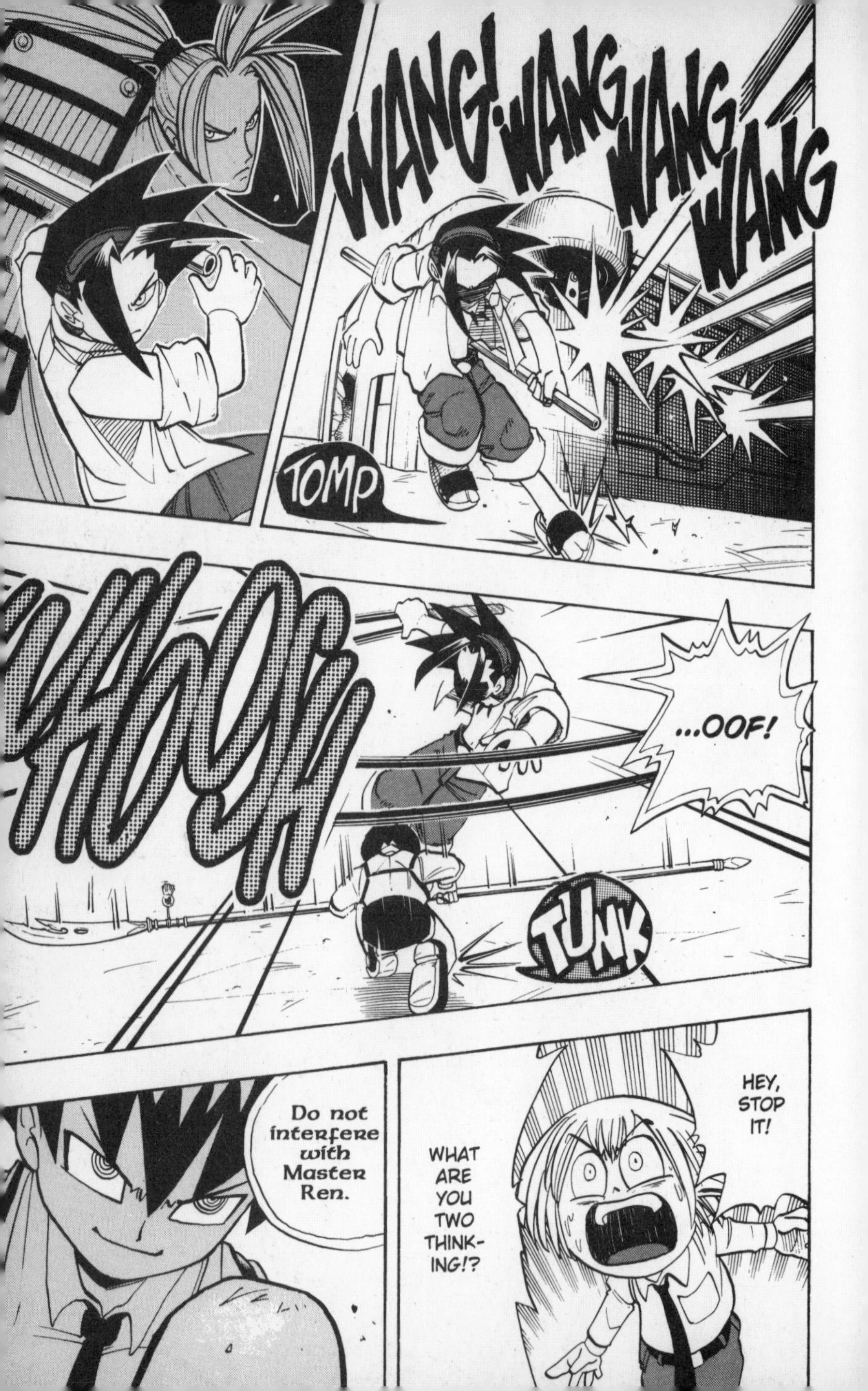
WANG! WANG WANG WANG
TOMP
...OOF!
TUNK
HEY, STOP IT!
WHAT ARE YOU TWO THINK-ING!?
Do not interfere with Master Ren.

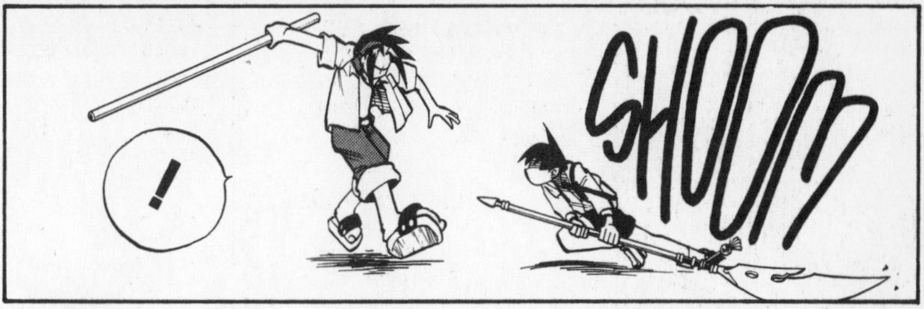
SHOOM
!
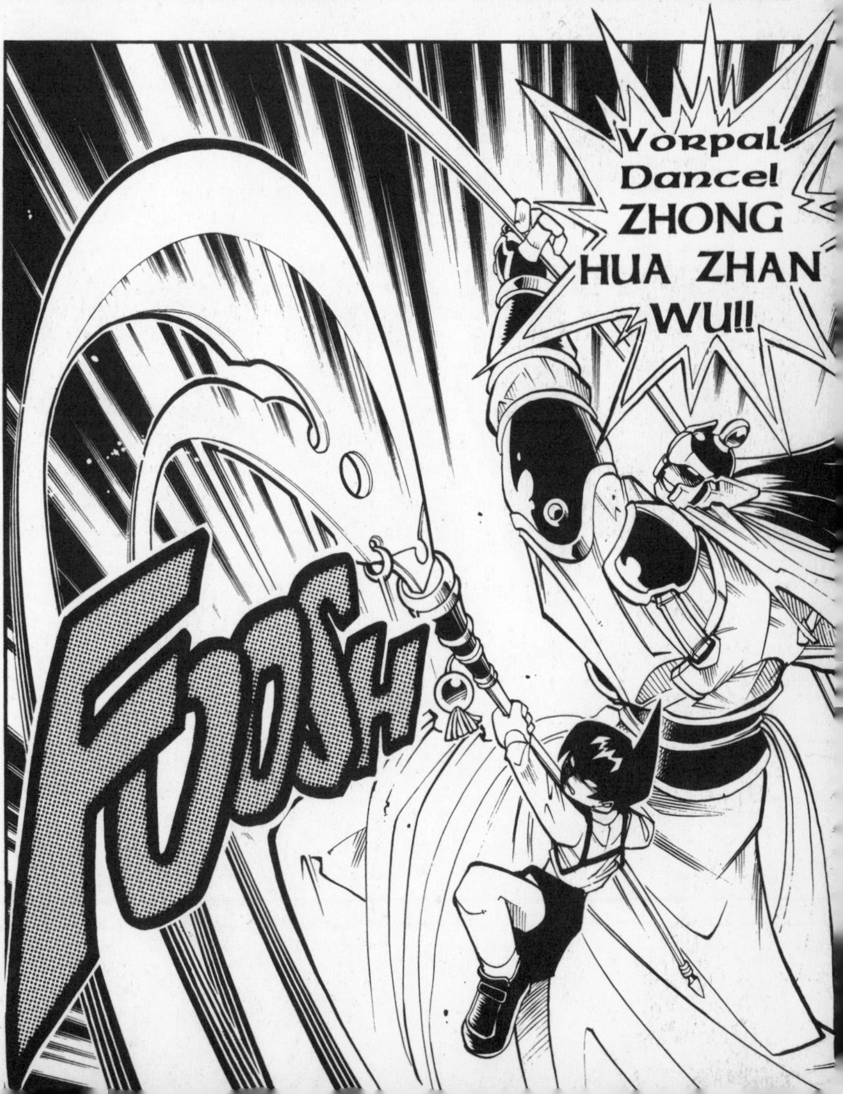
Vorpal Dance! ZHONG HUA ZHAN WU!!
FOOSH

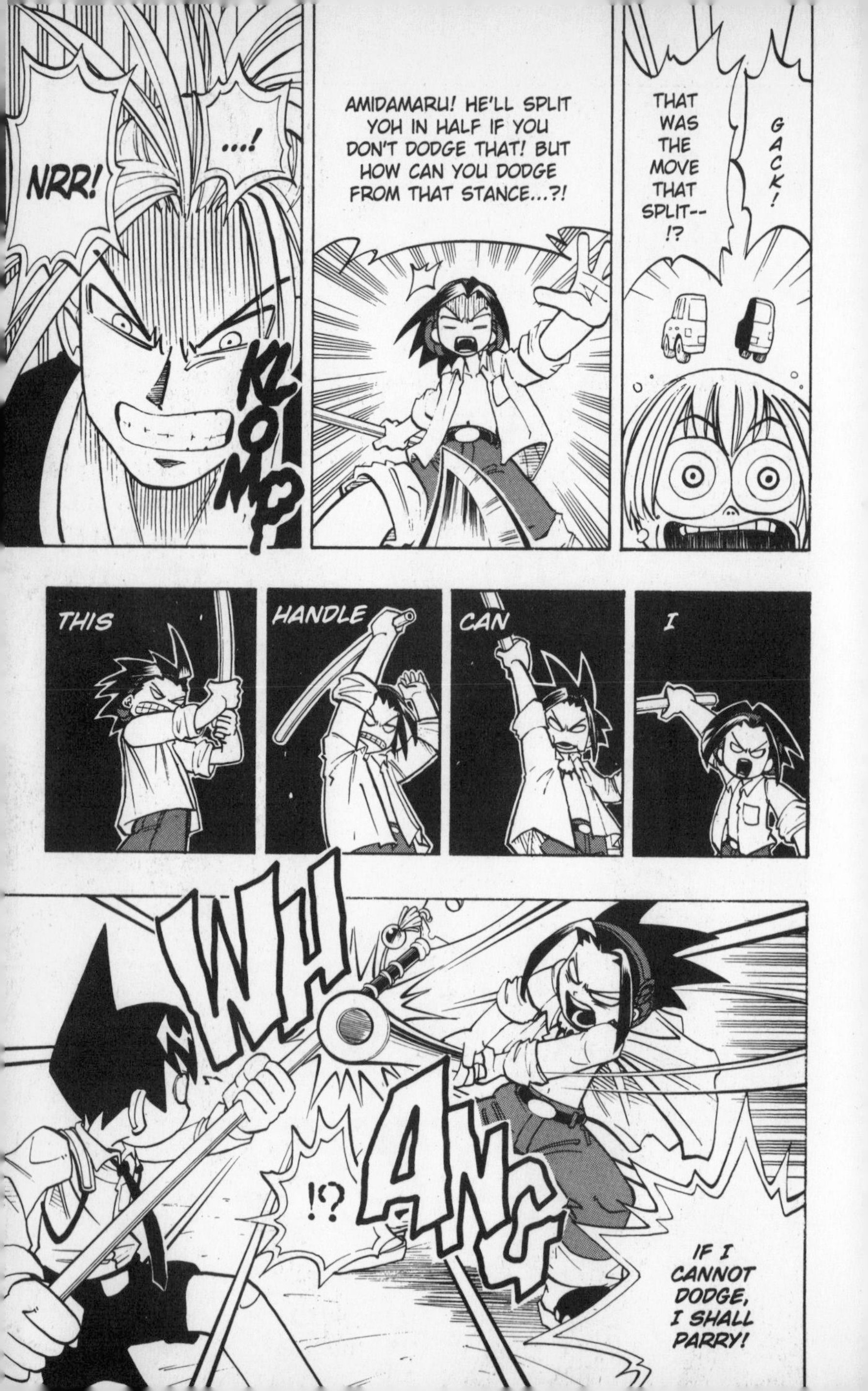
THAT WAS THE MOVE THAT SPLIT-- !?
GACK!
AMIDAMARU! HE'LL SPLIT YOH IN HALF IF YOU DON'T DODGE THAT! BUT HOW CAN YOU DODGE FROM THAT STANCE...?!
...!
NRR!
I
CAN
HANDLE
THIS
IF I CANNOT DODGE, I SHALL PARRY!
WHANG
!?

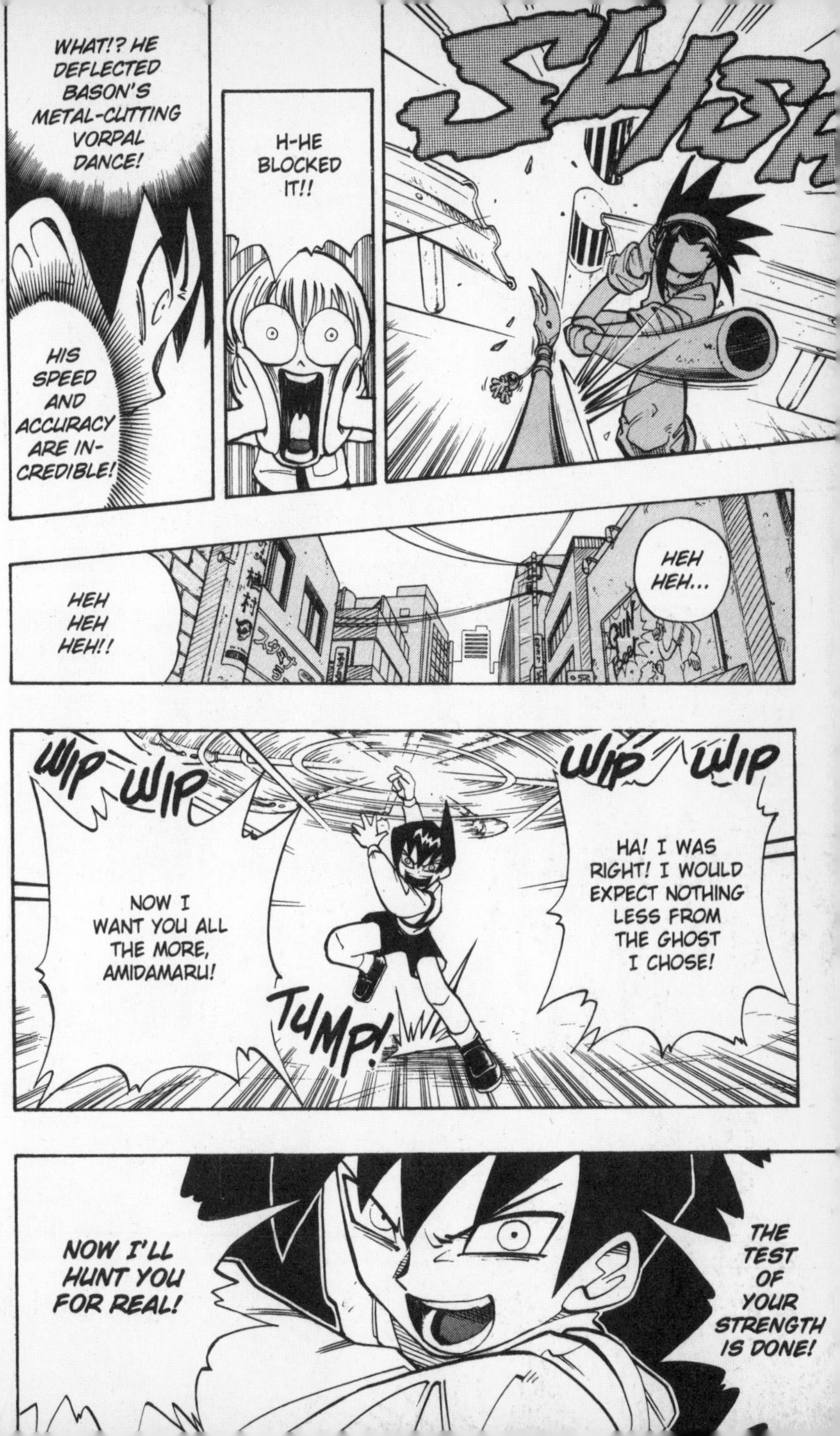

H-HE BLOCKED IT!!
WHAT!? HE DEFLECTED BASON'S METAL-CUTTING VORPAL DANCE!
HIS SPEED AND ACCURACY ARE IN-CREDIBLE!
HEH HEH...
HEH HEH HEH!!
WIP WIP
HA! I WAS RIGHT! I WOULD EXPECT NOTHING LESS FROM THE GHOST I CHOSE!
WIP WIP
NOW I WANT YOU ALL THE MORE, AMIDAMARU!
TUMP!
THE TEST OF YOUR STRENGTH IS DONE!
NOW I'LL HUNT YOU FOR REAL!

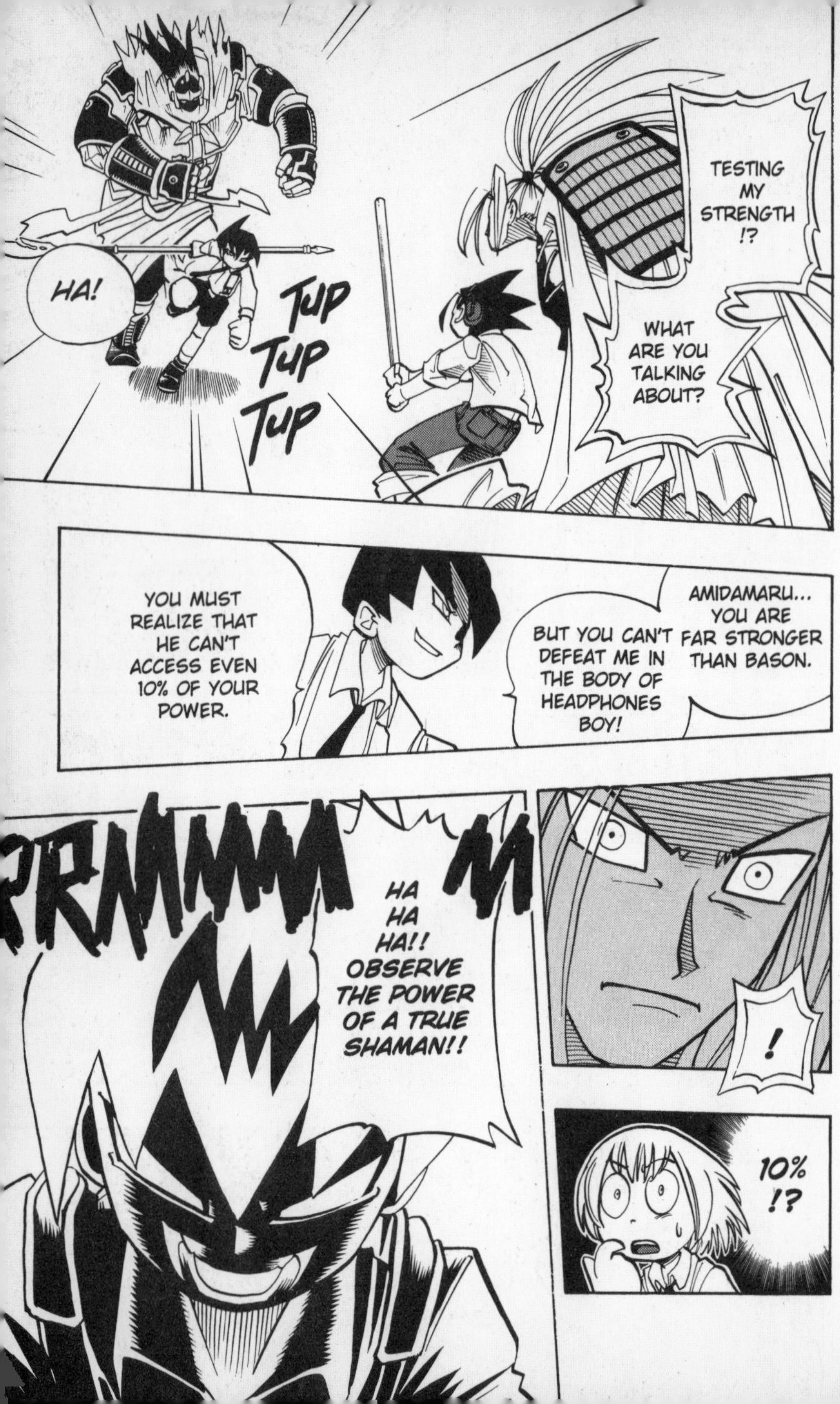
TESTING MY STRENGTH !?
WHAT ARE YOU TALKING ABOUT?
TUP TUP TUP
HA!
AMIDAMARU... YOU ARE FAR STRONGER THAN BASON.
BUT YOU CAN'T DEFEAT ME IN THE BODY OF HEADPHONES BOY!
YOU MUST REALIZE THAT HE CAN'T ACCESS EVEN 10% OF YOUR POWER.
!
10% !?
RMMMMM M
HA HA HA!! OBSERVE THE POWER OF A TRUE SHAMAN!!

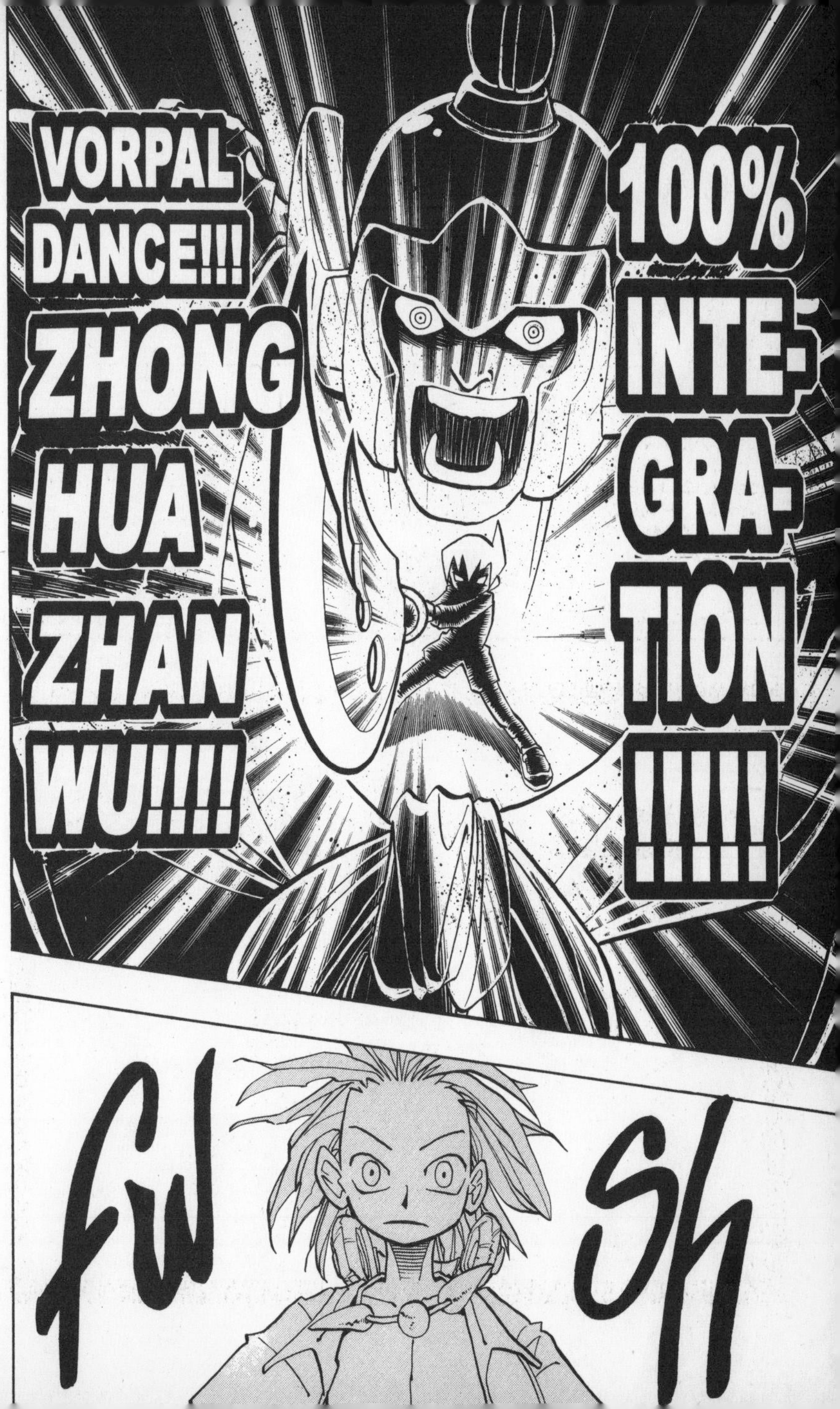
100% INTE-GRA-TION !!!!!!
VORPAL DANCE!!!
ZHONG HUA ZHAN WU!!!!
Fw Sh

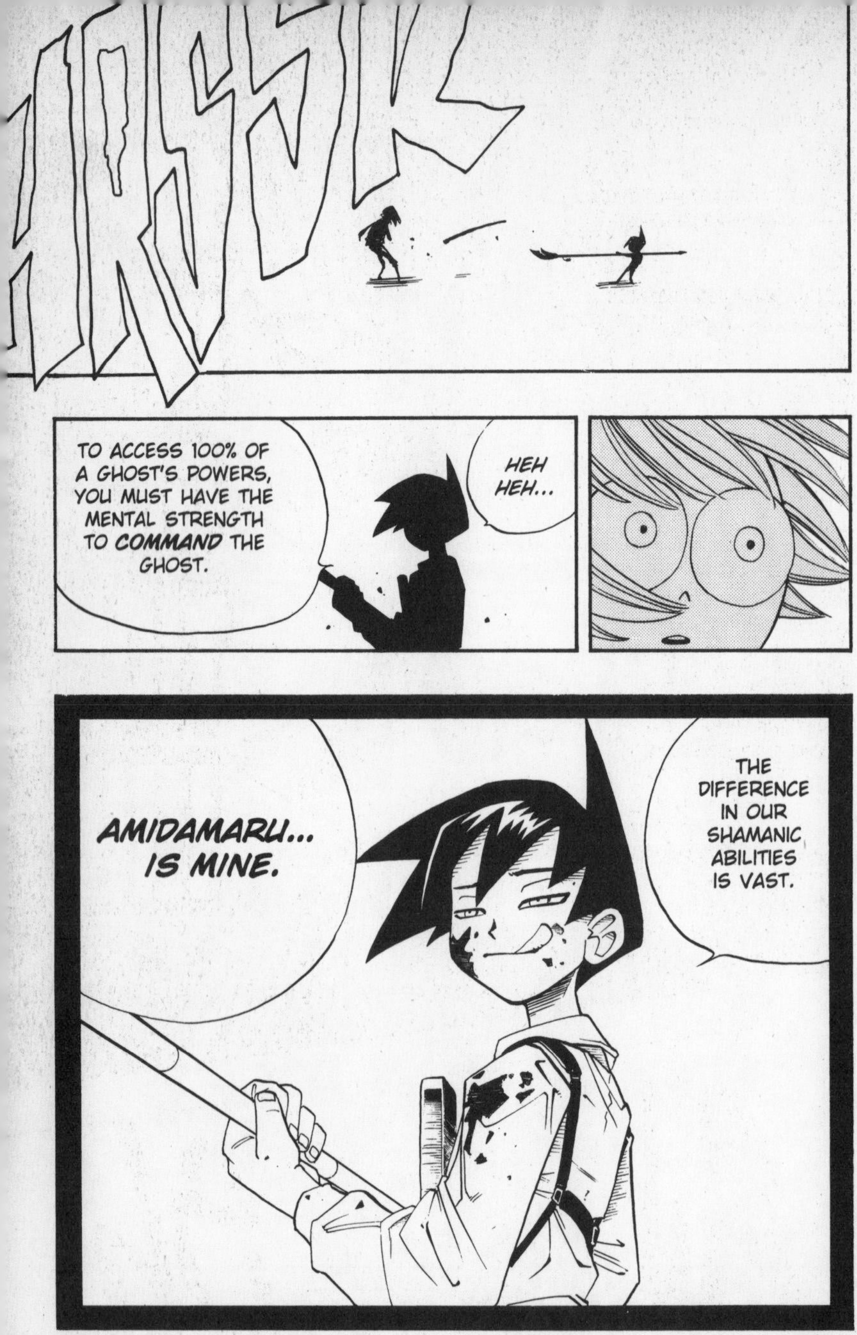
HEH HEH...
TO ACCESS 100% OF A GHOST'S POWERS, YOU MUST HAVE THE MENTAL STRENGTH TO **COMMAND** THE GHOST.
THE DIFFERENCE IN OUR SHAMANIC ABILITIES IS VAST.
AMIDAMARU... IS MINE.

SHAMAN
KING
1

**BATHROOM
SANDALS**

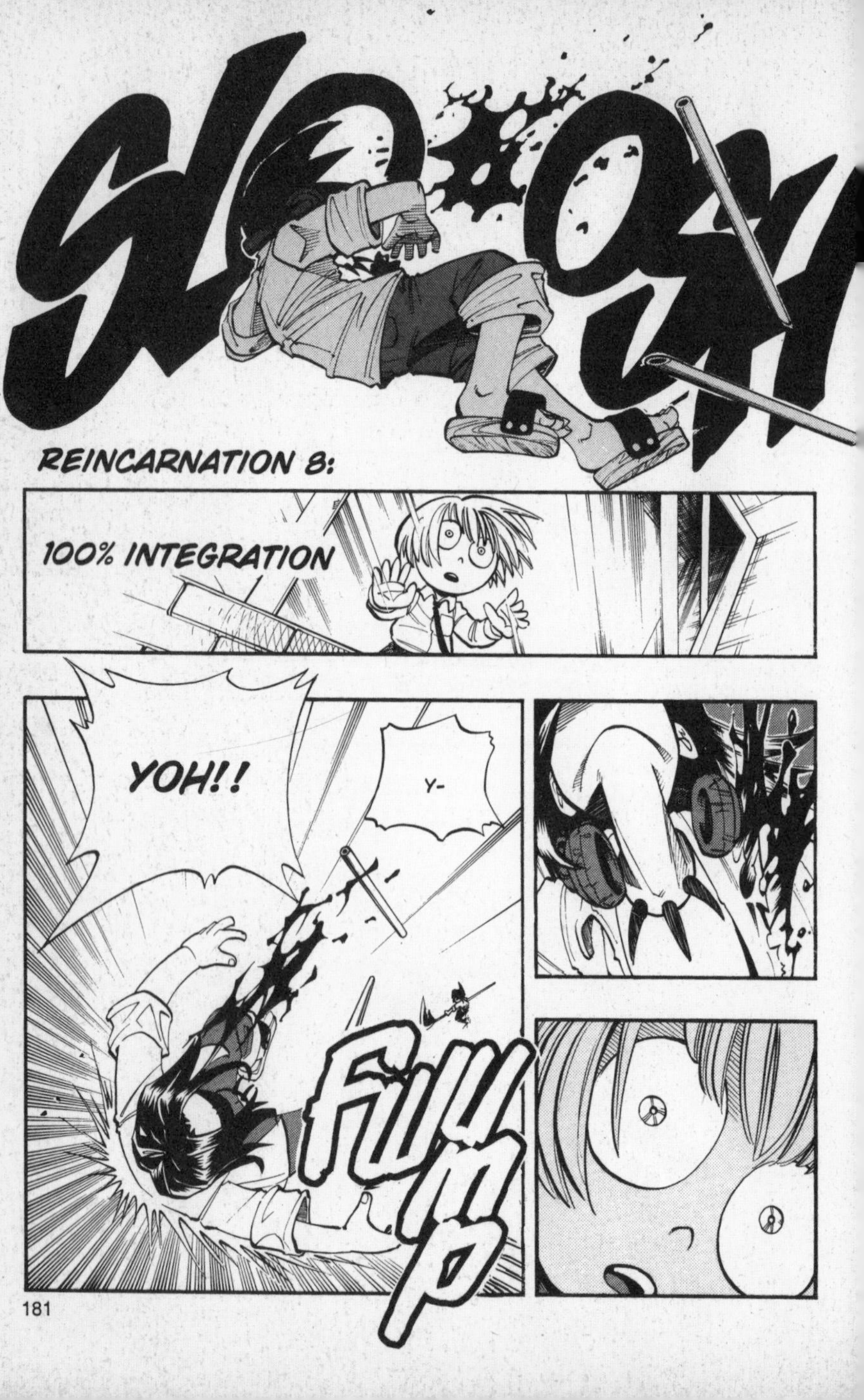
SLOOSH
REINCARNATION 8:
100% INTEGRATION
Y-
YOH!!
FUMP

READ THIS WAY

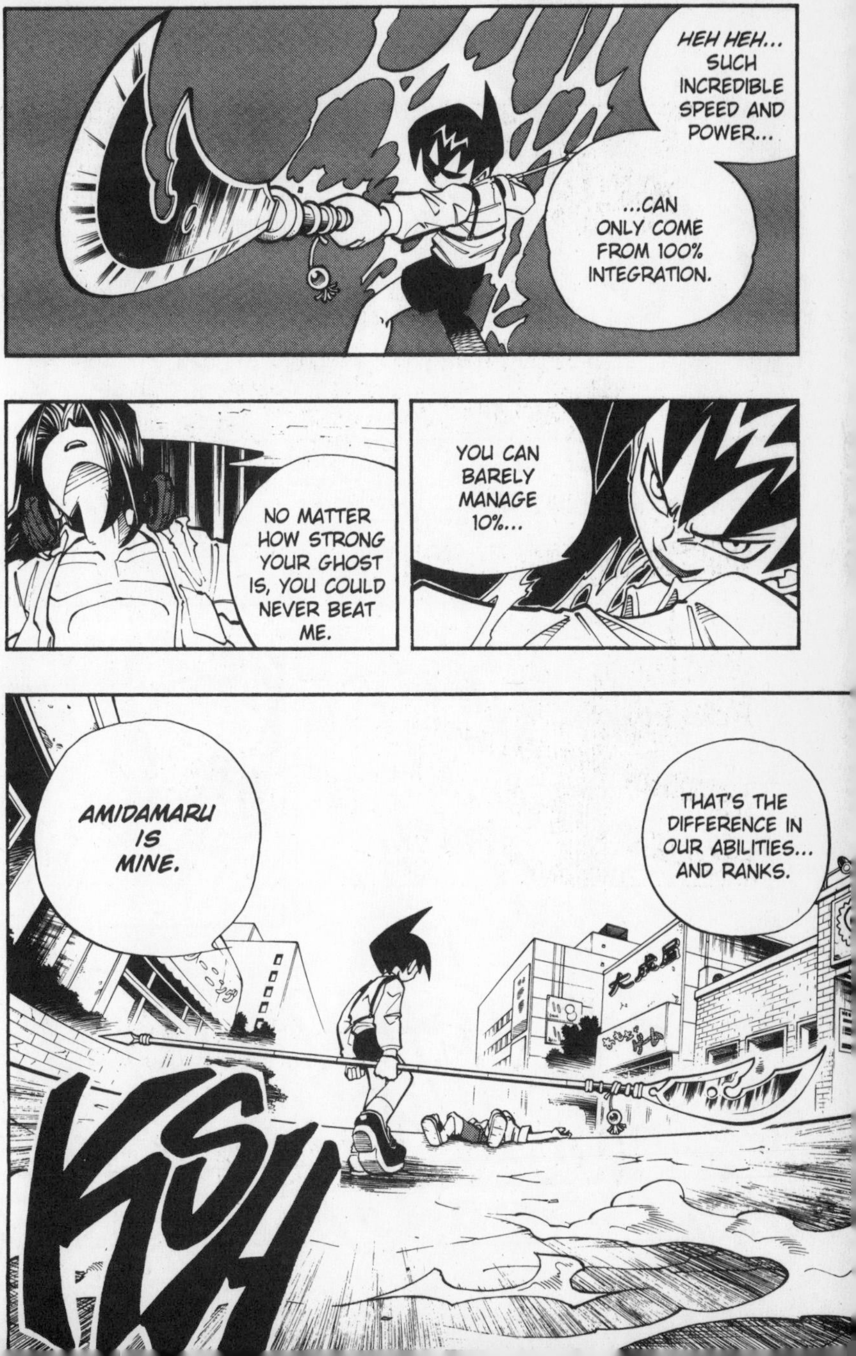
HEH HEH... SUCH INCREDIBLE SPEED AND POWER...
...CAN ONLY COME FROM 100% INTEGRATION.
YOU CAN BARELY MANAGE 10%...
NO MATTER HOW STRONG YOUR GHOST IS, YOU COULD NEVER BEAT ME.
THAT'S THE DIFFERENCE IN OUR ABILITIES... AND RANKS.
AMIDAMARU IS MINE.
KSH

Reincarnation 8:
100% Integration

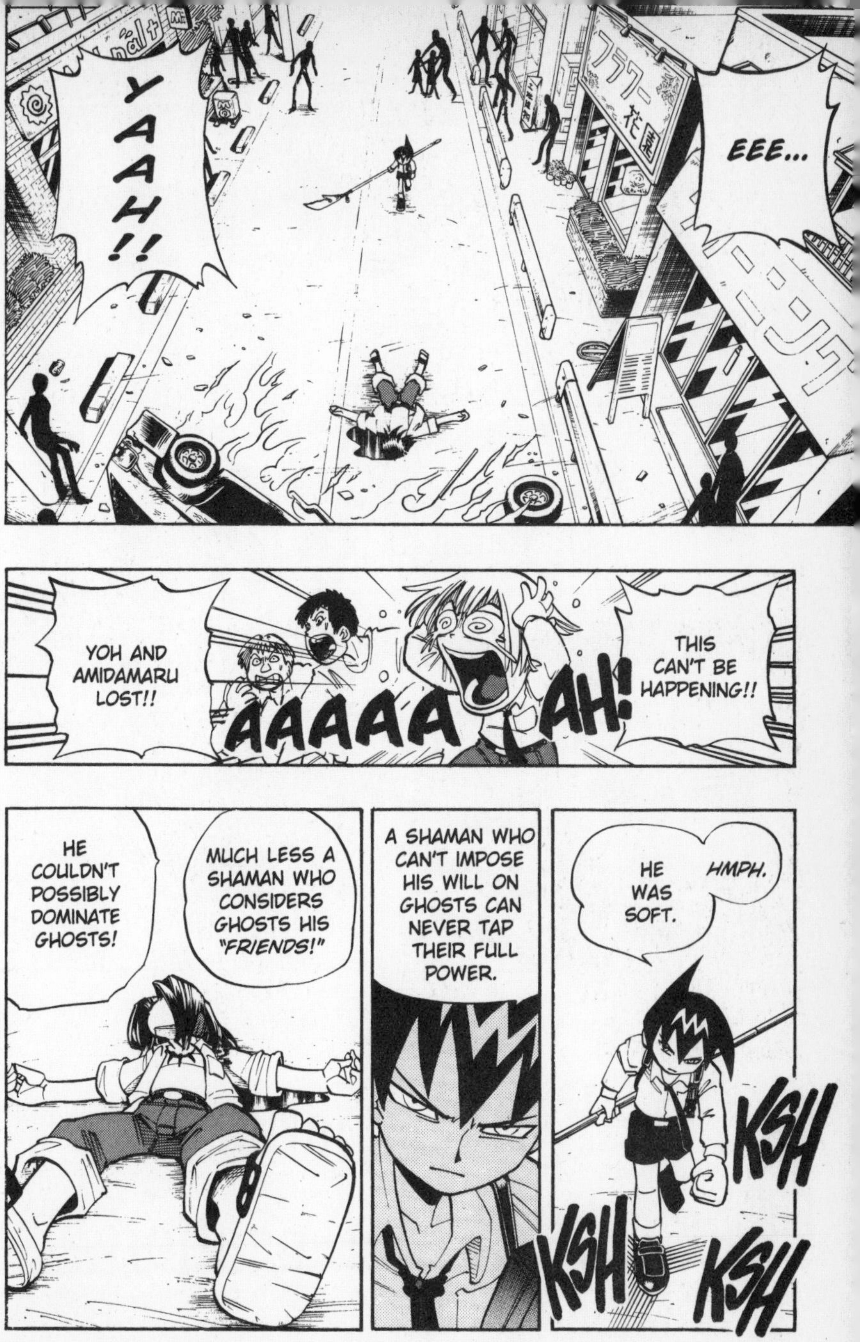
EEE...
YAAAH!!
THIS CAN'T BE HAPPENING!!
AAAAAAH!
YOH AND AMIDAMARU LOST!!
HMPH.
HE WAS SOFT.
KSH
KSH
KSH
KSH
A SHAMAN WHO CAN'T IMPOSE HIS WILL ON GHOSTS CAN NEVER TAP THEIR FULL POWER.
MUCH LESS A SHAMAN WHO CONSIDERS GHOSTS HIS "FRIENDS!"
HE COULDN'T POSSIBLY DOMINATE GHOSTS!

READ THIS WAY

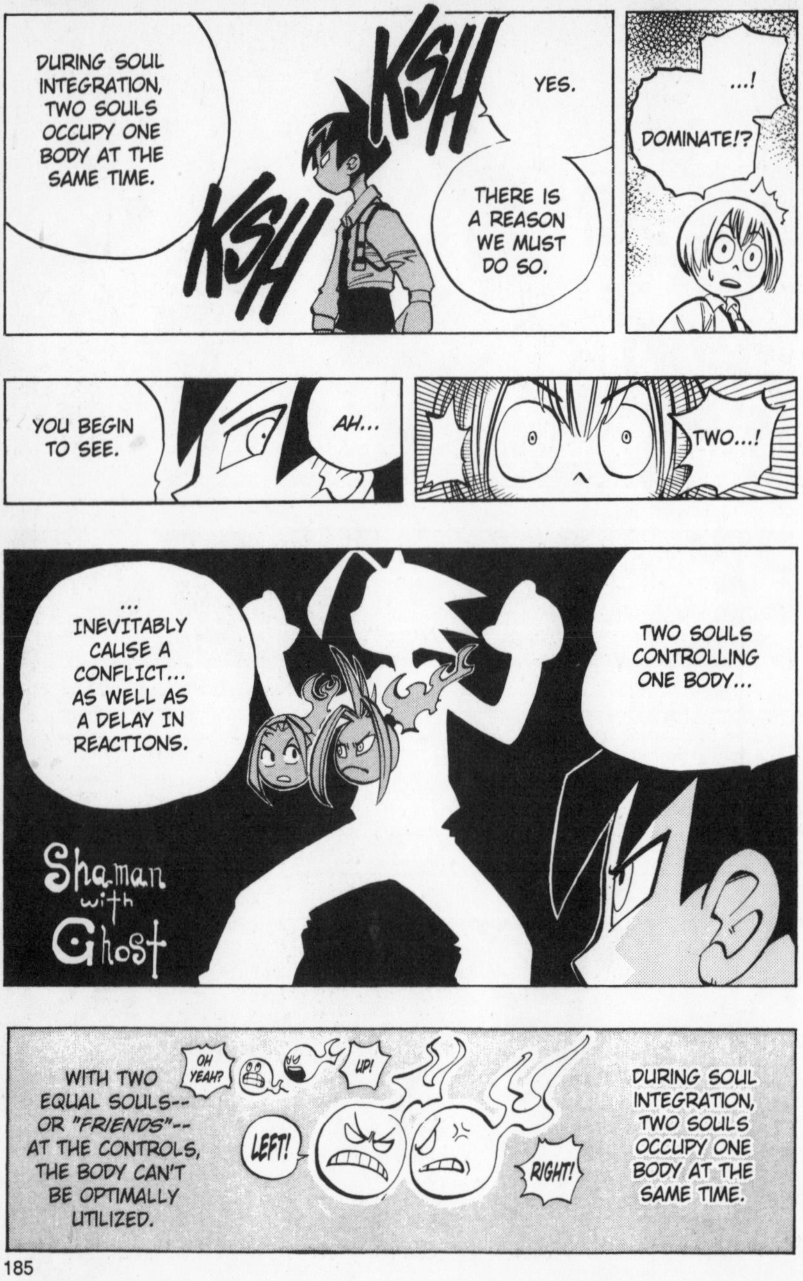

...!
DOMINATE!?
YES.
KSH
THERE IS A REASON WE MUST DO SO.
KSH
DURING SOUL INTEGRATION, TWO SOULS OCCUPY ONE BODY AT THE SAME TIME.
TWO...!
AH...
YOU BEGIN TO SEE.
TWO SOULS CONTROLLING ONE BODY...
... INEVITABLY CAUSE A CONFLICT... AS WELL AS A DELAY IN REACTIONS.
Shaman with Ghost
DURING SOUL INTEGRATION, TWO SOULS OCCUPY ONE BODY AT THE SAME TIME.
UP!
OH YEAH?
RIGHT!
LEFT!
WITH TWO EQUAL SOULS-- OR "FRIENDS"-- AT THE CONTROLS, THE BODY CAN'T BE OPTIMALLY UTILIZED.

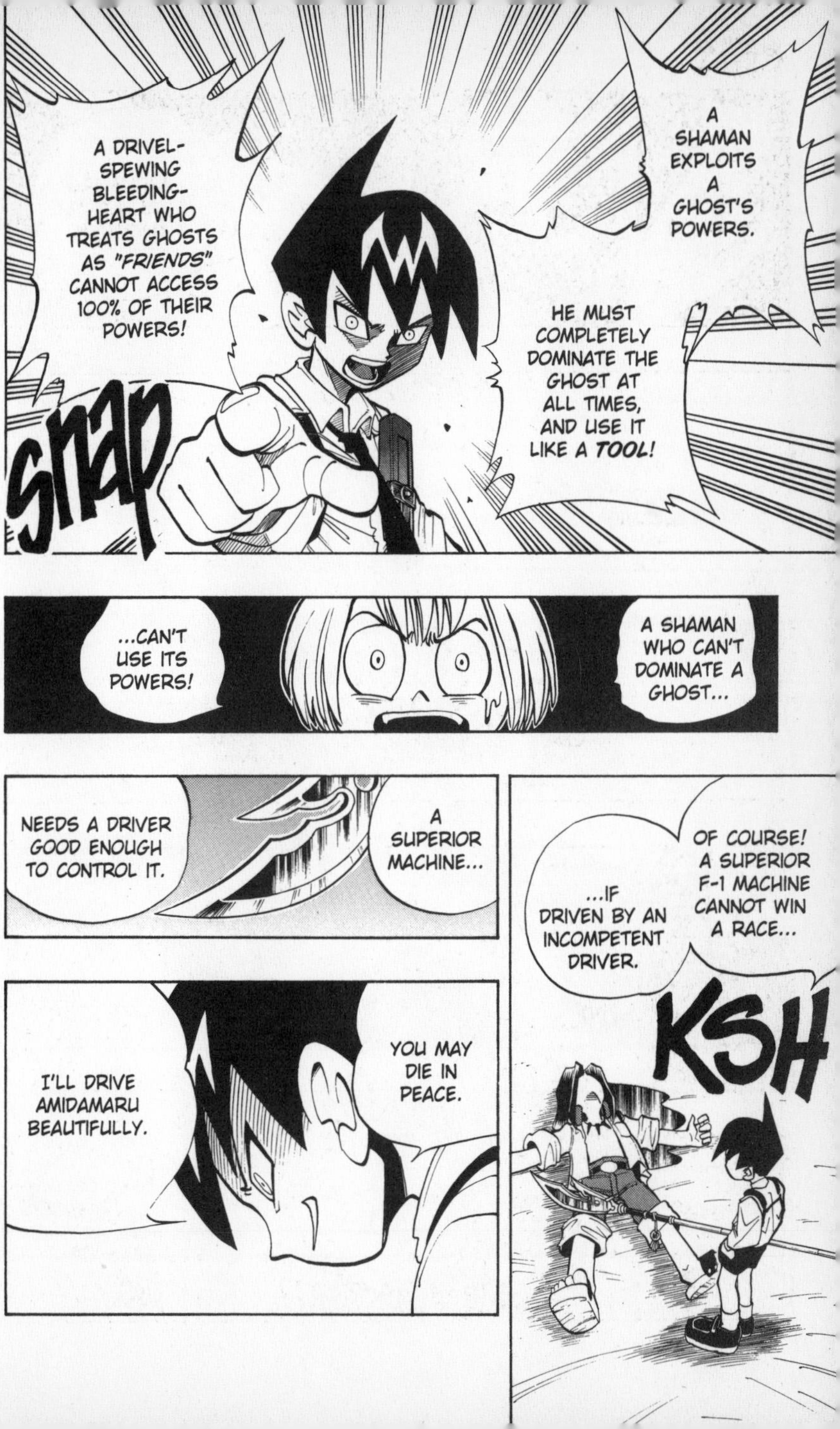
A SHAMAN EXPLOITS A GHOST'S POWERS.
HE MUST COMPLETELY DOMINATE THE GHOST AT ALL TIMES, AND USE IT LIKE A *TOOL*!
A DRIVEL-SPEWING BLEEDING-HEART WHO TREATS GHOSTS AS "*FRIENDS*" CANNOT ACCESS 100% OF THEIR POWERS!
SNAP
A SHAMAN WHO CAN'T DOMINATE A GHOST...
...CAN'T USE ITS POWERS!
OF COURSE! A SUPERIOR F-1 MACHINE CANNOT WIN A RACE...
...IF DRIVEN BY AN INCOMPETENT DRIVER.
KSH
A SUPERIOR MACHINE...
NEEDS A DRIVER GOOD ENOUGH TO CONTROL IT.
YOU MAY DIE IN PEACE.
I'LL DRIVE AMIDAMARU BEAUTIFULLY.

READ THIS WAY

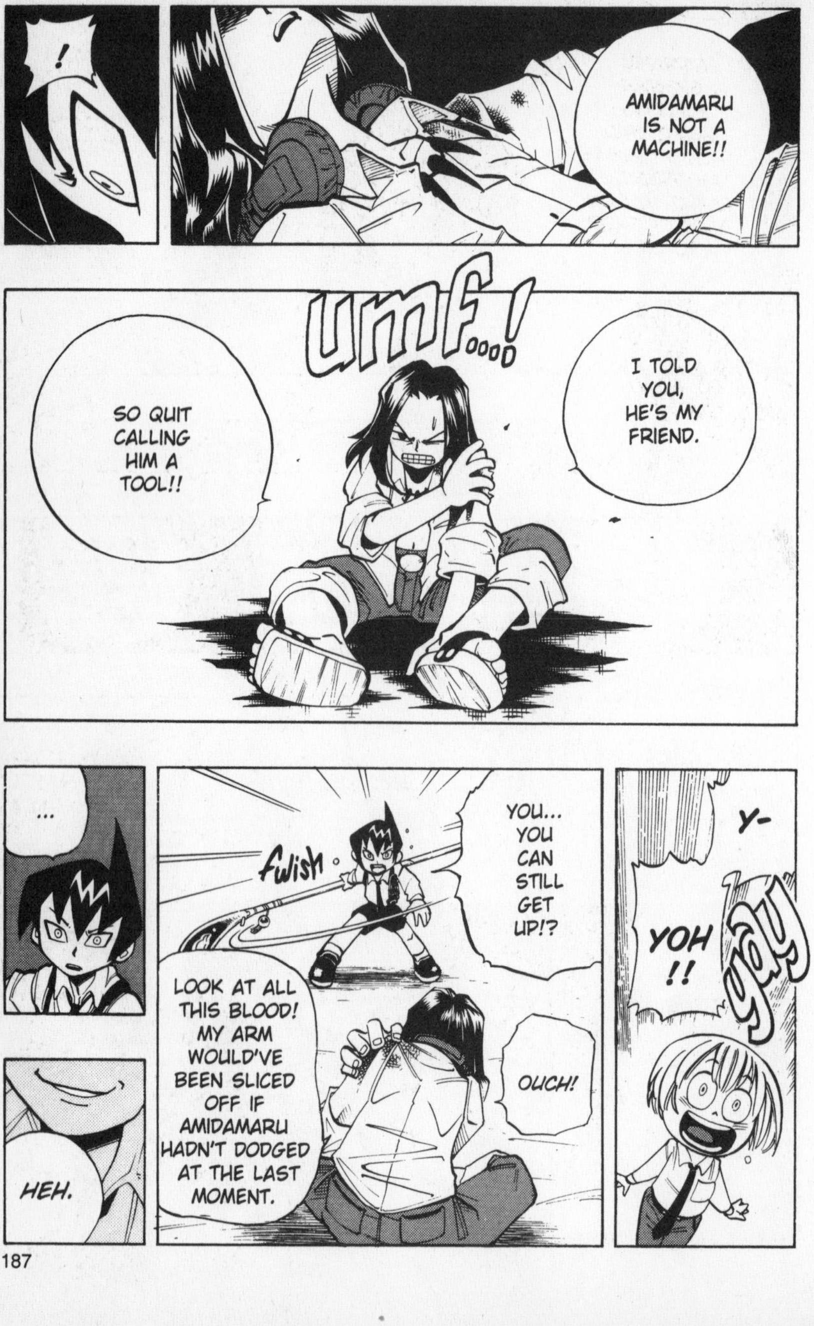
AMIDAMARU IS NOT A MACHINE!!
!
umf...!
I TOLD YOU, HE'S MY FRIEND.
SO QUIT CALLING HIM A TOOL!!
Y-
YOH!!
yay
YOU... YOU CAN STILL GET UP!?
fwish
OUCH!
LOOK AT ALL THIS BLOOD! MY ARM WOULD'VE BEEN SLICED OFF IF AMIDAMARU HADN'T DODGED AT THE LAST MOMENT.
...
HEH.

READ THIS WAY

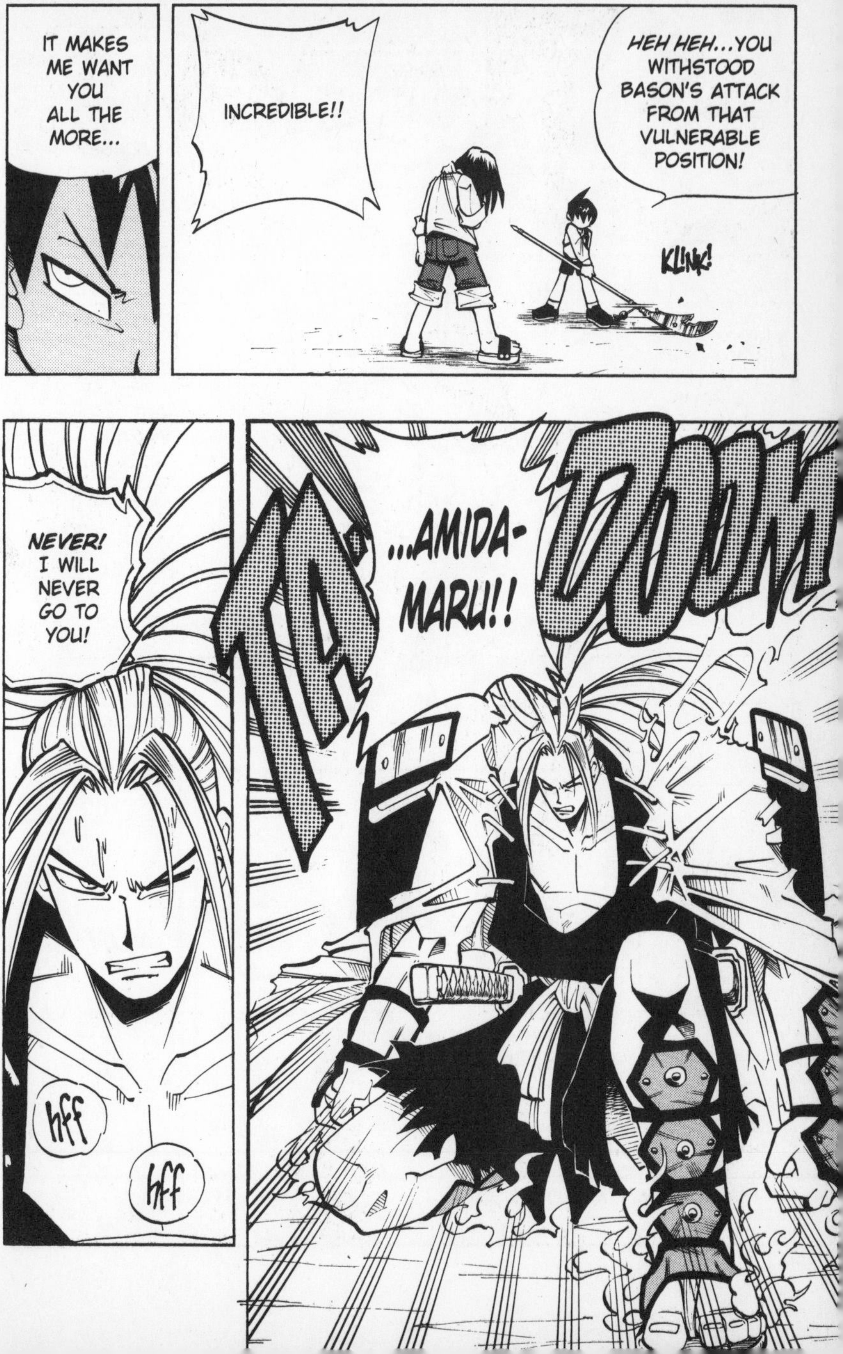
HEH HEH...YOU WITHSTOOD BASON'S ATTACK FROM THAT VULNERABLE POSITION!
KLINK!
INCREDIBLE!!
IT MAKES ME WANT YOU ALL THE MORE...
DOOM
...AMIDA-MARU!!
TA
NEVER! I WILL NEVER GO TO YOU!
hff
hff

READ THIS WAY

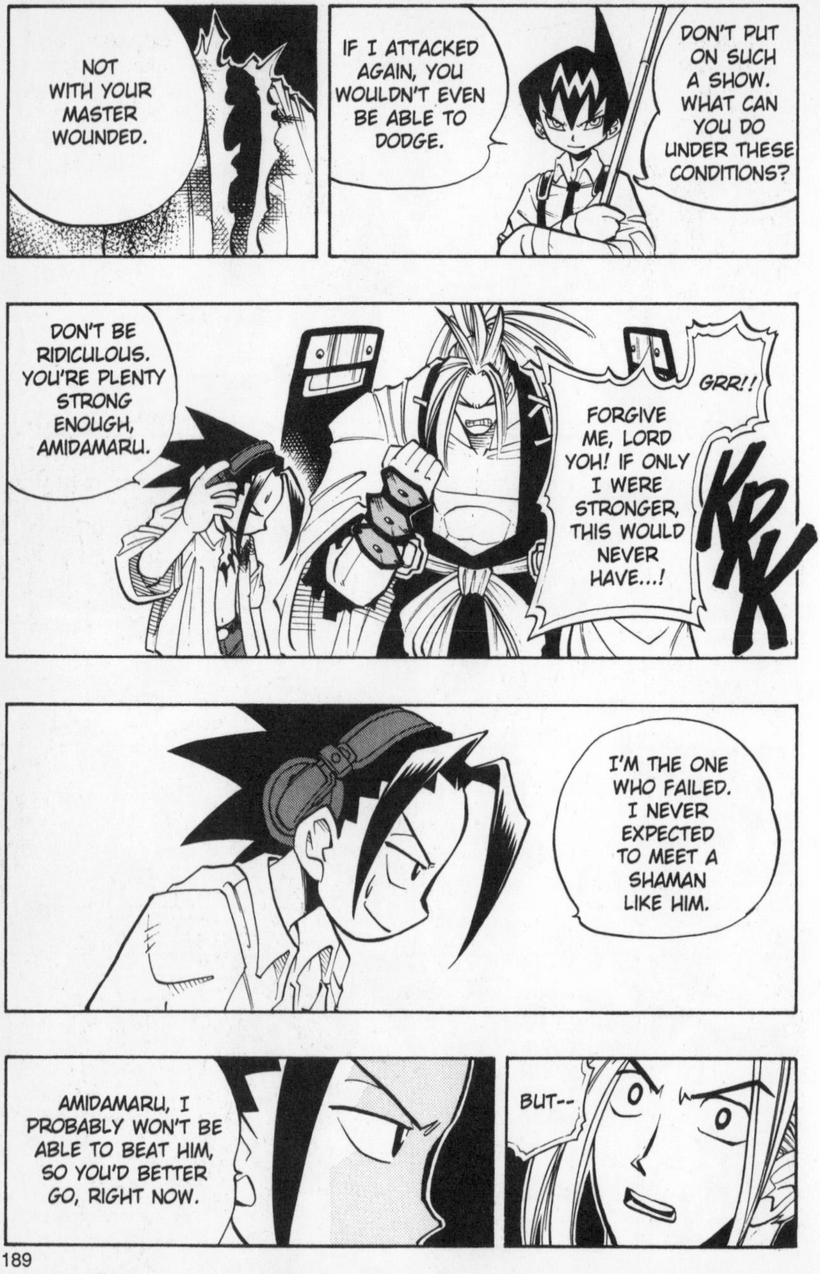
DON'T PUT ON SUCH A SHOW. WHAT CAN YOU DO UNDER THESE CONDITIONS?
IF I ATTACKED AGAIN, YOU WOULDN'T EVEN BE ABLE TO DODGE.
NOT WITH YOUR MASTER WOUNDED.
GRR!!
FORGIVE ME, LORD YOH! IF ONLY I WERE STRONGER, THIS WOULD NEVER HAVE...!
KRK
DON'T BE RIDICULOUS. YOU'RE PLENTY STRONG ENOUGH, AMIDAMARU.
I'M THE ONE WHO FAILED. I NEVER EXPECTED TO MEET A SHAMAN LIKE HIM.
BUT--
AMIDAMARU, I PROBABLY WON'T BE ABLE TO BEAT HIM, SO YOU'D BETTER GO, RIGHT NOW.

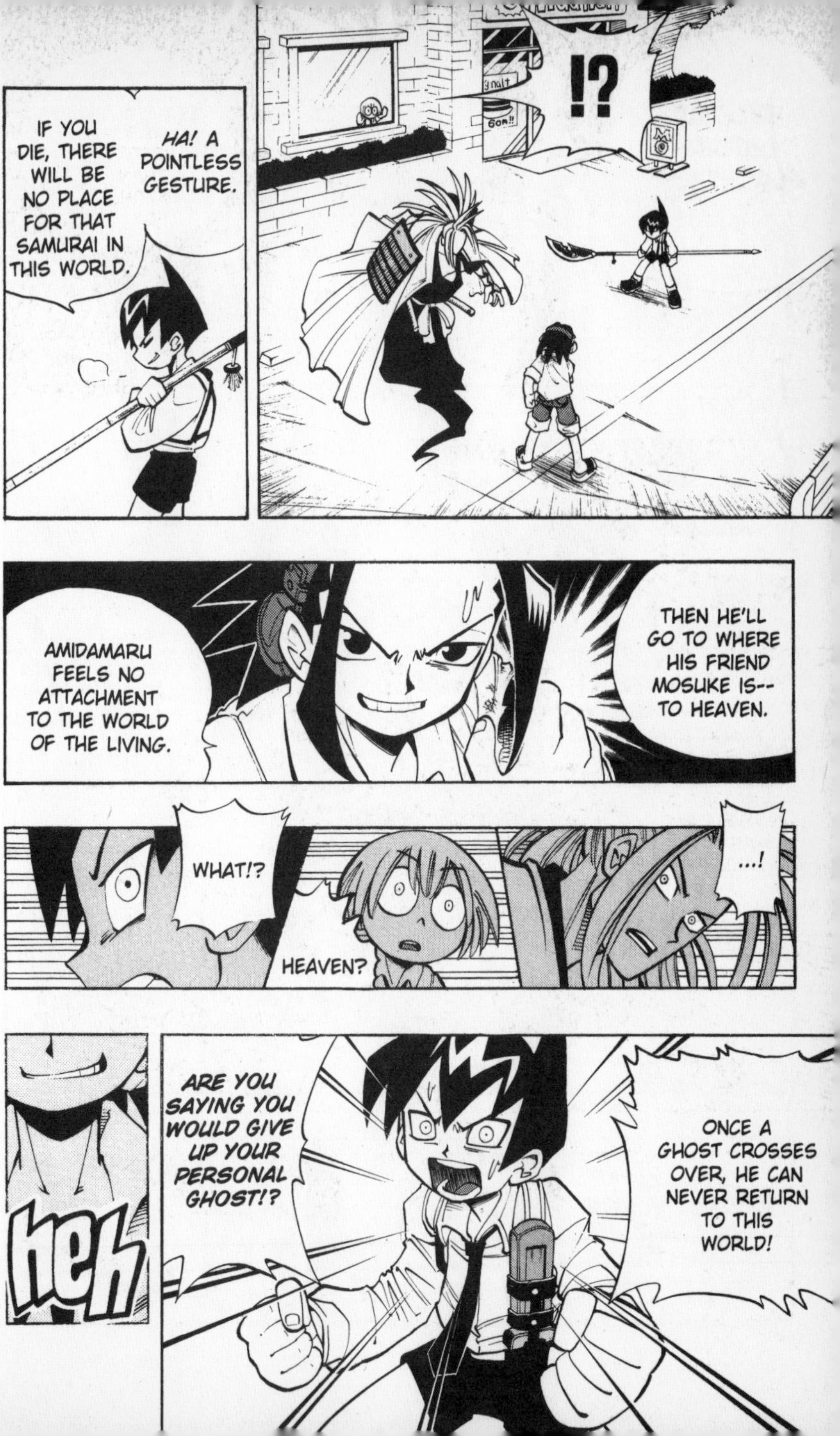
!?
HA! A POINTLESS GESTURE.
IF YOU DIE, THERE WILL BE NO PLACE FOR THAT SAMURAI IN THIS WORLD.
THEN HE'LL GO TO WHERE HIS FRIEND MOSUKE IS-- TO HEAVEN.
AMIDAMARU FEELS NO ATTACHMENT TO THE WORLD OF THE LIVING.
...!
HEAVEN?
WHAT!?
ONCE A GHOST CROSSES OVER, HE CAN NEVER RETURN TO THIS WORLD!
ARE YOU SAYING YOU WOULD GIVE UP YOUR PERSONAL GHOST!?
heh

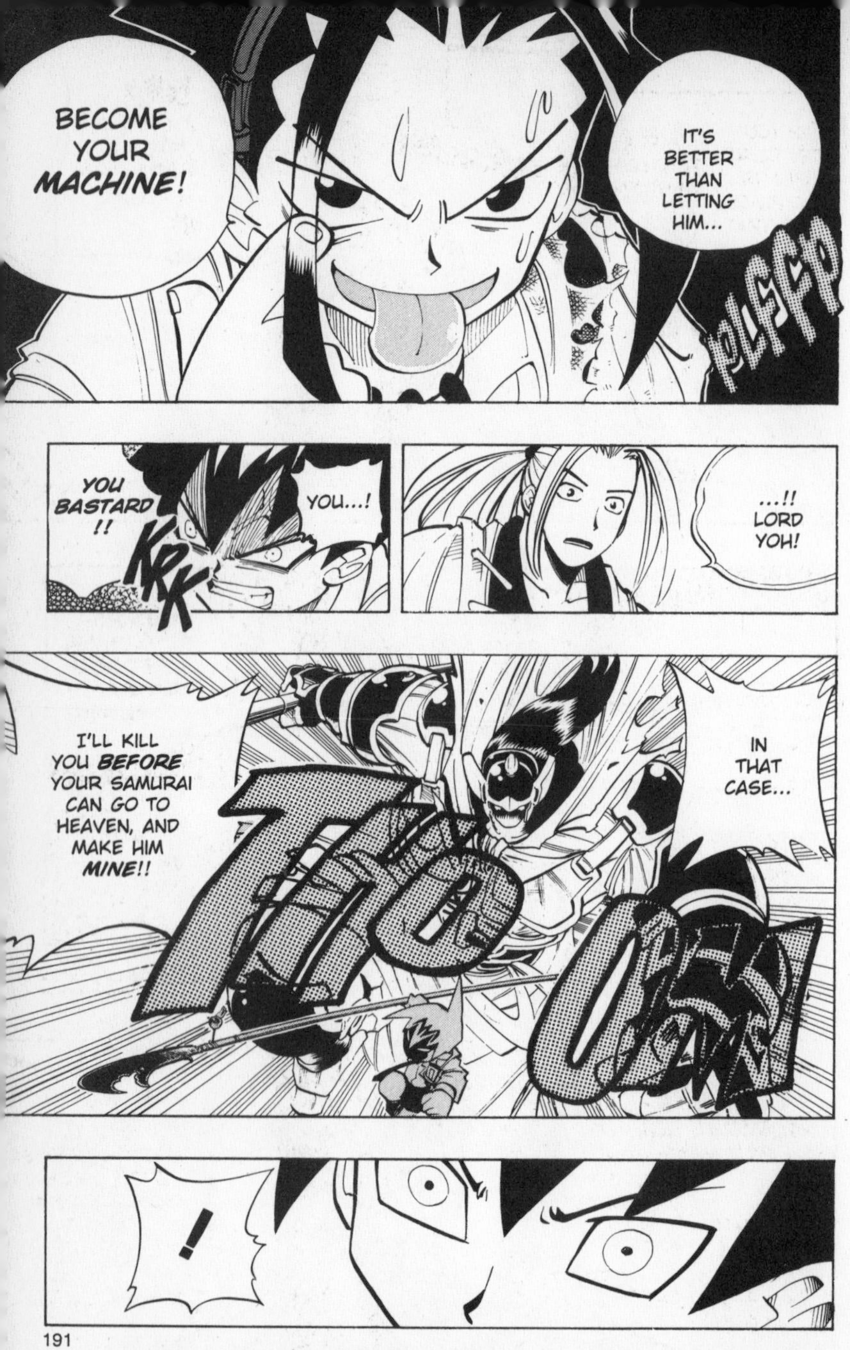
IT'S BETTER THAN LETTING HIM...
PLFFP
BECOME YOUR MACHINE!
...!! LORD YOH!
YOU...!
YOU BASTARD!!
KRK
IN THAT CASE...
I'LL KILL YOU BEFORE YOUR SAMURAI CAN GO TO HEAVEN, AND MAKE HIM MINE!!
!

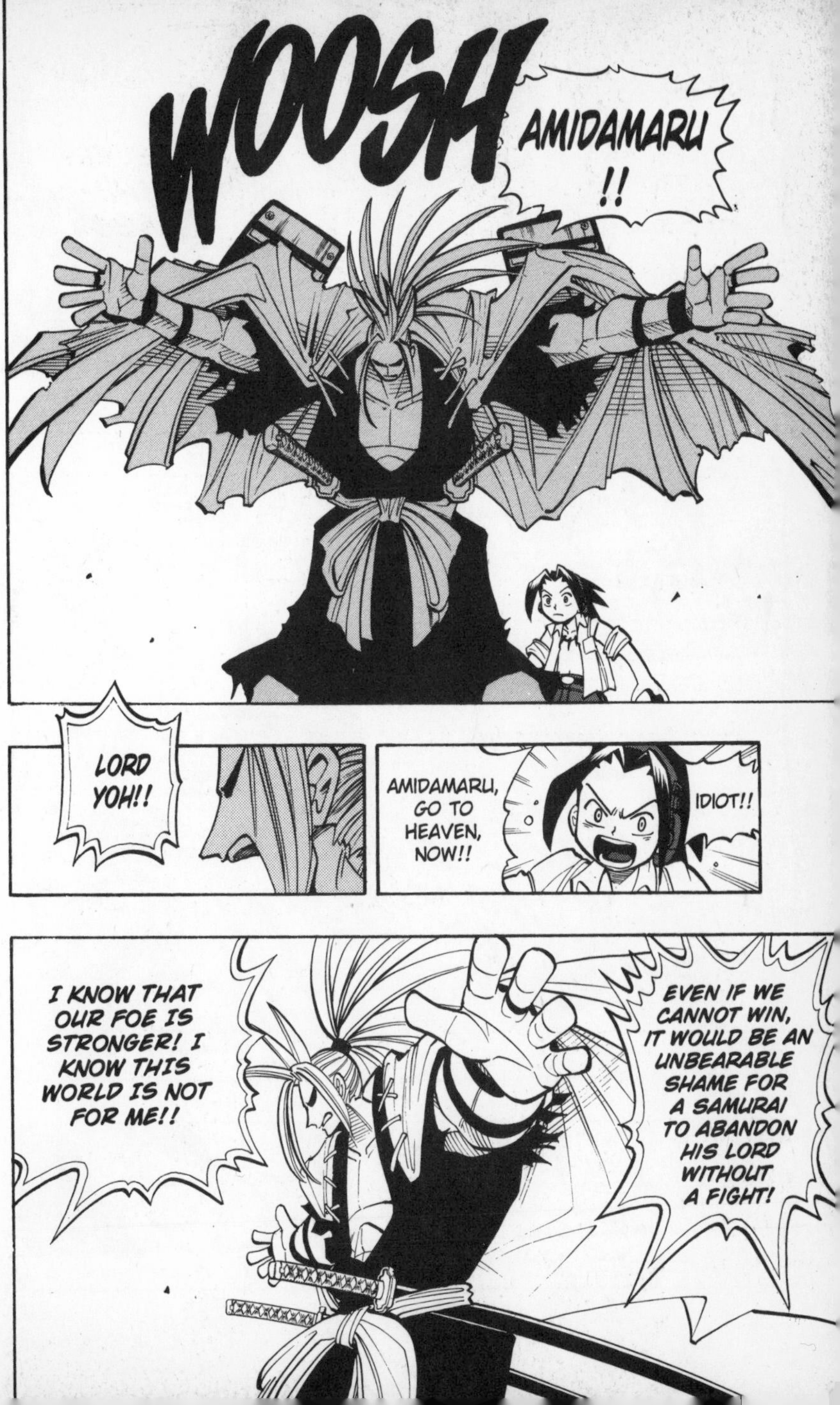
AMIDAMARU !!
WOOSH
IDIOT!!
AMIDAMARU, GO TO HEAVEN, NOW!!
LORD YOH!!
EVEN IF WE CANNOT WIN, IT WOULD BE AN UNBEARABLE SHAME FOR A SAMURAI TO ABANDON HIS LORD WITHOUT A FIGHT!
I KNOW THAT OUR FOE IS STRONGER! I KNOW THIS WORLD IS NOT FOR ME!!

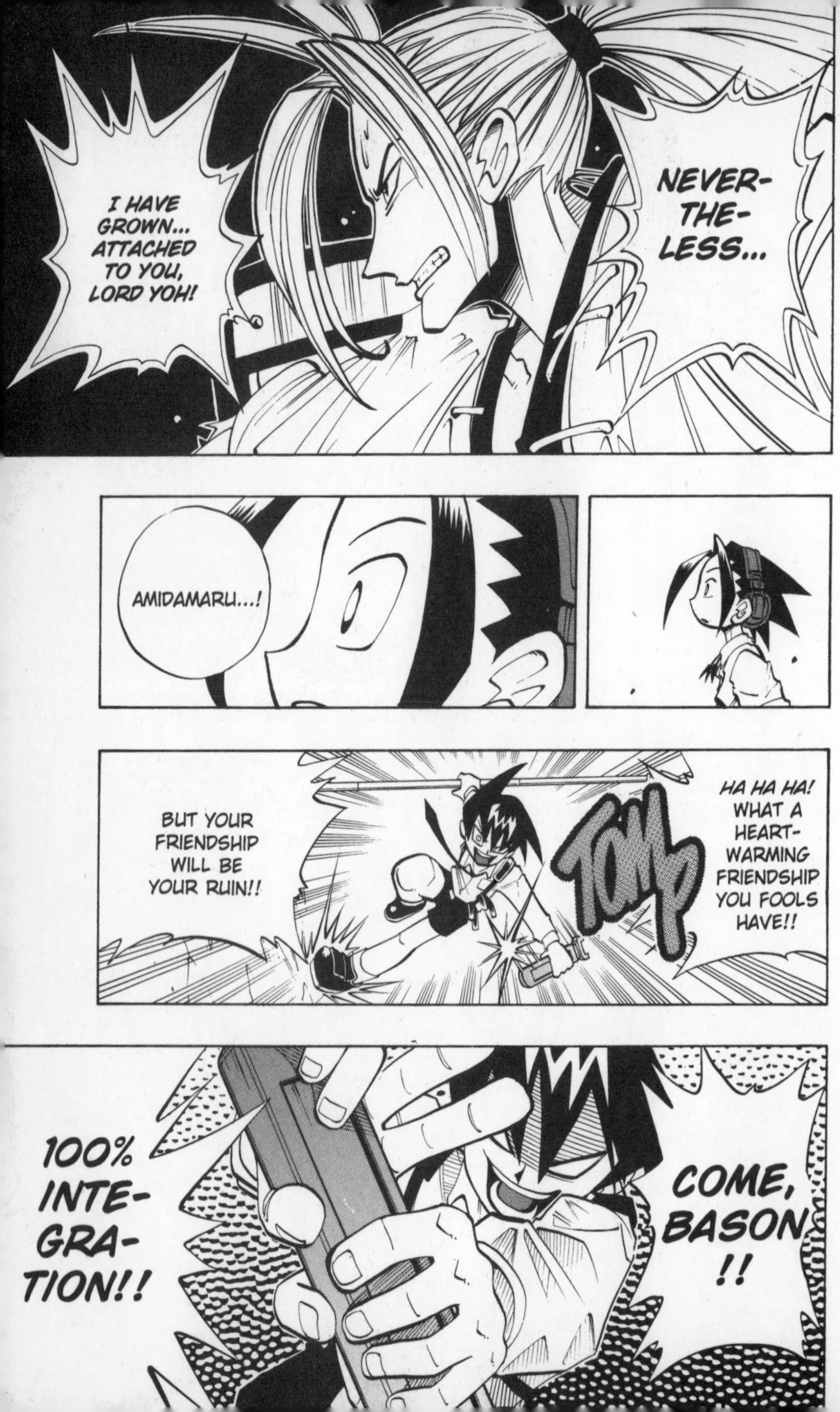
NEVER-THE-LESS...
I HAVE GROWN... ATTACHED TO YOU, LORD YOH!
AMIDAMARU...!
HA HA HA! WHAT A HEART-WARMING FRIENDSHIP YOU FOOLS HAVE!!
TOMP
BUT YOUR FRIENDSHIP WILL BE YOUR RUIN!!
COME, BASON!!
100% INTEGRATION!!

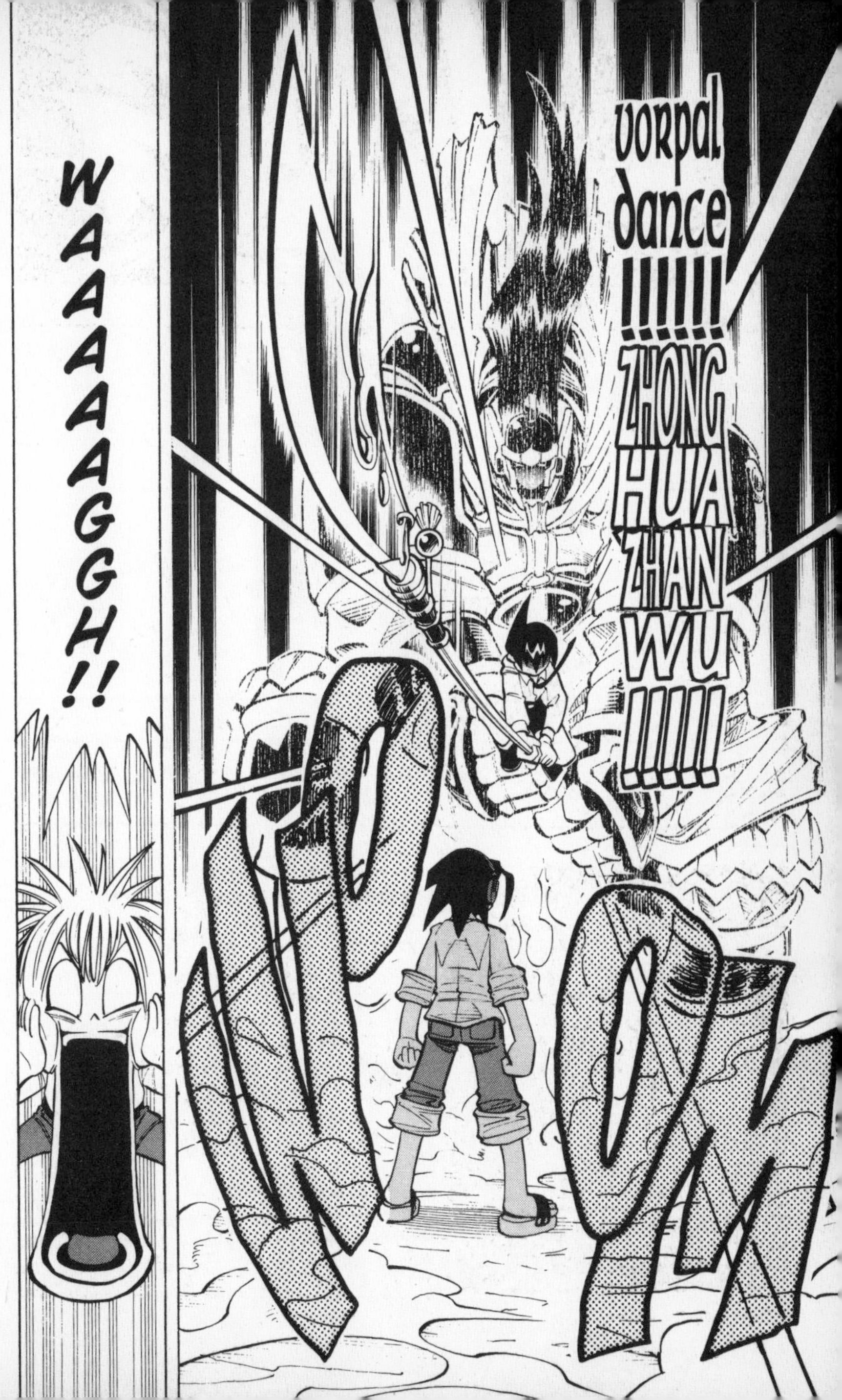
Vorpal dance !!!!!!!
ZHONG HUIA ZHAN WU !!!!!
WAAAAAGGH!!

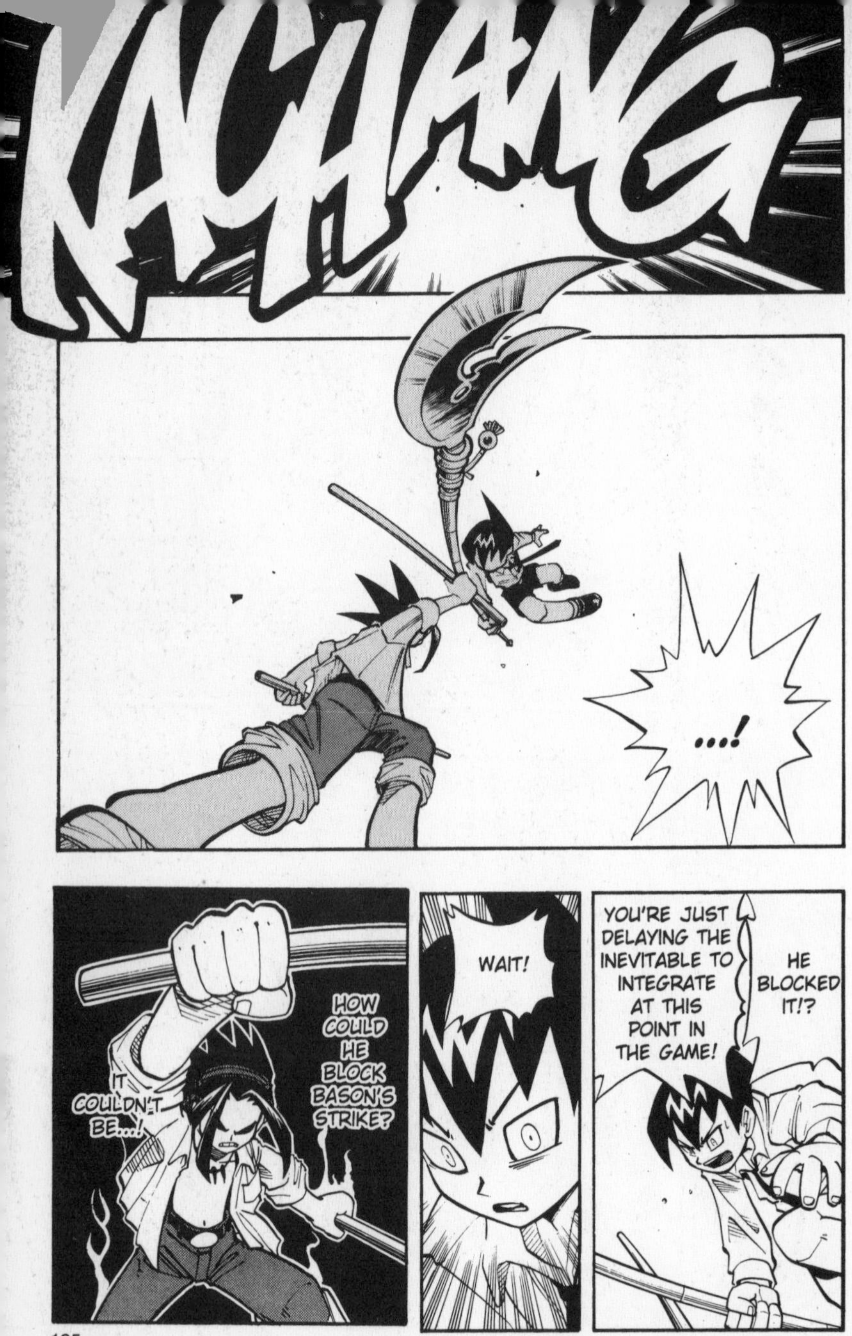
KACHANG
...!
HE BLOCKED IT!?
YOU'RE JUST DELAYING THE INEVITABLE TO INTEGRATE AT THIS POINT IN THE GAME!
WAIT!
HOW COULD HE BLOCK BASON'S STRIKE?
IT COULDN'T BE...!

READ THIS WAY

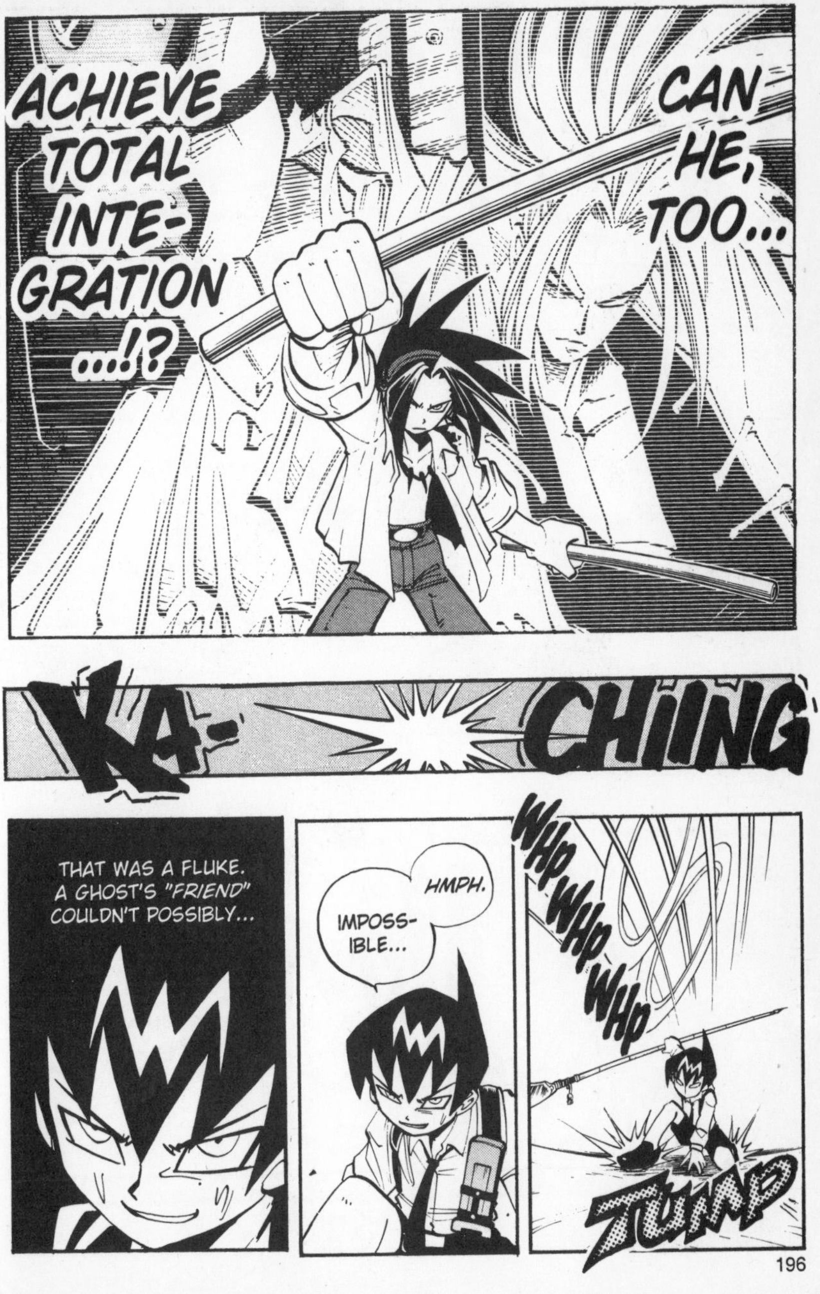
CAN HE, TOO...
ACHIEVE TOTAL INTE-GRATION ...!?
KA-CHIING
WHP WHP WHP WHP
TUMP
HMPH.
IMPOSS-IBLE...
THAT WAS A FLUKE. A GHOST'S "FRIEND" COULDN'T POSSIBLY...

READ THIS WAY

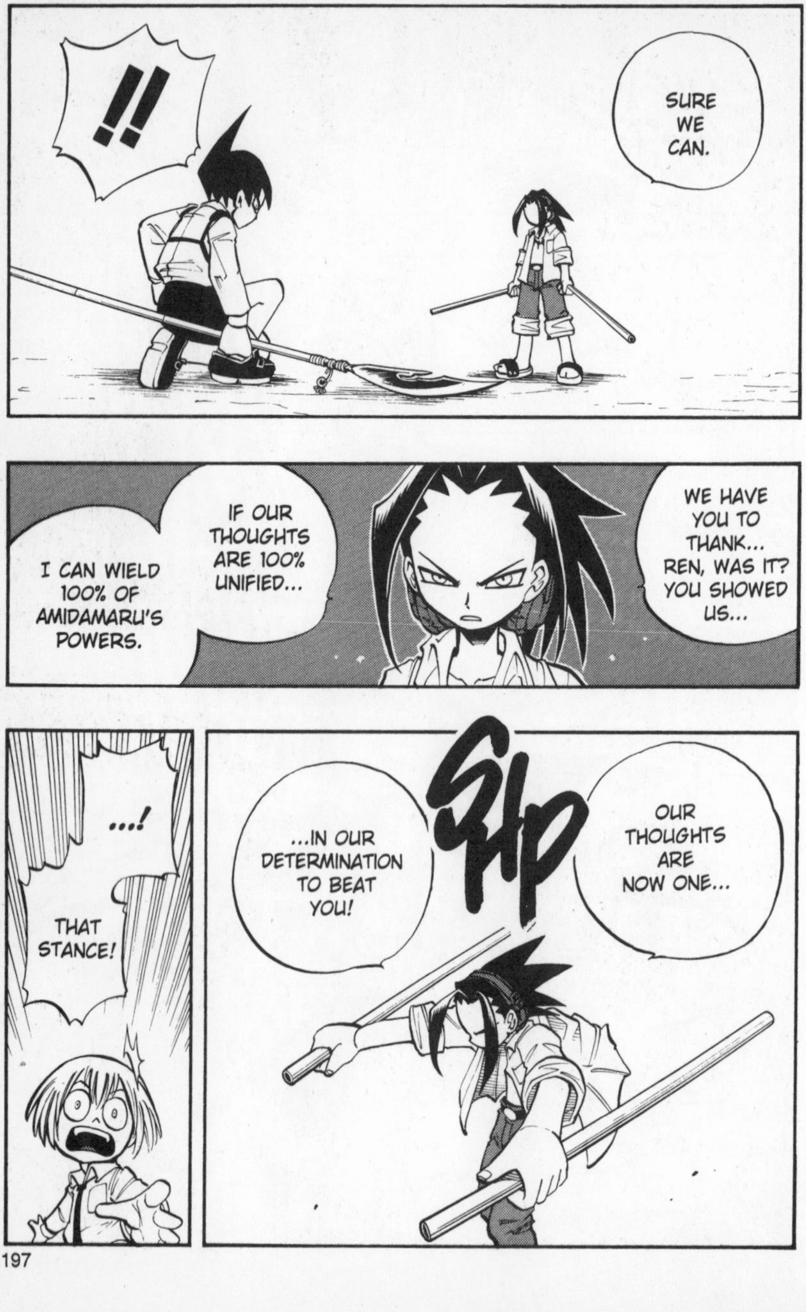
SURE WE CAN.
!!
WE HAVE YOU TO THANK... REN, WAS IT? YOU SHOWED US...
IF OUR THOUGHTS ARE 100% UNIFIED...
I CAN WIELD 100% OF AMIDAMARU'S POWERS.
OUR THOUGHTS ARE NOW ONE...
SHP
...IN OUR DETERMINATION TO BEAT YOU!
...!
THAT STANCE!

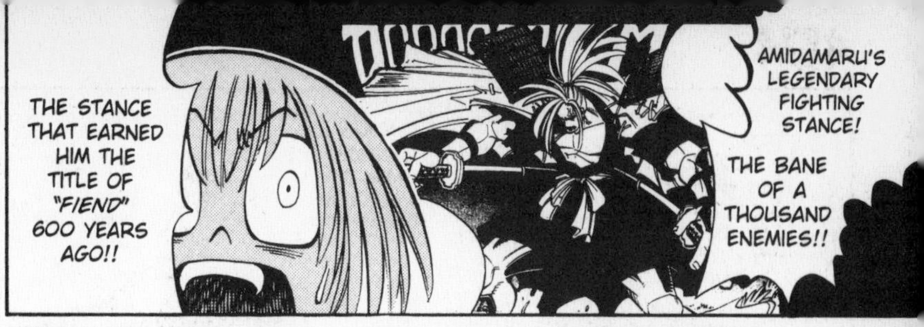
AMIDAMARU'S LEGENDARY FIGHTING STANCE!
THE BANE OF A THOUSAND ENEMIES!!
THE STANCE THAT EARNED HIM THE TITLE OF "FIEND" 600 YEARS AGO!!

* ONE OF THE NAMES OF BUDDHA

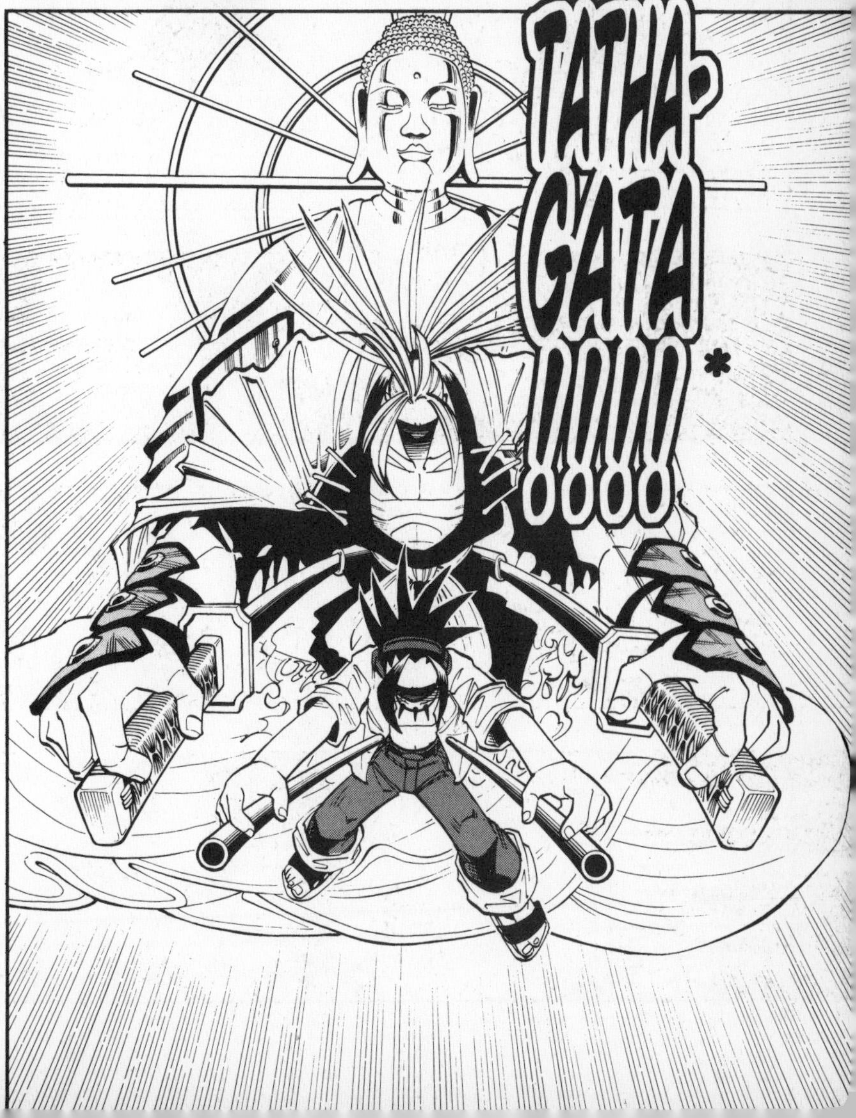
TATHA-GATA!!!!*

READ THIS WAY

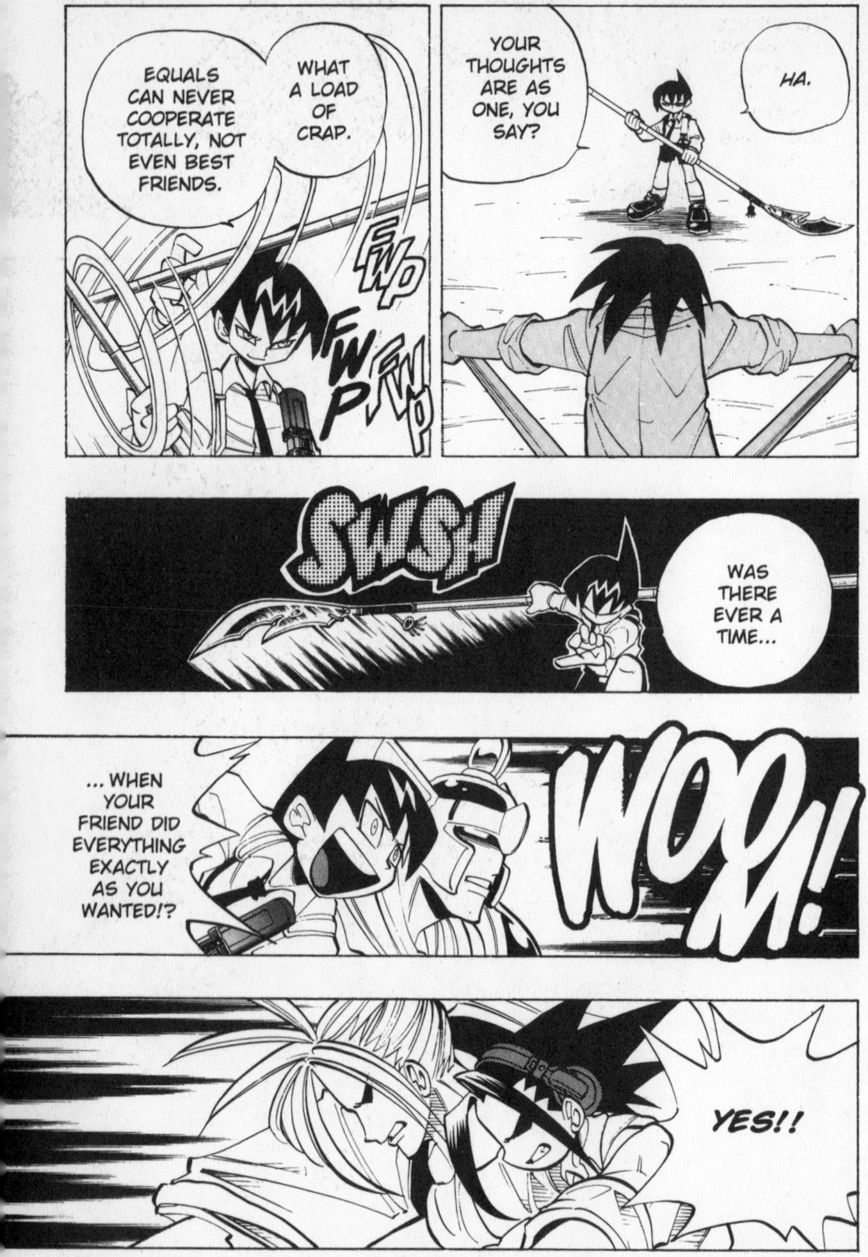

HA.
YOUR THOUGHTS ARE AS ONE, YOU SAY?
WHAT A LOAD OF CRAP.
EQUALS CAN NEVER COOPERATE TOTALLY, NOT EVEN BEST FRIENDS.
FWP
FWP
FWP
WAS THERE EVER A TIME...
SWSH
WOA!
... WHEN YOUR FRIEND DID EVERYTHING EXACTLY AS YOU WANTED!?
YES!!

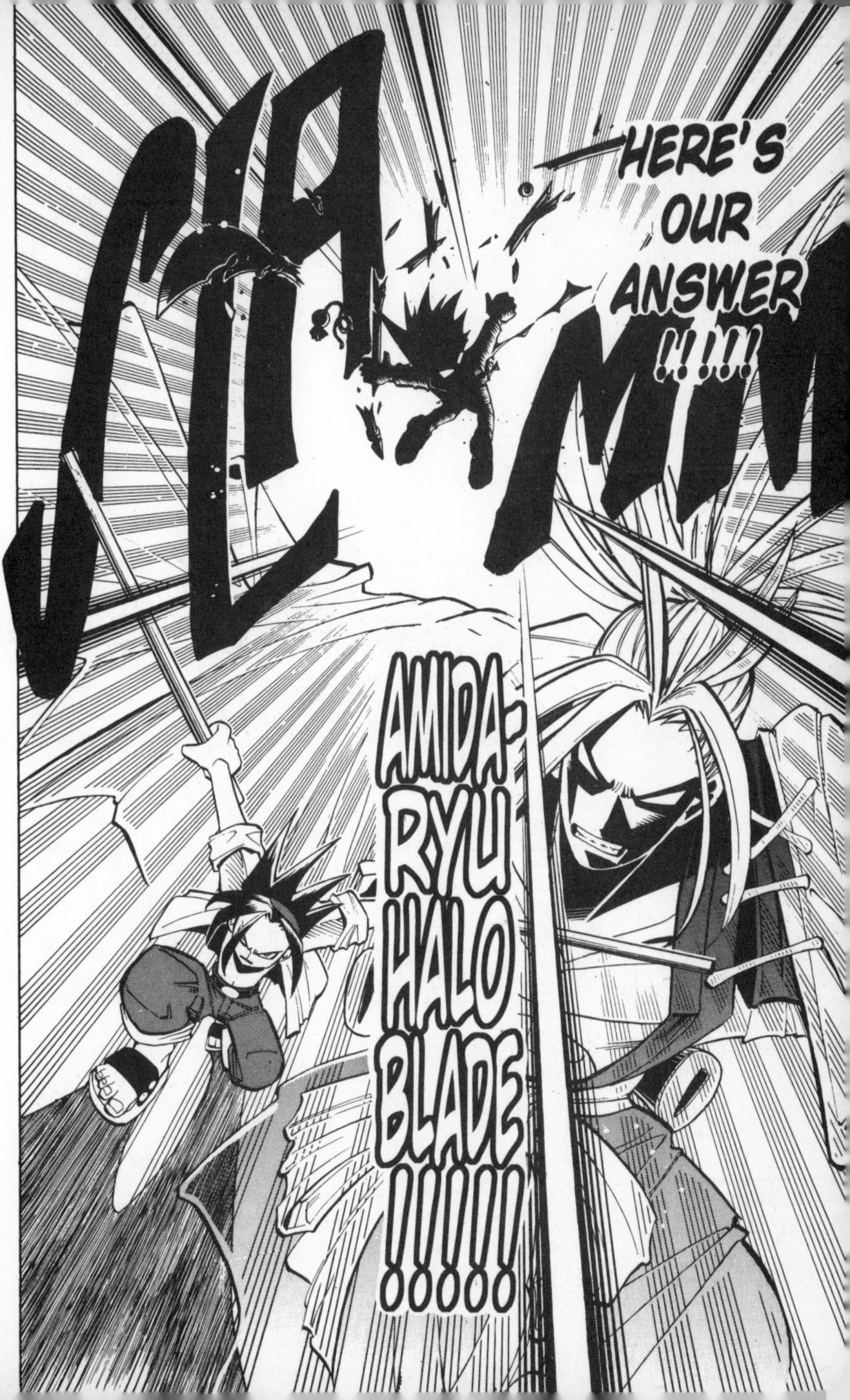
HERE'S OUR ANSWER !!!!!
SLAM
AMIDA-RYU HALO BLADE !!!!!

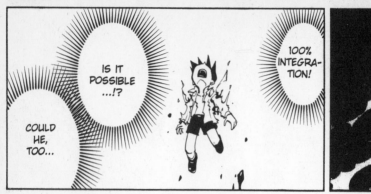

READ THIS WAY

100% INTEGRATION!
IS IT POSSIBLE ...!?
COULD HE, TOO...
HAVE THE POTENTIAL...
...TO BE THE SHAMAN KING?
REN WAS DEFEATED--BUT THERE ARE MANY UNANSWERED QUESTIONS.
WHAT IS A "SHAMAN KING?" WHO IS YOH, REALLY?
I STILL KNOW SO LITTLE ABOUT SHAMANS.
-MANTA

TO BE CONTINUED IN *SHAMAN KING* VOL. 2!

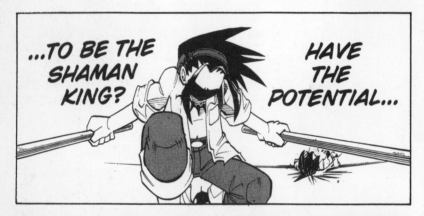

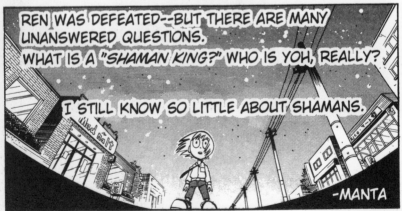

BONUS PAGE!
SHAMAN KING CHARACTER FILE No.4

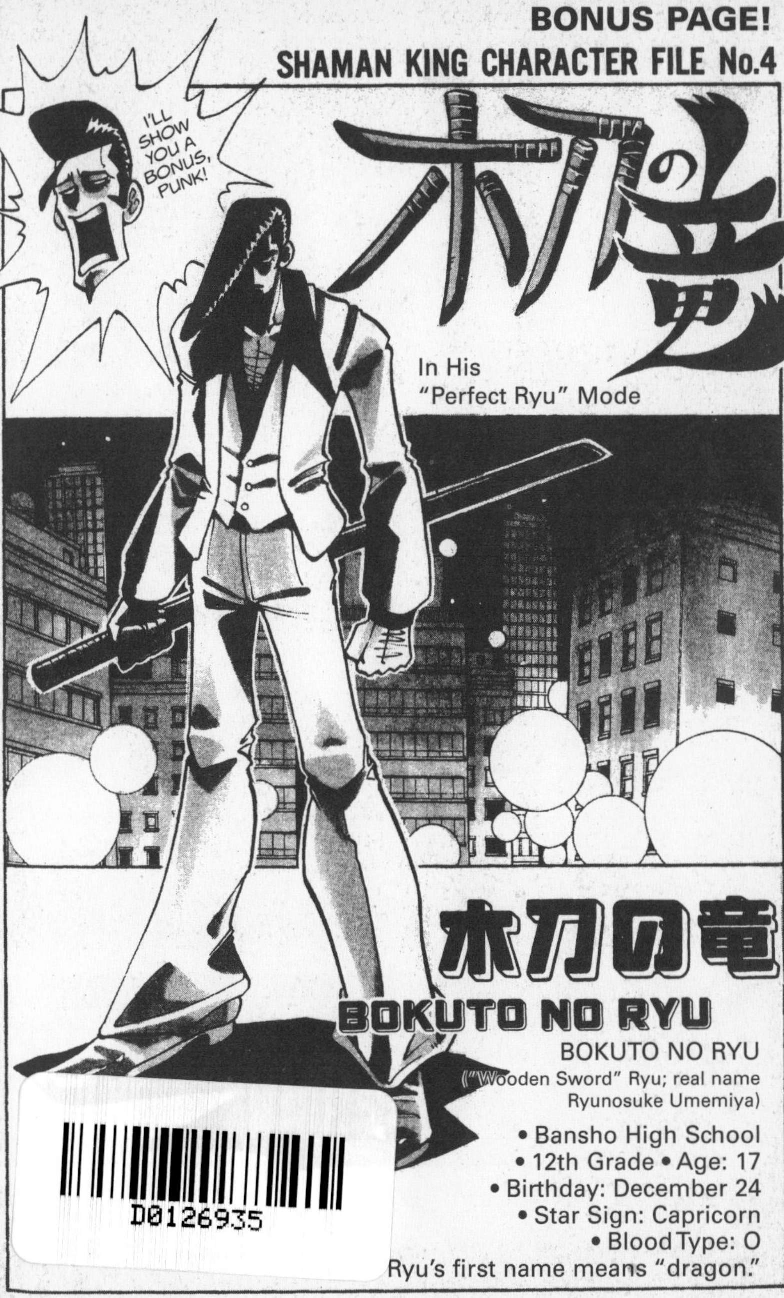
I'LL SHOW YOU A BONUS, PUNK!
木刀の竜
In His
"Perfect Ryu" Mode
木刀の竜
BOKUTO NO RYU

BOKUTO NO RYU
("Wooden Sword" Ryu; real name Ryunosuke Umemiya)

- Bansho High School
- 12th Grade • Age: 17
- Birthday: December 24
- Star Sign: Capricorn
- Blood Type: O

Ryu's first name means "dragon."